Competition and Cooperation in American Higher Education

Edited by
Thomas M. Stauffer

AMERICAN COUNCIL ON EDUCATION
Washington, D.C.

© 1981 by American Council on Education
One Dupont Circle, Washington, D.C. 20036

Library of Congress Cataloging in Publication Data
Main entry under title:

Competition and cooperation in American higher education.

1. University cooperation—United States—Addresses, essays, lectures. 2. College students—United States—Psychology—Addresses, essays, lectures. 3. Competition (Psychology)—Addresses, essays, lectures. 4. Cooperativeness—Addresses, essays, lectures. I. Stauffer, Thomas M.
LB2331.5.C646   378'.104   80-23201
ISBN 0-8268-1450-6

9 8 7 6 5 4 3 2 1

Printed in the United States of America

Contributors

Alexander W. Astin
PROFESSOR OF HIGHER EDUCATION, UNIVERSITY OF CALIFORNIA,
LOS ANGELES; PRESIDENT, HIGHER EDUCATION RESEARCH INSTITUTE

Louis T. Benezet
PROFESSOR OF HUMAN DEVELOPMENT AND EDUCATIONAL POLICY,
STATE UNIVERSITY OF NEW YORK AT STONY BROOK

Gene A. Budig
PRESIDENT, WEST VIRGINIA UNIVERSITY

John J. Connolly
PRESIDENT, DUTCHESS COMMUNITY COLLEGE

Eileen M. Egan, S.C.N.
PRESIDENT, SPALDING COLLEGE

Jan V. Eisenhour
DIRECTOR, EXECUTIVE SECRETARIAL SCHOOL, DALLAS, TEXAS

Porter L. Fortune, Jr.
CHANCELLOR, UNIVERSITY OF MISSISSIPPI

Sally M. Furay, R.S.C.J.
VICE PRESIDENT AND PROVOST, UNIVERSITY OF SAN DIEGO

Donald Grunewald
PRESIDENT, MERCY COLLEGE

John R. Haire
PRESIDENT, COUNCIL FOR FINANCIAL AID TO EDUCATION, INC.

Charles L. Hayes
FORMERLY PRESIDENT, ALBANY STATE COLLEGE; PROFESSOR OF
EDUCATION AND COUNSELING, NORTH CAROLINA AGRICULTURAL
AND TECHNICAL STATE UNIVERSITY

Thomas R. Horton
IBM DIRECTOR OF UNIVERSITY RELATIONS, IBM CORPORATION

Dennis L. Johnson
PRESIDENT, JOHNSON ASSOCIATES, INC., OAK BROOK, ILLINOIS

Gerald B. Kauvar
EXECUTIVE ASSISTANT TO THE PRESIDENT, BOSTON UNIVERSITY, 1979;
SPECIAL ASSISTANT FOR EDUCATION, OFFICE OF THE SECRETARY
OF DEFENSE, AUGUST 1978—JULY 1979 AND APRIL 1980—

Contributors

Brent Knight
PRESIDENT, TRITON COLLEGE

Leslie Koltai
CHANCELLOR, LOS ANGELES COMMUNITY COLLEGE DISTRICT

Ben Lawrence
EXECUTIVE DIRECTOR, NATIONAL CENTER FOR HIGHER EDUCATION MANAGEMENT SYSTEMS

Allan W. Ostar
EXECUTIVE DIRECTOR, AMERICAN ASSOCIATION OF STATE COLLEGES AND UNIVERSITIES

J. W. Peltason
PRESIDENT, AMERICAN COUNCIL ON EDUCATION

George H. Robertson
PRESIDENT, MOHAWK VALLEY COMMUNITY COLLEGE

Morris L. Norfleet
PRESIDENT, MOREHEAD STATE UNIVERSITY

John W. Ryan
PRESIDENT, INDIANA UNIVERSITY

Gloria M. Shatto
PRESIDENT, BERRY COLLEGE

John R. Silber
PRESIDENT, BOSTON UNIVERSITY

William P. Snyder
ASSOCIATE PROFESSOR OF POLITICAL SCIENCE, TEXAS A&M UNIVERSITY; FORMERLY VISITING PROFESSOR OF POLITICAL SCIENCE, U.S. ARMY WAR COLLEGE

Thomas M. Stauffer
DIRECTOR, DIVISION OF EXTERNAL RELATIONS, AMERICAN COUNCIL ON EDUCATION

F. W. Steckmest
CONSULTANT, PUBLIC AFFAIRS, SHELL OIL COMPANY

Robert A. Stone
DEPUTY ASSISTANT SECRETARY, PROGRAM MANAGEMENT (MRA&L), U.S. DEPARTMENT OF DEFENSE

Dean E. Tollefson
EXECUTIVE DIRECTOR, UNION OF INDEPENDENT COLLEGES OF ART

LeVester Tubbs
ASSOCIATE VICE PRESIDENT FOR STUDENT AFFAIRS, UNIVERSITY
OF CENTRAL FLORIDA; FORMERLY VICE CHANCELLOR FOR STUDENT
AFFAIRS, UNIVERSITY OF MASSACHUSETTS AT BOSTON

Neil J. Webb
PRESIDENT, ST. NORBERT COLLEGE

Clarence G. Williams
SPECIAL ASSISTANT TO THE PRESIDENT, MASSACHUSETTS INSTITUTE
OF TECHNOLOGY

Contents

Foreword, *by J. W. Peltason* xi

Acknowledgments xv

    Competition and Cooperation in Higher Education 1
    THOMAS M. STAUFFER

COMPETITION

1. Competition for Students—The Marketing Issue

The Case for Nonprofit Marketing
at Colleges and Universities 9
DENNIS L. JOHNSON

Three Rs of Higher Education Marketing 16
SALLY M. FURAY, R.S.C.J.

Marketing Higher Education—
The Survival Value of Integrity 22
JOHN R. SILBER

Marketing, Management, Mobility—
College Admissions in the 1980s 29
MORRIS L. NORFLEET

2. Competition for Students—Recruitment and Retention

Strengthening Student Recruitment
and Retention—Some Ideas from Research 35
ALEXANDER W. ASTIN

Strategic Planning to
Improve Recruitment and Retention 42
BEN LAWRENCE

Throw All the Darts—The State
of the Art in Recruiting and Retention 49
NEIL J. WEBB

Partial Prescription for Institutional Vitality 55
BRENT KNIGHT

3. Competition for Students—The Military and the Campus

The Garrison *versus* the Academy? 62
WILLIAM P. SNYDER

Citizens, Soldiers, Students   68
GERALD B. KAUVAR

The Volunteer Force, the Draft, and National Service   75
ROBERT A. STONE

Competition Between the Military and Higher Education   80
JOHN J. CONNOLLY

4. Competition Among Institutions—Acrimony or Accommodation?

Two-Year *versus* Four-Year Colleges—
Competition Likely to Escalate   89
GENE A. BUDIG

Two Years *versus* Four—Wrong Battle, Wrong Timing   92
LOUIS T. BENEZET

Cooperation—Key for the 1980s   96
LESLIE KOLTAI

Lifelong Education as a Rationale for Colleges   99
GEORGE H. ROBERTSON

Growth in a Time of Steady State   103
DONALD GRUNEWALD

Toward Cooperation
Among Public and Private Institutions   108
ALLAN W. OSTAR

A Common Goal—Profit and Nonprofit Institutions   113
JAN V. EISENHOUR

COOPERATION

5. Cooperation Through Networks and Associations—Costs and Benefits

The Indiana University Experience—
And Some Admonitions   119
JOHN W. RYAN

P2E IB F4Z—Identifiers
for Twenty-first Century Learning Communities   126
DEAN E. TOLLEFSON

Patterns of Leadership for Changing Times   132
J. W. PELTASON

6. Cooperation with Private Philanthropy—Raising Money in the Eighties

Voluntary Support in the 1980s   139
JOHN R. HAIRE

Corporate Support of Higher Education   145
THOMAS R. HORTON

7. Cooperation with Business and Government—Building Coalitions

Renewing Cooperation and Building Coalitions   151
GLORIA M. SHATTO

Creating Coalitions for Cooperation—A Case History   155
F. W. STECKMEST

Cooperation with Government—Forced   162
CHARLES L. HAYES

8. Cooperation in the Human Dimension—Blacks on White Campuses

The Journey Begun, The Journey Ahead   165
PORTER L. FORTUNE, JR.

Black Students, White Campuses—
Variables That Affect Performance   172
LE VESTER TUBBS

Black Students on White Campuses During Retrenchment   177
CLARENCE G. WILLIAMS

Black Students, White Campuses—
Student Perceptions and Institutional Response   184
EILEEN M. EGAN, S.C.N.

Foreword

AMERICAN ACADEMICS bow to certain values almost automatically. One such value is the pluralism among institutions of higher education in the United States. With 4,500 accredited colleges, universities, and other postsecondary institutions, of which about 3,200 are identified as nonprofit, what emerges is a crazy quilt matrix of categories. Often a division is made between public and independent institutions (roughly 1,600 of each kind among accredited, nonprofit colleges and universities), but that distinction is a gross oversimplification of academic pluralism. In scale, control, tradition, spirit, and direction, vast differences can be observed among the publics and the independents. Without question, the variety is much greater than anywhere else in the world.

This pluralism is a product of the American experience. It has not been imported from Europe or elsewhere. The national experience is defined largely by emphasis on private initiative, open markets for ideas and organizations, academic freedom, pragmatism, the freedom of religion and speech, and the propensity of Americans to work through organizations to accomplish their goals. From these impulses, higher education in the United States has moved in a multiplicity of directions to meet the needs of a dynamic, multiculture society. The result is the world's largest academy: it enrolls one out of four college students in the world, even though this nation accounts for only slightly more than 5 percent of the global population. The two competing higher education models for the organization of higher education are the British and Continental European. Neither has produced a similar scale or diversity until the last decade or so when the Continental European model in particular began to incorporate features of the American system of higher learning.

Pluralism has also meant competition among institutions and categories of institutions. In large measure the competition has been healthy, forcing colleges and universities to remain responsive to changing needs of students, research requirements, and demands of the society. Higher education's experience in the United States proves once again that nothing is to be gained by restraint of trade. The efficiency, productivity, and quality of American colleges and universities stand as testimony to the virtues of the free market in which they must operate. This attainment is sufficient reason for academic leaders to resist excessive encroachment into their affairs by government agencies. There is a thin line between holding institutional leaders accountable for effective performance and interfering in the free academic market. However well intentioned, state "coordinating boards" and federal agencies must not force restraint of trade. For whatever short-term gains may be realized, dangers and long-term losses are unavoidable, as comparisons with the experience in other countries will attest.

Although competition is a strong force, voluntary cooperation remains a significant tradition in the American academy. Again, cooperation is a part of the American experience, imbedded in democracy. Without the cooperative instincts of the citizenry, democracy will not work. Without cooperation, intellectual intercourse in any academy will not work. Most often in higher education, cooperation occurs within categories of institutions, such as institutions with heavy research commitments or institutions sponsored by a particular religious denomination or related by some other unifying interest. The cooperation is most effective when it does not restrain trade and does share assets to mutual benefit.

The pull and tug of competition and cooperation is at the forefront of the agenda of the American Council on Education. Inasmuch as the Council represents almost all categories of institutions, competition is manifest. The largest categories are represented in Washington by their own associations, and the Council works through and with them. It convenes leaders of these associations, and, in trying to address issues among them, often takes the blame when they are unwilling to cooperate. But such is the Council's appropriate role: to get vexing issues on the table, to push for agreement, and to articulate agreements to disagree when that course becomes necessary. What is remarkable is the extent to which agreements are reached on governmental policy, academic, and other issues. Nine times out of ten, broadly based agreements are hammered out. Unfortunately, it is the tenth issue that almost always attracts media attention, often giving the impression that deep divisions tear at the American academy. In fact, the American tradition of fair play and consensus prevails. Remarkable cooperation is the result.

It is in the mission of the American Council on Education to help both competition and cooperation to prosper. The Council does so by working principally as a coordinating agency among the education associations. Competition and cooperation continue to give American higher education its distinctive character. Although they can be countervailing forces, competition and cooperation more likely are mutually reinforcing impulses which benefit the fifteen million Americans who at any given time study or serve as staff in our colleges and universities.

This volume, a product of the 1979 Council annual meeting in Houston, Texas, represents an effort to clarify the nature and outcomes of competitive and cooperative pressures. Many of the issues are difficult, but, to repeat, this task is much in the tradition of the American Council on Education. The Council's Board of Directors has asked staff not to avoid the most troublesome issues dividing the academy. Harmony will most likely be achieved, it has said, if the Council fosters open address to real problems. This book, I am confident, is a balanced representation of major problems, with strong emphasis on solutions and new directions. In particular, the focus is on problems faced by campus leaders. They are the ones who must keep their institutions competitive, cooperate with others, and continuously build the strength for which American higher education is known.

J. W. PELTASON, *President*
American Council on Education

Acknowledgments

MUCH CREDIT FOR THE QUALITY of the papers in this volume is owed to the leaders of American higher education who journeyed to Houston, Texas, late in 1979, for the annual meeting of the American Council on Education. The meeting convened around the theme "Competition, Cooperation, and Quality—Challenges to Higher Education." Experts were commissioned to prepare papers for forums, where they spent most of their time exchanging views with colleagues in the audience. Many papers in this volume appear as modified following those discussions.

This volume is not a proceedings of the meeting. (A companion book, *Quality—Higher Education's Principal Challenge*, treats "quality" as a separate theme.) Some very good papers are not included here because they ranged beyond the book as designed to emphasize a cohesive discussion of the issues. Rather, the volume is a compendium of papers that develop important, if rarely discussed themes. It is also the result of the careful work of others, which I freely acknowledge.

Olive Mills merits special praise and recognition for her work in editing this volume. The quality of her editing has long been praised by authors who have worked with her. It is unlikely that there is a more professionally competent and cheerful editor in all of American higher education. But beyond the usual kudos, it must be noted that this is the last volume she will develop as the senior editor of the American Council on Education. She retired at the end of 1980, after thirty-five years at the Council. Earlier, she was an editor at the University of Chicago Press.

In a letter to her, upon announcement of her retirement, I wrote:

> Good editorship is like good leadership: its absence is more often noted than its presence. And therein hangs the essence of your historically important role in American higher education. The United States leads the world not only in its emphasis on higher education but also in the development of a literature about the academy. The American Council on Education has led in the development of this literature, which has been the vehicle for the worldwide ascendancy of the American higher education model. Even proponents of the other models increasingly are borrowing features of American higher education as a basis for reforms in their own systems. As the arbiter of quality in substance, style, and grammar of Council publications, your role in these developments has been central. Without your stewardship toward Council publications, the respect and hence the spread of literature on American higher education would

have been less likely. Your colleagues in the academy already know that you have always been very, very good at what you do; they also recognize how important your career has been to the American Council and to higher learning.

Others whose assistance was crucial in preparing this volume include Marcy Massengale, director of the Publications Department of the American Council on Education, and her staff who provided important guidance and technical assistance. In addition, a national design committee of almost a hundred persons helped develop ideas on the basis of which the papers were commissioned. Finally, Council President J. W. Peltason encouraged the development of the cooperation and competition theme. His letter to the Council's membership about this idea recognized risk in dealing with these issues because so many were controversial or even divisive. He wrote,

> This period of stringent, if not declining resources increases the risk that the issues dividing us will become so intense that normally healthy competition will end in bitter conflict. If this outcome is realized, then the quality of our institutions, of first importance to us all, will suffer. Looking ahead in the 1980s, we now face crucial options. Our disposition on these choices should determine how our stewardship of American higher education will be judged in the future. I believe it is appropriate for the Council to encourage reflection and decision as a guide for the next ten years, and I am confident thoughtful persons in the higher education will want to address these choices for action.

THOMAS M. STAUFFER
American Council on Education

Competition and Cooperation in Higher Education

THOMAS M. STAUFFER

AMERICAN VALUES permeate American higher education. American ideas about liberty and equality, material well-being, and experimentation, for example, find expression in the structure and behavior of the American academy. American academics, notably those without foreign experience, tend to take these values and their effects on colleges and universities for granted. Yet these values make American higher education's character unique, a character that is now observed and emulated worldwide to a degree beyond any other national higher education system.

American higher education has had the freedom to operate and to serve diverse constituencies. Resources have been available more times than not to do what needed doing. And the American propensity for experimentation has fostered a scale and diversity in postsecondary education that are without parallel. Many categories of colleges and universities, with similar historical roots and contemporary structures—such as liberal arts colleges, community colleges, research universities, and sectarian institutions—are represented among the nation's 4,500 accredited institutions.[1]

Martin Trow has reported that diversity in higher education was present from the beginning of the Republic. By the time of the American Revolution, nine colleges had been founded in the Colonies whereas there were only two in the much more densely populated England. Trow notes:

> The United States entered the Civil War with about 250 colleges, of which over 180 still survive. Even more striking is the record of failure: between the American Revolution and the Civil War perhaps as many as 700 colleges were started and failed. By 1880, England was doing very well with 4 universities for a population of 23 million, while . . . Ohio, with a population of 3 million, already boasted 37 institutions. . . . By 1910, we had nearly a thousand colleges and universities with a third of a million students—at a time when the 16

---

1. Sherry S. Harris, ed., *1980–81 Accredited Institutions of Postsecondary Education* (Washington: American Council on Education, 1980).

universities of France enrolled altogether forty thousand students, a number nearly equalled by the faculty members of the American institutions.[2]

American higher education's scale and diversity, with both the willingness to experiment and the political and economic freedom to do so implied, has fostered an environment which many educators now seem to fear—if their rhetoric is to be believed—as they look toward the last two decades of this millenium. In their view, competition increases are exacerbated by financial squeeze, enrollment and demographic shifts, government intrusion, and economic and political changes that are less than favorable to higher education. For many reasons, they say, higher education's "golden age" is past and the best that can be hoped for is partial control of the damage. An array of opinion about future prospects is hotly debated.

On the more positive side, the final report of the Carnegie Council on Policy Studies in Higher Education attacked

> discussions of the future of higher education [which are] dominated by gloom and doom, even by a sense of panic: all certain changes are said by some to be for the worse, and uncertainty additionally is said to be unlimited. Some of these observers seem to have been unprepared for any unfavorable changes in the status quo ante. . . . [T]hey seem to have forgotten the age-old cycles of advance and retreat, the long history of new problems following on old solutions.[3]

The Carnegie Council goes on to plead with educators to look realistically at the academy, to be pragmatic in their search for solutions to problems. Realistic viewing requires an understanding of the competitive pressures among American colleges and universities; looking pragmatically requires an understanding of the opportunities for cooperation which exist. Diversity is a product of competition, but diversity, used advantageously, can be a basis for cooperation.

Competition among institutions and its converse—cooperation—are among the principal facts of life in higher education in the 1980s. The competition is bound to become more intense. The contradictions in competition and cooperation pose challenges to postsecondary education, both as problems and opportunities. This volume seeks to direct attention to questions arising from competition and from the pursuit of cooperation. Both values, whose roots were apparent early in the American experience, offer a basis for enhancing institutional quality.

---

2. "Aspects of Diversity in American Higher Education," in *On the Making of Americans*, ed. Herbert Gans et al. (Philadelphia: University of Pennsylvania Press, 1979), pp. 271–72.

3. *Three Thousand Futures: The Next Twenty Years for Higher Education* (San Francisco: Jossey-Bass, 1980), pp. 7–8.

At the outset of the new decade, competition (conflict, in some cases) may have a depressing effect on academic quality and on traditional kinds of cooperation in American higher education. Competition for students and competition among categories of institutions, adversarial relations between faculty and administration, with government at different levels, and with sectors such as proprietary institutions and the military, the dilemma of rising costs and declining enrollments—all threaten the good will and prospects of the academy.

Times may be difficult, but, ten years from now, heightened competition may indeed be viewed as helping to force cooperation and qualitative improvements in higher education. Competition, after all, is cut from the same ideological cloth as the free market and autonomy. A shake-out of programs and, unfortunately, of institutions, such as occurs among business corporations in a recession (in business, a shake-out is usually seen as the foundation for new real growth), may well occur in higher education.

There is reason, however, to approach this time with a sanguine spirit. The experience with the elementary and secondary grades in recent years may be instructive. The lower birth rate—the increasing numbers of Chicanos in the Southwest, for example, demonstrate that the phenomenon is not uniform nationwide—has forced program cuts at the K–12 level and the necessity to rethink assumptions and to take new bearings. The human and financial costs have been heavy, but school systems have remained innovative and budget levels supportive.

Higher education, which has some advantages in infrastructure compared with the lower grades, may reasonably expect a similar fate but—the important point is—not necessarily. Educators who are concerned about the role of colleges and universities in American society must rededicate themselves to the complex task of working together on their problems. Inevitable competitive pressures need not inevitably push aside the natural impulses of American scholars and institutional administrators to cooperate and to strive for excellence in the academic enterprise. The possibility of hanging separately, if there is no unity, should add inducement.

Competition is frequently ignored in analyses of higher education though it is a factor widely understood by educators. Institutions and individual professors and administrators do compete for students, resources, and prestige, but it is considered bad form in academic culture to draw public attention to competition. Competition thus tends not to be recognized in the literature as a principal motivating factor in American higher education.

Competition exists at micro and macro levels. Within institutions, students compete for class standing (not to mention social standing); faculty members compete for appointment, promotion, tenure, grants, and publication of research results; administrators compete with various constituencies to influence academic policy; faculty unions, where present, compete with administrators or governing boards; schools, departments, and programs compete for scarce resources; governing bodies compete with one another and various institutional constituencies; and at the professional, social, and athletics levels, competition is simply part of academic life. Institutions, as a whole, compete with other institutions for many items of value: institutions compete for the philanthropic dollar and governmental appropriations; institutions compete for students, quantitatively and qualitatively; institutions compete for attention in press, academic, and professional circles; institutions seek recognition by opinion leaders and their own alumni; institutional rivalries in intercollegiate sports are part of American folklore.

At a meeting of about a hundred and fifty college and university presidents, sponsored some time ago by the Academy for Educational Development, a question was raised about how presidents could help one another. And the suggestion was made that presidents need to share private advice. The presidency is a lonely office, and peer involvement would be likely to improve the effectiveness of all participants, it was agreed. Then, upon reflection, one president added that an important qualification had to be included: No president could advise another president if their campuses were within five hundred miles of each other. Exposing institutional secrets while exchanging advice represented too great a risk. Institutional competition would be too great a factor.

The alleged lack of competitiveness of American business in international markets is said to be at the root of decline in the U.S. productivity rate, inflation, and other economic maladies. The effect of federal regulation on the competitive position of the U.S. automobile industry, for example, was hotly debated in the 1976 and 1980 presidential campaigns: how really free is a market bound by environmental, economic, management, social, and other federal and state regulations?

As these national debates are thrashed out, academic leaders need to be cognizant of their stake not only in the national debates but also in the effects of competitive pressures on colleges and universities. In recognizing competition for what it is and how it can help or hinder institutional progress, these leaders can seek to overcome the adverse effects while enhancing positive outcomes of a free marketplace, in and outside an institution. Although safeguards are needed in free competition, efficiency can increase and quality will more likely prevail once competition is recognized and understood. Competition has a secure place in American higher education, and healthy competition needs to be encouraged.

Cooperation is not the reciprocal of competition; it results from competitive pressures. Because both institutions and persons need to effect efficiencies, opportunities for cooperation are explored and implemented. The extent of interinstitutional relationships is difficult to measure; full understanding would require a Leontief-style matrix analysis of inputs and outputs. One study of about a hundred and fifty institutions by the American Association of Community and Junior Colleges identified a low of 20 "cooperative arrangements" for a small college and a high of 1,700 by a multicampus district, the average being about 100 per institution. Lewis D. Patterson in a 1979 report lists 65 examples of academic, administrative, community, and student-related cooperation. Further, he counted 51 descriptors in the ERIC Clearinghouse on Higher Education system under "interinstitutional cooperation" and "consortium," and lists 35 areas of cooperative activity among libraries.[4] Whatever the actual count, cooperation appears to be extensive through consortia, within states and locally, within and across institutional categories, through national and other associations, and through government programs and private compacts.

Just as the costs and benefits of competition merit understanding, so too does cooperation. Since competitive pressures seem likely to increase as enrollments and financial resources stabilize or decline, cooperation can be a safety net for many institutions. There may be cost advantages; duplication can be avoided; efficiency can be increased; and other benefits may accrue. Cooperation also recognizes interdependence within the American, not to mention the world, academy. The overall health of institutions is bound by similar economic, demographic, political, philosophical, and social pressures. Pretending to avoid these pressures through noncooperation is to misunderstand the value and historical context in which higher education operates.

In academic trade in the United States, the free market is more pronounced than any restraints on it. Most countries have state-controlled higher education systems where freedom in the academic marketplace is not at issue—cooperation is directed rather than voluntary. American values have oriented the nation's higher education system toward com-

4. *Survival Through Interdependence* (Washington: American Association for Higher Education, 1979), pp. 7–9.

petition, access, and diversity. Academic leaders can experiment within this framework. Such experimentation is rare in the world, and it behooves American academic leaders to work together to seek solutions to the myriad problems and opportunities created. They also need to appreciate the liberty that makes it all possible.

COMPETITION

1. COMPETITION FOR STUDENTS—THE MARKETING ISSUE

The Case for Nonprofit Marketing at Colleges and Universities

DENNIS L. JOHNSON

COMPETITION FOR STUDENTS AND DOLLARS in the 1980s has the potential to improve the quality of higher education. The education industry can react positively and control its destiny, or it can allow external influences to force changes that are unsound. Education managers can no longer assume that higher education enjoys credibility and confidence among its many publics, some of whom are asking difficult questions. Reactions by institutions in postsecondary education must be, not defensive, but, rather, needs-oriented. The emerging education managers must convey that they understand the education marketplace. To do so, the educator in the 1980s must learn a new approach to planning—nonprofit marketing.

The term "marketing" should not be an issue; instead the emphasis should be on understanding marketing. Leaders should not allow false perceptions of marketing to become an obstacle in developing new skills for management. Postsecondary education has always marketed itself, but the approach was often "sales-based." Delivery was through promotional personnel using admissions, public relations, development, lobbyists, and others as means. Rarely were *product, place,* and *price* combined with *promotion*. These four Ps must become the fundamental basis of the marketing process for education managers and planners. Until recently, the law of supply and demand favored the institutions. However, pressures brought on by demographic changes, inflation, fiscal support restraints such as Proposition 13, college attendance trends, and other challenges urged that new skills in institutional management be developed.

As recently as 1978, a Gallup poll reported that 82 percent of the public still felt that higher education was very important or fairly important.

Yet, as of February 1979, only 33 percent of those polled felt that postsecondary education leadership was doing an acceptable job. In 1966, the figure was 61 percent, followed by a precipitous drop to 31 percent in

1976. Fortunately, that figure rose to 41 percent in 1977 and 1978.[1] These seemingly contradictory poll results present great opportunities for the 1980s. If the public maintains or improves its attitude about the need for postsecondary education, and postsecondary education improves the way the public perceives its management and leadership, the education industry may attain recognition as a student-centered industry. If not, postsecondary education may become entrenched in its negative position, with public support further eroding. Obviously, the nation can ill-afford that development, nor can it afford an educational system that functions without direction, quality, and positive change.

Defining Education Marketing and Research

If nonprofit marketing is to be accepted in higher education, it must be understood. In fact, nonprofit marketing has its marketing problem of not being understood. Too often, a "liberal attitude," voiced in publications and speeches, disappears when the subject turns to marketing postsecondary education. Many educators see nonprofit marketing as a Madison Avenue, coercive, and business-related process that has no place in education. Nonprofit marketing has been best defined by Philip Kotler:

> Marketing is the analysis, planning, implementation, and control of carefully formulated programs designed to bring about *voluntary* exchanges of values with target markets for the purpose of achieving organizational objectives. It relies heavily on designing the organization's offering in terms of the target markets' needs and desires, and on using effective pricing, communication, and distribution to inform, motivate, and service the markets.[2]

Kotler responds to those who question whether marketing is ethical, wastes the public's money, or is intrusive and manipulative when he states that nonprofit marketing "learns the needs and wants of people and their attitude toward the organization's current products so that the organization can deliver greater satisfaction to its target publics."[3] Kotler's book should be required reading for any leader in higher education. Perhaps nonprofit marketing should be a required course for students in departments of higher education at universities and colleges. Dealing with decline, change, attitude shifts, delivery of goods and services, and how the public feels, all will be important functions for the educational leader of the future.

1. 1979 survey on public confidence in higher education, conducted by Louis Harris Associates, New York.
2. Kotler, *Marketing For Nonprofit Organizations* (Englewood Cliffs, N.J.: Prentice-Hall, 1975), p. 5.
3. Ibid., p. 12.

Drucker has made a good point about the role for marketing: "Consumerism is the shame of marketing. Consumerism is a response to the failure of business leaders to base their business and their management on the values, expectations and wants of the consumer. It is the failure to *practice* marketing."[4]

The same could be said about postsecondary education. The emergence of student consumer groups and the recently developed Center for Helping Organizations Improve Choice in Education at the University of Michigan, headed by Joan S. Stark, are potential trend setters. As the traditional student becomes more sophisticated and as the adult learner demands better teaching, postsecondary education must respond.

Product, Price, Place, and Promotion

Postsecondary education must reestablish its case, and nonprofit marketing is a proper tool to chart the future. We have failed to counteract the negative media of the last several years. The negativism began with Caroline Bird's *The Case Against College*[5] and continues with Lansing Lamont's *Campus Shock*.[6] Lamont's book, though sensational in title, can benefit the educator. The final chapter has some important statements, one of which is, "We are entitled to expect good teachers, sympathetic advisors, and demonstrable concern for the students that is equal to the concern for endowments and scholarly research."[7] Nonprofit marketing centers on the exchange relationship between an institution and its publics, especially students. The value of postsecondary education must be accurately perceived, understood, and realized.

As already noted, nonprofit marketing, in its simplest sense, deals with product, price, place, and promotion. It is based on research. *Product*, in postsecondary education, can be seen as the learner's development resulting from exposure in the classroom or to the learning environment. The student deserves to be challenged and, it is hoped, benefits from the experience. Postsecondary education is unique in its product, which is, in a sense, dual. While the product, education, is being offered through the relationship with a teacher, the student becomes an improved *product*. As a learner, the student needs the skills necessary to learn beyond college. In the 1980s, the "buyer's" assessment of "outcomes" expectations will

---

4. Peter F. Drucker, "Marketing and Economic Development," in *The Great Writings in Marketing*, ed. Howard A. Thompson (Tulsa: Petroleum Publishing Co., 1977), p. 35.
5. New York: David McKay, 1975.
6. *Campus Shock* (New York: E. P. Dutton, 1979).
7. Ibid., p. 131.

increase as an important factor when the student considers the costs in terms of dollars and cents invested.

Price, as related to product, assumes significance for nearly all students. Price-satisfaction trade-offs will become more critical as discretionary income becomes more limited in an inflation-dominated economy. Financial aid of all types will, for many "prospects," be seen as a crucial element in college choice and attendance. Financial aid has not been marketed well by institutions and throughout postsecondary education. The poor, disadvantaged, minority, middle-class, nontraditional, and adult students have yet to be adequately informed and served.

Place has changed greatly in the last several years. Where, when, and how learning takes place is an especially important variable for the future. Modern technology and the changing role of student learning are apt to force postsecondary institutions and faculty members to modify delivery systems. The change in *place* may be as significant as the change made by the banking industry when it had to adjust to competition from savings and loan institutions, finance companies, credit unions, and other forces. "Banker's hours" became "customer convenience hours." The work place, shopping centers, homes, and the campus may well share as "place" in the learning society of the future.

Promotion cannot work effectively over the long term unless it is preceded by product, place, and price. Analysis of these elements calls for an accurate data-based program. Nonprofit marketing research is the key that will permit the educational leader to control the whole process. Any successful promotion effort must include an understanding that student needs and wants are more important than those of the institution. The disjointed promotional efforts of the past should be replaced by a market-based plan that is cost effective and that is based on market segmentation. Taxpayers, parents, students, voters, alumni, and governing board members have come to expect institutions to justify expenditures. Accountability is a reality for the 1980s, and the research developed through a nonprofit marketing process offers direct answers to probing questions. Vague responses will not satisfy the demands of the 1980s.

Goals for Education Research and Marketing

Enrollments and student recruiting are often viewed as the only purpose for marketing. If this false perception is allowed to prevail, nonprofit marketing cannot produce the necessary long-term benefits; for example, at some institutions, enrollment increases are an improbable dream. Yet, the nonprofit marketing analyses and process could point toward some specialization, new markets that ought to be explored and served (such as education for the aging), and the need for innovative and creative funding methods. A move away from the use of enrollments as a base for financing could happen if postsecondary institutions were to demonstrate its case to its various publics through a program that carefully documents the needs assessment. In some instances, student outcomes and teaching quality, rather than quantity, would be supported. A planned retrenchment and decline could well build public support if accurate, significant information were made available to the institution's various publics. In addition, market planning and research can benefit fund raising, development, image, and the perceived value of education, They can help improve public confidence.

Nonprofit marketing will not promote positive change as a process if the criterion for success or failure is limited to increasing enrollments. Attrition and retention should receive higher priority at some institutions—even higher than recruitment. Attrition and retention are two components in *internal* marketing. Internal marketing is sometimes more difficult than external marketing. Even basic understanding of, and commitment to, an educational philosophy that emphasizes helping nontraditional students requires internal research and education of many staff members. Behavior modification of the people who make up the faculty, staff, and administration of an institution is a difficult task. Unless administration, staff, and faculty members share both the positive and negative facts regarding what the publics feel about the institution, departments, or even a discipline, they will operate in an information void that is counterproductive to positive change. Nonprofit marketing offers all employees of an institution a chance to understand and help influence their own and the institution's destiny. It is a democratic, yet objective process.

Theodore Levitt, in his classic article "Marketing Myopia," discussed the difference between marketing and selling processes:

> The difference between marketing and selling is more than semantic. Selling focuses on the needs of the seller; marketing on the needs of the buyer. Selling is preoccupied with the seller's need to convert his product into cash; marketing with the idea of satisfying the needs of the customer by means of the product and the whole cluster of things associated with creating, delivering, and finally consuming it.[8]

Understanding the critical difference between the definitions as they

---

8. In *The Great Writings in Marketing*, p. 46.

apply to postsecondary education may make a great difference in the acceptance or rejection of nonprofit marketing in postsecondary education. The balance between what the student's needs are and what society perceives to be essential will determine whether or not an institution will have the opportunity or ability to deliver. In the 1960s, the student's "perceived" needs, and the public's willingness to cooperate, created a proliferation of courses, programs, and social regulations that often added little to the life- or job-preparation process. Today, students of all ages tell us they need assistance with writing, reading, other communications skills, career choice, and guidance. Many institutions, including Harvard, are responding with quality "back to basics" courses. This move does not suggest that postsecondary institutions must revert to the pre-1960 era. It does imply that the various publics are concerned about the unfortunate cycle of courses that lead to social promotion. The classroom experience must be seen as one of quality—a quality product.

Guidelines

Competition may release the creativity and genius that exist on any campus. Nonprofit marketing can help break the cycle of adversary relationships that have developed within institutions and between institutions with different missions. Public and private institutions cannot afford to air their differences and concern for their "piece of the financial pie" in the media or other public forums.

Both public and private institutions have their strengths and weaknesses. The prevailing sameness of institutions ignores the differing needs of our emerging learning society. The Oxford model or even the university or liberal arts model will not succeed at all institutions. The innovative American system of educational opportunity for all requires that institutional differences be encouraged and supported. College management too often does what is needed for its own preservation because it sees itself as being in the education business rather than in the "opportunity" business. If postsecondary education wages the funding battle in the press, all will be harmed. The potential learner is too fragile to be involved in a feud for market share.

There are so many unmet learning needs. The American Society for Training and Development estimates that $40 billion is being spent by American business in training and educating employees. Postsecondary education has reacted wholly insufficiently to a need that has a significant dollar value as well as a social and corporate benefit. Business is doing much of the work that secondary and postsecondary education should be doing. The competition in the 1980s will not be simply between institutions; it will also be between traditional learning organizations and the corporate learning programs that are filling a void which postsecondary education left unfilled.

In a recent column, Drucker discussed redundancy planning. There are faculty, staff, and administrators who are redundant for future needs. This practicality suggests the need for strategic market planning because, in Drucker's view, to "create and find productive jobs for knowledge workers will be the first employment priority for this country."[9] Retraining, career change, and the creative use of good minds in a productive way will be a major challenge for institutions. Tenure, academic freedom, unionization, and teaching will be examined and may have to change if institutions are going to be able to react and adjust. Learning, whether it be by students or educational leaders, will never be redundant.

Frank Borman took Eastern Air Lines from a nearly bankrupt state, with the industry's least productive employees, to a profit position in 1978–79. He accomplished this feat with great courage and by sharing the crisis with his employees. He worked with unions, the public, and all the employees to overcome morale and financial hurdles. This example and others in the corporate and college worlds provide a basis for optimism. Nonprofit planning and marketing must involve governing boards, faculty, staff, administration, and other key publics.

The chief executive officer must lead in implementing nonprofit marketing. The American Council on Education is a leadership organization whose membership is represented by education leaders. The ACE report *Adapting to Changes in Characteristics of College-Age Youth* encourages colleges and universities to consider marketing. This courageous recommendation must move onto the campuses if marketing is to become a positive force in the future learning society.

Woodrow Wilson once stated, "I would rather fail in a cause that will ultimately succeed than succeed in a cause that will ultimately fail." Postsecondary education has had some failures, but it must ultimately succeed. If not, all of society will fail.

9. Peter F. Drucker, "Planning for 'Redundant' Workers," *Wall Street Journal*, September 25, 1979.

Three Rs of Higher Education Marketing

SALLY M. FURAY, R.S.C.J.

CONSCIOUSLY OR UNCONSCIOUSLY, colleges and universities have always been involved in a marketing function. Most of them were founded because formal or informal "market research" demonstrated a need for certain types of educational opportunities. The earliest seminaries of Colonial days, the numerous church-related or nonsectarian liberal arts colleges, the land-grant schools, the expanding comprehensive universities, the community colleges, the research institutions, the professional schools—all these and many others have been developed because individuals, organizations, and legislatures discerned a need which they had the capacity to meet. Students flocked to take advantage of the educational opportunities. "For generations, higher education . . . had an assured market, and as long as colleges were operating in a seller's market, it was unthinkable to view [higher education] as a product to be 'sold.'"[1] Such high demand can create an indifference to the "nuances of demand, competition, and customer satisfaction,"[2] and an unawareness of vulnerability.

When the seller's market began to shift to a buyer's market, with grim predictions about the declining number of high school graduates and escalating tuition costs, colleges commenced "to recognize the similarities between themselves and business organizations" and "to accept marketing responsibility."[3] College and university administrators have developed intense interest in marketing concepts formerly unfamiliar to most of them, and have begun to explore developments in market research, advertising, selling, distribution. There is currently close examination on the part of administrators of the "set and sequence of activities that are under the control of the college and can affect the size, quality, and preferences of the applicant pool."[4] The result is a growing awareness of the necessity to develop marketing plans as institutions compete for a declining number of students.

Essential to the success of any marketing plan for an institution of higher education are what I have chosen to designate the "three Rs": *Raison d'être*

---

1. Philip Kotler, "Applying Marketing Theory to College Admissions," in *A Role for Marketing in College Admissions* (New York: College Entrance Examination Board, 1976), p. 54.
2. Ibid.
3. Ibid., pp. 54–55.
4. Ibid., p. 56.

or *reason for being*, the nature of the institution and the profile of students it seeks to serve; *Responsibility*, the institution's obligation to the profession of education itself and to the students who seek its education; *Retention*, the institution's achievement of a reasonably low attrition rate as a marketing tool.

Raison d'Etre

The French expression *raison d'être* connotes somewhat more than its usual English translation, "reason for being." As applied to institutions of higher education, it not only suggests that a college or university explore and articulate its own institutional mission, but also implies that honest questions be regularly raised about why the institution exists at all and what it accomplishes. Efforts to be all things to all persons are futile in our increasingly complex, rapidly changing society. At minimum, it is too expensive for one institution or agency to try to meet all possible needs and wants. Nor can institutions remain static in an evolving society. Hence, each college or university must continually ask itself a wide variety of questions: Why was it founded? with what special purposes, if any, in mind? Is the reason for its founding still valid? Into what has it evolved from its original concept? Is it needed? What are its strengths? Its weaknesses? What group or groups can it serve competently? What are its actual and potential human, financial, and physical resources to serve those groups? Is it duplicating what others in its area are doing? Is such duplication needed and purposeful? What are the effects of its geographical location? of its surroundings?—And so on.

Any college or university asking such fundamental questions must be prepared to take the consequences of its honest answers, which may range anywhere from closing its doors, to merging with a counterpart, to expanding or shrinking its scope, to shifting or reaffirming its institutional mission, and numerous variations in between. Consequences may even include such fringe benefits as providing a rationale for disapproving the establishment of another of the burgeoning institutes or centers, which sometimes fulfill the function of a "pet rock" for certain faculty members.

For my own institution, the University of San Diego, asking such questions back in the late 1960s resulted in the corporate consolidation of previously independent colleges for men and women and a coeducational law school. Many of the issues raised by the questions above had to be dealt with and resolved. The advantages of single-sex education to future women leaders, abundantly demonstrated by research, had to be weighed against the greater educational strength and diversity stemming from combining two small institutions. The most fundamental issue of institutional mission was not at stake: both institutions were Roman Catholic. Indeed, a cogent argument favoring merger was the fact that there were no other Catholic institutions of higher education south of the Los Angeles area, and none in Arizona. Hence, it was deemed very significant that the single institution growing from the merger would be educationally stronger, more diverse, and thus provide expanded opportunities for those seeking Catholic higher education in the southernmost portion of the nation's most populous state.

Another institution, asking the same questions about the same time in another region of the country, decided to close (even though it was still running in the black) because there were two sufficiently similar church-related institutions in its immediate, not heavily populated geographical environs. This institution concluded after serious study that three such colleges were not needed in its area, and that the presence of three created a situation wherein the college in question was becoming too small to afford a high quality education.

It is sadly ironic that a season of declining enrollments often affects most adversely those smaller colleges which, because of their institutional mission, are in the best position to personalize higher education in an era when—despite the pronouncements of E. F. Schumacher and his disciple, the incumbent governor of California—small is not generally perceived as beautiful. Splendid recent advice to such institutions (and indeed to all institutions) reads: "The small college which intends to survive the eighties must choose very precisely what it intends to do and be; it must be very certain that those things need doing; it must do them well; and it must learn to communicate those intentions and accomplishments to its many publics with skill and imagination."[5]

Responsibility

Just as an institution must know its own nature and purpose in the light of its history, its location, its resources, and its opportunities in order to market itself to the public, so also must it recognize its responsibility to the profession of which it is a part, and to the students it seeks to serve. Without such overt and well-articulated responsibility, institutions of higher edu-

5. Jack L. Engledow and Ronald D. Anderson, "Putting Small College Admissions in a Marketing Mode," *College and University*, Fall 1978, pp. 7–8.

cation risk debasing themselves and their role within society. The college or university's dual responsibility to the profession and to its students is to be competent in what it does and to provide quality education. If an institution of higher education has clearly articulated what it is about and concentrates on that institutional mission—whether it be a traditional or nontraditional approach to education, or some combination thereof—it runs less risk of falling prey to what might be called the "survival syndrome." "Survival at any cost" can never be an objective of a responsible college or university.

If an institution comprehends the nature of the advancement and perpetuation of knowledge, understands its own strengths and weaknesses, and recognizes and accepts its responsibility to maintain standards appropriate to the profession of education, that institution is less likely to overemphasize the "need of the seller to sell the product,"[6] and hence does not debase the currency of the realm (academic credit) by distributing it too readily for too little work or background. Colleges or universities entrapped into inappropriate stress on the "hard sell" not only fail in their responsibility to the profession, but also sell the student short by giving him or her a false sense of accomplishment. Of course, some students want and are willing to pay high prices for "quick and easy credit," but the college or university that respects itself as a member of an honored profession will not degrade that profession by catering to such shabby desires, either in its marketing concept or in practice.

My institution terminated its participation in several off-campus graduate programs rather than water down its offerings. This action came through the initiative and with the agreement of USD's full-time faculty involved in those programs, because students continually complained about having to do reading and writing assignments for USD when others required them only to show up for class in order to receive credit. The issue is not traditional versus nontraditional learning. That it is possible for a college or university to fulfill its responsibility both to the profession and to the students, and also offer university credit and degree programs in nontraditional formats, is amply demonstrated by the many institutions offering well-monitored, high quality programs in one or other of these modes. The issue is rather, quite simply, professional responsibility for quality of learning at a level appropriate to the credit being offered.

6. Kotler, "Applying Marketing Theory," p. 56.

Retention

The third R is retention, which underlies recognition that a low attrition rate is one of the best marketing tools in the institution's shop. What management consultants sometimes call "institutional fit" is at the heart of the marketing issue in higher education, and retention is one of the best indices of institutional fit. The first two Rs deal with what the particular college or university claims to be and do, and with the institution's responsibility to the profession that the claim be suitable and that the college or university implement its claim. Incoming students have been told something about the institution, directly or indirectly. They come expecting to find that what they were told is accurate for the most part. They stay if their expectations are met. They leave if disappointed or angered by a hiatus between marketing claims and institutional reality. Hence, a high rate of retention is, in a partial sense, an indication of student satisfaction and of institutional performance. Obviously, it is also the least expensive means to maintain enrollment. Students who remain have already been recruited. It has recently been noted that nationally "only half the students who enter a private four-year college or university graduate in four years. And only 35 percent graduate from four-year public institutions in four years."[7] A revolving door is very costly for the college or university.

The reasons students drop out or transfer elsewhere are myriad. Many such reasons cannot be controlled, for example, change of financial status, inability to get a desired major, boy friend or girl friend elsewhere, shift in family exigencies. But every institution that cares about its academic quality and its student enrollment (in that order) should be using retention as a marketing tool through a continuing examination and evaluation of those factors which are controllable. Is there a person or committee responsible for monitoring attrition rates? for following up students who drop out? for ascertaining any problems with the advising system, the scheduling of classes, the availability of financial aid? Are students able to get the courses they want and need, or do they have to hope they can "crash" their classes? Are there advance surveys to determine what courses students need? Marketing consultants query, "Are course times and numbers of sections designed for the convenience of the faculty or the students?" and conclude that such scheduling problems are "a critical factor (and a common

---

7. David W. Barton and David R. Treadwell, "Marketing: A Synthesis of Institutional Soul-Searching and Aggressiveness," in *Marketing Higher Education*, ed. David W. Barton (Washington: Jossey-Bass, Spring 1978), p. 82.

complaint) at small colleges who sing the song of individualized programming and tie up upperclassmen with red tape."[8]

In the early 1970s, the University of San Diego, alarmed at what seemed to be a climbing attrition rate, instituted, through the office of the director of academic services, a program called "Project Keep." Faculty and administration worked together to interview students about gaps between what we say and what we do. A semesterly analysis of students who drop out (as distinct from those who graduate or flunk out) was established, with follow-up letters to all dropouts who were full-time students asking them to help us aid future students by giving us reasons for their departure or transfer. Serious problems surfaced with the general education program, subsequently revised by the faculty.

Other controllable issues were identified and solutions found.

Prominent among causes was a severe difficulty with freshmen advising: we were doing a poor job in this significant endeavor. As a result the faculty inaugurated the freshman preceptorial program, designed to provide an academic orientation to university life. Each freshman must enroll in a three-credit course of fifteen to seventeen students, which fulfills one of the general education requirements. The teacher-preceptor becomes the academic adviser for the student until he or she declares a major, thus providing immediate and continuing contact between students and caring faculty members. The semesterly survey continues, with no "pattern" of dissatisfaction apparent for about three years. Most of the reasons given for departure are not controllable by the institution.

Institutional responses to the retention problem will vary according to the size, the needs, the purpose of the institution. But the goal remains the same: to influence student satisfaction by making the institution the kind of place it told the student it was when he or she chose to come. Then, if there is no "institutional fit," it is because the student chose unwisely, not because the college or university made unrealistic or even false claims.

An examination of what I have called the "three Rs" will reveal that they keep the college or university looking at itself, not at its supposed "competition." Instead of competing for students, it endeavors to create an educational environment where students of the type it serves will want to come and stay. Its emphasis is on the student, not on the so-called com-

---

8. David W. Barton, "Marketing: A Consultant's Evaluation of What Colleges Are Doing," *College and University*, Summer 1978, p. 559.

petitor; its responsibility is toward that student and toward the profession of which its enterprise is a part. Hence, educational quality always remains a primary priority, and the college or university retains its integrity.

Marketing Higher Education— The Survival Value of Integrity

JOHN R. SILBER

"COMPETITION FOR STUDENTS—THE MARKETING ISSUE" reflects a willingness on the part of the higher education community to concede that we are, after all, businessmen and that our business is producing and selling education. We are a business with very different standards and procedures from other industries, and our product is intangible and hard to identify. Nevertheless, our institutions are, *inter alia*, businesses, and, as such, our operations include marketing as an essential part.

These ideas, however obvious, we still perceive as alien and repugnant. As academics, we are accustomed to the idea that we have special ethical obligations. As administrators, we may also recognize special administrative ethical obligations. But we do not like to think of ourselves as businessmen, concerned with selling, and few of us have thought directly and hard about the ethical constraints on marketing in higher education, that is, about marketing ethics.

Marketing ethics in its most obvious sense deals with avoiding conviction under the fraud statutes. In another sense, marketing ethics deals with avoiding the dubiously legitimized dishonesties of some commercial advertising. We should hope that colleges and universities are supplied with the qualities of intellect and character to keep them on the narrow path. As teachers and administrators, however, we must meet a substantially higher standard than narrow legitimacy. We have special ethical obligations not to oversell our own institutions relative to others and to deliver on the fundamentals of what we offer. These are ethical problems implicit in most marketing, although they are often joyously ignored.

Higher Education or Postsecondary Education?

There are other ethical problems in marketing higher education that are less obvious but no less real and perhaps more compelling. Our first obligation as businessmen in higher education, it seems to me, is to ensure that what we sell is really higher education—"higher education" rather than "postsecondary education."

The minimum standards for purveyors of postsecondary education are somewhat laxer than for those of higher education, which is probably why the phrase is gaining currency. Anyone in postsecondary education, either as a provider or a consumer, is spared having to answer that embarrassing question, Higher than what? There is, for those who have no answer, a certain honesty in declining the use of the term "higher education," but I presume that almost all colleges and universities are willingly involved in the business of higher, rather than postsecondary, education.

Higher education is infinitely complex and elusive, but I presume that it must ultimately depend on an interaction between a person to be educated and a system for educating him. Herein lies our first dilemma, the one that resides in the admissions office. We must ask ourselves whether absolutely everyone can plausibly avail herself or himself of higher education. If the answer is no, we must devise a responsible system for screening those who cannot buy our product, no matter how much and how often they pay for it in coin and in sweat.

I do not oppose open admissions: I have no objection to that trend in itself. It does not greatly matter at what level a student is admitted to college, provided he does not receive college credit until he can do college-level work and provided he is not graduated until he reaches a level of accomplishment that is equivalent to four years of college study. It may be just as well to admit unprepared students freely and provide remedial work to qualify them for college studies; such a policy would have the decided advantage of not denying anyone educational opportunity. It would put an end to the surreptitious use of racial criteria in the admissions process. But at minimum we should be prepared to warn those students whose prognosis is ultimately grim, Travel at your own risk. One of the greatest moments in the lives of teachers and schools is when such a student triumphantly proves the experts wrong and finishes the course. On the other hand, unless we are to be callous and sadistic, we should not encourage applications from those who are almost certain to end in utter failure.

Within the next decade we may have not only open admissions but also open graduation. At that point "postsecondary education" will probably replace "higher education" altogether. At long last, what we do may not be higher than anything.

The American public will not, in my opinion, stand still for this abandonment of standards. Already they show an increasing reluctance to send their children to college and are beginning to ask whether the people who will be responsible for their children's education are good enough to be worth the price. The movement toward open admission, open promotion, and open graduation will increase public disillusionment, and the public's reaction could be swift and devastating.

But let us make the optimistic assumption: we shall resolve the coming demographic crisis with an admissions policy such that we offer higher education only to those who have some minimal chance of achieving it, and a retention policy that makes graduation something less than automatic. We are left with the far thornier ethical problem of ensuring that what we offer our students has an optimum chance of affording them higher education.

From Content to Methodology: Leeching the Curriculum

We have, I trust, passed the mad period when higher education was being defined as whatever a student wanted to do for the first four years or so after high school. The most unfortunate hangover from that time is our widespread abandoning of the foreign language requirement. This is a marketing issue not merely for higher education but for all of American industry: how can we generate a favorable balance of trade if American salesman do not speak the language of their foreign customers? As for higher education, it is hard to believe that anyone is truly educated who has not learned enough of a foreign language to comprehend in full the dependence of thought on language. Comprehension cannot be gained by a fleeting, confused "exposure" to a foreign language, and colleges and universities that are not prepared to provide a genuine encounter with foreign language are more honest to drop it altogether. The practical deficiencies of uneducated students detract less from the idea of higher education than our proclamation that someone forever locked in the intellectual prison of his own language can be called "educated."

But we have escaped by and large—and not a semester too soon—from the fraudulent position that higher education is not dependent on a curriculum. Unfortunately, we have not always chosen a curriculum that is consonant with the possibility of higher education for our students. The recent attempt at reforming the undergraduate curriculum at Harvard College is an excellent example of how far we have drifted. The "Report on the Core Curriculum," presented to Harvard's faculty of arts and sciences and approved by them, says:

> We do not think there is a single set of Great Books every educated person must master, and we do not think an inevitably thin survey of the conventional areas—humanities, social sciences, natural sciences—is any longer useful.

That last part is harmless enough. The first part is a cultural statement of the greatest importance: "We do not think there is a single set of Great Books every educated person must master." This declaration means that a person may receive the benefits of a Harvard education and be proclaimed a member of the company of educated men without having read the Bible or Homer or Sophocles or any of Shakespeare or Plato or Aquinas.

The statement that there is no set of great books that an educated man must read may be satisfactory for the development of the undergraduate curriculum at Harvard. For Harvard has immense advantages in the recruitment of a student body who will continue to educate themselves despite the obstacles and deficiencies of any curriculum. But the statement, in my view, endorses a principle inconsistent with the survival of higher education at most colleges and universities. In the development of undergraduate curricula, most colleges and universities must be animated at all points and at all times by the conviction that an educated person can read, with comprehension and without recourse to a reference library, the works of readily accessible poets such as Milton, or at least A. E. Housman.

Milton's sonnet "On His Blindness"—

> When I consider how my light is spent,
> Ere half my days in this dark world and wide,
> And that one Talent which is death to hide
> Lodg'd with me useless, though my Soul more bent
> To serve therewith my Maker, and present
> My true account, lest he returning chide; . . .

makes perfectly good sense to one who has read the parable of the talents, and no sense at all to one who has not. A student who has not read the Gospels, in trying to understand this sonnet, may require access to a research library. Or this:

> Methought I saw my late espoused saint
> Brought to me like Alcestis from the grave
> Whom Jove's great son to her glad husband gave
> Rescued from death by force though pale and faint.

Who is Alcestis? The student must return to the research library to find out. These well-known poems, high school requirements in the nineteenth century all over the Midwest and in other benighted areas of the nation, may now be beyond the educational expectations of the graduates of our foremost university.

Consider the confusion of the student who is assigned the following lines:

> Loveliest of trees, the cherry now
> Is hung with bloom along the bough
> And stands about the woodland ride
> Wearing white for Eastertide.

The puzzled student will have to repair again to the library where he will find: Easter—a ceremony sacred to Christians, symbolized by the Easter lily (Lilium Harrisii), white of color.

In such a sterile educational tradition, we will be in the educational equivalent of the position described by Saint-Exupéry in his *Flight to Arras*. Anticipating a mission from which he was unlikely to return, he wrote:

> And as I sat there longing for night, I was for the moment like a Christian abandoned by grace. I was about to do my job . . . honorably, that was certain. But to do it as one honors ancient rites when they have no longer any significance. When the god that lived in them has withdrawn from them.[1]

Or like Evelyn Waugh in his final despairing days, feeling like "a sentry at Buck House . . . posted with no possibility of his being employed to defend the Sovereign's life."[2]

The new Harvard curriculum does not so much seek to teach students a subject as to teach students *about* a subject:

> Our goal [the committee reports] is to encourage a critical appreciation of and informed acquaintance with the major approaches to knowledge, not in abstract but in substantive terms, so that students have an understanding of what kinds of knowledge exist in certain important areas, how such knowledge is acquired, how it is deployed, and what it might mean to them personally.

It goes on to describe what this means in practice:

> A Literature and the Arts requirement will acquaint students with important literary and artistic achievements and will aim to develop a critical understanding of how man gives artistic expression to his experience of the world.
>
> A requirement in Social and Philosophical Analysis will introduce the central

---

1. Antoine de Saint-Exupéry, *Flight to Arras*, trans. Bernard Lamotte (New York: Harcourt Brace Jovanovitch, 1942), p. 24.

2. *The Diaries of Evelyn Waugh*, ed. Michael Davie (London: Weidenfeld and Nicolson, 1976), p. 793. (Published in the United States by Little, Brown & Co., Boston.)

concepts and ideas of social science and moral and political philosophy and will develop students' analytic skills in addressing fundamental aspects of individual and social life in contemporary society.

Finally, a Science and Mathematics requirement will acquaint students with basic principles of the physical, biological, and behavioral sciences and with science as a way of looking at man and the world.

Thus, one does not necessarily learn a science; one learns something about a science and "how it is deployed." The presence of the buzzword "deployed" indicates the committee's indecision and lack of conviction. In my opinion, such a program is not education. It is rather today's equivalent of the grand tour obligatory for all well-finished young gentlemen a hundred years ago—a month in France, two months in Italy, perhaps a week in Constantinople. The tour of cities and continents is replaced by a tour of the intellectual metahorizon—an acquaintance, not with the subject, but with its principles and methodology.

This conception is a very unfortunate example of the solipsism that was once thought to disfigure only the schools of education, wherein content was put on the back of the shelf to be covered up with studies of methodology, technique, and process. It is a bizarre notion, that students can understand the structures and behavior of elephants and what elephants "might mean to them personally," when they have no idea what the elephant looks like. The time was when we understood that the methodology of science was something to be studied and understood once one was competent in one or more sciences, and the methodology of literature was something to be studied after one had read extensively in one or more literatures.

To criticize such a program is not to engage in the sort of Harvard-bashing that is always tempting for the less fortunate and perhaps therefore envious. It is rather to suggest that we have so lost our way that what is arguably the greatest university in the world has lost a part of its belief in higher education.

If American higher education continues along such a track—and where our greatest university leads, many will inevitably follow—our schools and colleges shall soon be little better than the schools of Athens when the Emperor Justinian finally closed them.

The Survival Value of Integrity

I believe that many of us, if not put to a public test before a board of trustees or before some foundation from which we wish to extract money, will admit that what Saint-Exupéry said is true of our campuses. We find that the god has withdrawn from the ceremonies that we celebrate and from the principles for which we allegedly stand. This withdrawal is no fault of ours, or our fathers or our predecessors, or the previous president of our institution, or some vile board of trustees. The fault lies neither in our stars nor in ourselves, but in the cultural decline that marks this age.

In such a state, we may well wonder whether we are capable of offering higher education even to those who genuinely wish it. We, as representatives of institutions, as people who teach in and work in and administer those institutions, must decide whether we will go with the cultural drift of our age, measuring the decline in our civilization by the decline in our expectations for our students and for ourselves. Or will we resist this current, and set much higher standards in curriculum and requirements that will identify us as the institutions in our society that stand for something?

We are doubtless obligated to do so as academics, on all the high and noble grounds that we are accustomed to invoke when we set ourselves apart from the vulgar and meaningless bustle of the great world. But we are no less obligated to uphold high standards as a matter of simple marketing ethics. For that is what people expect of us. The reputation of higher education has been damaged by the turmoil of the past decade, the erosion of standards, and the rise of a faculty unionism that places the teaching of classes somewhere about third—behind economic self-interest and personal self-dramatization. Nevertheless, that reputation is based precisely on the assumption that we maintain high standards and maintain principles even when it may be inconvenient to do so.

If we abandon the principles of academic integrity—without a public declaration announcing the fact—we shall be engaging in a very serious piece of marketing fraud. We shall certainly be found out at length, and we may expect that retribution will follow, partially in the form of boycott and partially in the form of control. Both are in the air even now: we have had our warning. If we foolishly insist that the quality of our product is whatever we say it is (and if we cannot state it short of a twenty-page committee report), the consumers—our students and parents who demand truth in selling from others—will at length turn their full attention to us. It is not clear that even businesses that serve the public well at declining costs can withstand such an examination, but let us at least hope that we shall deserve to pass the scrutiny more or less intact. If we maintain our integrity, we shall have grounds for optimism.

Marketing, Management, Mobility—
College Admissions in the 1980s

MORRIS L. NORFLEET

WHEN A NEW UNIVERSITY PRESIDENT takes office and finds that the full-time enrollment of the institution has been dropping for the last three years while the headcount enrollment remained relatively stable, what does he or she do? Danger signs emanate from the computer. The "soft" enrollment picture created by part-time students amounted to 20 percent of the total headcount.

At Morehead State University, the new president brought to his job a background in research and some limited experience in marketing. The circumstances, reinforced by the published success stories of community colleges in marketing their admissions, led the university into a serious study of marketing principles and concepts applicable to admissions in a four-year institution of public higher education. Staff in admissions and public affairs, consulting with administrators in all other areas of the university, sought answers to several basic questions: Where do our students come from? What do they think of our academic programs and student life activities? How can we communicate with prospective students and influence them to consider Morehead State in their career planning? From the prospective student's viewpoint, what are the institution's strengths and weaknesses? And, perhaps most important, how is the admissions effort being coordinated to maximize use of resources and to obtain objective evaluation of the entire operation?

The consensus was that Morehead State University must develop a marketing approach to admissions, using the concepts of market research, marketing strategies, and ongoing evaluation. Although skepticism was obvious, particularly in academic quarters, the decision was made to proceed with a marketing plan for all admissions activities, starting with the 1978–79 school year. The results were surprising, and the original skeptics were pleased that their fears of marketing leading the university to hucksterism had been unfounded. An organized effort to "sell" higher education did not destroy the university by likening it to proprietary schools that advertise in pulp magazines and on late night television.

Morehead State University's commitment to a marketing approach to admissions has produced an 8 percent increase in enrollment during the first year and an increase in full-time freshmen in the second year.

But marketing alone, despite its sophisticated application of organizational and selling principles, will not be sufficient for most institutions of higher education that face the grim prospects of declining population and the growing tendency of young persons to opt for other career alternatives. In the admissions world of the 1980s, institutions must be prepared and determined to utilize marketing and management and to cope with the mobility of American society, particularly those of college age.

Marketing Can Make the Difference

The marketplace of higher education admissions, like the marketplace of the business community, is changing constantly as buying (enrollment) patterns fluctuate and new markets (potential students) emerge. For example, the marketing plan at Morehead State University is undergoing several changes during 1979–80 because market research has made us aware of the potential for stabilizing enrollments by attracting nontraditional students such as employed persons preparing for a mid-life career switch. The elderly, stay-at-home mothers, and certain high school students also fall into these virtually untapped markets in our region of Kentucky. This new thrust, we hope, will produce more part-time students, on campus and off. One basic component is a bolstering of our commitment to noncredit community education (continuing education), which has been shown to have a spin-off effect on credit courses. Strategies are being developed with the goal of achieving an enrollment increase as early as the spring term of 1980.

At Morehead State, we are convinced that marketing can make the difference between stabilization and retrenchment; there really is no other choice for colleges and universities that wish to remain viable in the 1980s. Without the cost efficiency of admissions marketing, we could not afford to be competitive in the admissions arena. Marketing is compatible with higher education's basically conservative image with most of its publics. The selling techniques of the marketing approach can be employed without sacrificing institutional integrity, academic quality, or the dignity of academe.

Marketing is selling, pure and simple, but the marketing of higher education must be recognized as vastly different from the marketing of laundry detergent. Our product, obviously, is intangible. Its utility is eternal and universal because education is the cornerstone of our society.

The so-called hard sell of the huckster cannot be effective over the long run in higher education because the consumer (student) must live with the product (education) forever. On a more practical note, attempts to "hustle" someone in college admissions—be it through inaccurate publications, misleading advertising, or other device—will place the institution immediately at cross-purposes with consumer protection agencies on the local, state, and federal levels. At Morehead State, we have no desire to add the Federal Trade Commission to the list of government agencies with which we are required to communicate and even litigate.

Marketing professionals make much ado about "positioning." The need to improve the seller's position in the marketplace presented the first hurdle for Morehead State's marketing plan. As the only public university in Appalachian Kentucky, the institution had a primary market where only about 38 percent of the high school graduates plan on postsecondary training, and the figure is as low as 28 percent in certain counties. Thus, the institution's admissions staff must market the idea of higher education in general and higher education at Morehead State University in particular. The twofold objective is to provide information to show prospective students that the college experience is worth while and that the university is a reliable, progressive institution that strives to prepare its students for careers with a future.

Although situations may differ from campus to campus, the keys to successful admissions marketing invariably requires (1) research, (2) planning, (3) implementation, and (4) evaluation.

Market research, to be effective, must be unending. In addition to determining how the institution is perceived by its constituents, market research also must measure public opinion on the worth of the product, the projection of the messages, and the effectiveness of the delivery systems. By identifying misconceptions and marketable strengths, the institution can more easily select the means effective for reaching various target constituencies.

To illustrate this point, the first market research at Morehead State revealed that a nationally recognized teacher education program and the heritage of a teachers college had created a misconception in the marketplace. Teacher education remains a vital program, but the institution offers many other programs. However, we learned that our academic offerings, specifically in the technologies and business, were widely unknown to certain groups, especially parents who are natives of the region. A low-key and cost-efficient series of messages, appearing primarily in the form of newspaper, magazine, and radio advertising, has largely corrected this identity problem.

Ongoing programs in community relations, press relations, governmental relations, and faculty-staff relations ensure that the university's principal publics are aware of the institution's diverse curricula. Similar programs supported the viability of a college degree as a career preparation option and the personal rewards of the student-life experience on campus.

Graduates of high schools and two-year colleges are the main consumers of higher education in senior institutions. Various studies have shown that guidance counselors, parents, alumni, peers, and ministers are the "influentials" in the decisions of these consumers. Accordingly, these persons must be central in all efforts to disseminate information about the institution. Moreover, an informed "influential" can reinforce indirect marketing strategies such as direct mail and mass media.

When all the procedures have been followed carefully and when all the creative messages have been sent and received to some degree, we at Morehead State University have learned that the success of the marketing approach still depends on the timely employment of the most basic of all sales tools—the personal touch. A soon-to-be-published study by David W. Chapman of the School of Education, University of Michigan, involved college admissions and high school guidance counselors at more than 1,300 schools. In the opinion of a majority of the respondents, of twenty-seven generally practiced "admissions activities," the high school visit by the admissions representative remains the most effective.[1] Ranking second was campus visits by prospective students. Both activities consist mainly of personal selling, either by the admissions representatives and faculty or by university students serving as campus hosts or guides. Hence, the admissions marketing plan at Morehead State will continue to utilize new strategies but the underlying emphasis will be on support of the personal selling activity.

Management by Any Other Name

"If it ain't broke, don't fix it" is a common expression in rural Kentucky, especially in reference to the sometimes strange activities of government bureaucrats, including some on college campuses. In the case of admissions at Morehead State, management was in need of fixing: we overhauled the organizational structure and intensified the management process. Two previously separate staffs were consolidated, and the admissions office was upgraded to division status, with the director reporting to a vice president

---

1. Chapman et al., "Effective Admissions Practices: A National Survey" (August 1979).

and also having direct access to the president. Financial resources were increased modestly and reallocated, as prescribed by the various strategies in the marketing plan. The executive management group of the university became more involved as the marketing program required campuswide coordination of all admissions activities. At Morehead State, we insist that all administrators, from the president down, make time for the nitty gritty of admissions such as receptions, letter writing, handshaking, and the like. No other activity has a higher priority.

Management, by any other name, still involves imagination, sound decision making, and, in the parlance of the athlete, mental toughness. The unpredictable admissions area, with its spiraling costs, inordinate time demands, and potential for disaster, represents a managerial challenge equal to any other in higher education, public or private.

Institutions with team-oriented management systems should have no major difficulty in implementing the marketing approach to admissions. A collaborative effort is required in each step of the process and particularly in evaluation, where candor is vital.

Perhaps the thorniest of all management problems related to admissions is retention of students. Why do institutions work so diligently to attract students only to see that, sometimes, as many as half of them leave within three semesters? The attrition rate at Morehead State, as at most other institutions, is too high, but now it is getting center stage attention through improved academic advisement, personal counseling, and a renewed emphasis on developmental studies. Aided by a new federal grant, we are moving to implement a "diagnostic-prescriptive" approach to postadmissions, which is intended to identify and prescribe corrective action for academic deficiencies, particularyly in reading, mathematics, and written and spoken communications, which new students bring with them to the university.

Attrition rates can be reduced substantially without lowering academic standards or encouraging further grade inflation. Management of the postadmissions processes, if innovative and if sufficiently financed, can and will solve the attrition problem in higher education.

In Search of Something

Mobility, a social phenomenon of our times, is becoming a consideration in college admissions today and, if the trend continues, will be even more so into the 1980s. Morehead State University certainly is not unique in its concern about students who fail to report after being admitted or who voluntarily interrupt their college studies and, in many cases, return to the campus after lapses of one to four years. Identified usually as "no shows" and "stopouts," respectively, these persons can be encouraged to return if the admissions staff maintains or reestablishes personal contact. At Morehead State, we have experienced frustration and, on a limited scale, a degree of success in this venture. Central to this endeavor and the rest of the admissions effort at Morehead State is TISAD (Total Information Services for Admissions), a data bank which has as much pertinent information as can be obtained on prospective students, past or future.

It is becoming more evident with each year that the competition for students in higher education will become more intense as the market dwindles in size during the 1980s.

With the bold, yet practical application of marketing principles and solid management practices and with an awareness of mobility—and a little luck—Morehead State University will be among those institutions surviving the next ten years without a significant enrollment decline and without being forced to dilute quality academic programs which serve its region, the Commonwealth of Kentucky, and the nation.

2. COMPETITION FOR STUDENTS—RECRUITMENT AND RETENTION

Strengthening Student Recruitment and Retention—Some Ideas from Research

ALEXANDER W. ASTIN

DISCUSSIONS ABOUT RECRUITING STRATEGIES with persons representing several different types of institutions presents a dilemma. To a certain extent, institutions compete with each other in their quest for students; one institution's success may be another's failure. Of course, effective recruiting by a large number of competing institutions may serve to increase the total pool of prospective students by encouraging some young people who might otherwise not attend college to apply. My impression is that most recruiting, particularly that done by four-year institutions, focuses on students who are already college-bound.

My own research suggests that the public institutions played a major role in fostering the competition for students; and the shortage of applicants that many private institutions experienced in the 1970s was directly traceable to the rapid expansion of the public sector during the 1960s.[1] As a tangential note, a select subgroup of private institutions do compete with each other for that limited pool of the very brightest students. Still, in sheer numbers of students affected, competition from large, low-cost public institutions represents by far the biggest threat to private colleges.

Recruitment

Although the suggestions offered here about recruitment could theoretically be of value to any institution, the private colleges are probably in a better position than the public institutions to act on them. The greater hope, however, is that better recruiting by all institutions will eventually serve to increase the total pool of applicants.

As I was deciding which elements of my research would be most useful

---

1. A. W. Astin, C. E. Christian, and J. W. Henson, *The Impact of Student Financial Aid Programs on Student Choice*, Final Report submitted to the Office of Planning, Budgeting and Evaluation, U.S. Office of Education (contract No. 300-75-0382) (Los Angeles: Higher Education Research Institute, 1977).

to institutional administrators, it occurred to me that *no* recruiting strategy is likely to be entirely successful unless it is based on some conception of how and why students pick their colleges. So rather than presenting a handy-dandy list of the latest recruiting strategies, I shall emphasize some findings from a national study of college *choice* to identify those characteristics of the student and of the student's environment that influence the type of college the student chooses.[2]

Early choices. The study involved a longitudinal analysis of changes in the college preferences of students between the eleventh grade and college entry. The sample included about 725,000 eleventh-graders who were followed up in the twelfth grade. About 150,000 of these students were also followed up at the time they actually entered college. Thus, information on the students' choices is available at three points: early in the eleventh grade, midway through the twelfth grade, and at the time of college entry. The nature of the sample makes the information derived from the study applicable only to the recruitment of students directly out of high school.

First, what do we know about students' early choices? It appears that the choices of many students beginning the eleventh grade are constrained because of money. That is, very early in the game, many of the economically poorest students opt for the cheapest public institutions, thinking they cannot afford to attend more expensive private institutions. Clearly, these students are not aware that enormous resources of state, federal, and institutional financial aid exist. Thus, one immediate conclusion is that private institutions should band together to ensure that poor students understand that they can afford to attend even the most costly private institution—provided, of course, they offer certain other attributes.

As students revise their choices between the eleventh grade and the time they actually apply, they move in the direction of cheaper, less selective, public institutions, particularly two-year colleges. These trends suggest that many potential students are lost to the private institutions sometime between the beginning of eleventh grade and midway through the twelfth grade. While we do not know all the factors involved in these changes, widespread ignorance among high school students about the availability of financial aid is certainly one factor to consider.

Student characteristics. Without question, *high-ability* students are the hardest to recruit. Most such students limit their choices to expensive and highly selective institutions located far from their homes. While family income plays some role in determining whether a student picks a private

2. Ibid.

college, ability is a much more important factor. Also, parents' education operates much like student ability in affecting institutional choice. Students whose parents are highly educated tend to opt for selective and expensive colleges located far from home. Probably an imitative process is at work here, whereby parents who went to private colleges encourage their children to go to the same types of institutions. This relationship may spell more problems for the private institutions in the near future, since the proportion of parents who went to private institutions is declining sharply. That is, the children of parents who completed college during the massive expansion of public higher education that began in the 1950s are just now reaching college age, and during the next twenty years the proportion of college-age students whose parents went to public rather than private institutions will increase steadily.

Our research documents a number of interesting differences among ethnic groups in their college preferences. Asians are heavily concentrated in selective and expensive colleges located far from home (particularly universities); they tend to avoid community colleges. Moreover, the college choices of Asians are more stable between the eleventh grade and college entry than are those of other ethnic groups. Blacks who live in a region where the traditionally black colleges are located are relatively likely to attend these colleges, but very few black students from other regions travel a long distance from home to attend black colleges. Blacks and American Indians are the most unstable in their college choices between eleventh grade and college entry. One especially provocative finding concerns the college preference of Chicanos. Unlike the other disadvantaged minorities, Chicanos tend to be strongly attracted to private institutions. It seems, then, that private institutions might find a rich pool of prospective students among Chicanos provided this pool can be reached by sophisticated recruiting techniques.

Geography. The single most important factor in determining whether a student is able to carry out early (eleventh grade) choices is the distance of the early choice college from home. The closer it is to home, the greater the likelihood that the student will actually attend that college.

Private institutions are at the greatest disadvantage in attempting to recruit students when a public university or a public four-year college is located nearby. Similarly, the public institutions also compete with each other. A public two-year college, for example, is particularly threatened in its quest for students when it is located near a public four-year college or a nonselective public university. The public two-year colleges, in turn, are likely to frustrate the recruiting efforts of sectarian colleges if the two types of institutions are located in the same vicinity.

Financial aid and tuition. Our study revealed some interesting differences from state to state with respect to the relation between financial aid and college choice. In general, a very generous state financial aid program seems to encourage high-ability students to attend private institutions and low-ability students to attend public two-year colleges. Though not entirely clear, this finding may well reflect the fact that some state aid programs have a merit component.

Another clear-cut effect of a generous state financial aid program is that it encourages students to attend colleges within the state rather than to migrate to neighboring states.

Our research also throws some light on the so-called tuition gap (difference in the average costs of a public and a private institution). Nonselective private institutions are most adversely affected by a substantial tuition gap; the more elite private institutions suffer very little.

Probably our most important findings concern how competing financial aid offers affect college choice. When a student is trying to choose between competing offers from two different institutions, the weightiest factor is the relative size of the *grants* in the aid packages. The other components of the aid package (loans, work-study) make little difference in the student's eventual choice.

When the choice involves competition between a public and a private institution, the most important consideration appears to be the private institution's *net tuition* (the difference between the tuition charged by the institution and the amount of financial aid offered). Apparently, students choosing among competing private institutions or among competing public institutions pay little attention to their relative costs. But when the choice involves competing public and private institutions, the student becomes conscious of how much the private institution will cost. These results suggest that, in attempting to influence student choice through offers of financial aid, institutions must be aware of the student's *choice set*.

The president's role. Before leaving the topic of recruitment, I would like to mention one other recent study that has yielded some valuable information.[3] This study, conducted in the mid-1970s, examined the behavior of college presidents at fifty private liberal arts colleges. Although

---

3. A. W. Astin and R. A. Scherrei, *Maximizing Leadership Effectiveness* (San Francisco: Jossey-Bass, 1980).

most of these colleges had either stable or declining enrollments during the period of the study, enrollments at two of them increased sharply. As it happens, these two colleges were the only ones where the president *personally* participated in the recruitment process. In both instances, the involvement took the form of meeting with prospective students and their parents when they visited the campus. Although presidents of the larger institutions would probably find it difficult to meet every prospective student who visits the campus, presidents of smaller institutions might be well advised to calculate the costs and potential benefits of allocating some of their time to this activity. Even at relatively large institutions, a certain amount of the president's time might be productively devoted to meeting prospective students.

Under these conditions, the admissions office would probably have to select judiciously only those students who are genuinely on the fence. It should be kept in mind that students and parents considering a small college are frequently looking for an environment where the student will get more personal attention than is normally the case in a large institution. My hunch is that nothing would impress such people more than a personal visit, even a very brief one, with the chief executive.

Retention

During the past fifteen years, considerable research on student retention has used longitudinal data from the Cooperative Institutional Research Program (CIRP). This continuing series of studies has highlighted a number of factors that bear on student persistence or attrition in higher education. For instance, it seems that one of the best ways of keeping students in college is through part-time jobs. Undergraduates who are employed part time stand a better chance of completing their degree programs than do comparable students who do not have outside jobs. Here is an instance where the research evidence contradicts the folklore, which holds that having to work while attending college impedes the student's academic progress. On the contrary, working while in college can enhance academic progress. I hasten to add a note of caution: the beneficial effects of outside employment diminish when students work more than twenty hours a week; if the student has a full-time job, the effect is reversed. In other words, students who must work full time are less likely to finish college than are those who have no jobs. Thus, jobs represent a potentially effective way of combating attrition provided the number of hours is limited and the job is on campus.

Another highly effective way for students to reduce their chances of dropping out is to get away from home and live on campus in a dormitory. The positive effects of dormitory living on retention occur in all types of institutions and apply to all types of students regardless of sex, race, ability, or family background. In fact, our data show that the absence of residential facilities is a main reason for the relatively high attrition rates among community college students.

In addition, students who join social fraternities or sororities are less likely to drop out, as are students who participate in extracurricular activities. Involvement in sports—particularly intercollegiate sports—has an especially pronounced positive effect on persistence. Other activities that enhance persistence include participation in honors programs, in ROTC, and in professors' undergraduate research projects.

The students most likely to persist are those who are heavily involved in their academic work and who interact frequently with faculty. On the negative side, students who seldom or never make contact with faculty members or who have little involvement in their academic work are good dropout prospects. If ways could be found to involve these students more deeply in their studies and to increase their interaction with faculty, attrition rates might be significantly reduced.

Do these findings suggest any specific actions that institutions might take to increase retention rates? I think that they clearly do. Perhaps more important, they also suggest a general *theory* about persistence which might be useful to administrators as they consider how to design programs for reducing attrition. The key construct in this theory is student *involvement*. Briefly, the theory maintains that, the greater the student's involvement in the academic experience, the greater the chances that the student will remain in college and complete a degree program. In essence, "involvement" refers to the amount of time and of physical and psychic energy that the student invests in the educational process. Some of the factors already mentioned that enhance persistence appear to reflect greater student involvement: having a part-time job on campus, living on campus, joining student organizations, participating in extracurricular activities, and so forth.

As a general operating principle, college administrators and faculty members should encourage students to get more *involved*, to invest more of their total time and effort in the educational process. But what does this mean, in more concrete terms, for institutional policy and practice?

Perhaps the first step should be a thorough examination of the institution's *information system*. How much is known about how involved or uninvolved are the students at a particular institution? Is information concerning student involvement (or lack of it) available to key institutional personnel? Do classroom instructors and faculty advisors regularly have access to data on students' academic involvement? Do students personnel administrators periodically receive information on students' extracurricular participation? Do appropriate data get disseminated in a comprehensible form and in time to take appropriate remedial action? Does the administration regularly take the initiative in serving faculty and staff needs for better information on student progress and development? Since probably few institutional administrators could respond affirmatively to all these questions, evaluation and improvement of the institution's information system offers a useful way of encouraging greater student involvement.

I want to emphasize again that the findings reported here were derived primarily from studies of students who enrolled full time in college directly after graduating from high school. Since involvement of the type that I have described is probably a more serious issue for these students than for adults or part-timers, it may be useful for those institutions with large nontraditional student populations to make some special effort to differentiate the eighteen-year-olds from other student groups. My impression is that many students coming directly from high school into large commuter institutions often get lost in the shuffle. Such students might well benefit from special orientation, academic advisement, career counseling, and other support programs. More important, these students probably merit much more intensive *monitoring* through the institution's information system than do other student subpopulations.

Institutions with large commuter populations are faced with another serious problem. Lacking adequate residential facilities, how can such institutions be administered so as to maximize student involvement? Is it possible to *simulate* the residential experience, at least for those eighteen-year-olds coming directly from high school in pursuit of a bachelor's degree? As a beginning, commuter institutions should distinguish clearly among their different categories of students. The special programs for enhancing involvement will be less costly to implement and more likely to be effective if they are targeted specifically at such students, rather than at students in general. The range of possible programs for enhancing student involvement are numerous: weekend or week-long residential "retreats," more cultural events on campus, improvements in parking facilities, required office hours for faculty, regular conferences between students and advisors, organized study groups, improvements in campus recreational facilities, expansion of on-campus employment opportunities, and expansion in number and scope of student clubs and organizations. Suggestions for dealing with the special problems of commuters are given in a recent report from the Educational Facilities Laboratory, *The Neglected Majority: Facilities for Commuting Students*.[4]

My final suggestion is one that might be expected of a researcher: I urge institutions to seize every opportunity to experiment and innovate. From the laundry list of possible approaches for reducing attrition, try to figure out which ones offer the most promise for your particular situation, and try out one or two of them on an experimental basis. Find out if they actually work. Be sure to collect enough systematic data during the trial period so that you will be able to judge whether the new policies are really effective and whether they should be instituted on a permanent basis.

Strategic Planning to Improve Recruitment and Retention

BEN LAWRENCE

COLLEGES AND UNIVERSITIES GENERALLY ARE SEEN to have four basic ways of dealing with the declining size of the potential college student population in the 18–24 age bracket in the coming decade. The first is to economize, cut back, even close the doors. But evidence is building that smaller is not necessarily cheaper and that what little is gained by efforts to economize may be more than offset by the erosion of quality.

A second alternative is for an institution somehow to obtain a larger percentage of the pool of high school graduates. But higher education will not be served well by competition among institutions to win a zero-sum game. With respect to public institutions, funders are no more enthusiastic about such a prospect than are the colleges and universities themselves.

A more sanguine prospect is that our campuses can maintain themselves by attracting larger numbers of students beyond the age of twenty-four, through enriched continuing-education programs and other offerings designed for adults of all ages. Institutions must be prepared, of course, for the fact that the establishment of such programs and accommodation of

---

4. Educational Facilities Laboratory, *The Neglected Majority: Facilities for Commuting Students* (New York: The Laboratory, 1977).

such students—the great majority of whom will attend only part time—will entail significant and perhaps massive reallocation of resources, radical curriculum changes, administrative upheavals, and human dislocations.

So it makes sense for almost any institution to look to yet another course, which is to increase student retention rates. Although the dropout rate is not known with certainty, it seems to be roughly 50 percent, with less variation among institutions with differing admission standards than might be expected. In any case, an institution with an attrition rate of 30 percent, say, for an entering freshman class could do much to stabilize itself financially and academically if that rate could be halved. Few institutions today would regard as insignificant a 15 percent increase in overall enrollment.

In reality, however, retention is not a cure-all, and it is not divorced from recruitment. For practical purposes, recruitment and retention are two sides of the same coin. If recruitment is careful as well as energetic, retention will benefit. Moreover, an institution with a higher-than-average retention rate can make the most of that virtue in its recruitment efforts. We should include recruitment and retention as elements in an overall concept of marketing, along with curriculum and program development, faculty development, and resource allocation and reallocation. However, college and university administrators commonly view recruitment and retention as discrete activities. Consequently, they divorce these functions, both from one another and from the other factors that affect marketing and that are integrated in the strategic-planning process.

Two Assumptions

My argument proceeds from two assumptions. The first I have already stated—that recruitment and retention are two sides of one coin. Recently the staff of the National Center for Higher Education Management Systems, in investigating the need for better information for prospective students, encountered administrators with similar convictions. For example, an admissions director at a private school said the institution had learned that providing misleading information to prospective students can increase attrition. It also had learned that the student who drops out because of unmet expectations spreads the word among relatives and friends, with definitely negative effects on future recruiting.

My second assumption is that marketing is a valid, ethical activity for colleges and universities. Cut-throat competition that degenerates into head-hunting in the zero-sum jungle, we all condemn. If we are wise, we will eschew the advertising tactics of the commercial marketplace not only because misrepresentation boomerangs but also because it does untold harm to the victimized students and to our own sense of worth and high mission. Higher education must survive for a purpose other than survival itself. In higher education, marketing appropriately constitutes communication with potential clients and is in itself value-free.

Higher education is in competition with other public services for public dollars. But none of the competitors seeks a profit except in the form of benefits for clients. I see nothing improper and much that is socially, financially, and politically wise in higher education making vigorous, responsible marketing efforts. When, because of our marketing efforts, potential students and the public understand exactly what we offer and at what price, we have done nothing more than provide information needed for intelligent decision making. Failure to do that would not be in the public interest.

Preparing for the Future

How, then, can strategic planning improve recruitment and retention of students in higher education? The potential is inherent in strategic planning as it is usually defined: holistic planning that (1) integratively considers purposes, environment, and capacity, and (2) formulates strategies that either satisfy the constraints posed by these factors or determine how one or more of the constraining factors should be modified.

At NCHEMS, where we are beginning a four-year research and development project on strategic planning in higher education, we emphasize the proactive nature of such planning. That is, strategic planning considers purposes, capacity, and the environment to be constraints only initially. If an effective future is not envisioned for the institution when these factors are viewed as constraints, strategic planning calls for developmental plans to change one or more of those factors. We are extremely cautious about drawing analogies between higher education and business and industry, where strategic planning is relatively well developed. But the areas for strategic-planning decisions in business and industry probably are duplicated in colleges and universities, remembering that our behavior within each of these areas may be, and should be, distinctively different.

The first area of strategic-planning decisions generally is labeled organizational *mission, purposes, and objectives*—or, as we call it in higher education, mission, role, and scope. It involves decisions about the *market-product mix*, that is, decisions about what clients the organization seeks to attract and serve, in what geographic area, and with what products, programs, and services. One may list markets and products separately, but obviously they are interaactive and matchable. In addition, strategic planning includes decisions about *resource mix*, that is, what resources will be provided to produce goods and services and by what processes and techniques they will be produced—in the corporate world, called production function. Decisions in this area take into account financing as well as human and material resources. Finally, there are decisions about *pricing*.

In each of these decision areas, three sets of criteria are frequently employed to evaluate individual decisions. The first set consists of three questions: What are the competitive implications, the differential advantage being sought by the institution? Will the decision in question make the institution more distinct from other institutions, or more like them? How will the increased difference or similarity help (or hinder) the institution's competitive position?

The second set of criteria comprises these questions: How will any one decision affect other functions and components of the institution? Will it increase or build upon an existing strength or capability? Will it take the institution in a new, unsupported direction? Is synergy possible, or will diffusion result?

The third set of questions: Are there opportunities that are consistent with institutional capabilities but are not now being pursued? Will the decision maintain or diminish the institution's ability to realize other future opportunities?

In short, strategic planning requires the institution to set its course with due regard for its external environment and with consideration for its internal capabilities. It identifies decision areas that are critical to the formulation of institutional strategy, and it establishes competitive advantage, synergy, and maximizing of opportunity as essential considerations in each decision.

The strategic-planning project at NCHEMS initially has identified seven tasks associated with recruitment and retention: (1) using evaluation and outcomes information effectively; (2) identifying and assessing needs of constituents; (3) clarifying the purposes and objectives of the institution as a whole and of its various programs; (4) comprehensively identifying and assessing the institution's capacity; (5) building on existing strengths and improving marketing through targeting, positioning, and segmentation; (6) providing better information to students and communicating it more effectively; and (7) getting full participation within the institution in the efforts to improve recruitment and retention.

Effective Use of Outcomes and Evaluation Information

Before colleges and universities can learn to make the most effective use of information about the quality of their programs and the benefits deriving from a college education, they are going to have to acquire a great deal more of this kind of information than they now have.

A few months ago, NCHEMS and the College Board established the Student-Outcomes Information Service, from which colleges and universities can acquire much of the information and consultation they need to conduct outcome studies and analyze the results. Much work remains to be done on ways to measure a full range of outcomes, however, and the NCHEMS strategic-planning project will be working on ways to apply outcomes information to planning. In passing, I want to observe that higher education cannot afford either overzealous skepticism or too-fastidious diffidence with regard to outcomes information. It will never be complete, or pristinely valid and reliable, any more than is the information now obtainable about the value of medical care or aid to dependent children. In the political arena in which higher education must compete for funds, it either must make the best case it can or risk getting less than its fair share of public money.

Identifying and Assessing Student Needs

Most studies of student needs have attempted only to identify the needs. For planning purposes, however, it is just as important to assess the extent of needs, determine why they exist, and determine the extent to which they may reasonably be met. Most work in this area has been done at the elementary and secondary levels. At the postsecondary level, NCHEMS recently published two books on assessment of student and community needs. Other recent work deals with how to conduct market surveys of potential demand, with demand considered to be an indication of probable need.[1]

Clarifying Purposes and Objectives

Too often, the goals and objectives of institutions and their programs are communicated in such global and abstract terms that they have little meaning either to constituents who are trying to understand the institution's

---

1. See JoAn S. Segal and G. Roger Sell, *Needs Assessment Information System* (Boulder, Colo.: National Center for Higher Education Management Systems [NCHEMS], 1978) and Oscar T. Lenning et al., "Identifying and Assessing Needs in Postsecondary Education," staff paper (Boulder, Colo.: NCHEMS, 1979).

aims or to those in the institution who are responsible for planning. Conrad has observed that the goals of an institution function in several ways: as standards for judging accomplishment, as a source of legitimacy for justifying activities, and as a means for defining organizational needs and priorities, units of output, clientele, and the nature of the relationship between the institution and society generally. Conrad adds that "in most universities, goals are often implicit, residing in an extended body of collective understandings rather than in explicit statements."[2]

Considerable attention is now being paid to developing clear, comprehensive statements on mission, role, and scope as well as formulating procedures for identifying, articulating, and measuring progress toward institutional goals and objectives.[3]

Assessing Institutional Capacity

Primary determinants of an institution's ability to achieve its goals reside in its tangible capacity (physical facilities and equipment, finances, personnel, and students) as well as its intangible resources (curriculum and program offerings; the knowledgeability, leadership capability, vitality, and flexibility of its faculty and administrators; decision processes; staff morale; and institutional reputation). All these resources must be analyzed, so that they can be employed in ways that exploit opportunities and advance progress toward priority goals. Little work has been done on analysis and organization of institutional capacity, and the literature is narrow in scope, with little attention given to many of the intangible resources.

Segmentation, Positioning, and Targeting

In the current fiscal environment, colleges and universities cannot afford to spread themselves too thinly in the name of comprehensive programming. In coming years, most institutions are likely to find that they are better off focusing on their strengths and relinquishing parts of the market that they are not well equipped to serve. The marketing terminology *segmentation*, *positioning*, and *targeting* is self-explanatory. The trick is to understand the interrelations of these activities when making strategic-planning decisions that will guide recruitment and bolster retention. Ten

2. Clifton Conrad, "University Goals: An Operative Approach," *Journal of Higher Education*, October 1974, pp. 505–15.

3. See McManis and Associates and University Associates, *A Guide to the Development of Mission, Goals, Objectives, Performance Evaluation Measures and Milestones* (Washington: McManis and Associates, University Associates, n.d.), and J. Kent Caruthers, *Handbook for Mission, Role, and Scope Studies* (Boulder, Colo.: NCHEMS, forthcoming).

years ago, the Danforth Foundation took the position that a private college should be unique, at least in some respects, to deserve existence.[4] Recent studies testify to the wisdom of that outlook.

Better Information for Students

Numerous studies have shown that prospective college students often receive inadequate information on which to base their selection of institution and program, and that what information they receive often is ineffectively communicated. Work at NCHEMS has shown that these information deficiencies have serious consequences with respect to student access, equality of opportunity and choice, adjustment, satisfaction, and accomplishment.[5] Obviously, there are negative consequences also for the institutions.

The Education Amendments of 1976 mandated that colleges and universities provide prospective students with certain information. The National Task Force on Better Information for Student Choice, organized by the Fund for Improvement of Postsecondary Education, developed a guideline on how to meet the general information needs of prospective students. At the University of Michigan, project CHOICE did similar work. However, little is known about the special information needs of minority groups and other groups of disadvantaged students. Little attention has been given to the information needs of enrolled students, faculty and staff, funders, and the concerned public.

Getting Full Participation

Recruitment and retention will prosper to the extent that faculty, administrators, support staff, alumni, and students themselves are motivated and guided to contribute fully and appropriately to the enterprise. One task of strategic planning may be to analyze and organize appropriate approaches to improved recruitment and retention of students. But successful implementation may well depend on an understanding of motives and effective incentives in the academic world—a subject not yet explicated in the literature. At NCHEMS, we are assessing the state of knowledge regarding organizational performance in higher education, which thus far falls far short of the theoretical, conceptual, and developmental knowledge

---

4. Danforth Foundation, "A Report: College Goals and Governance," *Danforth News and Notes*, November 1969, pp. 1–9.

5. Oscar T. Lenning and Edward M. Cooper, *Guidebook for Colleges and Universities: Presenting Information to Prospective Students* (Boulder, Colo.: NCHEMS, 1978).

available to management of business and industry. We are considering whether we must undertake basic research on organizational behavior and change in order to support our strategic-planning project. We are under no illusions: This is a high-risk area for research and one in which few have ventured over the past quarter-century. But it is high time that we learned more about what makes people in higher education tick.

To prescribe strategic planning as a way to improve recruitment and retention while admitting that strategic planning in higher education is in its infancy is to risk a certain loss of credibility. But strategic planning does have a good record in other sectors of endeavor and it has, in my mind at least, a compelling logic. Strategic planning has three foremost aims: (1) to achieve the optimum match between student and institution and student and program, (2) to optimize the institution's research and scholarship capabilities, and (3) to optimize public service.

Thus strategic planning aims to make higher education at once effective and efficient. It is the way, I am confident, to achieve the greatest good for the greatest number, and when higher education can do that and prove it, perhaps we will turn public attention away from the productivity mongers who care nothing about the value of a college education and are reserving their enthusiasm instead for cost cutting at any price. To the extent that strategic planning can maximize recruitment and retention in higher education, it will ensure not only the survival of colleges and universities but also the survival of what they stand for and what they provide in our society. That is the main reason that over the next four or five years, NCHEMS will put much of its resources into a comprehensive study of the potential for strategic planning in higher education and on investigation of ways to capitalize on that potential.

Throw All the Darts—State of the Art in Recruiting and Retention

NEIL J. WEBB

A SURE WAY TO STRIKE TERROR in the hearts of college presidents is to mention the 1980s decade and the projected decline in the eighteen-year-old population. The concern is well founded: higher education expects to lose a fourth of its college-age population base in the next thirteen years.[1]

---

1. U.S. Bureau of the Census, *Current Population Reports*, series P-25, nos. 529, 601, 643.

In short, the survival and prosperity of most colleges and universities in the 1980s will depend on improved recruitment and retention practices.

The experience at St. Norbert College offers some optimism for improvements in recruitment and retention. Among the top priorities in an overall fourteen-point action program launched in 1972 to prepare for the 1980s were improved recruitment and retention of students. The basic strategy in both areas was to try a number of approaches gleaned from research findings and the experience of other colleges in the hope that some would work.

The action programs, now in effect for seven years, have proved moderately successful. In recruitment, applications for admission increased by 45 percent. In 1972, the college generated 745 applications for admission, and in 1979 a record number of 1,080 applications were received. By holding the new student enrollment stable, the increase in applications provided the hoped-for opportunity for greater selectivity.

The activities designed to improve retention have also been successful. Attrition has been reduced by about 12 percent. Although the improvement rate may not seem significant, in enrollments annually it represents 186 more students returning who did not flunk out, drop out, or voluntarily transfer. With an opening-day enrollment of about 1,550 students, the 186 more continuing students have also had a felicitous effect on the budget. The improvements in recruitment and in retention, it is worth noting, are related.

Recruitment Strategies

Improvements in the overall attractiveness of a college's educational programs, in its physical facilities, or both will enhance recruitment. During the past seven years at St. Norbert College, considerable progress has been made in building much-needed new facilities and in generally improving the quality of the academic offerings and the demands made on the student. The upgrading has undoubtedly contributed in some way to the gains in recruitment and retention though their direct effects cannot be readily measured. In addition, more specific strategies were employed.

Clearly establish institutional identity. Considerable time and effort were devoted to establishing a clear statement of institutional objectives, using, in part, the *Institutional Goals Inventory*.[2] A year-long study resulted in a consensus statement of goals and objectives. From this document, a summary was prepared describing the college and establishing its identity.

2. Princeton, N.J.: Educational Testing Service, 1973.

Personnel: admissions director. Another important strategy was the hiring of a top-notch dean of admissions. The college found a person who was experienced, well prepared, respected, and expensive. After seven years he is still among our highest paid administrators and ranks among the highest paid admissions officers for schools of our size. He has improved his skills by becoming more market-oriented, a better user of research data, and a good educational counselor. The admissions job is too important to hire an inexperienced person to manage the recruitment effort.

Market definition. Few schools today have a national market; therefore, it is important to define a primary market area carefully. St. Norbert College defined its geographic area for market concentration and, within the area, further defines targets. Each year the admissions office attempts to present the college to a wider audience within its market area. New market areas are opened only after considerable study and then only if they have some relationship to the primary market area.

Market segmentation. Work on market segmentation has helped the college secure applications from prospects who are likely to be a good match between what the college has to offer and what students and their parents want from a college. The objective is not merely to generate large numbers of applications, but, rather, applications from those students with the characteristics to persist to graduation. The college has identified forty-eight main feeder high schools that supply over 50 percent of the new freshmen each year. The characteristics of students from those schools who do well at St. Norbert College are useful in selecting new students.

Market orientation. Good marketing essentially begins and ends with the consumer. Systematic information from our consumer—the students at our schools—can contribute to a positive and honest portrayal of a college's strengths. A survey for seniors, designed to gather information from students about crucial aspects of their college experience, is distributed annually at St. Norbert. The one-page instrument and a letter from the president asking for an open, candid response is distributed to senior class members during their final semester. The responses, when tabulated and analyzed, provide a consumer view of their four-year experience. Placed alongside the goals and objectives of the college, the results also provide direction for improvements. Responses to one question on overall student satisfaction have been particularly helpful: the level of student satisfaction after four years at college. That is, satisfied students and parents are excellent recruiters in their home communities.

Use research data. A variety of data is readily available to assist in recruitment research at most institutions. To illustrate, most institutions belong to the Cooperative Institutional Research Program initiated by the American Council on Education. The annual reports on the characteristics of entering freshman and transfer students offer a wealth of information useful in recruitment.[3] The national norms permit comparisons between the characteristics of new students at a particular school and those of the national sample. Longitudinal studies can be done as well on selected variables important to an individual school. For example, why do students select a particular college? How do these reasons compare with those given at other schools, and how have the reasons changed over the years?

Another example of easily available information useful for recruitment studies may be obtained from the national testing organizations. The shared prospective applicants report provided by the Educational Testing Service, for example, is helpful in gathering data about how prospective students view a college or university. The list of twenty-five schools where enrolling students have also applied can provide valuable information about a particular college's institutional identity.

Financial aid. Student aid obviously can be an effective way to assist in recruiting students. Most schools have some discretion in financial aid and can use their discretionary funds to select students who have the potential to become campus leaders. Most colleges and universities have no-need money available for distribution to these special students. For some groups of students the recognition is more important than the money. The danger, of course, is that scarce student aid funds may be awarded to students who can afford the tuition and who would come without it.

Make a fair presentation of institution. One final point on recruitment should be made before moving on to retention. To be successful in increasing applications, the institution should be presented as attractively and fairly as possible. "Attractively" because colleges want to call attention to their strengths and advantages. But "as fairly and honestly as possible" because accuracy is a good way to help ensure retention. If printed or other material about a college or university is presented unfairly or is exaggerated, the school may create expectations by students that are unrealistically high. When students enroll and find the institution is not as advertised and their expectations are not met, they will be disappointed and are likely to become an attrition statistic for the institution. And the message they take to their

---

3. Alexander W. Astin, Margo R. King, and Gerald T. Richardson, *The American Freshman: National Norms for Fall 1979* (Los Angeles: University of California, Los Angeles, Graduate School of Education, Cooperative Institutional Research Program).

parents, high schools, and friends will not help the institution's future recruitment efforts.

Studies using the College and University Environment Scales (CUES) have shown that freshmen perceptions of a college change during their first year. At entrance freshmen students have views that mirror the school's promotional materials, but by the end of the first semester their perceptions conform more closely to the real culture of the institution. Ideally the two perceptions should be closer together than is often the case. Furthermore, inflated or misleading advertising will probably result in greater government regulation in this area.

Retention Strategies

Recruitment and retention are closely related. Many areas noted as significant in recruitment are also important for improving retention. The leading factor in improved retention at St. Norbert College was undoubtedly the opportunity to select more carefully which applicants to admit. As might be expected, there is a high positive correlation between high school achievement and persistence in college. If a school selects the better students as indicated by their high school performance, attrition should improve—and typically it does.

The national record for persistence in higher education, however, leaves much room for improvement. The education community must better the current figures, which estimate that 60 percent of the students will drop out, or stop out, and not graduate within four years from the college they entered as freshmen.

A costly problem. The cost of recruiting a student ranges from an average of about $200 to $800 each depending on the type of institution, its location, and so forth. A high attrition rate definitely has an adverse economic effect on a college or university. At St. Norbert College enrollment in 1978–79 was up by 72 students, while the freshman class remained the same size as in the preceding four years. The increase can be attributed to better retention.

Awareness of the problem. If attrition is a problem at a given institution, a vital element is to have a plan or program to do something about it. Some universities designate a retention officer whereas others assign the task to one of several administrative officers. Communicating to faculty and staff the importance of improving retention and some action strategies for doing so seem to be crucial. Studies clearly show that faculty and staff attitudes about students can make a big difference in retention. A caring attitude for students among faculty and staff is positively correlated with better retention rates.

Use research findings. A major effort at St. Norbert College also derives from research findings. The strategy is to offer students a variety of opportunities to become personally involved. This strategy is once again in accord with our institutional goals. Academic and social clubs, musical and dramatic productions, athletic competitions, campus ministry activities, government, campus employment—all are ways for students to get involved. At a residential college, this kind of involvement is fairly easily available to students, but new opportunities, whenever possible and realistic, are added.

Research demonstrates that living on campus increases chances of persisting as well as of assisting students in important areas of personal growth. A few years ago at St. Norbert College an effort was made to encourage local residents to live on campus rather than commute. Now, each year seventy-five to eighty-five local students attend college by living in the residence halls rather than commuting.

Better teaching and advising. High quality teaching and advising have become even more important factors in faculty appointment and promotion at our institution. From our experimental program called education-by-objectives, we now have a cadre of trained advisors. They approach advisement from a life-planning perspective, stressing personal values and a broader view of life before bringing into the process the student's four years of college and possible career goals. An early warning system for students in academic difficulty, with mandatory follow-up contact with advisors, also has proved to be effective in reducing attrition.

A snowballing effect. Better retention of students, like many other phenomena, seems to have a snowballing effect. As good retention practices become accepted by staff, and as they become characteristic of life on campus, attrition decreases even more.

Many colleges and universities will have tried or adopted most of the practices outlined. At this stage of the game we don't know everything that will work, or which activities will work best on a given campus. It is much like throwing darts at a target. The target is vitally important—the target of improved recruitment and retention. Some ideas or darts will seem right for certain types of institutions and programs; other plans and variations will also be tried. Considering the importance of recruitment and retention, a good strategy might be to throw all the darts in the hope that some will be effective and hit the target.

Partial Prescription for Institutional Vitality

BRENT KNIGHT

STUDENT RETENTION HAS ALWAYS BEEN a topic of at least theoretical interest among educators. Today, as colleges face a shrinking pool of college-bound high school seniors, the interest has become more practical. The realization that many colleges will be forced to close or substantially curtail their operations in the next decade is already affecting all kinds of institutions—large and small, public and private, two-year and four-year, baccalaureate and vocational-technical. And within some colleges and universities, the radical changes projected for enrollments are already influencing strategic planning and the allocation of resources. During the 1980s the emphasis will be on competition for students and on their retention.

The structure of higher education today and the environment in which colleges and universities operate are such that the vitality or even the survival of some institutions to the mid-1980s is being determined by the leaders who head them. Increasing dependence on funding from the federal and state governments and bureaucracies, the extreme difficulty in achieving curriculum changes, and the recent growth of collective bargaining agreements, all greatly extend the lead time it takes to transform new program ideas into operating programs. Like other bureaucratic organizations today, colleges and universities are unable to respond rapidly to changes in their environment. Therefore, it has become imperative that they develop sophisticated systems for anticipating the kinds of programs and services required in the future. At the top of the list, effective recruitment programs are essential for maintaining institutional vitality. However, long-term vitality is possible only if students stay once they are enrolled.

Background for an Action Program

Triton College, founded in 1964, serves a population of approximately 400,000 persons in the densely populated near-west suburbs of Chicago. As a comprehensive public community college, its funding comes from local property taxes, state funding based largely on enrollment, and student tuition and fees. Recent demographic studies project a stable population for the college district over the next decade, but with a 50 percent decrease in the number of graduates from the public high schools of the district between 1980 and 1990. Because recent high school graduates account for 50 percent of current full-time equivalent enrollments, it is obvious that without an active institutional response to the projected decline, the future is indeed ominous.

Triton's action response to its ominous future is based on three principal assumptions: The overall mission of the college is to provide a broad array of postsecondary educational programs and services to meet the diverse needs of the people of the district. Education leaders can affect the future vitality of their respective institutions to a considerable extent by the decisions they make today. The long-term vitality of a college can be achieved only by simultaneously doing many things well.

A Comprehensive Program

In 1977, Triton initiated an action program whose primary goal is to make the college the comprehensive, open-door institution it purports to be in its mission statement. Pursuant to that goal, the following changes have occurred or are under way.

Institutional advancement program. In 1978, the college established a collegewide task force whose charge was to recommend methods and procedures for informing the community about the educational programs and services available at Triton College and for helping students clarify and achieve their educational goals. The task force screened more than 150 recommendations and actually acted on 113 different strategies designed to affect promotion and retention. Examples of these strategies are: develop a peer recruitment team to assist high schools in articulation efforts; announce and promote the career planning and testing services of the Career Center; develop a Triton viewbook; expand tutorial services to a broad range of students; develop a series of short-term workshops and seminars in specific areas designed to help students who have learning problems; review course prerequisites.

The action program also included a broad effort to educate the Triton college community to awareness of the enrollment changes expected in the 1980s and of the need for a collegewide response to the changes.

Following its report, the task force was replaced by two committees headed by the dean of student affairs—the Promotion Committee and the Retention Committee. These broad-based committees are now responsible for coordinating the overall institutional marketing and student retention activities.

College and community research. The office of college and community research has been assigned the task of establishing a student tracking system to obtain information needed by managers throughout the college. The office also conducts studies to identify the factors related to student attrition and retention. Cohort survival studies reveal the enrollment patterns of each student in a particular group over the course of several semesters. These studies have shown, for example, that adult education students generally do not subsequently enroll in related regular college degree programs.

Triton research now enables us to know our market penetration in each of our twenty-four municipalities by major program. We know exactly how well we draw from each of our sixteen high schools. Market research enables us to formulate our promotional objectives based on hard data.

A comprehensive community needs assessment is being prepared which will, we hope, provide a sound basis for developing new programs and services, especially in the areas of continuing education. The research staff will carefully analyze the 1980 census data to identify any demographic changes that may have program implications.

Developmental education. The high attrition rates in community colleges attest that, for many students, the open door has indeed become a revolving door. The Developmental Education Program and the Learning Assistance Center were established in 1978 as Triton's response to high attrition rates. Today all entering degree-seeking students, both full time and part time, participate in a mandatory preassessment program, which determines their need for developmental courses.

The Developmental Education Program is characterized by small classes, individualized instruction, and differentiated staffing. The developmental mathematics classes are self-paced, with the opportunity for variable entry and exit. In the Learning Assistance Center all students may obtain tutorial assistance in a variety of disciplines. During 1978–79, more than forty tutors in a variety of skill and content areas worked directly with developmental education students and with students referred to the center by instructors of college-level courses.

In the first year of operation, the substantial investment in developmental education has begun to pay dividends in increased retention rates. An evaluation of the program after the first semester of operation showed that the retention rate for the high-risk developmental education students is higher than for all university transfer and career education students. Of 1,489 students entering in the fall of 1978 who were enrolled in one or more developmental education courses, 78.9 percent were still enrolled at Triton College at mid-semester of spring 1979. And of 240 students classified as academically disadvantaged, physically handicapped, economically disadvantaged, or having English as a second language and, therefore, considered to be an extremely high-risk group, 81.7 percent completed two full semesters.

The early successes of the Developmental Education Program are being attributed to the special tutoring and counseling services for students and the direct involvement of the developmental education staff in determining course content and methodology.

Adult Reentry Program. This program offers assistance to adults who are returning to college, changing careers, or returning to the work force. Its primary purpose is to facilitate a smooth transition to college and to alleviate the anxiety that adult students often experience when they begin college or return to college. The program was established in 1976. By 1979 it had grown from fourteen courses and workshops attended by 1,500 people to sixty-six courses, seminars, and workshops involving 5,000 people. Because many adults who are thinking about returning to college lack confidence in their study habits or their abilities in reading, writing, or mathematics, the program offers skills workshops before the start of classes and at midterm. Adult Reentry also offers a variety of day and evening seminars on life planning, individual goal setting, stress management, and other personal development topics.

The Adult Reentry Program allocates 50 percent of its operating budget to promotion and recruitment activities, which include press releases, advertising, publications, and personal outreach. Approximately 4,300 semester hours were generated from counselor contacts during the 1978 academic year.

The Tuesday-Thursday College has also been established to meet the special needs of many adult students who cannot attend college on a full-time basis. Through the Tuesday-Thursday College, students may earn the two-year associate degree in three years through attending classes only two days each week.

Employee Development Institute. The institute was established to provide a wide array of education and training programs for persons and organizations in the community. Special programs are designed for various forms of employee development. The college has recently employed three program developers whose primary task is to contact employers throughout the college district, assist them in identifying their education and training needs, and design special programs to meet those needs. Triton College believes that its mission is to provide a wide range of educational programs and services within the broad statutory limits under which it operates. And as it increases its share of the lucrative employee training and retraining market, these new students will help offset enrollment decreases in other markets.

The V.I.P. Program. In spring 1979 an experimental program was undertaken to test a hypothesis. The program explored whether highly personalized support services for new students, beginning with their initial contact with the college and continuing through placement, would result in a higher matriculation rate, a larger average course load, and a higher retention rate than for students who go through regular procedures. To test the hypothesis, an experimental and a control group, each comprising 300 persons, were randomly selected from persons who had not previously enrolled at the college. Each group was composed of degree- and non-degree-seeking, full-time and part-time students.

Each student in the experimental group was assigned to an admissions specialist who served as his or her primary contact person with the college and who provided personalized assistance with program planning and registration procedures. The student was also exposed to a series of activities and events, ranging from telephone calls and letters to assistance with financial aid and schedule changes. All the activities were designed to increase the probability that the student would enroll and then proceed toward some educational goal. Throughout, the emphasis was on personal contact between the prospective student and one person at the college.

Preliminary data for the fall 1979 semester showed that the program was successful at least several ways. A significantly greater percentage of the experimental group matriculated than did those in the control group. Students from the experimental group enrolled for more hours of credit than students in the control group. The retention rate for V.I.P. students through the middle of the 1979 fall term was considerably higher than for the control group.

President's Scholar Program. The honors program was established in fall 1978 to attract academically gifted students and to provide for their needs. Together with the Developmental Education Program and the regular college-level classes, the honors program is helping the college move toward its goal of meeting the educational needs of every student it enrolls.

Counseling-advising program. Over the past two years Triton has attempted to build a student counseling-advising system to provide support services from admission through transfer or job placement. Pursuant to that end, the following steps were taken.

The functions of academic advisors and counselors were clarified. A staff of advising specialists has been established to help students construct their schedules and understand academic information. Counselors have been freed of onerous, repetitive tasks so that they may concentrate on life and career planning and help students master learning skills.

In addition, all student intake procedures were reviewed and revised to achieve simplicity and efficiency for students. Student assessment and screening procedures were expanded to include part-time and nondegree students. A testing center was established. A career exploration center, which included a computerized career exploration program and a support system for area high schools, was established. Counselors are more and more being assigned to specific student groups or functions that are clearly critical to retention outcomes. Special counseling services for the handicapped and for students with academic difficulties have been established.

Professional review and program review. A comprehensive faculty evaluation system, which is tied to a professional growth plan for each instructor, was implemented in the fall 1978 semester. A program review system was recently developed by a joint faculty-administration committee and is currently being field-tested with volunteer programs. Both programs are intended to assure that all academic programs are current and are of the highest quality possible. We are convinced that the most important element in a comprehensive student retention program is academic excellence in the classroom. The primary goal of both faculty evaluation and program review is to assure that the quality of instruction and the curriculum contribute to the maintenance of a staying environment at Triton College.

Assessment for the Future

Over the past three years, Triton College has been preparing for the 1980s. We believe that future institutional vitality will depend on our ability to do simultaneously many things well. Effective recruitment and retention programs are essential but they are not sufficient. They must be combined with equally effective support programs and with high-quality instruction. In short, college student retention is a campuswide responsibility requiring nothing short of institutional renewal.

The prognosis for higher education requires action now. College presidents cannot afford to permit bold new program ideas to lie dormant or languish in committees. Direct presidential intervention may be necessary to translate new program ideas into operating programs. College presidents must promote an attitude of service to students at all levels in their institutions. They must also continue to develop new markets, expand both the scope and the quality of institutional research, and strive for the institutionalization of change if they hope to meet the challenges of the next decade. And despite the best efforts, even the most successful colleges will be buffeted severely and will suffer occasional setbacks in the years to come.

In any event, colleges must move quickly to implement activities that will be critical to institutional growth and vitality: new programs for new groups of students; excellence in all programs; a sophisticated collegewide marketing program; staff development at all levels; and appropriate financial and accounting controls.

3. COMPETITION FOR STUDENTS—THE MILITARY AND THE CAMPUS

The Garrison *versus* the Academy?

WILLIAM P. SNYDER

THE BABY BOOM OF THE DECADE AFTER World War II, which fueled the expansion of American higher education in the 1960s, has faded into history. It has been replaced by a baby bust that portends a 25 percent decline in the college-age population over the next fifteen years. Higher education has already felt the effects of this demographic shift: some fifty smaller colleges have closed in recent years, in large part because they could not find enough students; an equal number of institutions are on the verge of shutdown. Only academically prestigious and financially sound institutions can hope to avoid the consequences of this demographic reversal.

In response, educational institutions have attempted to expand the market for higher education, primarily through adult education programs and increased enrollment of foreign students. Many schools have also turned to marketing experts for help in devising new recruiting and admissions programs. These changes have been accompanied by curriculum revisions designed to provide more career-related courses and beefed-up counseling activities to assist in job placement. Many of the institutions that employ these techniques have, thus far, managed to avoid enrollment declines. When all institutions use such an approach, however, the payoff to individual institutions will largely be negated.

During the past decade, the 18–21-year-old cohort, from which both higher education and the armed forces draw most of their personnel, has been sufficiently large to support both activities. But as attempts to maintain enrollment levels extend to admitting more students of average ability, higher education may possibly begin to compete with the recruiting activities of the armed forces. For this reason, educational administrators should be aware of the nature and potential challenge posed by military personnel procurement policies. Further, educational administrators may want to ensure that the interests of higher education are taken into account by defense policy makers as changes in military recruiting policies are considered in the near future. What is the background for this potential challenge, and what are the implications for higher education of possible changes in military personnel procurement policies?

Status of the All-Volunteer Armed Forces

The all-volunteer force dates from 1970, when a presidential commission recommended that the military draft be replaced by a volunteer system that relied on economic incentives as the major inducement for service. Based on this report, the Nixon administration ordered the Defense Department to move as quickly as possible to an all-volunteer force. To facilitate this shift, military pay was increased in 1970 and armed forces recruiting activities were expanded. By the end of 1972, with an adequate number of volunteers entering the services, the administration decided to allow induction authority under the Selective Service Act to expire in mid-1973.

The all-volunteer experiment achieved excellent results during its initial years. Volunteers in sufficient number to meet overall personnel requirements were recruited by the military services. The quality of volunteers was generally satisfactory as well. By the middle of the decade, however, some disturbing trends had appeared. First, the enlisted ranks of the armed forces became somewhat unrepresentative of American society. Specifically, blacks in the enlisted force far exceeded their proportion in the population. Soldiers from lower income families were also overrepresented. These trends raised the possibility that minorities and the poor would bear an inordinate share of the burden in any military involvement. Volunteers from middle-class backgrounds, in contrast, were underrepresented. This latter group was particularly missed by the armed forces: during the draft years, men in this group had often filled key technical and administrative jobs within military units. Finally, and in sharp contrast to the experience of the active (or regular) forces, reserve component units were generally unable to obtain enough volunteers; further, the quality of reserve enlistees was poor.

The undesirable trends that first appeared in the mid-1970s have worsened since early 1978.[1] The quality of enlistees has continued to decline. Roughly one of four new enlistees does not have a high school diploma; almost half of all new enlistees reads at ninth-grade or lower levels; and slightly over one-third of the recruits entering the services fail to complete their initial period of service. This decline in quality is taking place at a

1. For a discussion of the status of the all-volunteer force, see "Son of Sad Sack," *New Republic*, July 5–12, 1980, pp. 20–23.

time when military equipment and procedures require higher technical skills and greater initiative.

The extent to which the armed forces are socially unrepresentative has also increased. Blacks now constitute about 18 percent of the enlisted force, as compared to about 12 percent nationally, and the percentage is likely to rise over time. Some combat formations in the Army and Marine Corps have from 40–50 percent black members. Personnel from lower socioeconomic backgrounds continue to be overrepresented.

Reserve component recruiting continues to encounter great difficulty. Army reserve units are now at roughly 90 percent of the strength levels authorized by Congress, with some formations at less than half strength; the quality of enlistees remains well below that of recruits to the active force. One element of the reserves, the Individual Ready Reserve (IRR), which is intended to provide individual replacements during an emergency, has a strength of less than 400,000, as compared to 1.5 million a decade ago. This situation in 1979 prompted the Department of Defense to recommend youth registration, which would shorten by several months the time that the active forces would have to wait for trained replacements. Finally, for the first time since 1972, the active forces are failing to meet their recruiting quotas. Currently, active force strength is about 25,000 below authorized levels, and many military leaders fear that the services will be unable to maintain even present strength levels.

The problems described above, when viewed in the context of demographic projections for the next decade, have prompted widespread concern. In Congress, there have been calls for reinstituting the draft and for enactment of a broadly based national youth service program. Both houses of Congress have had lengthy discussions on the status of the all-volunteer force for several months. Similar concerns have been expressed by prominent academic analysts. Most troubled of all are armed forces leaders, perhaps because they are so keenly aware of the many problems posed by the all-volunteer force. In short, the difficulties being encountered in the all-volunteer approach have begun to attract widespread public interest. A national debate on the future of the all-volunteer force, possibly leading to changes in policy, seems likely within the next two or three years.

Youth and Military Personnel Requirements

Before examining the alternatives to the all-volunteer force that are being discussed, it will be useful to summarize the recruitment requirements of the armed forces. Currently, the enlisted ranks[2] of the active forces number about 1.8 million. To maintain this force level, the military services must enlist about 400,000 new recruits each year. (An additional 100,000 enlistees are needed by the reserve components; these reservists undergo only brief training and they continue to be available for work or schooling in their home communities.) The mix of men and women among new enlistees is roughly nine to one; most new recruits sign three- or four-year enlistment contracts.

This annual requirement for new enlistees could conceivably be reduced by having smaller armed forces, by substituting civilian employees for military personnel, and by recruiting more women. For various reasons, however, these approaches are not appropriate. Smaller forces are especially unlikely—the services now have fewer personnel than at any time since mid-1950. Moreover, in the judgment of most defense analysts, conventional military capabilities, which have a large manpower component, are badly in need of strengthening. Similarly, a considerable amount of civilian substitution has taken place in recent years, to the point where observers believe the armed forces have lost some of their ability to respond in a crisis. Finally, women enlistees, plentiful until recently, are now as hard to recruit as their male counterparts. Thus the prospect of any significant lowering of the annual accession requirement through these approaches is not good.

The implications of the military personnel requirement can be illustrated more clearly by numbers of high school graduates. As noted above, three of every four recruits are high school graduates. Thus, in 1979, roughly 300,000 recent graduates, of whom 260,000 were men, entered the armed forces. These men represented about 12 percent of recent male graduates. Assuming current military strength levels are maintained, and there is no change in the percentage of teen-agers completing high school, the military will want to enlist 15 percent of male graduates in 1985. By the early 1990s, the percentage rises to about 18 percent. The comparable figures for higher education, assuming it attempts to maintain present enrollment levels, is 45 percent in 1985 and 52 percent in the early 1990s, as compared to the present level of 40 percent. Individually, these increases are not dramatic; taken together, however, they suggest that future high school graduates,

---

2. The armed forces have been able to recruit an adequate number of officers except health care professionals, and changes in officer recruitment are not now being considered.

particularly students of moderate ability, will be the object of increasingly intense recruiting efforts.

Options in Personnel Procurement

As of late 1979, three alternative methods of military manpower procurement were being discussed. The first option, and the most likely approach for the immediate future, is to continue the all-volunteer approach but to provide increased pay and benefit levels so as to attract more enlistees and enlistees of slightly higher quality.[3] Such an approach would cost from $2–$3 billion annually when initiated, with costs increasing in the mid- and late-1980s.

The second option is to return to the military draft. Volunteers would be permitted, but draftees would be inducted to meet any quantity or quality shortages. A reinstituted military draft would probably rely on a lottery system to select those who would serve and severely limit deferments and exemptions. Slight cost savings might accrue if a military draft were reinstituted.

The third option is national youth service. National youth service would presumably require some period of service from all young Americans. Those not electing to enter the military would be expected to engage in work similar to that now performed by volunteer groups and agencies such as ACTION. The flow of young people into the military would be guaranteed by higher pay and educational benefits or by a shorter period of service. The cost of a mandatory national youth service program is estimated at about $25 billion per year. A *voluntary* national service program would be less expensive, but would do little to solve the recruitment problems of the armed forces.

Implications for Higher Education

Any of the broad alternatives described above would enable the armed forces to deal effectively with the problems that now plague the all-volunteer force. But each has different implications for higher education.

Retaining the all-volunteer approach, but with added economic incentives to obtain more personnel as well as personnel of higher quality, would have the least effect on higher education. The number of enlistees required each year would not change. To the extent that incentives were tailored to attract youth from higher socioeconomic strata and those with higher

---

3. For an insightful discussion of the policy actions that might be involved, see Charles C. Moskos, "How to Save the All-Volunteer Force," *Public Interest*, Fall 1980.

test scores (possibly through the mechanism of educational benefits after completing military service), a small number of potential students might be attracted into the armed forces. Many of these young people would probably enroll in college after completing military service. Overall, this alternative would have few adverse consequences for higher education.

Reinstitution of the draft would have a greater effect on higher education. The period of required service under a draft would probably be two years, instead of the three or four years now required of volunteers. As a result, accessions into the active force would increase, perhaps by one-third, to roughly 500,000 annually. Further, because of the lottery selection and limited exemption-deferment features of the draft, many potential students would be required to serve. The *prospect* of being drafted might also provide an incentive to enlistment that is not now present, thereby prompting additional potential students to enter the armed forces. Of the potential students who did serve, most could be expected to enter higher education after completing military service. Since more potential students would be diverted to military service, the impact on higher education would be greater than in the case of continuing the all-volunteer force. Adoption of this alternative might also revive antidraft sentiments and complicate the problems of educational administration.

A mandatory youth service alternative along the lines described would undoubtedly have a serious consequence for higher education. Proponents of national service, such as Congressman Paul McCloskey, clearly intend that national service contribute to broad societal and morale goals, with resolution of military manpower problems a distinctly secondary concern. But assuming that such a program was phased in over several years, the ultimate effect would be to defer college enrollment for entire age groups for one or two years. The absence of total age groups for even a limited period would probably cause many smaller institutions to close. It is also likely that some potential students, as a result of satisfying work experiences during the national service period, might decide to forgo college completely. To the extent that the experience was satisfying, community colleges and technical school enrollments would be affected more than enrollments in four-year institutions.

A national youth service program, if properly administered, might return substantial benefits to the nation and its young people. However, this alternative would cause considerable disruption in higher education, at least for a three- or four-year period, and would probably reduce somewhat the total number of students likely to seek higher education.

Each of the options examined above has powerful and articulate proponents. Politically, the most acceptable at this time appears to be the first one—strengthening the all-volunteer force through the mechanism of higher economic incentives. Continuing the all-volunteer force will be more costly than a military draft, but it appears to be less disruptive of higher education than either of the other broad alternatives.

Whichever approach emerges as the ultimate solution to the military manpower problem, it seems indisputable that the needs of higher education and the armed forces will intersect in the coming decade. Elsewhere, I have suggested that this relationship might be competitive.[4] The degree of competition will depend not only on the option that is finally selected but also on the extent to which the armed forces are given the means to obtain higher quality personnel. It is also possible that a deteriorating international situation may prompt national leaders to increase the size of the armed forces. In any event, the interests of higher education ought to be represented in decisions on military personnel procurement policies.

Citizens, Soldiers, Students

GERALD B. KAUVAR

ASSUME IT IS OF CRITICAL IMPORTANCE to prepare young adult Americans to contribute to a world in which the future is uncertain, a world in which new technology is introduced at an accelerating pace and where the knowledge and skills learned in school decay at an accelerated rate: a shrinking world which emphasizes our global economic and political interdependence. Assume, too, that education should strive for a critical understanding of the forms and values of our own culture, strive to produce citizens who are able to alter those forms and values as the good of the Republic requires, and who are prepared to defend the forms and values of the culture they share and cherish. If these assumptions are correct, then there is no competition between the goals of the military and the larger society which it serves and defends.

4. "Military Personnel Procurement Policies: Assumptions, Trends, Context," in *The All-Volunteer Force and American Society*, ed. John B. Keeley (Charlottesville: University Press of Virginia, 1978), pp. 28–29.

This paper was prepared when the author was Executive Assistant to the President of Boston University. He was and is Special Assistant for Education, Office of the Assistant Secretary of Defense. The views expressed here are personal and are not intended to represent Department of Defense policy.

Nevertheless, during the last half-decade a sense of competition has persisted between the military and postsecondary education. A few years ago, some unauthorized speculation by a Department of Defense education representative gave rise to the belief that the military would need to enlist one out of every three or four male eighteen-year-olds during the early 1980s. The eighties, of course, are also the decade that education planners have been warning institutions to prepare for: The 1960s birth rate leads directly to a highly predictable decline in the number of young adults who might be interested in pursuing postsecondary education, particularly directly after graduation from high school.

The DoD representative who speculated was in error on several grounds—he was not a manpower economist. Because he estimated accession rates from the draft experience rather than from the early years of the all-volunteer force, because he underestimated retention rates, and because he discounted the role of women, he concluded that, to maintain current force levels, 25–33 percent of eighteen-year-old males would have to be accessed into the armed forces. Another erroneous assumption was that the force structure and level mandated by military doctrine would remain what it had been.

A DoD study, *America's Volunteers*, demonstrates convincingly the error of the original speculations.[1] A brief analysis of recruiting patterns during the first years of the all-volunteer service should help dispel unwarranted fears of competition.

Characteristics of Volunteers

The armed services prefer to enlist high school diploma graduates. Their reason is more the motivation than the education. The young high school graduate has shown an ability to complete an assigned task that provides no immediate gratification but promises deferred benefits. The lower attrition rate of high school diploma graduates makes them attractive to the military services.

Among the unattractive candidates for recruitment are high school graduates who intend to go directly on to college. Such young adult Americans have decided the course of their immediate future. But these young Americans are valuable future additions to the officer corps of the services. The benefit to society and the military is that the officer corps has been educated at the same time and in the same way as their college

1. Office of the Assistant Secretary of Defense (Manpower, Reserve Affairs, and Logistics), *America's Volunteers, A Report to Congress* (December 1968).

contemporaries. Thus the officer corps will have a tested, secure sense of and belief in the values it is obliged by oath to defend.

Of those young Americans who volunteer for military service, countless surveys have shown and continue to show that their primary reason for enlisting is to obtain training and education. Even when the surveys distinguish between training and education, education retains its recruiting power: education is the second most important reason cited by people joining the uniformed services.

It is worth pausing here, before describing the educational benefits offered to servicemembers, to ask whether the 400,000 accessions per year who volunteer are qualitatively as good as those who comprised the armed services prior to the all-volunteer force. As *America's Volunteers* shows, in almost every way the all-volunteer force is more representative of America than was the force at any time during the draft. Especially worthy of note to the higher education community is that there are more accessions in the higher mental categories than during the draft. (The military is concerned about overaccessing persons in the higher mental categories because not all the military tasks require persons in the higher mental categories. It is also concerned, as is the civilian education community, about the decline in ability among holders of the high school diploma.) Even in discipline and attrition, the all-volunteer force has a significantly better record than did the force during the latter part of the draft. In one area, the force structure is unlike that during the draft. Persons in the highest mental categories are not enlisting at the rate the military would like. The most influential incentive used by the military to recruit people in these categories is educational benefits.

Since the beginnings of the all-volunteer force a profound change has taken place in the thinking of the recruiting commands and the manpower planners in the Department of Defense. Because military doctrines have been changing and because new technologies will require abilities from personnel different from those needed for recent technology, increasing attention has been paid to force structure. When the more sophisticated weaponry was introduced, it was expected to require more service members from the higher mental categories. For many years this expectation did not prove accurate in fact because the increasingly sophisticated technology was so designed that more and more parts could be replaced rather than repaired. A new module could be snapped to replace a malfunctioning unit. People in the lower mental categories could perform quite adequately in the military despite the sophisticated electronics of the weaponry. The higher technology that will be introduced in the armed forces during the next few years, however, may in fact demand a brighter, and better trained, and better educated force.

Education Offerings by the Military

The military has an enormous investment in training and education. The most conservative estimate I can make is $6 billion a year. The figure may even be doubled if all the nonapparent and indirect costs are included. The military, sensitive to cost-benefit analysis, has recognized the economy and wisdom of retaining trained personnel in the military service rather than accessing and training new recruits. The sophistication and skill gained by long-term service is invaluable.

Because retention has improved, recent accession shortages have been less serious than they appear when taken out of context. It was recently reported that for the second quarter of 1979 the military services reached only about 85 percent of their recruiting objective—85,000 accessions rather 100,000. What was not reported was that retention had increased, with the result that the total number serving was what manpower planners thought was needed and that in many ways the mix of skill levels was improved. All the services are actively considering ways to change the assignment and promotion systems of the last decade in recognition that the force structure required in the future will be different from that required in the past.

The military may be fairly regarded as not in competition with institutions of higher education in that the military produces consumers of education. Each year, well over 800,000 active duty military pursue postsecondary education in off-duty hours. Many of these students have their first experience with postsecondary education while in the military. The education, funded by the government, is offered on some five hundred bases and in countless remote locations around the globe. The educational services are provided by civilian institutions which cooperate with the local bases. If only from a morale and welfare standpoint, education is one of the most attractive features of nonduty hours. To military planners, it is attractive primarily because it promotes the skills and a comprehension of society that the military needs, quite aside from providing a better use of free time than some of modern youth's diversions.

Education in the military takes many forms. In addition to the voluntary off-duty programs, the military also fully funds study at both undergraduate and graduate levels as a benefit because the skills acquired during the funded study are needed in the modern military.

The benefits available after military service have been demonstrated to generate enrollments in postsecondary education. The GI Bill induced enrollment in institutions of higher education. One expects no less from the current Veterans' Educational Assistance Program. Thus the military attracts young adults who were "turned off" by school and provides the motivation, opportunity, and funds for education both during and after active duty. The point is worth repeating: for 20–25 percent of young adult Americans, any interest in postsecondary education is likely to be that acquired while in military service.

Interplay Rather than Competition

The real bone of contention between the education community and the military may be the distribution of students rather than their numbers. Looking at the steps that postsecondary education has taken to retain what it euphemistically calls "full enrollment" when there are fewer eighteen-year-olds, we see a remarkable and sudden interest in adult, continuing, or lifelong education, of which military education is a major component. This interest is not always inspired by noble educational motives, nor is it always characterized by academically respectable programming. Some recent pronouncements from higher education on competition with the military have emphasized a so-called "fair share" of the number of eighteen-year-olds each year. I'm not sure what education's fair share is, unless it means at least the enrollment "my" institution had last year. Given parallel declines in the rate of college attendance and military recruiting, it may be that this competition is a scapegoat rather than a fact: a scapegoat for our failures to demonstrate our value to a skeptical public.

The military and postsecondary education are neither obviously nor inherently in competition for those eighteen-year-olds who decide on immediate continuation of their education. In fact, the military may have a competitive edge in the overall youth market. Recent data from the National Center for Education Statistics show a continuing decline in the number of high school diploma graduates who intend to enter postsecondary education within three months of graduation. Note that the declining rate of postsecondary education prospects coincides with the shortages in recruitments. These parallel declines are taking place in a period of economic recession and relatively high youth unemployment. Yet federal monies are available for people who wish to continue their education, and the military services offer the certainty of at least adequate pay. These parallel trends contradict the conventional view: during periods of uncertainty and recession, the military and those educational institutions that can afford financial aid will prove successful competitors for young people because the job market is in a sorry state. Many Defense Department officials believe that the most significant reason for the volunteer force's inability to meet its recruiting goals is the lack of an attractive salary and fringe benefit package. This country may be wiser to debate the price and value of an all-volunteer force rather than the benefits that are supposed to inhere in a draft or in the alternative of national service.

Youth Service and Higher Education

The effect on higher education of either a return to the draft or the alternative of national service would be to worsen the likelihood of maintaining current levels of enrollment. If the country again resorts to a draft to supply the armed forces, the military would experience increased turnover and decreased retention in comparison with the all-volunteer force. A counterbalance would require a continuing raid on the market of eighteen-year-olds. If the number of eighteen-year-olds who wish to go to college continues to decline, the military and education may not be looking at the same eighteen-year-old market. But if the college-bound cohort stabilizes, then the military and higher education may well indeed be recruiting the same youth.

Any scheme for national service will have to include provision for staffing the armed services. In a rational society, such a scheme would ensure that the mix of abilities required by the armed forces is obtained. It seems to me that, for higher education, any national service program is even more threatening than a draft. National service would have to be either financially attractive or compelled, and in neither case is it likely to provide the future educational benefits offered by military service. It is even more unlikely that educational benefits would be provided during a period of service, a practice the military considers essential. National service is not at all likely to increase the supply of potential students, as the military has demonstrated its ability to do.

Because the Congress and the Department of Defense recognize the value of education both during and after service, studies are under way of additional educational incentives to offer people who join the military on a voluntary basis. Such a plan is not bad news for postsecondary education—it is good news. It is good news because civilian institutions will have a growing market of students in the military, and the environment in which these potential students live and work will encourage participation in postsecondary education, unlike the environment in which many potential students now find themselves. The military must and will rely on civilian institutions to provide the sensitivity to our society and its values that is mandatory for volunteer forces in a democracy. I believe the military should and will continue to offer training and education in those specialties where civilian institutions do not offer comparable programs. However, it is my experience at the Department of Defense and my sense of the Congress that there is no enthusiasm for creating competing programs within the military when civilian institutions are equipped to provide the required education.

For all these reasons it is incumbent on the military to ensure that the educational opportunities it offers are at least as good as those that can be freely chosen by an intelligent consumer interested in quality. The postsecondary education community must ensure that it provides high-quality education or programs to citizens in uniform. One of the most debilitating forms of competition that I think could exist would be for either the military or postsecondary education to resort to unethical recruitment, because then all of society, not just these two institutions, would suffer. In a society, where civilian control of the military is a principle, it would be tragic if false issues of competition limited the opportunities for the military and civilian educational institutions to cooperate and learn from each other.

The military's interest is in providing a quality education at every level, from vocational and occupational, even avocational, to the most sophisticated Ph.D. programs in the high technologies and the sciences. The military properly rejects overtures from institutions that are interested in peddling diplomas rather than providing education. The military has little interest in competition for educational service based solely on price. But colleges and universities are faced with competition from some of their less serious confreres. The military has a common stake with higher education in principles of fair practice and in developing outcome measures which will prove that we are in fact providing a quality education to our clientele.

A rational society will perceive no competition between the military and the education community. A rational society will perceive the utter mutuality of interests and of forms of cooperation discussed here. A rational society whose principles include civilian oversight of the military will work to ensure that citizens in the armed services—because they are citizens and because they are in the armed services—have available the best education and training our institutions can offer. A rational military has identical objectives. Our society must be prepared to recognize that for many young adults to merge three roles—citizen, soldier, and student—is an investment in the most profound form of national security.

The Volunteer Force, the Draft, and National Service

ROBERT A. STONE

SINCE 1973, THE UNITED STATES has manned its active forces without resorting to conscription. We moved from a force composed largely of draftees to a force composed, in peacetime, entirely of volunteers. So bold an initiative inevitably inspires debate and warrants continued review and appraisal. We in the military establishment welcome debate on this vital issue. However, much of the debate has been simplistic: Some people are certain that the all-volunteer force is a success. Others are equally certain that the all-volunteer force is a failure. Rather than adopt either of these views, I find it preferable to identify specific manpower supply problems and discuss the specific solutions.

The Volunteer Force

Active forces. The active forces were originally expected to pose the most serious problems in an all-volunteer force. Concerns were that not enough young people could be recruited and that quality might drop sharply.

These potential problems have not materialized in the six and a half years since the draft ended. The armed forces have never been more than 1.5 percent below authorized strength. This level is all the more remarkable because at times during the draft we fell more than 1.5 percent below authorization. In fiscal 1979 we were within 32,000 of authorization, a deviation of just over 1.5 percent from our goal of 2,050,000 military people.

Quality is hard to define, let alone measure. We define it as ability and willingness to learn military skills and to perform successfully as members of military units. We use two objective measures: educational achievement and score on aptitude tests. With respect to education, 73 percent of enlistees in 1979 were high school graduates compared to 68 percent in 1964 and in the last draft year, 1972. Of our officer corps of 275,000, about 88 percent have at least a bachelor's degree. Even more remarkable, more than 30 percent of the officers have advanced degrees, most earned during military service.

To measure mental ability, aptitude tests are administered to all recruits. We are not recruiting as many high-aptitude personnel as we would like, or as many as we had thought we were. We recently discovered an error in our entrance test score calibration affecting test scores of accessions from January 1976 to the present. In 1964, 15 percent of the recruits scored "well below average," roughly the lowest one-third of the population. In 1968, 25 percent scored "well below average." Last year 30 percent of the volunteers scored well below average rather than the 5 percent originally reported. The services have always enlisted and drafted those "well below average," taking larger proportions during the Korean war and the Vietnam conflict. Preliminary analyses of the job performance of those accessions whose test scores were inflated because of the miscalibration of the test suggest that most of the low-scoring people are performing adequately. The services have intensified their efforts to recruit as many high-scoring people as possible.

Even though we are within 1 percent of authorized strength, we have had some problems with numbers of recruits. In 1979 all four services for the first time failed to meet recruiting goals. They recruited only 93 percent of the number planned. Fortunately, retention rates were higher than expected; thus we ended the year at 99 percent of authorized strength, but 7 percent short of recruiting goals. We don't have a complete explanation for the recruiting shortage but think a number of factors are responsible: We have set very high quality goals. Postservice educational benefits are not as valuable today as they were, and, moreover, they must compete with other federal educational assistance programs. Entry salaries for servicemen have declined compared with entry salaries in the civilian sector. Youth unemployment has declined. The popular image of military service has been unfavorable.

We don't know whether recent recruiting problems represent an isolated deviation from our strong recruiting experience or whether they show the beginning of an adverse trend. We are watching recruiting results carefully. In 1980 all services exceeded their recruiting goals. For the Department of Defense as a whole, we recruited 50,000 more people—15 percent—in 1980 than in 1979. In the long run, we face the challenge of a declining youth population—15 percent in the next ten years. We will need to manage skillfully and to get the continued support of Congress and the American people in providing the recruiting resources we need.

Reserve Forces. In contrast to the active forces, our reserve and guard units have not been able to maintain strength since the draft ended. The Navy, Air Force, and Marine Corps are getting the people they need, but a significant decline has taken place in the Army Reserve and the Army National Guard. The total actual strength, officer and enlisted, for these two components at the end of September 1980 was 573,200—4 percent above the congressional authorization of 553,100 and about 55,000 below what the Army would like to have. The September 1980 strength does, however, represent an increase of 48,200 above the low point of August 1978.

Recruiting for the reserves is somewhat a new experience for us. When we had the draft, young people flocked to the reserves, many to avoid being drafted into active service. We are learning to recruit and now have a comprehensive program to increase reserve manning. It is too early to predict whether manning above current levels can be achieved.

Mobilization Needs

Trained manpower. Mobilization would call for us to add people who have already been trained. They would be needed to bring active and reserve units from peacetime to wartime strength and to provide replacements for losses during the initial months of a conflict. We do not now have enough already trained people to meet our needs, although the strength decline of the past few years has begun to turn around. We are accordingly making substantial efforts to raise the number of already trained people available to us.

Untrained manpower (draftees). The Selective Service System now has registered over 3.5 million young men. This pool will grow substantially during the coming months. Registration will allow the Selective Service System to begin delivery, if necessary, of potential inductees to our Armed Forces Entrance and Examining Stations within twelve days after a decision is made to mobilize. This schedule represents a significant improvement from last year and will allow the Selective Service System to deliver over 100,000 inductees within the first month of mobilization. As a result of this improved delivery capability, the Department of Defense can now expect the first inductees to be trained and available for assignment to units almost one-hundred days after a decision is made to mobilize. Our mobilization plans now can include these individuals to offset manpower shortfalls that were expected to occur at that time.

Peacetime Draft—Better than the Volunteer Force?

When we compare the peacetime all-volunteer force we have with a draft we don't have, we should avoid a "grass-is-greener" syndrome. For example, it is tempting to conclude, because we have voluntary manning and because we have force management problems, that if we did not have voluntary manning, we would not have force management problems. Most people would recognize in this a very elementary fallacy in logic.

We shouldn't assume that a peacetime draft we don't have will solve the problems of the peacetime volunteer force we do have. The draft would reintroduce its own problems. For example: Draftees serve shorter terms than volunteers. The draft would lower the experience level of the force at a time we need more experienced people to man modern weapons systems. Military discipline is better now than it was in the last draft years. We have no reason to think that drafted soldiers, serving involuntarily, will be more amenable to military discipline than volunteers.

The late Chief of Staff, General Creighton W. Abrams, said, "The decision to adopt a volunteer Army offers us opportunities for professionalism and stability which we have not had in the recent past. We can build a strong, capable, effective Army with volunteers as long as we have a foundation of pride."

Neither the draft nor the volunteer force is without problems. We in DoD are working to resolve the problems. I believe they are resolvable within the context of a peacetime volunteer force. But there is no guarantee that we shall be successful in keeping our forces up to strength. If we are not, the department at that time would support a return to the draft.

Competition Between the Military and Higher Education

The military competes, and will continue to compete, with higher education for young people. To some extent, however, we work opposite sides of the street. While both attempt to attract bright high school graduates, higher education recruits mainly among young people who know they want to go to college now. The military recruits mainly among young people who know they do not want to go to college now.

Higher education should welcome Defense as a competitor for two reasons. First, like many competitors, the military brings "business," to higher education—far more than it takes—by creating a demand for education among high school and college graduates. The military creates this demand by encouraging and paying for postsecondary education courses for people in military service. After leaving service, many veterans continue working toward a degree that they would not otherwise have sought.

Second, success of the military as a competitor is necessary to the nation. The armed forces share the basic values of the nation, and its very reason for existence is to protect the nation.

National Service

Certain proposals before the Congress would require some form of national service by America's young people. Defense manpower requirements can be met in the absence of national service. Therefore, the decision on national service should be based, not on the needs of the armed forces, but on the needs of the youth of the nation and on its cost relative to other national objectives. But if the nation moves to national service, Defense needs must be considered carefully in designing and implementing it.

Defense needs are a highly important consideration because a voluntary national service program would compete with the armed forces for young people. It would compete by offering young people some of the same things that the armed forces offer now: the opportunity to serve the nation, the opportunity to learn a trade or get an education, and, finally, the opportunity to grow up. Some recruits today enlist to gain these opportunities. I would expect some of them to be attracted to a civilian national service system that offered the same opportunities.

Mandatory national service is another matter. It would meet Department of Defense manpower needs just as a draft would, because a draft would be a part of a mandatory national service system. But there are other problems with mandatory national service. Of these, two are most significant: finding enough meaningful work, and paying 4–8 million youth each year. The military can employ about 10 percent. Perhaps 1 percent could be used in the national forests. The McCloskey bill would use national service workers on farms, but even that would probably leave over 80 percent without meaningful work. At minimum wage, the cost would be more than $20 billion per year in wages alone.

Defense is concerned about national service for another reason: some of the national service proposals involve drastic reductions in pay for military recruits. The McCloskey bill, for example, would cut military basic pay for new recruits from $449 per month to $192 per month, well below minimum wage.

National service is thus a potential threat to the volunteer force. If national service lessens the attractiveness of military service—either by offering other attractive choices or by reducing pay of military recruits—it well could lead to return of the draft.

Competition Between the Military and Higher Education

JOHN J. CONNOLLY

FIRST, A BASIC QUESTION: Is there competition between the military and higher education? The question can be answered by one statement that ensures an affirmative response: It is estimated that by 1990 the military must recruit one out of three male high school graduates in order to maintain the projected manpower needs of the all-volunteer armed forces.

The implications of this projection are staggering. The consequences of the massive recruiting necessary to achieve such a goal will be dramatically felt in all sectors that provide opportunity for high school graduates—higher education, the labor force. Further, the economy, the military itself, and the basic value system of American society will all be influenced and, perhaps, altered if one of three American male high school graduates does select the military as his post-high-school entry career. Thus, it is not sufficent to suggest that colleges and the military compete only for potential students-recruits; they compete in other spheres of American life as well. The competition for the student-recruit is fierce and portends a questionable future for American society if allowed to continue unchecked. Less subtle, but perhaps of greater magnitude, are the various arenas of competition for public funds, for education programming and services, and, ultimately, for shaping the condition of a democratic society in the years ahead.

The competition for students is the most blatant and perhaps the simplest to analyze. The military, like higher education, is an institution of youth. Sixty percent of military enlisted personnel are under twenty-one years of age. Only 12 percent are over thirty-five. In 1972, 2 percent of high school graduates in the country entered the military directly from high school, 42 percent entered college (two year or four year), and 35 percent entered the labor market. The remainder married, entered vocational schools, or were looking for work.[1] Similar data for New York State for the same year showed 2.2 percent of high school graduates entering the military. This percentage is now 3.2 percent. In October 1979 General Edward C. Meyer revealed that the Army may finish the 1979 fiscal year with a shortage of between 13,000 and 15,000 volunteers. If the military is to achieve the manpower goals of the All-Volunteer Armed Forces, it clearly must ag-

---

1. Department of Health, Education, and Welfare, *1972 Longitudinal Study of High School Graduates* (Washington: Government Printing Office, 1975).

gressively recruit high school graduates from other postsecondary career options. How it does this, and the cost of doing it, should be of concern to responsible educational, military, and political leaders.

Military Recruitment Practices and Costs

Military recruitment is viewed by some critics as an extremely "hard-sell" effort and by others as a subtle soft-sell, almost to the point of being insidious. The truth probably resides only in the eyes of the beholder. Nonetheless, one point that can be well argued is that military recruitment is frequently creative, multifaceted, and expensive. Recently, the Department of the Army awarded a $45 million contract to a New York advertising firm for a recruitment public relations campaign.

The military recruitment pitch is also pervasive. Billboards, direct mail, recruiters at county fairs, radio, television, newspapers, popular magazines—name it and the military uses it. Much of the recruitment stress is on "choice" and "career training." Particularly with the advent of the Community College of the Air Force, educational opportunity rather than military service has become a recurrent theme. As high school seniors approach graduation, they are inundated by mail with expensive brochures describing the advantages of the military. Recruitment officers call homes and even visit potential prospects.

Most college admissions officers would be envious of the vast resources available to military recruiters. Access to name and address lists of high school graduates is a useful tool, usually unavailable to the college recruiter. One way the military obtains valuable recruitment information—unavailable to educational institutions—is through use of the Armed Services Vocational Aptitude Battery (ASVAB). The ASVAB (vocational tests) are administered in many schools, at one time were required in the State of New Hampshire and in Cincinnati, and are used but not mandated in many other communities. In 1978–79, an estimated 963,000 students took these examinations. Once a student takes the exam, the military has access not only to his name and address but also to expressed career interest and abilities. Although the tests are touted as a good way to help students find the right career, internal military documents describe them as a way "to motivate high school and junior college students to enlist in the military by providing a free test service."[2]

2. United States Navy Recruiting Command, *Standard Operating Procedures* (Arlington, Va.: The Command, 1975).

The military uses more subtle approaches to high school students as well—bands, sports clinics, participation in career awareness days, films, and the Junior ROTC. The Junior ROTC was introduced into the nation's high schools in 1916, and the program was limited to 254 Army units until a change in 1974 raised that limit to 1,200. Junior ROTC is presented to schools as a form of citizenship and leadership training, but the ultimate purpose and utility to the military is to gain acceptance of the armed forces and to enlist recruits. The Junior ROTC program concentrates on drill, ceremony, and military subjects. It is taught by retired officers and noncommissioned officers, and it now permits women to join. Its influence is strong in schools where it has become established, and it offers a unique, powerful recruitment tool.

Another practice used by the military, but unavailable to most institutions of higher education, is flying high school guidance counselors to visit the military academies. The Air Force expanded this practice when the Community College of the Air Force was at Randolph Air Force Base, and flew high school guidance counselors to that base, to inform, entertain, and shape the attitudes of those whose responsibilities included helping high school graduates decide on the first important step after graduation.

The cost of these various recruitment programs is tremendous. In 1977, the military budgeted $68.8 million for advertising. Recruiting operations cost an additional $78 million, and National Guard and reserve recruitment cost $258.7 million. In addition, enlistment bonuses cost $53.5 million. It was estimated that in 1977 the cost of recruiting male high school graduates capable of scoring average or above on standardized entrance exams ranged from $870 a recruit for the Air Force to $3,700 a recruit for the Army.[3] Furthermore, the effort and costs of military recruitment have vastly increased with the advent of the all-volunteer forces.

In a recent study conducted by the General Accounting Office, the cost of implementing the all-volunteer armed forces was shown to be over $4 billion in 1976 alone, and, cumulatively, from 1971 to 1976 cost American taxpayers more than $15 billion.[4] This figure reflects the costs of premilitary service (recruiting operations, enlistment incentives, and so on), military service (higher pay, education incentives), and postmilitary service (retirement, etc.). These figures are not the total cost of these operations, but merely the *additional* costs created by the all-volunteer forces. During the

3. Martin Binkin and Irene Kyriakopoulos, *Youth or Experience?: Manning the Modern Military* (Washington: Brookings Institution, 1979).

4. Elmer B. Staats, *Additional Cost of the All Volunteer Force* (Washington: General Accounting Office, 1978).

same period the federal government gave less than $15 billion to colleges and universities for direct institutional support. In other words, simply the *increase* to the military for these purposes was more than the *total* support to institutions of higher education.

The massive amounts of public funds needed to fuel the growing recruitment operations of the military are funds that, in theory at least, could be used for other public purposes, including higher education. However, most people recognize and accept the basic defense and other purposes of the military as vital and necessary. My contention is that military training would be more cost effective if greater use were made of the staffs, equipment, and physical plant resources currently in place in colleges and universities. Degree-granting authority and education are rightfully in the domain of educational institutions and not the military. It seems unnecessary and wasteful, as well as of questionable educational merit, to duplicate these resources.

Military Education Activities Costs

The related issues of recruitment practices and costs lead to the matter of competition in the realm of education. The military is unquestionably one of the nation's largest purveyors of education and training at all levels. Historically, the higher education community has shown little concern that the military educated the dependents of its personnel or educated many of its officers in the various military academies. The former activity is clearly not in competition with local school districts, as it takes place overseas. The latter has been integral to the national educational scene since George Washington recognized the need to train engineers during the Revolutionary War, a thought which ultimately led to the creation of the U.S. Military Academy at West Point (now a Hudson Valley neighbor to Dutchess Community College, with which I am associated).

The massive educational effort of the military is far-reaching and expensive. Though most of the programs are not viewed as competitive to civilian education programs, they nonetheless make the military an educational enterprise of vast scope. In FY 1976, for example, the Department of Defense spent an estimated $1,198 million on educational activities in the following areas: elementary and secondary education, military service academies, ROTC, graduate and professional education, adult basic and extension education, training of federal military employees, and foreign education activities.[5]

5. Office of the Assistant Secretary of Defense, Department of Defense, *Military Manpower Training Report for FY 1978* (Arlington, Va.: Department of Defense, 1977).

Since the sole source of the military's financial support and an important source for colleges and universities is one and the same—the federal budget—the military and higher education are competitive education systems. What is allocated to one clearly cannot be allocated to the other. Thus, competition for the federal dollar does occur.

Education and training have always been important phases of military operations. Certainly, one must train new recruits to bear arms, if nothing else. Moreover, as the structure of military occupations changed over time and, like the rest of society, reflected increasing specialization and greater use of technology, it also became necessary to train new recruits and experienced servicemen to use the new technology. As work in the military evolved to meet needs created by technological change, it became more like civilian work: the modern military demanded computer programmers, electronic technicians, and medical specialists. Thus, military work roles also have come to reflect more closely civilian work roles. And, inevitably, military education and training have come to reflect more nearly civilian education and training, a trend that has resulted in less distinct lines between military and nonmilitary training. The outcome is overlap, demand from the military for civilian recognition of its education and training programs, and, ultimately, competition for students to fill classes and quotas. The competition has led the military to assume the guise of one of its prime competitors—degree-granting colleges.

Military Encroachment on Higher Education's Responsibilities

My primary concern is not really for total dollar amounts spent on educational programs or the provisions for elementary and secondary education for military dependents. Rather, my concern is for the intrusion of the military into an area traditionally reserved for institutions of higher education in this country—with very few exceptions, the granting of degrees. The military always has and always will train many of its own people. It is reasonable to expect some of its training to be applicable in civilian life and jobs. Only since 1972, with the creation of the Community College of the Air Fore (CCAF), with more than 80,888 students currently enrolled, however, has the military competed so directly with higher education by granting degrees. The military has historically, but to limited extent, offered degrees for some of its specialized training. The military academies are examples, but the practice has been in effect in other specialized military schools as well. The Army Staff and Command College is a less familiar example of degree granting by the military.

The case of the CCAF is unique in many ways. First, and most important, it is the only military degree-granting organization designed to serve large numbers of people in degree majors not limited to military specialization. Second, it is the first military degree-granting operation designed primarily as a recruitment tool and not as a new education program. Third, it is the only military degree-granting effort that has violated the understanding of the 1955 "Federal Policy Governing the Granting of Academic Degrees by Federal Agencies and Institutions."[6] Last, and of less significance, CCAF is the first federal attempt at granting the associate degree.

The CCAF clearly competes with higher education. It is designed to recruit students who might otherwise attend community colleges and perhaps four-year colleges by offering the opportunity to complete military service and training *and* to earn an associate degree, *concurrently* and at no cost. The need, from the perspective of the Air Force, is critical. The Air Force attempts to recruit the cream of the crop, those interested in skilled trades, technical fields, and a good education. The CCAF takes specialized Air Force training, such as missile maintenance, wraps a few general education courses around it (as few as twelve credits taught by civilian institutions or by the Air Force), and awards an associate degree. Obviously a powerful recruitment tool, it was played up in recruitment ads in the mass media even before its approval for implementation by the U.S. Office of Education.

The creation of CCAF is a story in itself. It was not created through a piece of major legislation, widely discussed and hotly debated as befits a major change in federal policy. Its creation was so subtle that the higher education community, Congress, and most of the federal government hardly knew what was taking place. The CCAF was created by a sentence or two in Public Law 94-361, a military appropriations bill. The Department of Defense denied initiating the move for degree-granting authority, claiming it was promulgated by "friends of the Air Force."

The approval by Congress of degree-granting powers for what had been a record-keeping center was a dramatic move. Even more dramatic, for the first time Congress approved legislation granting a federal agency the authority to award a degree prior to receiving a recommendation from the Commissioner of Education, an action in direct violation of procedures mandated by the 1955 "Federal Policy Governing the Granting of Academic Degrees by Federal Agencies and Institutions." The Commissioner's opinion was solicited after the fact, but could he be expected to say no after Congress had approved the concept?

6. Statement by the U.S. Office of Education in *Higher Education*, May 1955.

The CCAF exists today at Maxwell Air Force Base. It still offers no courses, but "credits" Air Force training toward the associate degree, which it awards. In addition to standard occupational Air Force programs (for example, Religious Institution Management, Heavy Equipment Technology, Metal Working Technology, and Intelligence Imagery Analyses), the student may take other Air Force courses such as Business English, Technical Writing, and Persuasion as required or elective courses. Some of these same courses also may be taken at nearby colleges and universities. The CCAF determines the amount of credit its courses are worth and does not follow the recommendations of Office on Educational Credit of the American Council on Education. The different credit values recommended for the Air Force courses by the Office on Educational Credit may have been one factor underlying the creation of CCAF. For example, CCAF grants twenty-two academic credits, over one-third needed for the degree, for its course in Missile Maintenance Technology. ACE recommends to colleges and universities that the same course be given the equivalent of two or three college credits. It is hardly surprising the Air Force felt it could do a better job of recognizing the value of its own courses, particularly when the interest was to show high school seniors the wisdom of choosing to enter the Air Force and earn a degree instead of attending an institution of higher education to achieve the same end.

Yes, in order to recruit new manpower to meet the goal of the all-volunteer forces, the military does compete with higher education. It does so, in at least one instance, by assuming the shape and form of a community college. Not the true shape and form of a community college, for the basic characteristics of the institution are markedly different from a community college, and the resemblance is in name only. But the similarity is played up and exploited. Admittedly, the competition as an educational institution is surface only, a veneer, for the ultimate competition is for student-recruits.

The Department of Defense had been considering a proposal for a Community College of the Armed Forces, to encompass all the armed services in a program similar to the CCAF. However, the proposal was shelved (in fact, denied) when it received a cool reception from the Navy and early resistance from persons in the higher education community who were aware of the idea.

Competing Value Systems

Particularly in this kind of competition, the question of competing values comes into play. Sociologists have examined the value systems of both institutions, higher education and military. Even the most naïve Sociology 101 undergraduate would probably see these value systems as dramatically different. Patently, they embrace different goals and processes. In doing so, and in being major aspects of American life and culture, these value systems compete.

On the surface, this situation does not appear to be at all bad. I, for one, do not believe there is a single acceptable value system, nor—as much as I embrace and admire the values found in institutions of higher education—do I believe the military value system to be "un-American" or unacceptable. On the contrary, it is probably satisfying and beneficial to many people. Although such a value system has its place in a diverse American society, it should not *predominate*. Many of its ideals are opposed to principles of American democracy as we know them, and an infusion of these concepts into our culture can only make it a more closed and, ultimately, a weaker society. We do need a military and a strong one. But we do not need a militaristic society.

Thus, the competition for influence on American values exists. Each of these value systems strives for primacy in the hierarchy of American values. It is not simply to attract more new bodies or to gain more financial support that they compete—these are simply indicators of the relative standing of the institutions—but instead they compete to influence the minds and values of Americans.

Despite the concerns among professionals, higher education has fared well in this country, and its values have had great influence on American culture and values. But when I think of one of three American males entering the military after high school and, more important, receiving all or a portion of their "higher education" in that environment, the specter that comes to mind is the success of some state universities with their legislatures: success exemplified by strong financial support and undying loyalty to "old State U." How, I wonder, will that process evolve in Congress when a significant portion of its members have received their higher education in the military and fondly recall "old CCAF." How will the values of criticism and of open and free inquiry, the principles of academic freedom be modified to achieve a livable compromise in a military setting? Bruce Dearing, University Professor of Humanities at the State University of New York Upstate Medical Center, after participating on an ACE's site visitation team to the Community College of the Air Force commented:

> Justice, equity, and social good require that appropriate means be provided for facilitating service personnel in receiving proper recognition for postsec-

ondary education achievement. Conceivably the most cost-effective and desirable in terms of social policy would be the extension of degree granting authority to the Armed Forces and other Federal agencies conducting extensive programs of postsecondary training and education. However, in view of the potential cost of duplicating significant portions of an educational system already in place, it would be preferable to seek ways of making the present Federal non-Federal partnership in higher education more efficient and effective.[7]

The federal government must carefully consider the issues generated by permitting the military to compete directly with higher education both for students and in the offering of degrees. It should consider even more thoroughly the implications of a significant portion of American youth earning a "college" degree for participating in military training. The policy may help meet military manpower needs, but it will not help meet the intellectual manpower needs of the nation in the years to come.

7. Bruce Dearing, letter to Victor Hurst, chairman, site visiting group, CCAF, San Antonio, Texas, October 29, 1976, p. 5.

4. COMPETITION AMONG INSTITUTIONS—ACRIMONY OR ACCOMMODATION?

Two-Year *versus* Four-Year Colleges—Competition Likely to Escalate

GENE A. BUDIG

EARLY IN THE 1970s, many four-year colleges and universities began to realize the impact of the community college movement. In California, for example, two-year colleges accounted for a stunning 60 percent of all public and private college enrollment.[1] Academic administrators suddenly saw the community colleges as one of the prime sources for prospective students.

They saw other significant trends, too. More and more high school graduates were entering the labor market directly, and record numbers of them were choosing job-oriented postsecondary institutions. Two-year campuses were prospering. In 1972, the greatest growth in American higher education came in first-time enrollments and in numbers enrolled in public colleges offering vocational and technical programs of less than bachelor's degree level.

Meanwhile, the increase in freshman enrollments of four-year colleges were slowing two or three years before the expected time. Educators such as Ronald B. Thompson of Ohio State University were telling their colleagues in spring 1973 that "since 1957, the number of births has declined steadily and consequently the number of college-age youth will soon begin to decline at least until 1987, when we may expect the college-age cohort to be only 83 percent of the number in 1978."[2]

By 1973–74, most four-year colleges were working aggressively with community college leadership on the varied problems of articulation. The four-year colleges and universities were presenting packages in many academic fields that would encourage the community college graduate to move on to a baccalaureate objective. Both two-year and four-year institutions hailed these developments in articulation, and they became popular politically. Administrators of some public colleges and universities even

1. *Los Angeles Times*, December 9, 1973.
2. Ronald B. Thompson, "Changing Enrollment Trends in Higher Education," *North Central Association Quarterly*, Spring 1973, pp. 343–48.

built budget requests around "increased articulation activities." Legislators were receptive, seeing this focus as a move toward more efficient use of academic programs and people. Countless community college students and faculty members were encouraged by the new-found interest in them and their enterprise. There was a general feeling of camaraderie, not competition, between two-year and four-year institutions in the mid-1970s.

But what about the 1980s? According to three two-year college presidents and three four-year college presidents from large, industrial states, the atmosphere already has changed—and not for the better.[3] They all agreed that competition between the two types of institutions has grown keen and at times unbecoming. Furthermore, they predicted more of the same for the 1980s. The three community college presidents were highly critical of alleged activities at the four-year campuses. Specifically, they accused the four-year institutions of attempting to recruit community college students before they completed their two-year programs; lowering admission requirements to attract students who would have attended community colleges; and moving into vocational-technical waters which the community colleges had charted and navigated.

"The four-year colleges and universities are raiding us," a community college president declared. "We have the students, and they need them." Another said, "We were ahead of the times. We built programs that prepared students to be productive in the world of work. The four-year institutions are taking a programmatic page from our book, but they want our students, too." One community college president claimed that the four-year institutions were dropping admission standards by allowing students to enter under "special program categories." He said, "This is questionable practice, but they are pulling out all stops to meet student quotas." The three two-year college presidents said the four-year institutions have moved dramatically into adult education. They look for intensified competition in this field because "this is where thousands of prospective students are."

Representatives from the four-year institutions were a bit defensive, but strong in the belief that community colleges have overreacted to increased competition. They countered with three principal points: Four-year colleges can do more for certain students who might have selected

---

3. The six presidents interviewed, in August 1979, asked to remain unnamed. They all regarded the general relationship between two- and four-year institutions as "strained" and "potentially explosive." The presidents were from major institutions in California, Illinois, and New York.

community colleges in the past, and the four-year colleges have a responsibility to tell them so through the recruiting process. Certain colleges and universities have liberalized admission requirements to assure a more representative student body. Four-year institutions must move more aggressively to meet the needs of the nontraditional student if they are to be deserving of continued public trust and support.

"There are many young people who would do better personally and professionally if they spend all four years with us," the president of a state university said. "It is a matter of being fair with them, and giving them a climate in which they can achieve their true potential." Another four-year college president noted that "of course, we have devised special programs to give disadvantaged students an opportunity to excel. Many of them have the intellectual potential, but not the academic record from high school. They cannot be denied the opportunity to attend a four-year college or university."

Only in the last year or so had many major colleges and universities been in a position to expand adult education opportunities, one president explained. "Before, we have been preoccupied with meeting the on-campus demands of the traditional student," he said. "Now we can concern ourselves with quality and service." The three presidents from the four-year colleges thought that increased competition could serve to enhance program quality. Their counterparts from the two-year sector disagreed.

Many community college leaders are concerned that increased competition between two-year and four-year institutions will be viewed by external agencies as unchecked duplication. Unwanted and unwarranted legislative intervention could result. Legislators from five midwestern states indicate there is reason for apprehension. As one state senator said, "if they [higher education] cannot adjudicate their problems, we [the legislature] will. No state government can afford program duplication today." The legislators also said that they were aware of the issue of increased competition between the two types of institutions.

There was unanimity on another major issue. The six presidents said that current financial assistance packages seemed to favor the four-year public colleges and universities. These packages, which often include state and federal dollars, can cover most, if not all, of the cost of education to the student. What these packages actually do is give students new mobility or the opportunity to pick and choose an institution of higher learning. They open the door to residential programs, which usually are found at four-year institutions. Community college programs are almost exclusively nonresidential.[4] The real change came with full funding of the Basic Grant Program in 1976–77, as well as with expanded state grants. Both developments were seen as a boon for women and minorities: with the dropping of financial barriers, more opportunities were created. Federal and state politicians point proudly to increased opportunities for persons from middle-income families. The politicians regard their commitment to financial aid to education programs as being exemplary.

The six college presidents agreed on several other significant points: Their institutions of higher learning had increased recruiting budgets significantly in the past two years. Community college graduates do very well academically at four-year institutions. Their colleges plan to place increased emphasis on programs that assure meaningful employment opportunities. Liberal arts programs will survive, but two-year and four-year institutions must reaffirm their public commitment to them. Graduates of liberal arts programs are able and adapt well to most jobs. Progress made through articulation programs must be protected for the sake of students. And, they remain uncertain about the future relationship between two-year and four-year institutions of higher education.

Two Years *versus* Four— Wrong Battle, Wrong Timing

LOUIS T. BENEZET

DEMOCRATIC SOCIETY, according to cultural historians and philosophers, bases its hopes for survival on providing a balance between two opposing urges, to compete and to cooperate. Anthropologists seesaw on the primacy of one over the other; and the American college, as the product of a Christian church founding for the most part, often is caught on the bridge between. It may depend on how closely one follows either Konrad Lorenz or Ashley Montague whether humankind is seen as a jungle full of born aggressors or as a garden, a rock garden to be sure, to be cultivated by people working together in the interests of all for survival.

College educators on the whole have grown up in places of mutual dependency. Still, when their proprietary interests are threatened with serious loss, they can be as competitive as any sales entrepreneur. Increased awareness of the competitive state in current higher education has sharp-

---

4. Interview with Neil E. Bolyard, president, National Association of Student Financial Aid Adminstrators on August 13, 1979. Mr. Bolyard is also director of financial aids, West Virginia University.

ened the edges of feeling between colleges of different levels and purposes. The feelings between proponents of two years and four years of postsecondary education have always had to skirt attitudes of hierarchy and status. Now that institutions face fewer prospective students from the 18–24 cohort than places to instruct and house them, those attitudes are being displayed in ways that may further alienate those persons who are already inclined to believe that college costs more than its benefits justify.

During the boom enrollment years of the late 1950s and early 1960s, colleges competed for students, at the upper levels of academic promise to be sure. The Korean Bill of Rights, P.L. 550, pitted private schools against public because the total monthly allotments included tuition payment rather than leaving tuition separate from subsistence as in the original GI Bill. By 1969 a dip in proportion of high school graduates going directly to college, followed by a mild recession, started trends of competitive recruitment tactics that grew more aggressive during the 1970s.

Competition and Students' Needs

A first type of competition can be illustrated. At a conference of presidents in 1973, some conferees were startled to hear a community college president accuse a four-year college president of lowering admission requirements so as to attract freshmen away from neighboring two-year colleges. Two-year private colleges have experienced worsening enrollments as four-year liberal arts colleges (including many of the better known) have eased freshman entrance requirements. A more successful arrangement is seen when a school like Hartford College for Women has specialized in preparing students for upper-division work in certain liberal arts colleges in the Northeast, particularly Mount Holyoke.

A second kind of competition centers on the student's purpose. The contest between community two-year and four-year state colleges should relate to the kind of preparation the student is looking for. Community colleges were developed (nearly twelve hundred today, with an enrollment approaching 4 million) to prepare students for postsecondary careers open after two years of college-level training and education. Still, at the University of California, for example, normally up to 40 percent of the upperclassmen come in as community college graduates. Pressure is then put on the two-year college to devote a larger share of its curriculum to prepare students for the rest of the baccalaureate course and enlarge academic programs rather than vocational offerings. The resulting stress must be blamed on a conflict of motives, which has, as far as I am aware, nowhere been well resolved.

A third type of two- versus four-year competition, community college versus four-year private college, invites even broader questions about the student's purpose. Is the student looking for a nearby nonresidential program of general and vocational courses at minimum cost; or does college present a development of social and personal competence in a twenty-four hour residential setting? It is incumbent on institutions to explore these questions thoroughly with the student before beginning recruitment efforts, let alone before entrance. Recent experience with students faced with these questions confirms my impression that the extra costs of a four-year residential college reflect careful thought and considerable family sacrifice. The differences in expectations from the college are commensurate.

A fourth competition may be briefly noted: between the two-year option in a four-year residential college with the associate degree as the award, and the full baccalaureate course. Presumably it depends on how much learning the individual can profitably achieve according to his or her aptitude, interests, funds, time, and needs. In practice, peers often apply pressure along the line "two years good, four years better" (to paraphrase Orwell's *Animal Farm*). The college is not impartial, since filling third- and fourth-year classrooms is economically desirable. Sophomore students may find it hard to qualify for an upper-division major or may simply prefer to step out after two years and enter the work field. Outside as well as inside influences don't always make this step easy or graceful.

The college race for enrollments, in brief, threatens to overrun distinctions among different types of colleges that were created in response to the traditional American call for diversity. The resulting disenchantment among observers in the public as well as in federal and state legislatures has accelerated movements to protect the student consumer. The Education Amendments of 1976 contain a section requiring full disclosure to prospective students regarding financial aid programs available. An interinstitutional consortium is furthering similar moves under the name, Center for Helping Organizations Improve Choice in Education.[1]

Toward Alleviating Competition

I have several suggestions, some already in operation, for reducing the more undesirable elements of competition while lending encouragement

---

1. Joan S. Stark and John V. Griffith, "Responding to Consumerism," in *Building Bridges to the Public*, ed. Louis T. Benezet and Frances W. Magnusson (San Francisco: Jossey-Bass, 1979), p. 93.

for renewed cooperative efforts in the interests of those we seek to serve. They are proposed, not as dicta, but as material for debate.

1. Increase state tuition equalization grants to widen public-private college choice for students who now cannot afford the difference.

2. Reduce interstate barriers to carrying a state scholarship to a college in another state.[2]

3. Increase fee differentials between the first two and latter two years of undergraduate college, thus reducing present lower-division subsidy of upper-division education.

4. Strengthen (with funds and closer supervision) college advisement both in senior high schools and in freshman and sophomore college years.

5. Make clearer the differences in subject matter and method of career-oriented courses in four-year college programs as distinct from their two-year college counterparts (e.g., accounting programs).

6. Promote better public recognition of the Associate in Arts and Associate in Science degrees.

7. A seventh proposal is perhaps more venturesome. Could we in higher education enhance cooperation by bringing closer together the aims and content of general education in the first two years of all colleges whether two year or four year? This suggestion may seem contradictory to proposal number 5. The contradiction is deliberate. A four-year college curriculum will approach career-slanted subjects differently from a two-year college where most students are being prepared to put their learning into practice in the third year. The situation, I submit, is not parallel to liberal learning in basic science, behavioral studies, art and literature. These subjects are needed to enrich every student's understanding of the world, whether they be learned in a two-year course or a four-year course. To downgrade a liberal general education in the two-year college is an error that is balanced in the four-year college by the error of tieing it too closely to departmental specialization.

My concluding suggestion is thus that all-out competition, tinged with hierarchicalism, between two- and four-year colleges could be moderated on a meeting ground where common aims of a general education for students beyond the high school are worked on in concrete terms. The search for a common approach to a contemporary general education for our times just could be the most critical educational problem we face. If that is even remotely true, then the time for genuine cooperation between two-year and four-year institutions of higher learning has arrived.

2. See David W. Breneman and Chester E. Finn, Jr., eds., *Public Policy and Private Higher Education* (Washington: Brookings Institution, 1978).

Cooperation—Key for the 1980s

LESLIE KOLTAI

NOT LONG AGO, THE VARIOUS SECTORS of American higher education coexisted rather peacefully. The strength of the higher education system has traditionally rested in its great diversity. Each sector has developed its distinct identity in response to specific student needs and expectations. Today, the situation is different. Dwindling enrollments have created an educational environment in which, many predict, increased competition for students will force colleges and universities to draw counterproductive battle lines.

As demographers continue to warn of a decreasing pool of prospective students, more intrusions into educational functions that were considered out-of-bounds are being seen. Four-year institutions have begun to tailor programs to attract the traditional community college student by increasing their offerings for the associate degree and by enrolling part-time students. Adult education classes, once the province of the secondary schools, are showing up on more four-year campuses, and the number of remedial courses offered for credit at these institutions has also increased. Two-year colleges, on the other hand, have begun to present more classes designed to appeal to other than lower-division students, a move that four-year institutions view as an invasion on their mission.

Strength Diffused by Competition

The range of common problems faced by those of us in two- and four-year institutions is, I believe, too great to diffuse our strength by inter-institutional competition. Besides decreased enrollment, we all face diminished public support, recorded legislative priorities, the effects of collective bargaining, competition from secondary schools, compliance with governmental mandates, lower student proficiency levels, and changes in the structure of financial aid programs. Student consumerism, a relatively recent factor, is causing educational policy to be dictated more and more by students. Additionally, the increasingly litigious student mood is going to call educators from their customary responsibilities to defend their policies and decisions in the courtroom.

Through cooperative effort, we educators can work to solve these common problems instead of using our energies to battle each other for bodies to fill our classrooms. And, I predict, the increased educational vitality emerging from such cooperation could also make our institutions more attractive to a whole new range of prospective students.

Educational specificity will be one key to successful adaptation in the future. While it is clear that our colleges and universities cannot be all things to all people, we must also recognize that soon we might not even be able to provide all that our students want. We must, however, continue to provide all that they need. We will have to balance limited resources against the realities of the student marketplace, attempting to provide relevant education that is also cost effective.

Warning Signals Outlined

As the matter of educational competition versus cooperation is being pondered, several points are worth considering. They may also serve as warning signals: (1) No two- or four-year college can escape the external pressures outlined above. Nor can they afford to spend the time, effort, and money on counterproductive competition when resources are needed for institutional growth and regeneration. (2) Faculty morale cannot but suffer in the strained environment of a competitive siege. (3) A workable partnership between two- and four-year institutions would result in better-prepared transfer students, who would then contribute to student retention at the four-year level. (4) The very integrity of postsecondary institutions would be threatened by the possible decline in academic standards caused by a battle for students. (5) If we in higher education cannot solve the problem of delineating the function, we may find that taxpayers indirectly do so by withdrawing their support. The public has little tolerance for functions that overlap. (6) Shared goals can best be reached if the "lifeboat" mentality of interinstitutional competition is rejected. (7) Unprofessional competitive maneuvers in postsecondary education could cause legislators to turn their funding mechanisms to other areas of public concern, leaving higher education to fight over the financial scraps.

Two- and four-year institutions *can*, I believe, forge a workable partnership. Efforts can be directed toward several specific areas, with the expectation of measurable success. Perhaps most obvious is the need for better communication between institutions in order to find more ways to assist each other.

Facilitating Transfer

A principal need in cooperation is for improved articulation agreements and clearer specifications on transfer requirements. Now, the educational road for the transfer student is hazardous. For example, a student enters a two-year college with the intention of pursuing the baccalaureate. Under the present "system," in order to ensure the transferability of course-work credits, he or she must choose, before matriculation, precisely which four-year institution to attend ultimately.

Students at two-year colleges can no longer be regarded as those who couldn't "make it" at a four-year institution. Community colleges are not the "halfway house" institutions in higher education. Students who meet admissions requirements for four-year institutions are often choosing to begin their college work at a conveniently located, inexpensive two-year college offering class schedules designed to meet their needs.

Two-year colleges could benefit immeasurably from follow-up reports on the academic performance of their graduates. By providing feedback on how well or how poorly students do after transfer, four-year institutions could give their two-year counterparts valuable data on which to evaluate programs and instructional modes. The four-year institutions would then reap the benefits of students who are more appropriately prepared for upper-division work. Conversely, two-year colleges could provide information about their student clienteles that would help four-year institutions to become more effective in recruiting two-year graduates.

The nontraditional student, once exclusively the client of the community college, is becoming the predominant student on many four-year campuses. The community colleges, by sharing insights into this type of student which they have developed over the years, could give the four-year institutions a head start in dealing with their changing clientele.

Sharing

Effective sharing of equipment and facilities is another area where I believe cooperative effort is needed, particularly in study areas requiring expensive technical equipment. Students could even attend classes at both two- and four-year institutions simultaneously, thus greatly improving utilization of resources.

And why not investigate the use of cooperative seminars and colloquia to advance common goals? Last spring, for example, the Los Angeles Community College District (LACCD) and the California State University and Colleges (CSUC) system cooperated in presenting a seminar on developmental education for appropriate faculty members and administrators from both systems. The experiment proved to be most effective, and additional cooperative ventures are being considered. The LACCD is also developing a program in conjunction with the CSUC system to train instructors from their institutions and the LACCD to implement basic skills education.

Many decision points lie ahead where, in light of available human and financial resources, each sector of postsecondary education will be forced to plan for growth in the areas it can handle best. Educational accountability requires that colleges and universities evidence quality and efficiency in the programs and services they provide. Only by honest self-analysis and self-appraisal can two- and four-year institutions effectively use their potential for providing meaningful education.

The criterion for evaluating the success and failure of postsecondary institutions must be based, not on the entry of, but on the education of the individual student. Competition can only hamper meeting that criterion.

Lifelong Education as a Rationale for Colleges
GEORGE H. ROBERTSON

SINCE THE GOLDEN YEARS OF EXPANSION have passed, most colleges have developed survival techniques based on the only thing their admissions departments know. They engage in more and more skilled and aggressive salesmanship, aimed at winning the required share of a traditional college population. But better and better salesmanship in the same market will no longer do the trick: the traditional market for higher education is declining by about 3 percent per year. Because colleges are no better at managing retrenchment than most other organizations, most institutions are reaching out to new markets in preference to winding down their operations. But there's the rub. Step by step, usually without much serious consideration, many colleges have moved into areas that have little to do with their original mission. Under the pressures of competition, actions by individual colleges are, almost incidentally, changing the basic form of higher education.

We in the higher education community might hope for some restraint based on cooperation. But given the independence and individuality of American colleges and the dire consequences of even the slightest enrollment downturn, voluntary restraint in competition seems unlikely. Cooperation is much talked about, but not much practiced. Even statewide systems and commissions seem powerless to curb institutional competition except by restricting financial support. But that usually only intensifies the competition to qualify for the dollars.

Institutional purposes can perhaps be determined effectively through an institutional Darwinism based on unrestrained competition. Yet higher education has an overall public purpose that needs to be explained to those who support our institutions. If the public sees our competition as desperation, survival tactics, we stand to lose their support. Surely a believable framework for our competition, a strategic rationale, can make competition acceptable, and permit each kind of institution to develop a case for its own existence within the higher education enterprise.

As a community college president exploring the competition between two- and four-year colleges, I feel particular need for such a framework. Our two-year colleges are exposed to public scrutiny through our local sponsors and local clienteles. Our need for a new rationale—a new market position—is intensified as other institutions, seeking survival, recruit and accept students who previously would have turned to the community college. To the extent that many traditional colleges have now embraced the Open Door or career and vocational programs, community colleges could regard part of their mission as finished or partially transferred to others. But in order to relinquish even part of that mission, two-year colleges need to know what comes next: we need to survive, too.

Relating Lifelong Education and the College Mission

Over the last year or so, community colleges have begun to develop a rationale that is both believable and socially desirable. We are beginning to recognize and act on the idea that American higher education is becoming a system for lifelong education. Traditional higher education may face declining enrollments. But lifelong education, by contrast, is surely a growth industry, with a large backlog of unfinished business. Given the prospect of growing demand, we are justified in engaging in energetic and aggressive marketing of college services. Colleges in America have a positive obligation to foster an educational economy of rising expectations.

Within a lifelong education concept, different colleges can compete in providing various kinds of services. Intellectual and personal development, manpower training, public service, and upward mobility through open access are all aspects of higher education that can be extended throughout life. Given a large unfilled demand for lifelong education, competition in an education marketplace has enough room for all the different colleges and their many different missions.

Any overall scheme of higher education must include some commonsense market segmentation. Geographical distance, mission and programs, and price are all specifics that can be applied to any given institution and its competitive position.

The great universities and their outriders in the elite liberal arts colleges will probably maintain their present academic standards for admission. Given inflated education costs and tuition levels, the elite institutions will probably develop even further the highly selective admissions patterns that are based on price as much as academic potential, particularly in the northeastern states. This policy may not be desirable, but seems likely.

Some other four-year institutions will probably shift toward the educational left, as they seek to maintain enrollment and revenues without the benefit of a prestigious national reputation. Many—perhaps most—four-year colleges will become more like comprehensive, open-access colleges. They will compete with two-year colleges for indifferently prepared high school graduates. As a result, two-year colleges will lose part of their present clientele to four-year colleges. But they will probably also attract substantial numbers of well-prepared students purely because of low costs. Both two-year and four-year colleges, in fact, will probably accommodate a broader spectrum of students than before.

New Programs, New Clienteles, New Problems

The measures that four-year colleges are taking to adjust to the new reality are well known. The problems that will arise from these measures get less attention than is needed.

Career programs are expensive to staff and equip. The typical four-year college will have difficulty in building a staff, especially when overall enrollments are stable or declining. Placement of graduates is not always easy, and the advent of large numbers of new specialized programs may soon create a glut of graduates in some areas now seen as most attractive—business, science-based careers, computer-based careers.

Any shortcoming in developmental and support services for marginally prepared freshmen will hurt. Support services are expensive and may be beyond the reach of institutions that most need to cope with enrollment decline. Relaxed admissions standards may prove quite efficient from a social point of view: many students will withdraw after an unhappy experience, having lost one or more years and perhaps even their appetite for education.

Four-year colleges, private colleges in particular, seem to make much of "quality education." In the long run, this assertion will become less credible as some of the self-designated "quality institutions" become less distinguishable from others.

Many four-year residential colleges will face serious difficulties in attracting adult students, especially part-time commuters. Experience in the adult education market shows that the first cut is the easy one. Sustaining a substantial program over the long haul isn't so easy.

Two-year colleges will have their problems too. The revenue patterns for community colleges present a particular problem: they are mostly enrollment-driven, and many are subject to local and often parochial control. The community colleges are most directly exposed to any public disillusionment with higher education.

In general, community colleges have had a rather poor image in academic circles. Their efforts to overcome that image by imitating other colleges have often inhibited efforts in their prime mission, which is to serve the public purpose of general or universal access.

The four-year colleges will probably find tough competition with the universities and thus will concentrate their recruitment and program adjustment toward the community college market and mission. The residential college is a powerful idea. Where the residence experience is important to a prospective student, community colleges cannot compete.

Advantages for the Two-Year Colleges

Nonetheless, the community colleges seem quite likely to do well in the future, even if they do vacate some of their turf to four-year colleges. They bring strengths to the competition: a strong and well-established commitment to career programs, arising in many cases from the technical institute tradition; program flexibility and diversity, with a taste for innovation which is absent in many institutions; a local base for commuters of all ages and circumstances; relatively low cost—especially important for the newly deprived middle classes; ability to relate to local schools, businesses, industry, and government in a more direct, uncomplicated way than regional or statewide institutions. Most important of all, they have a missionary zeal that focuses on the Open Door, the new students, adult students, individualized programs, experimental learning: the whole constellation of interests that can be summed up at "The Open Door to Lifelong Education."

For traditional students, the prime distinction between the two-year colleges and most four-year colleges will come to be the distinction between residential and nonresidential. Quality of programming or of students, however those may be defined, will cease to be a great issue for the community colleges, as other colleges continue to borrow programs, students, and philosophies from them.

Under the pressure of competition, the two-year colleges can and probably should shift into underserved segments of the education market. Among the new clienteles to be served: those who are below present college entrance thresholds; those who seek one or two years of preparation for a vocation; blue-collar workers; business and industry, through contract courses; adults seeking basic education; returning adult students, especially women and others in career transition; women in programs not traditional for women; transfers from four-year colleges; bright students with clear career objectives, who are unimpressed with the mystique of a four-year college residence experience and besides cannot afford it. For the last group, two plus two programs will become commonplace in fields such as accounting, engineering, nursing.

With the possible exception of adult basic education, none of these clienteles seems likely to add more than a few percentage points to each institution's enrollment. In aggregate, they will allow two-year colleges to maintain services at current levels of activity and revenues.

Lifelong education provides Mohawk Valley Community College with the rationale we need to fit ourselves into a long-range, large view of education. With this rationale, we can take a positive view of our collective future. While we cannot presume to speak for others, we do believe every college can have an important part in the scheme of lifelong education. Through competition, as well as minimum amounts of cooperation, each institution can assist in the long-term effort to help America become a learning society.

Too few of us see our work within an overall context for higher education. Urgent day-to-day adjustments at the local or state level distract us. Perhaps hard times do not permit statesmanship or consensus. Yet, if we are to maintain credibility with the public and among ourselves, we must look beyond our short-range problems toward some larger view of education in society. From the windows at my college we see lifelong education.

Growth in a Time of Steady State

DONALD GRUNEWALD

THE NEW YORK METROPOLITAN AREA is probably the most hazardous area in the country for the health and survival of the independent college. The City University of New York (one of the largest universities in the country) has been subsidized by billions of dollars of government—state and city—funds for construction and operations and has extremely low tuition levels. In recruiting activities, many city public school staffs seem to further access and support to admissions counselors from government-operated institutions. The nearby State University College at Purchase has a fine plant and low tuition. Other SUNY units, including community colleges, in the metropolitan area also have excellent facilities, low tuition, and large budgets for advertising, promotion, and other recruitment activities.

The government-sponsored institutions and the large independent universities also benefit from State Education Department regulations that particularly hamstring independent colleges. For example, any unit of the government-operated state university may refer to itself as part of the state university whereas in the independent sector only doctorate-granting institutions may use the designation "university." Unfortunately, many foreign-born persons think "college" means high school, to decided disadvantage in recruiting by the smaller independent institution. The State Education Department also requires an elaborate procedure of application and review for new programs before their implementation. The expense and sometimes long delayed decisions hamper smaller institutions in adapting to the changing needs of students. State restrictions on adjunct faculty also create financial difficulties for the smaller institutions in experimenting with new programs and new methods of delivering instruction. Several independent institutions in the metropolitan area have closed: Mills, Finch, Bennett, Briarcliff, Woodstock, and Mary Rogers Colleges, as well as Columbia College of Pharmacy. Others have consolidated (College of White Plains into Pace University, and People University into Touro College), affiliated (Parsons School of Design with New School for Social Research), or sell real estate (New York University sold its Bronx complex, and Manhattanville College sold part of its campus). Others have declined in enrollment and had to cut back programs.

A Case Report

Several independent colleges have, however, managed to survive and grow significantly. Mercy College is a case in point. In 1972, Mercy was a liberal arts college with teacher education programs, about 1,500 students, a faculty with only 25 percent earned doctorates, a library of 60,000 volumes, operating on a fifteen-acre campus with one building and an uncertain financial future. Mercy was founded in 1950 and became a four-year college in 1961 and nonsectarian and coeducational in 1969. By 1979, it had more than 8,000 undergraduate students in liberal arts and career programs, a much larger faculty (60 percent with the earned doctorate), libraries containing 275,000 volumes, operating on a main campus of fifty acres with four buildings and on a branch campus and five extension centers, and had built a quasi-endowment fund of almost $2 million. A joint program with Long Island University has brought graduate enrollment to more than 800 students at the Mercy College campus, compared with no graduate program in 1972.

Faculty, Facilities, Programs

How has Mercy achieved its growth and improved financial status in so short a time? First, our college has recruited an able faculty who have built a reputation for quality. Because the New York metropolitan area is the capital of the world, much brainpower is available on either a full-time or adjunct basis to colleges such as ours. We have been able to attract well-known academics on an occasional or regular basis. Many industries have furnished adjunct faculty who offer a "real world" background—usually rare in most full-time faculties—which is relevant and beneficial to adult students. Our salaries are number 1 on the AAUP scale for our type of institution and have helped us attract quality full-time faculty who enjoy New York and its cultural resources.

Good libraries and attractive but low-cost facilities are important in our success. Mercy has purchased three libraries from closed colleges at low cost to help build our quality library. With the support of Congressman Fish, Mercy was designated as a U.S. government partial depository library at the Yorktown campus, which has given our students and the pubic access to many government publications without acquisitions cost to us. All facilities other than at the main campus in Dobbs Ferry are rented: we rent space as programs grow and can contract if they shrink. Thus, we have avoided tieing up funds for capital expenditures or borrowing to finance building projects. This policy has given us flexibility to move in response to our needs and to avoid long-term losses when a given market declines.

Our faculty has developed sound, innovative programs in the liberal arts and in career education. Our career education programs now include business administration, social work, music, criminal justice, nursing, computer information systems, public safety, and fire science besides teacher education and medical technology initiated prior to 1972. Proposed programs in broadcast communications, nutrition, veterinary technology, and graduate professional psychology are undergoing State Education

Department review, and other new programs are being considered. Program development and reappraisal are constant activities. We have also tried to articulate our programs with those offered by graduate and professional schools so as to prepare our students for careers in law, health fields, business, social and government services, and higher education.

Accessibility

Gas shortages, other transportation problems, and varied work schedules make it important to offer courses at times and locations convenient to the students, rather than primarily to faculty members' preferences. We believe that scheduling should follow research into when and where students would like to take their courses. Faculty members are required to teach part of their regular load evenings or off campus, and most are happy to do so because our adult students are of high quality. We currently offer courses at six major locations: Dobbs Ferry (main campus), Yorktown (in a converted office building adjacent to a major highway), White Plains (in a downtown converted office building), Yonkers (in a converted hospital in the largest shopping center in Westchester County), in the Bronx (evenings in a private academy and days in a nearby converted supermarket), and in Peekskill (in a community center which also houses the public library and the senior citizens facility). Each facility has classrooms, a library, computer terminals, snack bar, and offices for faculty and counselors. We also offer courses in several prisons in New York State, in hospitals, and in corporate facilities as needed by the community. We find that most adult students will commute only four or five miles to class so multiple locations are needed if workers and homemakers are to be served.

Time is as important as place. We offer courses seven days a week from eight A.M. to eleven P.M. In fall 1979, we began experimenting with night owl sessions on our main campus, starting at one A.M., to serve shift workers in a nearby automobile assembly plant. Course duration is also adjusted to meet student needs. Some students prefer eight-week modules (class meets twice a week for two and a half hours); others prefer the semester (class meets once a week for two and a half hours or twice a week for one and a quarter hours). Parallel scheduling is arranged for workers whose shifts change regularly: students attend class in early morning or in evening, switching as needed. Student needs are primary unless some academic reason prohibits flexible scheduling.

Low tuition is also important to our growth. Mercy has been able to price its tuition somewhat lower than other independent colleges in the area, largely through economy measures: intensive use of facilities, lowered capital investment through renting only facilities needed, use of adjunct faculty where they are the most appropriate. Other cost-cutting measures include computerized registration, low expense accounts, secretarial pools, careful buying of library books and other major purchases, and avoidance of the hotel business (no dormitories). Our current tuition is $65 per semester hour of credit, and no fees. We announce tuition increases at least six months in advance. We offer a quality education at a reasonable price, and we deliver on this promise.

In keeping with our policy of low tuition is a student aid counseling program to acquaint students with sources of aid and to help them fill out the government aid forms. New York State has an excellent financial aid and tuition assistance program. Mercy College has been able, by adding from its scholarship funds, to offer free tuition to state residents who are full-time students provided their net taxable income is less than $10,000 per annum. We accept major credit cards and can arrange varied schedules for paying tuition.

Expansion at Low Cost

Joint programming with other institutions has proved another way to increase services and reduce costs. Mercy College has a joint major in music with the Westchester Conservatory of Music. Music majors take applied music courses at the conservatory, which has the instructors and facilities, and their liberal arts and music theory at Mercy. Thus, facilities and instructors are not duplicated, and each institution benefits by having more students. Similarly, we have brought graduate programs of Long Island University onto our campus in an arrangement whereby faculty are shared, libraries are linked, and other services are shared. Thus we can bring quality graduate programs to our area without the large investment in faculty, library, course development, and the like required to initiate graduate degree work.

Good programs, convenient locations and times, a qualified faculty, good libraries and other facilities, and a reasonable price are still not enough. Mercy College has carefully designed a program to inform prospective students about our offerings. Three times a year we use direct mail to send a complete schedule of our courses to more than 350,000 residences. Adult learners, in particular, find the mailer useful. They can quickly see what is offered, where, and at what time and price. The mailer seems to work better than newspaper advertising (we do some to reinforce our image) or any other media in part because advertising in metropolitan dailies is expensive. We also have an attractive catalog and brochures on each of our major programs available at each of our campuses.

A good counseling staff contributes to our success in attracting students or in counseling them where to go if Mercy's offerings are not appropriate to their needs. The counselors include representatives of major student cohorts such as an adult woman who has returned to education, a Hispanic, a veteran, a fairly recent college graduate, and others. Thus, potential students have someone comfortable to talk with who understands their needs and interests. Testing is provided to assist placement level and to aid students in identifying areas of interest. We visit schools, community colleges, and major employers. From time to time, a van serves as a mobile admissions information office in shopping centers. We follow up applicants on the telephone to make sure that questions about Mercy are fully answered. So far, these policies have enabled Mercy College to grow in size and continually improve what we offer our students.

The independent colleges can survive and serve their constituencies if they adapt to the rapidly changing conditions of higher education. I believe such institutions must not only survive but also prosper so as to provide diversity in education and freedom from political control as well as serve as a good yardstick for the costs and policies of the government-operated institutions and the independent multiversities. I believe that, all over the country, independent institutions such as Mercy College can often provide better education at a reasonable price than other choices. I believe independent institutions will survive to serve our citizens for many years to come.

Toward Cooperation Among Public and Private Institutions

ALLAN W. OSTAR

MOST COLLEGE AND UNIVERSITY ADMINISTRATORS could probably recite in their sleep a summary of the critical times for higher education: inflation, staggering energy costs, a smaller pool of entering freshmen, government regulation and its costs, the decline of collegiality, and growing public skepticism. There is no immunity based on classification, no reprieve because an institution happens to be a public or private college or university.

Perhaps the most worrisome pressure is a decline in the public's unquestioning faith in higher education. When war, politics, and economics jolted the nation awake from the American dream, more than government lost the public's confidence; all institutions were viewed with new, more skeptical eyes. As for higher education, credibility to manage its own affairs as it sees fit—to plan, to use resources effectively, to make intelligent financial decisions, to monitor its activities for refinements and improvements—is strained.

I am not among the gloomy who believe that higher education has entered an irreparable decline. I do think that we are in an era of delicate decision making. How carefully and how well we respond to current pressures will decide for the future the number and extent of restraints and constraints on our management and the influence we wield.

Against this background, cooperation between the independent and the public sectors is a necessity. Internecine policy pronouncements—the kind that periodically make good copy in the newspapers—fuel public speculation that public and private institutions are self-serving and make less than objective policy. When public and private institutions cooperate, they present a powerful presence in the community, in state planning commission meetings, in legislative sessions, in corporate offices, and in governors' offices. When they do not cooperate, the result is gaps in information and communication, gaps that permit external forces to enter and serve as facilitators, mediators, and decision makers.

Public and Private Institutional Missions

In order for public and independent institutions to cooperate fruitfully, several basic premises must be accepted about the nature of each sector.

One, public and private institutions are indeed different. They cannot be compared against the same yardstick, and they are not interchangeable. They are different basically because they were created to serve different purposes. Generally, private institutions were created to meet the special needs of students as members of a particular group. This construct holds from early national history—the founding of the nation's first colleges by churches—to the twentieth century, for such orientation as Parsons College for "problem students." Private colleges are, above all, oriented to particular student needs.

Public institutions, on the other hand, were created by the state to fulfill broad educational and educationally related objectives of the state. These objectives relate to the health and welfare of the state—its people and its economy. It was deemed good public policy to raise the education level of the state's citizens; therefore people must have access to educational opportunity they can afford; thus low tuition. Public policy also called for teachers, engineers, agrarian scientists, and health personnel. Good public policy called for resource centers that would provide continuing education to adults, extension services to farmers, and expertise to government agencies. The missions of public institutions are not directed at particular student needs; they are public missions.

Two, because public and private institutions have different missions and orientation, they are funded differently. Private institutions are funded primarily by the students they serve and by those who share the interests of that particular group. Public institutions are funded primarily by the state, with lesser percentages provided by students (although this percentage unfortunately is increasing in many places) and by those who may be interested in a particular mission of the institutions.

Public institutions have a unique need for institutional aid that private institutions do not have. If public institutions were deprived of state subsidy and were forced to depend on student tuition income, they would lose the flexibility needed to carry out the state's public policies. Their missions to provide educational opportunity, community and regional service, and applied research would be severely threatened.

Third, all institutions do not serve the public equally. The growing federal presence in student aid—awarded to students who may take the funds to public, private, or proprietary institutions—obscures this point. Does the public wish to support all institutions equally, regardless of the benefits it receives in return? I think not. There must be, then, public spending priorities, arranged according to the importance of the mission that is being carried out. It is not in the public interest to fund equally a small liberal arts college and a college with programs in urban planning, environmental waste control, and physical therapy. The same priorities must be applied to the issue of choice versus access. The state's first responsibility is to access. The state must assure that geographic distribution, tuition cost, and admissions policies provide equal opportunity for all citizens who have the potential to benefit from the education. The marginal public dollars—those spent to give students the choice to attend a more expensive institution—do not yield the same high return on the initial investment. It is less important to the public interest that some students can make a choice between differently priced institutions.

These premises constitute the framework in which cooperation should occur. To ignore the premises is to perpetuate some misunderstandings that will detract from the effort to cooperate. And cooperation is the key to maximizing the resources available to higher education.

A Pragmatic Approach to Cooperation

In 1978–79 a study on cooperative arrangements between public and private colleges was sponsored by the American Association of State Colleges and Universities in cooperation with the Council for the Advancement of Small Colleges. Its purpose was threefold: to demonstrate that the institutions can and do work together to their mutual benefit; to present models that would stimulate more consortium activity; and to interest governments in developing policies that would encourage, rather than inhibit, the development of such consortia. The resulting publication reports 100 distinct cooperative activities involving 775 institutions.[1] The study briefly notes the types of programs, their management and finance, factors contributing to success, and policy recommendations for further consortium development. The study gives glimpses into the access, services, and facilities that this kind of cooperation can provide—to particular student groups and to the public missions—and reveals a sense of the real loss from competitively lobbying the legislature for a larger piece of the action.

Fortunately, this latter situation is evident in few states and is not a national problem. The most extreme example, of course, is New York State, where private institutions received 25 percent more in state aid than was given by all the forty-nine other states combined. During the past five years in New York, the proportion of state aid to private institutions increased while that to public institutions decreased. The effect has been injurious to access, particularly for low-income and minority students; for example, when tuition was imposed at the City University of New York, enrollment declined by more than 50,000.

Institutional aid and the tuition assistance program have not been used to stabilize costs. Increases in assistance schedules have been followed by increases in tuition, leaving unchanged the gross dollar gap between average award and average tuition. This is questionable public policy, the kind that eventually loses the confidence of the public, which then questions the management, goals, and practices of higher education.

1. William J. McKeefery, *Cooperative Arrangements Between Private and Public Colleges: A Report on Current Practice and Recommendations for Policy* (Washington: American Association of State Colleges and Universities, 1978).

The AASCU-CASC cooperative study, it is hoped, constitutes the first step in a process that will multiply consortium arrangements by a hundredfold. Working together, the two associations hope to convene a series of conferences that will include representatives from public and private institutions, regional education boards, state higher education offices, and governors' offices. The purpose will be to examine state policies and develop and recommend policies in governance, finance, and related areas that will encourage institutions to maximize resources through consortium arrangements.

Another study in progress will complement efforts to take the long view of serving the public interest. The Ford and Exxon Foundations have awarded a $300,000 grant to AASCU, the American Association of Community and Junior Colleges, and the National Association of State Universities and Land-Grant Colleges to conduct a study on the financial health of public higher education. At present, no valid indicators are available to gauge what resources are necessary to meet public expectations. There is no litmus test for determining whether state appropriations or costs per student or faculty salaries are or are not appropriate. Higher education policy makers—at the state and federal levels—are thus trying to make important decisions about financial resources, student aid, and program development in an information vacuum. The study in its first year has issued a report on the financial status of public higher education[2] and, with this basis, will thereafter develop and refine financial indicators for use in planning and managing public higher education.

This study is linked with a parallel study being conducted by the National Association of Independent Colleges and Universities. By cooperating on data collection and analysis, the associations will obtain a much more accurate basis for comparing the financial situation of public and private colleges. Having the same, accurate information is crucial if we are to work within the larger framework of higher education.

Colleges and universities are the secondary aspects of higher education policy; they are the means, the vehicles for achieving the primary purposes. Access for citizens, well-prepared graduates, and public service programs are the ultimate goals and the prime concern of higher education policy. If institutions subordinate themselves to these missions, if they plan and act according to what best serves these missions, they will, in their sub-

---

2. Howard Bowen and John Minter, *Preserving America's Investment in Human Capital* (Washington: American Association of State Colleges and Universities, 1980).

ordination, gain a strength and an identity worth preserving. Conversely, if they put themselves first, they will find themselves subject to increasing controls and external direction.

A Common Goal—
Profit and Nonprofit Institutions

JAN V. EISENHOUR

A SIGNIFICANT FACT IN POSTSECONDARY EDUCATION is that the first business training institution in the United States was a profit-making institution—Harvard. The precedent established then has been the basis for an entire industry whose existence relies, not on tax dollars, but on students' tuition for financial support.

What is the difference between profit and nonprofit institutions? Or is there a difference? What are the specific differences in admissions? administration? faculty? student services? output?

Admissions

Admission differences are clearly disappearing. With the declining senior market, all institutions have become more competitive. The nonprofit institutions have studied carefully the successful marketing techniques used in the past by the profit sector. Billboard advertising, bus cards, radio advertisements, television commercials, shopping center promotions, direct mail—once scorned by the nonprofits as creating "high pressure enrollments"—are embraced as the race for students in the 1980s heightens. Seminars on how to recruit students are commonplace activities for community colleges, junior colleges, and even the universities that once turned applicants away. One Dallas community college has a policy of admitting students every Monday, thus emulating the traditional profit-making business schools. The business schools, on the other hand, are primarily on semester or quarter systems today, emulating the nonprofits. While the nonprofit sector is busily investing tax dollars and energy in marketing and in attempting to improve its recruiting results, thus copying the profit sector, the profit sector has strangely moved toward more low-keyed approaches to admissions.

The open-door policy of profit institutions is moving to a closed-door policy, requiring testing and various entry standards. Perhaps the reasons behind the change are the rigid regulations that have been promulgated by state and federal agencies on the profit institutions. These regulations frequently require that the institution either prove the student capable of benefiting from the training or provide statistics that verify the employment of the student in the field in which the student was trained. With the burden of proof on the institution, the selection process in admissions has tightened. Meanwhile, the nonprofits that once required SAT scores and other measures for selectivity are rapidly discarding them as admissions requirements and are, in fact, adopting an open-door policy. A role reversal is in the process, which is perhaps unhealthy for both types of institutions.

Administration and Faculty

The administration of nonprofit institutions has been plagued with bureaucratic responsibilities that continue to increase. The administrations of profit institutions, on the other hand, once simple and autocratic in nature, find themselves with more constituencies to which responses are necessary, thus increasing dramatically their bureaucratic duties. At one time the nonprofits envied profit-making institutions in their ability to respond to industry demands almost instantly. Now that margin of speed is reduced to a slight advantage in that the profit institutions find they cannot move until various state, federal, and accreditation agencies have been notified and satisfied.

The conclusion is that little difference exists. Both are engulfed in a paper jungle, and multiple details slow the educational process and frustrate the participants—profits and nonprofits.

The faculty differences are also diminishing rapidly. Accreditation standards and strict state regulations have affected profit institutions to the extent that profit and nonprofits resemble each other. In the state of Colorado, for example, the profit institutions cannot hire any faculty member until the state regulatory agency has approved that person's credentials. Even faculty unionism has become a norm in some geographic regions. Certainly, the input from the faculty on educational decision making in the profit institutions has increased, not yet equaling, but approaching that in the nonprofits. Faculty demands for increased professional benefits and increased faculty involvement are characteristic in both sectors.

The Student as Consumer and Product

Student services are far broader in the nonprofit area where more dollars are expended proportionately than in the profit institutions. While the demand for more student services is slowly increasing in the profit sector, the institutions are unlikely to devote a substantial portion of their budgets to this purpose. Frequently, the singleness of purpose and length of most programs—for example, secretarial or accounting training—limits the need for extensive student services.

The era of accountability adds a plus for the profit-making institutions that could not or would not exist had the output not satisfied the consumer. Almost instant accountability has been a fact of life for these institutions since their beginning. Until the early 1970s, most students did not measure the nonprofits with the same standards of accountability as they did profits. A college was a college was a college. However, in the 1960s when universities across the country graduated an excessive number of engineers, a cry of rage was raised by the unemployed, disillusioned graduates. Suddenly questions of accountability began to be asked of all educational institutions, questions for which a now wide-awake public demanded answers. Why train students for fields in which the purpose of the education cannot reasonably be attained? The public mandated that institutions give students the facts. As the 1970s progressed, accountability became the "in" word in all areas of education; thus the student as informed consumer entered the education marketplace—a very foreign being for the nonprofits and an old friend of the profits.

The Present and the Future

The battle cry from the profit institutions has been for recognition and acceptance of the postsecondary training they provide. Recognition has slowly emerged, with the profit sector realizing that recognition itself does not represent a panacea. For example, the transfer of credit policies in higher education confounds profit institutions that have not been taught the articulation game. "You accept mine; I'll accept yours" policy of some nonprofits confuses the profit sector, as does the power of registrars to make independent and sometimes arbitrary decisions, often to the detriment of the student.

The focus in all of education must be the student. Profit and nonprofit institutions must proceed with caution during the 1980s. The student of today and the future demands quality and accountability. The threat of government intervention in education is real. The Federal Trade Commission has promulgated a new regulation governing the profit-making institutions, which is having far-reaching results. Forward-thinking educators in the nonprofit sector recognize that any toehold into education threatens the concept of academic freedom for all institutions. Whether or not the FTC or other governmental agencies move further into regulating education, both the nonprofits and the profits had best plan to do what they say for the students and say what they can do for the students in the 1980s.

Acrimony or Accommodation?

Will the competition persist or will one group engulf the other? Unlikely the competition will cease. Will a peaceful coexistence develop? Unlikely the acrimony will disappear as both fight for the declining student population in the future. Will government regulations decrease? Unlikely.

Hopefully, both profit and nonprofit institutions will recall the advice a mother once gave her daughter as she left for her first dance: "Daughter, just don't forget to dance with the guy that brung ya." Perhaps both types of institutions will return to their original philosophies and stop emulating each other to the confusion of the public and themselves. For decades each has offered students a choice, and student choice is essential whether nonprofits and profits work side by side in acrimony or accommodation.

COOPERATION

5. COOPERATION THROUGH NETWORKS AND ASSOCIATIONS—COSTS AND BENEFITS

The Indiana University Experience— And Some Admonitions

JOHN W. RYAN

CONSORTIA IN HIGHER EDUCATION appear to be a fairly concrete concept until a close look, in order to determine their benefits and costs, reveals their diversity of purpose, size, and organization. I made the commitment to discuss consortia and networks with the welcome expectation that I would learn something valuable about my own university system—Indiana University. My first discovery was that no one seemed to know exactly how many networks and consortia we belong to. Besides the difficulty of defining networks and consortia is the complication that the university does not pay regular dues to some, and thus our financial records are incomplete. Some consortia are informal, do not require dues or contributions, are not governed by a presidentially appointed representative, and do not have a managing secretariat.

According to a study by the American Association of State Colleges and Universities and the Council for the Advancement of Small Colleges[1] there were then 170 cooperative programs in the United States involving 775 institutions. Indiana University must belong to a large fraction of the 170.

For purposes of my "case study" here, I have excluded organizations that essentially include all members of a class (the American Council on Education, National Association of State Universities and Land-Grant Colleges) or are primarily membership organizations for professions or disciplines (American Chemical Society, International Society of Nephrology, Indiana Academy of the Social Sciences), even though the university may make contributions to them from time to time. The elimination seems to have isolated for consideration those organizations or linkages of limited membership which the university has helped form or has joined with the expectation of some specific benefit to us.

---

1. William J. McKeefery, *Cooperative Arrangements Between Private and Public Colleges* (Washington: AASCU, 1978).

Selection of Examples

Further, I picked out fourteen consortia and networks to which Indiana University belongs and asked, for each organization, a knowledgeable member of the faculty or administration to give me his views on such questions as the governing mechanism of the consortium; its resources; membership; cost, including dues, contributions, released time, travel, space, etc.; benefits to Indiana University; expectations and objectives at time of joining, success or failure in accomplishing those expectations and objectives, and recommendations for changes in light of our experience. The consortia were chosen to represent a wide range of characteristics such as size, geographical distribution of membership, function (academic or academic supportive), scope and breadth of educational concern, disciplines involved, and length of participation by the university. The fourteen selections were:

American Universities Field Staff (AUFS)
Argonne Universities Association (AUA)
Association of Universities for Research in Astronomy (AURA)
Committee on Institutional Cooperation (CIC)
Consortium for Graduate Studies in Management
The Guest/Host Relationship on Indiana University Regional Campuses
Indiana Higher Education Telecommunications System (IHETS)
Indiana Conference of Higher Education (ICHE)
Indiana Cooperative Library Services Authority (INCOLSA)
Kentuckiana Metroversity
Midwest Universities Consortium for International Activities (MUCIA)
Midwest Universities Energy Consortium (MUEC)
Organization for Tropical Studies (OTS)
Public Broadcasting Service (PBS)

From this long list, I shall explore a smaller, representative group of six. But first should come some perspective on the diverse characteristics of the consortia and networks.

Characteristics

The smallest consortial arrangement is limited to the Indiana University regional campuses in a host-guest relationship which allows another university to offer courses using our facilities and vice versa—essentially a one-to-one relationship. The largest group is the Public Broadcasting Service, which in 1979 had 161 members. Our consortia, however, tend to be rather small, with six to 30 members.

Most of the consortia are limited to the immediate geographical region such as the state of Indiana or the Midwest; however, some such as AUFS, AURA, OTS, and PBS are nationwide.

Indiana University has been a member of the Indiana Conference of Higher Education since its establishment in 1945. The university helped form or joined most of the others in the late 1950s and 1960s. Most recently it helped establish the Midwest Universities Energy Consortium, which started operating in late 1979.

Benefits

The six consortia selected from the fourteen listed above will illustrate the various benefits that can be expected from consortial arrangements. I shall also use these examples to discuss the costs and to point out some potential problems.

The *American Universities Field Staff (AUFS)* was founded in 1951 by eight colleges and universities to enrich their faculties by jointly maintaining overseas a dozen or so faculty members. These faculty members write reports which are distributed on each campus and they also serve as visiting lecturers and course or seminar instructors during periodic visits to each campus. The benefits of having faculty members who are intimately acquainted with current conditions in overseas areas, especially in the developing countries, is partially offset by their limited availability on campus. The benefits depend to a great extent on the university's ability and ingenuity in devising ways to use an experienced visiting professor on a two-week tour. We have used them as lecturers at our regional campuses, where faculty members with overseas experiences are fewer than on our main campuses, and as visiting lecturers in courses on the main campuses. Since the AUFS associates have excellent contacts in the countries in which they reside, they have often been helpful to faculty members and graduate students who are doing research in those countries.

During the 1977–78 academic year, we had visits from three AUFS associates, who spent a total of thirty-four days on five of the Indiana University campuses. They gave thirty-two lectures to regular classes, twenty-three special lectures, met with more than seventeen individual faculty members and fourteen faculty groups, and produced two videotapes. One associate gave a two-week, two-credit intensive course for about ten students. The relationship is also two-way; during 1979–80, for example, under contractual relationships with AUFS, seven faculty members will be writing reports and the like.

The *Association of Universities for Research in Astronomy (AURA)* was formed by seven universities in 1957 to provide a way for the National Science Foundation to support the construction and operation of a national observatory. AURA now has fourteen members and operates three national observatories: at Kitt Peak near Tucson; at Cerro Tololo, in Chile; and a solar observatory at Sunspot near Alamogordo, New Mexico. The members of AURA have no special privileges on the telescopes. Our membership represents a public and professional duty. It does, however, keep our astronomers in touch with the forefront of developments in astronomical instrumentation and techniques. Over the years, four of our astronomers and about a dozen graduate students have used AURA facilities.

The *Committee on Institutional Cooperation (CIC)* was established by the Big Ten universities and the University of Chicago in 1958 to promote cooperation and exchange among the chief academic officers and to coordinate the activity of many other groups of representatives of these institutions. It has facilitated exchanges such as the traveling scholar program, which allows graduate students to work and study at another member university for a summer or a semester. During 1976–79, about two hundred fifty graduate students have been exchanged among CIC institutions. Of these Indiana University has sent twenty-two to other universities and received eighteen.

The CIC also promotes sharing scarce and unique facilities and exchanging information about such matters as salaries, new programs, pending budgets, structures, and personnel policies. It has attracted grants for worthy purposes such as minority graduate fellowships which probably could not have been obtained by any one university acting alone.

The Lilly Endowment has funded the CIC graduate minority program in the social sciences with grants totaling $1,745,989 over the period 1978–82, while the Andrew Mellon Foundation has funded the program in the humanities for the period 1979–81 at $340,000. So far there have been fifty-six CIC fellows, with six of these in residence at Indiana University. Incidentally, each university has agreed to support each graduate minority fellow for two years after the expiration of the initial support through the CIC.

The *Indiana Higher Education Telecommunications System (IHETS)* was established by the Indiana General Assembly in 1967. Its purposes are to aggregate institutional needs at the state's seventy-four public and private postsecondary campuses that can be at least partially solved through technology (primarily TV and communications networks); to expand the adult student's options to learn in the ways he or she best grasps and retains information; to provide the administrator with those tools that most nearly meet his needs in the management of higher education; and to serve as a catalyst and expediter for interinstitutional efforts in technology acquisition, programming, and utilization. It has been used by Indiana University to teach large classes and off-main-campus classes by TV, to communicate among peers, for business purposes of the institutions, and to operate a medical network serving campuses cooperating in the statewide medical program, including hospitals, doctors' offices, clinics, and sometimes even doctors' homes.

IHETS encompasses SUVON, a telephone network, which, through its bulk-buying of audio lines in Telpak, has cut the cost of statewide telephone, data, and computer communication by more than a third. For example, a typical three-minute telephone call placed by direct distance dialing within the state costs 99 cents, but over SUVON it is only 14 cents.

During the 1977–78 year, a beginning course in astronomy originating at the I.U. Bloomington campus was carried to two regional campuses, and the Approved Real Estate Salesman course went out to more than sixteen locations with approximately 6,000 students. In 1979 the School of Journalism, using IHETS, conducted a series of news forums throughout the state. Other uses included a forum on energy and one on school financing. Various tapes have been prepared for courses. Innumerable systemwide conferences have been held on the network and thus reduced travel costs. All the benefits of IHETS constitute a list much too long to enumerate here.

The *Kentuckiana Metroversity* is a 501 (c)(3) tax-exempt corporation organized in 1969 by six institutions of higher education in the Greater Louisville area to study the needs for higher education programs in the area, develop and present cooperative programs and activities, coordinate program offerings of the member institutions, promote the sharing of resources, and be the voice for higher education in the area. The Southeast campus of Indiana University (in New Albany) is a member, not the entire university. The Metroversity has arranged visiting student programs, reciprocal library privileges, and joint programs of study. It has promoted sharing of expertise as well as cooperative programs in curriculum, admissions, audio-visual materials, business affairs, educational technology, foreign studies, public relations, student records, student activities, faculty development, student government, and publications.

During the past two semesters, sixty students at Indiana University Southeast enrolled in courses at the other institutions in the Kentuckiana

Metroversity. Five student leaders participated in a Metroversity student leaders conference. Perhaps one of the most significant advantages, however, is the availability in the immediate area of library resources; I.U. Southeast has 140,000 volumes but the Kentuckiana Metroversity has total resources of 1,236,000 volumes, almost a ninefold increase.

The Midwest Universities Consortium for Internatioial Activities (MUCIA) was organized in 1964 by Indiana University, Michigan State University, and the Universities of Illinois and Wisconsin to promote knowledge about international affairs on campus through engaging in cooperative projects abroad, including joint endeavors with foreign institutions. It now has seven members. A grant of $3.5 million from the Ford Foundation provided the impetus and was used to provide graduate and faculty research opportunities abroad and to encourage and train faculty members to serve on technical assistance projects abroad. Although the Ford Foundation funds have been expended, the consortium continues and now operates several large technical assistance projects abroad, especially projects that require such a large number of faculty or such a wide variety of disciplines that no one university could handle the project alone. It is especially valuable in providing opportunities for Indiana University faculty members to serve abroad since we do not have colleges of agriculture and engineering, and most technical assistance projects today heavily involve these areas.

During the past twelve months one faculty member from Indiana University has been employed full-time as associate director of a MUCIA project in Indonesia, and another has been director of the MUCIA Program of Advanced Studies in Institution-Building and Technical Assistance Methodology (PASITAM) located on the Bloomington campus. This project also employs about ten professionals and graduate students and involves five to ten faculty members on an interim basis. In addition, two faculty members participate part time on other MUCIA projects, and ten to twelve faculty have received some financial assistance for overseas travel to international conferences and meetings.

Costs

The benefits cited above do not come without cost although a single university, without the consortial arrangement, would spend much more to obtain similar benefits.

Those consortia established in order to manage national facilities, such as AURA, the Argonne Universities Association, and Universities Research Association which manages Fermilab, usually are funded by a management fee from a federal agency. The cost to each university may be limited to the time spent in attending board and committee meetings by designated faculty or administrative members. Such time varies from one to two days to ten to fourteen days per year. Usually the university has committed itself, upon joining, to provide a limited sum of money should the consortium ever run into unforeseen financial difficulties. Often a part of this commitment is collected upon joining and is invested by the consortium to provide some interest which can then be used for purposes not covered by the management fee. This initial investment may run as high as $10,000, and the total liability can be several times greater. I know of no case where additional payments of the commitment have been requested.

Many consortia maintain a secretariat to handle the business affairs of the organization, arrange for board meetings, search for funding, seek contracts, and so on. In such cases the costs are usually borne by dues paid by the member institutions. Dues for the fourteen consortia listed above vary from nothing to almost $25,000 a year. The average for the fourteen is about $7,000 a year. In addition, the university is often responsible for the travel expenses of its board members. Such expenses probably average $125 per meeting or around $250 to $500 per year for consortia that do not pay such expenses from a management fee or from the dues collected.

In at least one case, the Indiana Conference of Higher Education, Indiana University acts as host institution for the secretariat of a consortium and, as such, provides limited office space, phones, secretarial help, duplicating services, and some released time for the executive secretary. These contributed and unreimbursed services can run to several thousand dollars per year.

Problems, Advice

When establishing a consortial arrangement, make sure that all commitments are carefully spelled out so that no surprises will arise. At the beginning it is prudent to have several financial officers as board members or advisors to help set up good financial policies consistent with the practices of the member universities. After a period of time these persons can be dropped from the organization. However, regular audits should be required.

In general, a university will reap benefits from a consortium in direct proportion to its input and interest. Faculty members must be made aware and be kept aware of the advantages to be obtained from the university's membership. Some university funds may be needed to promote relationships with a consortium, for example, travel to meet with colleagues at meetings or seminars arranged by the consortium, matching grants for faculty or students, publicity of consortia actions, released time for faculty participation in consortial activities.

It is wise to keep in touch with the actions of the consortium by reading the minutes and requiring frequent reports from representatives. Consortia change as time goes on; unwanted changes can be averted by timely action and concern.

The secretariats of consortia have a tendency to take over control and direction of the organization. Board representatives should be alert to this possibility and devote the necessary time to guide the secretariats' actions. The secretariat should be the servant, not the master, of the board. Executive secretaries or directors should probably be appointed for limited terms, and the secretariats' location can rotate from one member university to another on an established rotation scheme. Executive secretaries or directors sometimes become excessively involved in only one facet of a consortium's activities and neglect other facets. They need to be reminded of their total duties from time to time. An arrangement whereby they report on a regular basis to the presidents of their member organizations can be helpful. Secretariats also have a tendency to expand unnecessarily, and vigilance on this score is needed.

Except for consortia established to manage large national laboratories, it is wise to concentrate membership in a close geographical region. This step results in easier, cheaper, and more frequent communication between members, facilitates exchange of students and faculty, facilitates sharing of expensive equipment, and generally promotes common interests and bonds between the member universities.

P2E IB F4Z—Identifiers for Twenty-first Century Learning Communities

DEAN E. TOLLEFSON

THE ROAD AHEAD for postsecondary education is perilous. The extent to which it proves to be defeating or enlightening will depend greatly on the foresight and fortitude of the leadership in the journey. What is the evidence that college and university leadership is genuinely rethinking its position and moving to reorganize and reinvest resources to accommodate to economic and political pressures? Are there options for reinvesting talents, time, and money to pay greater dividends?

Retrenchment has begun, but too many institutions direct their evaluation and planning efforts mainly to their own needs and goals, ignoring other institutions' needs, interests, capacities, and resources. If needs and capacities were viewed comprehensively, suggestions for integrating some resources would be welcomed and viewed constructively.

With colleges and universities—whatever their resources—facing financial and other strictures, many have indeed been turning to interreliance among institutions of similar or complementary purposes. They have, to a growing extent in the last two decades, looked for interinstitutional cooperation that is cost effective and vitalizing to the programs and to the institutions participating.

Emergence of Consortial Relationships

Academic consortia are voluntary, formal, professionally administered organizations whose missions are related functionally and directly to the member institutions' goals and needs. They engage in multi-institutional programs, projects, and services that result from cooperative planning and shared resources. The formal consortium organization facilitates joint endeavor, and the cooperation enables members to use their resources to greater efficiency and effectiveness.

In the past two decades, substantial interinstitutional arrangements have emerged. The most recent *Consortium Directory* of the Council for Interinstitutional Leadership lists 115 academic consortia which involve over 1,343 public and private institutions.[1] These institutions participate jointly in more than 66 different kinds of programs in the academic, administrative, student, and community areas, and 1,926 separate programs were reported. These consortia also unite their resources in countless other activities and services in addition to the program reported and described in the directory.

Academic consortia—by definition, and as the term is used here—differ from other educational groups such as national higher education associations, accrediting agencies, state systems, state associations of private colleges and universities, international education cooperatives, interstate compacts, special- or single-purpose consortia, bilateral compacts, and informal neighborly groups. Institutions may participate in such groups and yet remain insular, apart from any community of institutions committed to a common goal, dedicated to mutual assistance, and joined in interreliance.

1. University, Ala.: The Consortium, 1977. 121 pp.

The consortium, as defined here, is a sophisticated relationship, beyond simply neighborliness. It is other than an opportunity to politicize or play power politics. Nor is it an opportunistic relationship to gain the most for the least investment, with no spirit of mutual support. A consortium is not a cartel, because its mentality—ethics and manners—is rooted in a concern for the human consequences of what is done with, as well as for, one another. Most consortia are not in business to build a supra-institution. In a consortium, interreliance is progressive as interaction increases. It works best when the institutions' presidents and trustees persist in eliciting substantial achievement, and staff and faculty hammer out strategies for it. It is an expression of what social psychologists call "organization development."

Beyond the philosophical and sociopsychological subtleties in genuine interreliance is the fact that it pays. It is cost effective. The Council for Interinstitutional Leadership, in a national study recently completed, documents many ways in which institutional investments realize benefits abundantly greater than the cost outlay. A report of that study, which was supported by the Carnegie Corporation of New York, is available from the council, either in full text or summary statement.[2]

Problems, Issues, and Strategies in Consort

In the problems and issues we seek to resolve, how does work in consort respond, especially in the more advanced consortia?

Consortial cooperation avoids unnecessary and thus costly duplication. Cross-college academic programs appear to be increasing among institutions joined in consortia with substantial experience in cooperation. The Five Colleges, Inc., in Massachusetts has a joint astronomy department. The cross-registration program of the Atlanta University Center clearly exemplifies interreliance in curricular offerings and teaching staff. In admissions work, the Union of Independent Colleges of Art shares publicity, personnel, and systems. The Auraria Higher Education Center in Denver promotes the sharing of facilities. Institutions in the New Orleans Consortium share a joint department of social work. The Quad-Cities Graduate Study Center in Illinois offers extensive graduate studies that reduce duplication among the public and private institutions in that region. The Greensboro Regional Consortium summer school is a joint program.

---

2. *Costing Collegiate Cooperation: A Report on the Costs and Benefits of Interinstitutional Programs, with Consortium Case Studies and Guidelines* (University, Ala.: The Council, P.O. Box 6293, October 1979), 430 pp.

Clearly, a consortium relationship, when conducted on a substantial level, offers an efficient alternative to duplication.

Cooperating institutions increase the quality of their offerings and services. The Boston Theological Institute and Five Colleges, Inc., are excellent examples. The film libraries of Tri-College University, in Minnesota and North Dakota, and the Union of Independent Colleges of Art assure a higher quality of instructional support through joint endeavor. In student services, graduate placement at the Atlanta University Center is outstanding. In health, accident, and life insurance, the plan evolved by the Council of West Suburban Colleges in Chicago is an unusual example of high quality coverage at lower per unit costs.

Institutions are increasingly concerned with the diversity and breadth of educational experience. Consortial relationships join this concern by providing students access to educational experiences. The New Hampshire College and University Council has significantly augmented financial aid to the students in that state. Theirs is truly an expression of imaginative leadership in overcoming a complex problem through joint endeavor and gaining for their institutions literally millions of dollars in tuition revenue. Access is also provided by cross-registration, nontraditional programs, and distance learning systems. Place-bound populations are served by cooperative outreach programs, new learning centers, and common market colleges, and persons previously inadequately served (minorities, women, the handicapped, the economically disadvantaged) have, in the last decade, been reached by new cooperative structures.

Cooperative endeavors have enabled institutions, as part of a cooperative structure, to obtain federal and philanthropic grants that, individually proposed, might not have been received. Notable examples are the Atlanta University Center and the Claremont Colleges, now enjoying over fifty years of imaginative leadership. Others, noted above, are the New Orleans Consortium's program in social work, the Five Colleges astronomy department, and the admissions and placement programs and film library of the Union of Independent Colleges of Art.

Cooperative programs reflect the educational needs and concerns of the member institutions. Yet, in structure, a consortium differs significantly from a college or university. It is an alternative system that does not replace existing structures but, rather, supplements and enhances the institutions in ways not otherwise open. The potential is not limited to this or that project. Consortia have been used for fast action when timing for achievement is crucial, and they have been used over long periods of time to assist institutional maturity. Examples of maturity are the institutions giving leadership to the Quad-Cities Graduate Center, which use their consortium as an alternative system for instructional delivery, and the John Wood Community College in Illinois where all programs, instruction, and services are obtained by contract. Coastline Community College contracts for its library services. The Kansas City Regional Council for Higher Education is an alternative system for the professional development of its member institutions' staff and faculty.

Competitiveness is a constant issue for institutions as they compete with one another for students and money. Curiously, one solution to uncontrolled competitiveness is the creation of a cooperative arrangement. Cross-registration programs, shared libraries, and joint purchasing help attract and serve students who might not otherwise be available to a particular institution. The programs in educational administration at Tri-College University in the Moorhead-Fargo region are an example. The West Central Wisconsin Consortium works with its members to harmonize their graduate-level offerings, thereby assuring adequate enrollment and quality offerings.

Financial efficiency is of perennial interest not only to those inside our institutions but to our outside detractors as well. All the programs noted have realized increased efficiency in curriculum, teaching, services, and administration. The degree of success depends on the experience, maturity, and quality of leadership within the institutions in consortial relationship. Worthy of note is the cost efficiency achieved in joint purchasing by the Hudson-Mohawk Association of Colleges and Universities and the Worcester Consortium for Higher Education, and the organizational efficiency of the joint registrar services used by the member institutions of the Graduate Theological Union in Berkeley. The computer services for both teaching and administration in the Associated Colleges of Central Kansas give still another example of efficient service.

The several outstanding models mentioned above are described in *Costing Collegiate Cooperation*, which makes for illuminating, if tedious, reading in detail of ways that substantial interreliance among institutions has been built. Institutional interreliance, then, helps participating institutions control their destinies. When free enterprise in higher education operates without a sense of community, institutions compete for students and dollars. In a cooperative arrangement, planning and open communication minimize laissez faire competition. For consortia, the cooperation is nonbureaucratic because the participants are the clients *and* the decision-makers. The consortium is a special kind of community where participation and self-direction facilitate achievement in ways that only mature communities can enjoy.

Premises for Consortial Cooperation

Two tenets in the higher education way of life, as we have come to know it, are at work in consortial arrangements: participants identify their own substantial interests in a comprehensive and detailed way; and they are able to discipline themselves in order to achieve those interests. The cooperative endeavor requires the best in statesmanly leadership from presidents, trustees, faculty, and administrative staff. Cooperative endeavor has a way of testing our will and capacity to apply in our work those humanistic values we teach. It is often a telling examination.

The management of cooperation is no different from that in an organization: Does the leadership define and insist on detailing the options open to it? Does it make the necessary decisions? And then does it allocate its human and financial resources to back those decisions?

A question often raised is, Where can institutions begin, or extend, their cooperative endeavors? Where can they gain greater interreliance? They can start with areas of greatest need, such as low enrollment or high costs or high-technology disciplines. Or they can start in areas where high systematization is possible, such as library and some student services. Most important, they can use their consortial relationship for faculty and staff development. They should begin, if possible, where interests and skills for cooperative endeavor are present among the participants.

The evaluation of substantial cooperation requires a level of discussion and planning not often found among us. Although developing interinstitutional cooperation is no easy process, rewards can be substantial. Communication and in-depth dialogue with colleagues at different institutions leads to development of new approaches to learning or operations and to mutual benefit.

Pericles, in offering his defense of Athenean democracy, said, "Instead of looking upon discussion as a stumbling block in the way of action, we think of it as an indispensable preliminary to any wise action at all." Wisdom of action is achieved in interinstitutional work, and it requires a truly creative interchange in realizing a greater good. Involvement among us will provide opportunity to explore identifiers for twenty-first century learning communities.

...is of Leadership
...hanging Times

W. PELTASON

HIGHER EDUCATION has perhaps never been more fully or better represented in Washington than it is today. (Clearly, this situation does not prevail simply because I am at the helm of the American Council, though I like to think that I've enhanced rather than hindered higher education's leadership role in Washington.) The evolution of a powerful postsecondary presence in the capital is owed directly to the determination by colleges and universities and their various regional and national organizations to stake out a claim on both the conscience and pragmatic interests of the federal government to recognize their needs and concerns. The organization which I am proud to lead has a mandate to coordinate this vast and vital representational effort. What makes the endeavor especially rewarding is that, far from being a narrow, parochial interest group, collectively we represent a unique social asset with infinite possibilities for helping to achieve human betterment.

Although we may be at the height of our prowess, I'd be remiss not to point out that we shall need all the collective wisdom we can muster to deal with the enormous federal involvement in our midst—an involvement that is likely to be more, rather than less assertive in the coming decade. I will not dot every *i* or cross every *t*, but simply say that in a time of fiscal uncertainty and social unease, federal auditors will not disappear; regulations will be increasingly disgorged by an executive branch often under heavy political pressure; a litigant-minded society will continue to challenge our institutions in the courts on all manner of issues, and our institutions will be increasingly viewed as instruments for social change.

There is no way in the world that in the eighties higher education can return to the ivory tower of pre-World War II days. In fact, I believe our figurative locale for the coming decade will bear closest resemblance to a fish bowl. Therefore, higher education should seize the initiative by attempting to add luster to its appearance and thereby be viewed in its proper light, ready and able to meet new challenges, yet determined to preserve its old institutional integrity and independence. How well we succeed will in no small measure be determined by our ability to articulate and orchestrate our positions on a broad spectrum of fundamental issues affecting higher education. Not for a minute do I mean that we should paper over the differences—reflecting different education values, missions, and orientations—of the variety of sectors of the academic landscape. We do and should speak at the appropriate times with the many voices inherent in our pluralistic system of higher education. But on such basic issues as autonomy, academic freedom, and the need for commitment on the part of our society to the values of knowledge and learning, we have, thankfully, far more in common than we have differences.

Representation and Service

The pattern of association representation, centered at One Dupont Circle in Washington, has evolved in a manner that provides the wherewithal to perform both of the critical functions I've outlined—service to the specialized needs of individual collegiate constituencies and to academe as a whole. The instrumentalities that make it possible are the some forty individual associations that focus on the first objective, and the American Council on Education, which has prime responsibility for the latter. At first blush, it appears to be a crazy-quilt pattern in which overlapping and duplication are sure to abound. But living with the system for more than two years has convinced me of at least one impressive fact: it works. Frustrating, at times, certainly. But productive—no question about that. Let me illustrate.

Two years ago, the then HEW Secretary Califano signed regulations for implementing section 504 of the Rehabilitation Act of 1974 which provided that there be absolutely no discrimination against the handicapped in programs receiving federal funds. Of course, our colleges and universities totally agreed with the objective, but they were concerned about having the know-how and funds to turn a noble objective into reality. The initial question put starkly was: Could a well-intentioned federal initiative be implemented by our postsecondary schools without their going broke? The eventual response by the higher education community through their associations was that indeed it could, but that individual colleges and universities would need all the help they could get. The assistance was forthcoming through HEATH (an acronym for Higher Education and the Handicapped), a united effort of twenty-three major higher education associations and consumer organizations of handicapped persons. They joined to provide the technical assistance needed for schools to comply cost effectively with the requirements of section 504. So well has HEATH succeeded that indeed it has become a model program of a type which HEW is urging others to adopt—the health care industry, elementary and secondary schools, and the social welfare systems. Incidentally, HEW joined with the associations in funding HEATH. Specifically, HEATH has provided, and is continually seeking new ways to provide, technical assistance that enables colleges and universities to make the physical and programmatic changes needed to bring them into compliance with section 504. Projects undertaken include the following:

- A guide to assist admissions personnel in the recruitment and admission of disabled students to colleges and universities; prepared by the American Association of Collegiate Registrars and Admissions Officers (AACRAO).
- A guide for the preparation of the transition plan to accommodate the handicapped required by section 504; produced by the Association of Physical Plant Administrators of Colleges and Universities (APPA).
- A series of workshops held throughout the country, open to all college and university personnel, to offer technical assistance in removing barriers to higher education for handicapped students and faculty; conducted by the College and University Personnel Association (CUPA).
- A technical bulletin describing and explaining section 504, and a guide to assist in preparing the institutional self-evaluation required under the section; prepared by the National Association of College and University Business Officers (NACUBO).
- A clearinghouse to aid higher education and the HEATH project in locating information about programs, resources, publications, training materials, and skilled personnel to meet the needs of handicapped students and employees; organized by the American Association for Higher Education (AAHE).

Late in 1978, the question of tuition tax credits suddenly came to center stage in the Congress. While the Carter administration, along with most of the higher education leadership in Washington, was convinced that the equitable way to move was to build up student aid, pressure was gaining in Congress to provide middle-income people with tax relief for helping their children get through college. The administration was not especially quick in recognizing that if it wished to block tuition tax credits, it would have to come up with a sound alternative. At this point representatives of higher education met under the leadership of Charles Saunders, Council vice president for governmental relations, to work out detailed legislative proposals for submission to Congressman William Ford, chairman of the House Postsecondary Education Subcommittee. With the leadership of

Chairman Ford and Senator Claiborne Pell, the legislation was pushed through Congress as the Middle Income Student Assistance Act. To be sure, the Carter administration played a central role in getting the legislation enacted. But had it not been for the knowledgeable forum provided by association staff, which was able to consider and test a range of options, a viable alternative to tuition tax credits might have been too long in coming. Differences within the higher education community were apparent as lengthy deliberations went forward. One association, for instance, had a strong preference for the tax credits. Others differed on the details of a proposal which eventually were worked out. The point is, though, the community was able to compose the major differences and to support a legislative package that Congress adopted and the President signed into law—a law that in my view is at least as important to the well-being of higher education as any enacted in recent years.

Let me cite another example of interassociation cooperation working its will to the benefit of all of higher education. Early in 1978, the U.S. Office of Education was faced with a small but growing number of what can only be described as horror stories of fraud and abuse in use of student aid monies. OE was swiftly moving toward developing and implementing regulations designed to assure that students are provided with fair and equitable treatment under college refund policies. Authority for the issuance of such regulations was contained in the Education Amendments of 1976. But as the agency moved ahead in drafting the regulations, it became clear to the associations that what was being developed was both impractical and overly restrictive. They persuaded the Office of Education to hold off on their development, pending an attempt by the associations to develop voluntary guidelines for the institutions. Under the leadership of Elaine H. El-Khawas, director of ACE's Office of Self-Regulation Initiatives, a task force of staff members from various associations was organized to consider the issue. It was decided that the National Association of College and University Business Officers (NACUBO) would have the lead responsibility for development of the guidelines. By June 1979, six months after agreeing to tackle the complex issues, a broad coalition of fourteen associations had approved the NACUBO guidelines for distribution to the institutions, including the United States Student Association. The then Commissioner of the Bureau of Student Financial Aid at the Office of Education commented: "There is no question in my mind the refund policy standards that NACUBO and ACE have put out are significantly better than the government could have ever put out. They are more equitable;

they are more practical; they are more liveable; and . . . the net effect is that we are not going to put out regs on refund policies."

At one point it seemed that Kornfeld's view would not prevail, but now it appears that the battle has been won. The Department of Education issued proposed regulations that adopt higher education's standards for a fair and equitable tuition refund policy.

Finally, during the 1978 session, a committee of the House reported out a new piece of legislation—on surface transportation. The bill provided that transportation research centers could be funded only at state institutions. Not a bad idea, I suppose, if viewed solely from the perspective of a state college or university. After all, competition for limited federal resources would be restricted. However, from the standpoint of higher education as a whole, that particular caveat linking research centers only to state institutions was grossly discriminatory to the private sector of the community. Once again, Charles Saunders convened the federal relations chiefs of other associations and obtained their support for a joint statement opposing the provision on the grounds that federal grants should be made on the basis of merit, not on form of institutional organization. The unanimous position of the community persuaded Congress to amend the legislation and drop the objectionable provision before final passage of the Surface Transportation Act. To the special credit of representatives of state institutions, they recognized the wisdom of the course pursued. I believe that ACE's role in pointing out a legislative anomaly and taking the initiative in remedying the matter was crucial. In the end, the best interests of the entire academic community as well as the public were served.

The HEATH project, enactment of the Middle Income Assistance Act, issuance of guidelines on student refunds, and elimination of discrimination toward independent institutions in the Surface Transportation Act, are but a few of the success stories involving interassociation cooperation that I've personally witnessed since coming to the Council. In each instance, there were various degrees of argumentation and, in some cases, bitter wrangling. In the end, though, the process triumphed. Narrow, parochial interests went by the boards in favor of overall needs and aspirations of our schools, our students, our faculty, and the nation.

Participation in Representation

The pattern of cooperation among associations is orchestrated through various informal and formal means. Of course, at times unanimity on a particular issue simply cannot be forged, as in the case of the Department of Education legislation. Here, differing positions were taken by some associations. Nevertheless ACE was able to play a constructive role in the development of the legislation by articulating the concerns of the various sectors and obtaining a number of changes in the bill which eventually became law.

The Council—through regular meetings with association executive directors, government affairs officers, and meetings with executive directors and chairpersons of boards of directors of associations—seeks to consider and compose differences on those issues that are vital to the higher education community as a whole. Also, at such meetings, individual associations are chosen to be the "lead" agent to work on a particular problem, as, say, NACUBO was for student refunds. In addition to the regular meetings, the housing of most of the associations at the Dupont Circle building assures frequent informal contacts among staffers. While the arrangement fuels the normal amount of gossip and rumors, proximity does in fact contribute significantly to strengthening the communication linkage among associations.

A formal study is to be conducted to ascertain whether there is indeed unwarranted duplication or unncessary competition between and among associations. The study will also look at the Council functions to ensure an appropriate balance between our service and coordinating activities.

For member institutions, many ways are available to participate in Washington activities. For instance, colleges and universities are welcome to involve persons from their campuses who have particular interest and expertise in issues being considered. The Council has advisory committees on self-regulation, academic affairs, and taxation, a Commission on Military–Higher Education Relations, and the Business–Higher Education Forum. Other associations have their committees and groups which work on matters or problems that are of particular concern to their constituency. The more knowledge and insight that all of us can bring to bear on problems or a given issue, the more powerful and persuasive we can be in presenting our case to those in the federal government where actions taken increasingly have impact on institutional life. Annual meetings, incidentally, are yet another point where members can make contact and become involved in the work of associations.

As we enter the 1980s, it will become even more essential that we are not merely reactive and that we are out front on issues about which we are able to offer compelling options for the panoply of problems facing us. On some issues, our sister associations will, perforce, have to go their own way and take a position on which a consensus cannot be reached. In so doing, we need to recognize, they truly will be highlighting just how important that matter is to their particular constituency. They will have defined their principal reason for coming into being.

Of greatest consequence to higher education is that its representation in Washington has created a climate in which we can agree to disagree and, at the same time, has maintained the capacity to present a united front whenever faced with an issue of transcendent importance to all our institutions collectively. There is a great deal of room for differences on many issues—manpower planning; youth policy; military–civilian educational relationships; profit-nonprofit educational relations; self-regulation; health education; the merging and closing of institutions; and the competition between public and independent institutions. Clearly, though, my experience in Washington has been that more often than not we will find common ground to stand on, to represent higher education in a manner commensurate with its importance to our society.

6. COOPERATION WITH PRIVATE PHILANTHROPY—RAISING MONEY IN THE EIGHTIES

Voluntary Support in the 1980s

JOHN R. HAIRE

PRIVATE GIFTS AND GRANTS have historically been an important source of revenue to the institutions of higher education. Between the legendary gift by John Harvard to a small school in the Massachusetts Colony in the early seventeenth century and the turn of the twentieth century, voluntary support was responsible for the founding, expansion, and preservation of more than a thousand colleges and universities. No comprehensive data are available that permit us to estimate the total of such support during those years, but the records of individual institutions indicate clearly that the dollar amounts were substantial.

Between 1910, when the U.S. Office of Education first collected such information, and 1950, private gifts and grants rose from about $23 million to more than $258 million, a tenfold increase.[1] In the twenty-eight years ending in 1978, voluntary support recorded another tenfold rise, to more than $3 billion.[2] Evidence for 1979 suggested an increase of about 15 percent, which implies that this source of revenue reached roughly $3.5 billion.

In relation to total expenditures of colleges and universities, this figure amounts to slightly more than 6 percent. While this proportion is less impressive than the 50 percent that reflects the importance of governmental support, it is a vital element in institutional revenues and represents the margin that is so critical to the independence and vitality of all higher

---

1. These data and a comprehensive discussion of factors affecting voluntary support are in Hayden W. Smith, "Prospects for Voluntary Support," in *The Corporation and the Campus: Corporate Support of Higher Education in the 1970s*, ed. Robert H. Connery (New York: Academy of Political Science, Columbia University, 1970), pp. 120–36; Hayden W. Smith, "Voluntary Support, Retrospect and Prospect," in *Students and Their Institutions: A Changing Relationship*, ed. J. W. Peltason and Marcy V. Massengale (Washington: American Council on Education, 1978), pp. 128–45; Hayden W. Smith, "Voluntary Support: The End Product of Fund-Raising Activities," in *Cost Effectiveness of Fund Raising*, ed. Warren Heemann (San Francisco: Jossey-Bass, 1979), pp. 1–21.

2. *Voluntary Support of Education, 1977–78* (New York: Council for Financial Aid to Education, 1979).

education. Moreover, voluntary support is of varying importance among the institutions and classes of institutions: for all private colleges and universities, for example, philanthropic support constitutes more than 12 percent of overall current and capital budgets, and for a few institutions it amounts to more than half of the total revenues. Voluntary support is, therefore, an important element in the preservation of density and quality in higher education.

As recently as the early 1960s, private gifts and grants were relatively twice as important as today.[3] Voluntary support regularly accounted for 10–17 percent of institutional expenditures in the period 1950–65. The decrease to 6 percent today is a reflection less of slow growth in voluntary support than of a very rapid growth in total expenditures. In the current steady state in higher education and the prospects of contraction in the next decade, voluntary support may grow in importance relative to institutional budgets. Potentially, this source of funds can regain the levels that characterized the years prior to 1965, and perhaps could go even higher.

For voluntary support to reach considerably higher proportions, however, the institutions of higher education must make a concerted effort to cultivate the sources of voluntary giving. This effort calls for the most sophisticated fund-raising techniques available, and they must be applied with knowledge and determination. Inevitably, increased attention must go to the task of institutional development if the educational system is to survive in its present form, if the quality of higher education is to be maintained, and if the freedom and diversity of the educational community is to be preserved.

Individual Donors—The First Priority

One virtue of voluntary support as a source of institutional revenue is that it is not monolithic. The money does not come from a single source, as do the funds from government; rather, it represents thousands of gifts and grants from individuals, private foundations, business corporations, and church groups. Thus, no single source of voluntary support is so large that it dominates the financial picture. Many private gifts are, of course, restricted for particular uses, but they do not impose undesirable and unwelcome restrictions on admissions, hiring, or curricula. Because each gift, bequest, or grant is typically small in relation to any institutional

---

3. *Corporate Support of Higher Education, 1977* (New York: Council for Financial Aid to Education, 1979), p. 6.

budget, it cannot be accompanied by burdensome regulations that impose donor-conceived standards on the operations of the academy.

Of great importance are the gifts and bequests of individual donors. Year in and year out, these funds account for roughly half of the voluntary support from all sources. Therefore, this source of private support must be given the highest priority in fund-raising efforts. This priority arises not only from the relative magnitude of support from individuals but also because individual giving is crucial to colleges and universities in obtaining support from foundations, corporations, and others. Alumni support is especially critical. No institution can command sustained support from other donors if its own alumni do not support it vigorously. Those who have received their education from an institution have a natural interest in its prosperity, in its ability to continue to provide a particular style of educational experience, and in its ability to survive in a competitive environment. Moreover, the potential for increased alumni support is manifest.

In terms of annual giving, less than 20 percent of all alumni participate. The record is a little better—25–30 percent—for private colleges and a little worse—10–15 percent—for public institutions. Yet higher levels than these are possible in both sectors. Some colleges, both public and private, receive annual support from more than 50 percent of their alumni; if they can do it, so can others. What is needed is careful, thoughtful cultivation focused on the natural loyalty of an alumnus or alumna.

Much the same is true of nonalumni—parents, friends, and others—who collectively give as much as do alumni. These are the citizens of this great country who recognize the importance of higher education to the well-being and future of society and who care enough to provide hundreds of millions of dollars annually to ensure that colleges and universities have the resources with which to carry out their high purposes. Only a small fraction of the potential levels of support from such sources is currently being realized; the challenge is to find it, cultivate it, and get it.

Taken together, alumni and nonalumni are likely to increase their individual support to higher education appreciably in future years if for no other reason than incomes are likely to continue to rise. As incomes increase, so also does individual giving. More important, the ratio of contributions to income appears likely to rise somewhat in the years ahead. It has risen modestly since 1950, and two important reasons suggest a continuation in the future. First, the upward movement of income per capita increases the proportions of persons at higher income levels where there is more discretionary power over the disposition of income. Much of the current growth in income is simply inflation, and to that extent the income effect is as illusionary for philanthropic giving as for college and university budgets. However, not all the increase in personal incomes has been offset by inflation; real incomes have increased somewhat, and this growth will continue as the growth in productivity continues.

Second, the progressive structure of personal income tax rates and the deductibility of contributions from taxable income reduces the net cost of giving at the margin, and this reduction increases sharply at higher income levels. There may be some decreases in the tax-rate schedule from time to time, and there may also be other reductions in the tax incentives for giving. The favored treatment of capital gains in both the income tax and the estate tax have long been targets for the tax reformers.[4] But tax reform can cut both ways; legislation is before the Congress to move the personal deduction for charitable contributions "above the line," so that all taxpayers can deduct their contributions regardless of whether they itemize or take the standard deduction.[5] The outcome of this and other efforts at tax reform is unpredictable. But given the existing structure of the income tax, it is almost certain that rising incomes will cause slightly larger increases in philanthropic giving.

Assuming that the combination of income growth and tax incentives does lead to a rise in total giving by individuals, what can be said about the share that will flow to higher education? Several factors are likely to operate favorably. The first is education itself. The appeal of higher education is basically rational, not emotional. Some degree of knowledge and sophistication is required to perceive and understand fully the benefits of voluntary support of higher education. Further increases in the level of educational attainment of the adult population will therefore raise indirectly the relative attractiveness of giving to higher education as compared to all other causes. This predisposition will be reinforced by growing numbers of college alumni, both absolutely and as a proportion of the working population. Given the high levels of enrollment, the total number of alumni will continue to grow. Given also any increase in the proportion of alumni making annual gifts, with no diminution in the size of the average gift, then the stage is set for a substantial rise in the share of higher education in the philanthropic dollar from individual donors.

4. *Voluntarism, Tax Reform, and Higher Education*, 2d ed. (New York: Council for Financial Aid to Education, 1975), pp. 11–23.
5. H.R. 1785 (Fisher-Conable bill) and S.219 (Moynihan-Packwood bill).

But, to reemphasize: voluntary giving will not grow without effort on the part of colleges and universities. However favorable the climate may be, increased support from individual donors can be attained only by persistent and intelligent development efforts at levels appropriate to the potentials and the needs.

Foundations—A Decreasing Resource

Until the early 1970s, foundation grants accounted for roughly one-fourth of the voluntary support received by colleges and universities. In the last five or six years, such grants have risen more slowly than support from other sources, with the result that foundations now provide about one-fifth of the total. Given the pervasive reasons, one may guess that foundation giving will continue to decline slowly in relative importance as a source of educational philanthropy.

Although total foundation giving has continued to increase, its rate of growth has decreased. Some of this slowing is caused by the provisions of the Tax Reform Act of 1969 and subsequent regulations, which have increased foundation mortality and inhibited the creation of new foundations. The slowed growth also reflects changed circumstances in the economy. The cyclical instabilities in the securities markets in the past decade have greatly dampened the long-run growth of foundation asset values, with the result that foundation income has shown relatively little growth in recent years.

For individual institutions, the most likely prospect is continued volatility in support from foundation sources. While the appeal of higher education in the grants programs of foundations may grow somewhat stronger in the 1980s, support from this source is inherently unstable. Foundation giving is generally unconventional, which means that innovative and experimental projects will continue to command an important share of foundation interest, perhaps even a growing share. General operating support of an unrestricted nature is becoming a rarity in the foundation community. While the institutions of higher education can continue to expect foundation support for well-conceived projects, the potential for growth of such funding is relatively limited.

Business Corporations—An Untapped Potential

Recent developments suggest that higher education is now looking to the corporate community for an increasing share of the funds needed in the 1980s. In part this turn represents a kind of "awakening" to the potentials of corporate philanthropy. While there is potentially more money to be obtained from business corporations, the amounts do not loom large in relation to college and university expenditures. The Council for Financial Aid to Education has for twenty-seven years focused its efforts on encouraging the corporate community to give more to higher education, and is now the authority on the amounts and purposes of such support.

Corporate support in recent years has averaged about one-sixth of total voluntary support or roughly 1 percent of institutional budgets. These contributions plus other support of an educational nature have typically amounted to between 0.35 and 0.40 percent of corporate net income before taxes, and roughly 36 cents of the corporate contribution dollar.[6] These facts must be kept in mind in any assessment of the corporate community as a prospective source of additional voluntary support.

The outlook, however, is optimistic if only because a relatively small fraction of all corporations have accounted for a disproportionate share of total business giving. Explaining the motivations and philosophy for corporate contributions more widely in that community will cause corporate giving to rise faster than corporate income, but probably only slowly. The evolution of corporate philanthropy indicates that businessmen have approached this activity cautiously, and with good reason. The purpose of business is to make money, not to give it away. However, a growing realization about the interdependence of business and society has led business to give at least limited support to those things clearly relevant to long-run business interests. This "enlightened self-interest" is the key to corporate giving; it can be cultivated, but the cultivation needs to be studied, perceptive, and realistic.[7]

Higher education as an area for corporate contribution has been strong since the early 1950s. Much of the appeal has been pragmatic: business has experienced chronic shortages in the supply of technical, scientific, and administrative talent and has turned to higher education for its needs. Some of the growth in business support to colleges and universities has, therefore, been an effort by individual firms to ensure that they will have competitive access to college graduates in their recruitment programs. Support to education has also been a concomitant of the "knowledge explosion," and for many firms the productivity of research expenditures has been much higher for university projects than for in-house efforts.

6. *Corporate Support of Higher Education, 1977*, p. 4.
7. DuBois S. Morris, Jr., "Corporate Support: More Money and Involvement," CASE *Currents*, October 1979, p. 37.

An important trend in corporate philanthropy is the change taking place in the organization for giving. Business firms now seek out, with full-time personnel and on an ever-growing scale, new opportunities for the effective application of their contribution dollars in all areas of philanthropy. Institutions of higher education have a slight competitive advantage over other recipients: they can provide the contributor not only with opportunities to make grants to worthy causes but also with opportunities to make intangible investments of a philanthropic character that yield demonstrable long-run returns to the donor comparable to the tangible investments of a conventional profit-oriented character.

As Goes the Economy, So Goes Voluntary Support

In the last analysis, the single factor most affecting the trend of voluntary giving to higher education is the state of the economy. Levels of giving are strongly correlated with levels of income, whether the donors are individuals, foundations, or corporations. The general expectation is that the U.S. economy will grow and that income levels will rise broadly during the 1980s. Although growth rates will fluctuate and inflation will impinge on all sectors of society, the dollar amounts of private gifts and grants will rise simply because more money will be available for giving.

An upswing in the *potential* levels of private support does not automatically result in an equivalent trend in *actual* support. Colleges and universities, like other recipient organizations, will have to work as hard as ever to attract the generosity of potential donors. In sum: there must be a resolve to apply sufficient determination, resources, and skill to the task of institutional development.

Corporate Support of Higher Education

THOMAS R. HORTON

CORPORATE SUPPORT TO HIGHER EDUCATION, in the aggregate, is seen to be substantial, over half a billion dollars annually. This contribution has recently tended to increase at a more rapid rate than has overall private support and at a more rapid rate than inflation. About one-third of corporate support is unrestricted, and, in general, the rest carries many fewer restrictions than do grants from most private foundations, let alone government grants. Hence, a college president or trustee who overlooks this potential source of support may be denying his or her institution some valuable resources. One sign that corporate support has increased in importance is the attention now given it by general welfare foundations. As economic circumstances continue to alter their expectations, "foundations have to work harder at being influential," says Alan Pifer, president of the Carnegie Corporation of New York.[1] This leading foundation has been exploring the possibility of cooperative funding endeavors with corporations.

Historically, education has had a somewhat favored place among the priorities of those corporations that maintain substantial programs of support. Approximately 36 percent of all corporate giving is designated for higher education, as opposed to 14 percent of all private giving.[2] From all of these perspectives, the corporate sector's contribution to the future of academic institutions appears impressively promising.

Looked at in another way, this support seems much less significant. Of the approximately $3 billion of total voluntary support received by colleges and universities in 1977–78, the contribution from business was $508 million; from foundations, $623 million; from alumni, $714 million; and from nonalumni individuals, $766 million. Thus, nonalumni of financial substance provide the most support; support from alumni exceeds that from foundations; and foundations in recent years have provided a somewhat larger contribution than business. Stated in another, less glowing, light, in total giving to *all* causes, about 83 percent of all gifts in 1978 came from individuals; 6.5 percent from bequests; 5.5 percent from foundations; and only 5 percent from corporations.[3] Even those who have departed from this world, one might say, make a larger contribution, through bequests, than do either foundations or business corporations.

Thus, the business contribution is substantial enough to deserve institutional attention. In fact, in 1979, for the first time, higher education received more support from corporations than from private foundations.

Variations Among Educational Enterprises

Obviously, the institutions best able to attract corporate support are those which are best known to business corporations: conduct research of relevance to industry, provide employable graduates, and provide com-

---

1. Roger B. May, "Foundations Are Reducing Spending as Economic Ills Shrink Their Assets," *Wall Street Journal*, August 10, 1979, p. 6.

2. Fred Schnaue, ed., *Giving USA* (New York: America Association of Fund-Raising Counsel, 1979), pp. 6, 16.

3. Ibid, p. 6.

munity services near the companies' headquarters or plants. Administrators of a rural liberal arts college located far from centers of industry and whose alumni generally pursue careers in other fields may be best advised to concentrate their fund-raising activities elsewhere—to look toward individuals rather than business firms for assistance. The type of institution that has been described, somewhat unhappily, as the "invisible college" is invisible indeed on the roster of corporate giving. And costly attempts of the "invisibles" to garner corporate support may be of little avail.

At the other extreme, the major universities, which represent leading national centers of research and graduate teaching, have learned well how to attract corporate aid and, in some cases, obtain as much as one-third of their total voluntary support from corporations. Between these two extreme examples lie a great range of institutions. Many of these enjoy a modest or even enticing level of corporate support. The question then is how to enhance this sustenance.

Variations Among Business Enterprises

Attitudes and actions with respect to contributions vary greatly from company to company, so there is really no substitute for getting to know the nature of a particular company which is the target of a college's attentions. Some large firms publish information about their grant programs, but most do not. Although there is great diversity among businesses, one characteristic is common to all business corporations: their mission, unlike foundations, is not to dispense money, but quite the opposite—to acquire it, to achieve earnings. While earnings should not be the entire *raison d'être* of a business firm, it must be a principal goal of any successful private enterprise.

Corporate grants to higher education typically rest on some basis of relevance between the business corporation making the grant and the institution receiving it. This "basis of relevance" need not be a *quid pro quo*, but there must be some reason for an organization whose mission is understood to be that of making money, to turn around and give some of it away. This basis of relevance is often as simple as physical location or a substantial number of employed alumni. If a university has outstanding competence in some technological field of importance, there must be companies for whom that particular technology has special importance. But this relevance, whatever it is, should be substantive and demonstrable, not something based only on transitory personal relationships. An early objective of a college president who is seeking corporate support should be to articulate the specific basis of relevance between an institution and the corporation whose funding is to be sought.

A New Climate for Cooperation

Several education associations are forging new links between business and higher education. For example, the Association of Governing Boards of Colleges and Universities has taken the lead with two other associations to develop a program to bring business know-how to bear on the problem of deferred maintenance of campus facilities. The American Council on Education has created the Business–Higher Education Forum. Increasingly, educators and particularly scientists are looking toward new types of relationships between education and business. At the 1979 meeting of the American Physical Society, the "Industry Connection" was described as being the wave of the future.[4] Certainly, one of the most significant new linkages is the twelve-year agreement between the Monsanto Chemical Company and the Harvard Medical School, under which Monsanto reportedly will provide $23 million for biological research on the "tumor angiogenesis factor." Another fresh initiative is being taken by California Institute of Technology in a unique program which involves visiting scientists and financial support from a half-dozen electronics companies in the Silicon Structures Project.

Increasingly, business leaders are publicly speaking out about the importance of university research. Reginald Jones, chairman of the General Electric Company, wrote in *The New York Times:* "One necessary element [to stimulate technological innovations] must be revitalized university research. . . . University grants and contracts must . . . be increased to cover full costs, or their research-and-development facilities will deteriorate to the danger point."[5] Similarly, Lewis M. Branscomb, IBM vice president and chief scientist, in testimony before the Senate Subcommittee on Science, Technology and Space, recommended new patterns of university support and the development of new kinds of constructive relationships between government, the private sector, and universities.

These evidences of mutual concern show that the climate for good relationships between universities and industry is favorable. But forging these links takes energy and commitment on both sides. They do not just happen.

4. Anne C. Roark, "Academic Scientists Eye the 'Industry Connection,'" *Chronicle of Higher Education*, April 30, 1979, p. 1.
5. Jones, "Progress, Remember?" *New York Times*, August 24, 1979, p. A26.

Contributions as Investment

Many business corporations will provide unrestricted grants or designated funds for the essential needs of the college, for example, scholarship support. However, in recent years some educational institutions, in their eagerness to be seen as deserving of corporate support, have created programs to fit the mold of what they think the companies would most like to support—chairs of free enterprise, for example. Even Milton Friedman has been quoted, perhaps somewhat in jest, as saying that some of these chairs give free enterprise a bad name. And whether this is true, they represent something not likely to be at the very top of a college's funding needs. It may be worth while first to seek funding for the institution's basic needs, especially if the corporation whose gift is being sought has no firm guidelines prohibiting such grants. The business firm's representative should want his or her company's investment in a college to be central to the institution's purpose, not peripheral to it.

Once one has established a sound basis for support, there is nothing mystical about what a proposal should be. A simple letter describing the purpose of the grant and funding requirements, accompanied by a budget showing anticipated sources of income and itemized expenses, supplemented by copies of the college bulletin and auditor's statement should suffice for most proposals. As in any English composition class, verbiage is no substitute for substance, and brevity, if not the soul of wit, is admired for its rarity.

Before writing a proposal, one should realistically assess the likelihood of its success with a particular company. The regionally prominent university can spend its time most efficiently with regionally based corporations. The college with only a local student clientele can probably do best by looking toward those corporations that have some special reason to support institutions in its particular community. Less likely is success to be gained by sending out broad requests to the large national and multinational corporations whose desks are covered daily with a new influx of proposals. After all, the large national corporations have an obligation to support the nationally important centers of excellence as well as those less prominent institutions located near their own facilities.

Apart from money, business corporations can provide another valuable resource, the assistance of their people. Many companies will permit some of their professional people to take leaves of absence to assist in teaching or administration. Obviously not all techniques of business management are transferable from the private to the not-for-profit sector, but some are.

Just as important, the involvement that results from these experiences can lead to strong and long-lasting relationships. Thousands of businessmen serve on boards of trustees of colleges and universities, yet some seem to be less than fully engaged in those responsibilities. Certainly more than merely good will should flow from the business corporation whose executives are engaged intellectually and emotionally in the cause of higher education.

Finally, one must recognize that a large number of business corporations provide little or no support to education. In the long run this group may offer the greatest potential. The college that stimulates such a company to make its first significant corporate grant aids not only itself but also higher education at large. The stimulus is most effectively applied at the top of a business corporation. In most cases, the history of a substantial corporate support program can be traced to a strong conviction and commitment to education on the part of a chief executive officer.

Although the potential for corporate support to a specific college or university depends critically upon the nature of that institution, few institutions of real quality should not be able to attract some form of company investment. And that is how corporate support should be regarded—as an investment in the future, not as just a charitable response to another "needy institution." Increasingly in the 1980s, business leaders will channel their support dollar to institutions that are seen to have a future, institutions which contribute to the quality of life and can demonstrate that they do. It is upon the skill of this demonstration that the future of an institution's corporate support depends.

7. COOPERATION WITH BUSINESS AND GOVERNMENT—BUILDING COALITIONS

Renewing Cooperation and Building Coalitions

GLORIA M. SHATTO

THE BUSINESS FIRM AND THE UNIVERSITY both reflect our nation's accomplishments, goals, aspirations, and values. Today, both institutions have great demands placed on them. Business firms have been assigned immense social responsibilities, and the corporation executive is expected to do much more than make a profit by producing goods and services, providing jobs, and dealing fairly with customers and employees. At the same time, colleges and universities are expected to educate students who will make the world a better place, and are still held accountable for helping to solve many of society's problems. Perhaps additional cooperation—combining some of the idealism and theorizing of higher education with the experience, wisdom, and pragmatism of business—will benefit both sectors.

Adam Smith laid the theoretical basis for partnership between business and education as part of the nation's capitalistic system by exhorting the business community to help improve education. In *The Wealth of Nations*, he went on record as opposing all forms of monopoly and chided business firms and business people for behavior that might lead to collusion. However, he made notable exceptions in two specific areas where, he advocated, business firms should cooperate to achieve their goals: to provide charity and to improve education. Smith recognized that our entire society benefits from education and therefore should support it, but he emphasized that he preferred fees and voluntary contributions from business firms to improve the quality of education.[1]

Colleges have come a long way toward fulfilling their roles in cooperation with business. The college today operates in marked contrast to its colonial period counterpart, whose constituents were the social, political, and occupational elite. Colleges and universities today strive to educate people for full and productive lives in a free society—a society in which there are

---

1. Smith, *The Wealth of Nations* (New York: Random House, 1937), pp. 128–30, 768.

opportunities for employment in a wide range of professional, technical, managerial, and service occupations.

Reasons for Cooperation

Colleges and universities are supported financially and politically by business and other sectors of society. In turn, the institutions of higher education serve the society that supports them. The business firm and the educational institution both hold the tenets of equal and fair opportunity for the individual, with rewards tied to individual initiative and accomplishment. An environment affording opportunity for each person to create, to grow, and to excel is consistent with excellence in education and success in business.

Both business firms and colleges find themselves in a world of rapidly changing values. Colleges continuously define acceptable performance for faculty in teaching, research, and professional service. In addition, each institution judges its progress by some external criteria and thus tries to improve its own performance. Similarly, the successful business firm is not merely operating adequately or meeting minimum legal requirements. Rather, the innovative and productive firms are seizing opportunities to operate on the frontiers of social change, just as enlightened colleges are.

Colleges and businesses have common goals: they want to be good citizens in their communities. Each describes its activities in terms that include social responsibility.

Both institutions face common problems. A timely example is the growth of government participation in both arenas. Moreover, both sectors face increasing public scrutiny and the concomitant demands for openness and accountability. Each agonizes over inflation. While business firms must struggle with efficiency and productivity, colleges must measure and improve cost effectiveness.

Avenues of Cooperation

The analogy of building bridges between business and higher education is not quite accurate. Rather, the relationship is comparable to a network or a cable with thousands of strands.

One avenue for cooperation between college and business today emerges from the main role of the university. Educated men and women are excellent ambassadors linking the academic halls to the business world. When they are successful in their businesses and professions, they provide significant input into the college—to their alma mater, to the colleges in their own communities, and to other colleges having the initiative to seek their cooperation. Business leaders have a genuine interest in curricula, programs, and quality of faculty in universities; their interest can be translated as the business sector's concern for hiring graduates who can think, can read with comprehension and communicate, and can analyze and solve problems. The myriad examples of cooperation include sharing costs for bringing outstanding speakers to the community, securing internships for professors and students in business firms, and providing lectureships for business leaders to contribute their expertise to some facet of higher education. It is essential that students look at business facts and study actual data; an early step in the understanding of business may be an actual visit to a firm, followed by subsequent contacts.

Schools of business administration around the country are resources to the business community continually in providing professional assistance, consultants, management development seminars, and numerous other exchanges. Students in business schools often ask firms for information and data. Some universities send teams of students, at the request of small businesses, to evaluate company procedures and to offer guidance—often refreshingly original.

Colleges and universities have faculty and facilities for lifelong learning. In the immense range of offerings, some courses are designed for specific groups, such as CPA reviews, management development, scientific and engineering update programs. At the same time, business executives and professionals provide leadership and expertise to the colleges, serving on boards and committees, as advisors, as lecturers, and in many other ways.

Universities perform a significant part of the basic and applied research from which new marketable products and processes are created to increase the viability of the private enterprise system. Business, on its side, supports that research by making available scientists and engineers, by sharing data and equipment, and by providing grants.

The college relates to the business sector by offering leisure-time activities, which enrich the quality of community life through music, art, drama, lectures, and athletic events. Members of the business sector enjoy these activities and respond by contributing their personal abilities to ensure the continuation of the programs. Business leaders, for example, contribute various talents to the college: their financial expertise, marketing skills, and managerial abilities. Those business abilities uniquely combined in a college setting with the creative talents of the musician, artist, dramatist, or English professor can help make the final presentation or production more successful, more creative, and perhaps even cost effective. This coalition is mutually beneficial in making the community a better place to live and helps corporations recruit workers and professionals to the area.

The 1980s will bring increased scrutiny to most institutions, including corporations and universities. Public demands for openness and full disclosure have been followed by demands for accountability and social responsibility. Both businesses and colleges are asked to examine their decisions and actions and then be prepared to justify the effects of each action. The university should be able to handle the critical examination of ideas and the open discussion of alternatives, and provide for free exchanges among all sectors; public forums with business executives and educators should identify some interesting areas for discussions.

As evidence of social responsibility, business philanthropy in the United States amounts to approximately $2.3 billion annually. *More than one-third of those coontributions go to education*. It is noteworthy that business firms rearrange their priorities for giving during business recessions in order to recognize the problems faced by colleges—primarily the private ones—during an economic downturn. In the three recessions prior to 1974, business firms increased the percentage of their total support to education. Thus, business firms' gifts to education were a greater percentage of their total corporate gifts at the bottom of the business cycle than at the previous peak.[2] Business contributions are even greater than the $2.3 billion figure just cited when the value of gifts-in-kind and employee-executive time donated during normal working hours are included.

Many other avenues of cooperation between business and college are available. New thrusts might include the variety of ways in which talents can be combined to help solve national problems. For example, declining productivity is a serious problem for the business sector and has adverse implications for the entire economy; prosperity and a high rate of economic growth nourish real progress in public and private education. Increasing productivity in every facet of higher education, although discussed in terms of cost effectiveness, is essential for private colleges in the 1980s, a decade that portends declining enrollments and decreasing *real* dollars. On many college campuses, research and projects are under way that contribute to improved understanding of various facets of productivity. The resulting information can be shared with the business community as well as contribute to campus efficiency. A dialogue between business firms and colleges with

2. *Corporate Support of Higher Education, 1974* (New York: Council for Financial Aid to Education, 1975), p. 5.

an exchange of knowledge about cost-cutting techniques and technology should prove conducive to improved productivity in both spheres.

Benefits to be gained from cooperation with business are immense. The first step calls for a serious attempt to understand today's business firm through holding discussions with decision makers, analyzing pertinent data, and genuinely seeking information and common ground. The avenues of cooperation are limited only by the imaginations of those on college campuses. The responsibility and the opportunity are ours.

Creating Coalitions for Cooperation—A Case History

F. W. STECKMEST

THE TRADITIONAL RELATIONSHIPS between higher education and business are many and various: placement officers and recruiters, development officers and foundation officials, continuing education courses and young aspiring executives, entrepreneurial professors and corporate clients, and university presidents as corporation directors and corporate presidents as university trustees.

These relationships serve reciprocal needs of both communities. They are part of the "business" of colleges and universities and part of the "business" of corporations. The relationships almost invariably create good will between counterparts in both communities. They have not, however, done enough to dispel an underlying suspicion between many key people in both communities—the professors and the business executives. While tension between campus and corporation is inevitable and, to some degree, desirable, many observers believe that the threshold of mutual trust is unnecessarily low.

I propose a new view on a largely dormant relationship, with the promise of raising the threshold of trust. The perspective is toward a nontraditional relationship wherein professors and business people voluntarily share intellectual and professional interests on a continuing basis. This relationship has its roots in similarities; many professors and business people have similar upbringings, similar educational experiences, similar values, and similar aspirations for society. It recognizes that an interacting relationship can help some professors be better teachers, some business people to be better managers, and some of both to be better-informed citizens.

This relationship of shared intellectual and professional interests was uncovered by several professors and business people who reached out to listen and talk with each other. As a participant in some of the events and an observer in others, I can report the case history of a nontraditional relationship that has led to or supported a variety of campus-corporation coalitions. The story begins in Houston with two chains of events—one local and one national.

The Houston Experience

Each year since 1971, we in Shell Oil Company have brought together a group of young professors and Shell people for a three-day meeting where they discuss public policy issues of common interest. We invite twelve leading universities each to select a young professor who has earned the students' respect as a teacher and as a person and who has had little or no direct exposure to business. The twelve company participants are promising managers or professional staff of comparable age.

The purpose of the annual Shell-Faculty Forum is to provide for an open exchange of ideas, attitudes, and experiences in order to develop understanding between potential future leaders of both communities. Equally significant is the sharing of views on how both communities can help meet the changing needs and expectations of society. Also, we believe it particularly important that our managers understand the role of the academy in the formulation of public policy. Subjects discussed are selected by forum participants from societal problems such as environmental protection, equal opportunity, energy, and the performance of government, business, and higher education.

What happens at the forums? After briefly sizing up one another, the participants become immersed in thoughtful discussion and intelligent debate. Before long, one has difficulty in distinguishing between the professors and the business people—whether in personal demeanor, intelligence, skill in discourse, or the nature of their social concerns. The participants learn a good deal from one another, not only about subjects discussed, but also in how others react to them, their ideas, and the institution they have chosen for their careers.

In short, the caricature of the professor as an impractical theorist and adversary of private enterprise and the caricature of the corporate manager as a single-minded profit-seeker and opponent of academic freedom are dissolved in the understanding that both communities have much more in common than in opposition.

The forum experience is characterized by this comment of a young professor:

> The Forum was highly informative, particularly the modes of thought, mores, and the public and private concerns of able young people in a major corporation. I was also impressed by their intelligence and striking candor.

One of the company participants, now a senior manager, volunteered this impression six years after attending a forum:

> I've had many educational experiences in acquiring three college degrees and in subsequent courses. Yet, the Forum has had the greatest single impact on my outlook concerning the role of business and higher education in enhancing our society, and my part in it.

In 1975, David Gottlieb, a professor of sociology and dean of the University of Houston College of Social Sciences, asked why Shell Oil did not have a forum with senior professors. He explained that from what he had heard about the forum, he had concluded that senior professors and experienced business people would equally benefit from a similar experience. "Indeed," said Dr. Gottlieb, "a number of my colleagues and I are ready. What can you and I do to bring our professors and your business colleagues together?" Within this imperative question lay an offer that we, as a corporate management, could not refuse. University people, quite properly, often ask corporate managers for financial support to do "their thing"; rarely is there an offer to do something together.

As a result, Dr. Gottlieb and I each brought five of our colleagues together and discussed our work, our personal and professional interests, and societal issues of particular concern to each of us. This initial meeting sparked a continuing relationship: we meet about six times each year from 4:00–10:00 P.M., rotating the site between the university and the Shell offices. Initially, we somewhat self-consciously called ourselves the "Town and Gown Group."

Soon we realized that many other business people and professors could benefit from the relationship we were experiencing, and the group was expanded. In the meetings the participants review and discuss their work in progress and key public policy issues, such as environment, energy, and federal regulation of universities. After several meetings, further coalitions developed. Several pairs of professors and managers undertook joint projects related to their professional work. These included papers on policy issues which became articles or chapters in books and materials for classroom lectures and company policy deliberations. One company participant became an adjunct professor of law, and a professor conducts a study course for Shell managers on business-government relations.

Beyond these developments, the Town and Gown Group organized a graduate course on energy policy in which the faculty and students are interdisciplinary and interinstitutional. In the first offering, the faculty members were professors of law, political science, sociology, and economics and managers whose work and experience involved manufacturing, scientific research, economic planning, and public affairs. The students were nine graduate students in political science, business, economics, law, and geology and six young Shell staff members. University of Houston officials believe this is the first credit course of its kind.

Because of their worthwhile experiences, group members began to consider how they could replicate the town and gown concept. In an effort to do so, they launched the Forum Club of Houston, a community platform for distinguished speakers.

The Town and Gown Group began this project by conducting a Distinguished Lecturer Series honoring the University of Houston on its fiftieth anniversary. The company members obtained a Shell grant, and the faculty matched it with campus facilities and services. The first three lecturers were David Broder, Pulitzer Prize–winning political columnist; Steven Muller, president of the Johns Hopkins University, and Fletcher Byrom, chairman of Koppers, Inc.

Before the third lecture, the Town and Gown Group concluded that community interest was sufficient to warrant phasing the lecture series into a community platform. While continuing the lecture series, members of the group invited Benjamin N. Woodson, chairman of the American General Insurance Companies, to serve as founding chairman of the Forum Club of Houston. Mr. Woodson, a nationally known business leader and a trustee of Rice University and the University of Houston, accepted with enthusiasm.

In one year, the Forum Club became a nonpartisan community platform for distinguished authorities to speak to members of the business and education communities, the professions, and other groups. In short order, Mr. Woodson formed a board of governors that included the presidents of the five universities in Houston, chairmen of several principal corporations, leading representatives of law firms, newspapers, and broadcast media, the head of the AFL-CIO, federal and local judges, and representatives of religious, professional, and cultural interests. Distinguished speakers have included university and corporate presidents, ambassadors, a Cabinet officer, a U.S. senator, and leading representatives of the media and the learned professions. The impact of such distinguished speakers before 500–1,000 members and guests is extended by television and radio broadcasts of the lectures.

In 1980, the Forum Club will move toward the replication of the Town and Gown Group by helping its members form similar groups to discuss public policy issues and, hopefully, to spawn more campus-community coalitions.

Coalitions at the National Level

The second, national chain of events developed from the 1975 Shell-Faculty Forum. On that occasion, participants zeroed in on common problems of the higher education and corporate communities, ranging from declining public confidence to excessive federal regulation.

Several months later, a faculty participant, Father Ernest Bartell, C.S.C., and I discussed the implications of the common problems of federal regulation. Father Bartell, as an economics professor, president of Stonehill College, and a trustee of Notre Dame University, had experienced, firsthand, the growing and adverse consequences of regulation. We noted that while a host of university administrators were delivering speeches on the detrimental effects of regulation, some business executives were chiding the academy with comments such as "Your chickens have come home to roost" and "You've encouraged government control of every other institution; why not yours?" We also noted that President Derek Bok, in his 1975 report to the Harvard Board of Overseers, forthrightly recognized the commonality of the regulatory problems of higher education and business.

Father Bartell and I decided to form an informal ad hoc coalition to help convey the common nature of regulatory problems to higher education and business leaders. In addition to ourselves, the initial members were Stephen R. Graubard, editor of the American Academy of Arts and Sciences, Walter A. Hamilton, vice president of the Conference Board, and Geno A. Ballotti, then managing editor of *Daedalus*.

The first activity of this town and gown coalition occurred in March 1976, when the American Academy of Arts and Sciences and the Conference Board cosponsored a meeting of university presidents and corporation chairmen to discuss the extent to which federal regulation was a common problem for their respective institutions. University presidents included Harvard's Derek Bok, Stanford's Richard W. Lyman, and MIT Chairman

Howard Johnson. Corporate chairmen included DuPont's Irving Shapiro, IBM's Frank Cary, Koppers' Fletcher Byrom, and Textron's William Miller, now U.S. Treasury Secretary. Others in attendance were Chicago law professor and former U.S. Attorney General Edward H. Levi, and Alan K. Campbell, dean of the LBJ School of Public Affairs and chairman-designate of the Federal Civil Service Commission.

This distinguished group discussed the similarities and differences of universities and corporations and concluded that federal regulation of both institutions is a common and growing problem. One point noted was that despite a great deal of academic research on regulation of business, little was being done on regulation of higher education. The presidents endorsed the efforts of the ad hoc coalition to develop understanding of the commonality of regulatory problems and to stimulate research to create alternatives to regulation and to improve the regulatory process.

In January 1977, Father Bartell returned to the Shell-Faculty Forum as the guest speaker. His speech, "Government Regulations Are Strangling Business and Education," was published in *Vital Speeches of the Day* and republished or quoted in several business journals. Incidentally, Father Bartell subsequently became director of the Fund for the Advancement of Postsecondary Education.

The next steps of the ad hoc coalition were to collect published materials on the regulation of higher education and to encourage more scholars to add regulation of higher education to their research agenda. In 1977, President William Baroody, Jr., included higher education in the regulation studies program of the American Enterprise Institute. Also that year, Robert Goldwin, an AEI scholar, joined our coalition.

In early 1978, the coalition met in Washington, D.C., reinforced by several guests, including Carl Kaysen, research director of the Sloan Commission on Government and Higher Education, Chester Finn, a Brookings Institution scholar, and J. W. Peltason, president of the American Council on Education. At this meeting, coalition members reported on the Harvard meeting of presidents, and the guests reported on their relevant activities. Also discussed was a national meeting that the AEI was planning on regulation of higher education.

In April 1978, the AEI held its meeting at the University of Alabama. Former President Ford was keynote speaker, and a panel discussion was taped for nationwide public service television, featuring David Mathews, University of Alabama president and former Secretary of HEW, Robert Wood, University of Massachusetts president and former Secretary of

HUD, and two of our coalition members, Stephen Graubard and Robert Goldwin. Meanwhile, on the recommendation of coalition member Geno Ballotti, Editorial Projects for Education prepared the article "The Entangling Web: Federal Regulation of Colleges and Universities" which was published early this year in several hundred university alumni publications.

Based on a suggestion by the coalition, the Institute for Contemporary Studies recently published *Bureaucrats and Brainpower: Government Regulation of Universities*. This book, on regulation of higher education and business, includes among its authors Stanford President Lyman, former HEW Secretary Casper W. Weinberger, now an officer and director of the Bechtel Companies, and Robert S. Hatfield, chairman of the Continental Group, Inc.

To return to the local chain of events, Dr. Gottlieb is now executive director of a University of Houston Commission on Non-Traditional Education. Again, he is bringing together a town and gown coalition, in this instance to facilitate the availability of lifelong humanistic and professional education.

Vital Initiatives

By raising the threshold of trust, these coalitions for cooperation are strengthening the traditional relationships of higher education and business in Houston and beyond. They are applicable in any community where colleges and corporations are in reasonable proximity. They are also applicable on a national scale.

I was delighted to learn in 1978 from Mr. Peltason that the ACE was establishing a national coalition of university and corporation presidents. The Business–Higher Education Forum already is establishing closer working relationships between leaders of the two communities. However, a relatively few leaders representing two large and complex institutions cannot alone achieve the objectives of the Forum. Logically, their principal role is an exemplary one—to encourage their respective colleagues to develop campus-corporate coalitions for cooperation.

Wisely then, the agenda of the ACE forum includes a project "to identify and disseminate models of campus-corporate cooperation to encourage interaction between the sectors." Based on "The Houston Experience," I recommend models that feature nontraditional relationships. As mentioned at the outset, the traditional relationships are among the established "business" activities of both communities.

The void that needs to be filled is the sharing of intellectual and professional interests by professors and their potential colleagues in the corporate community. The moving party in this model is the educator. Dr. Gottlieb's imperative question—"What can you and I do to bring our professors and your business colleagues together?"—contains an offer which cannot be ignored by any corporate management in tune with the times.

Cooperation with Government—Forced

CHARLES L. HAYES

IN THE YEARS TO COME, colleges and universities probably will have to depend on governmental grants for survival. The hundred-plus institutions that have closed over the past ten years are signals to the academy that reduction in alumni support and in enrollments and other factors, coupled with the high cost of living, will probably force additional institutions out of business. In all likelihood, federal grants will come to be relied on extensively.

Institutions, it appears, will have no choice but to pursue government grants to supplement and to sustain programs that are already experiencing declining enrollment and financial support. It could well be that where government regulations have been in instances quite stringent, some institutions have chosen not to bother seeking aid, but these are the extreme exceptions. In the case of certain high-cost programs, both private and public institutions are beginning to rely heavily on government grants as the prime source of support for continuation. The examples are many, particularly in all science and social science departments in the academy. The National Science Foundation, a government agency, has long been active in grants to higher education. Their grants have supported basic research and research in teaching, deemed necessary for a viable institution.

Seeking Funds by Competition or Cooperation

Institutions have had little choice but to compete for the funds. Certainly, few institutions can afford to sit still and refuse to participate in the competition for government funds and projects while other institutions devote significant effort and resources to the pursuit. If some of our prestigious institutions can boast they receive upward of 60 percent of their expenditures from outside sources, then other institutions could try for success—whether multiversities or small colleges; many institutions do qualify under agency guidelines. Competition becomes a volatile matter for institutions that have been unsuccessful in competing with old-line institutions which have had special facilities and staffs to service their grants and grantsmanship.

Among the high costs of pursuing government grants, certain items must be addressed. If an institution considers that the government is excessively stringent in its accountability requirements, then that institution may wish to give the grant or project further thought. The benefits derived from such grants must ultimately be measured by such matters of accountability to students and the respect the institution enjoys.

Because of the grave situation in financing the mounting costs in higher education, colleges and universities are adopting plans to share responsibility—in short, consortia. The idea is not new: about 25 percent of the nation's colleges either are or have been involved in cooperative arrangements, and the number of institutions and areas of cooperation are increasing. The most frequent areas of consortial cooperation are administration, curricula, faculty and staff, facilities, community affairs, and, in some cases, special-purpose projects. Many consortia have been funded by either private foundations or federal agencies on the basis of proposals that set forth the prime purpose as reducing costs through shared responsibility.

Under these circumstances, what can a developing institution do other than force itself into conformity with guidelines and regulations of cooperative foundations and, most specifically, the federal government? In short, there is no choice. Institutions in this category must cooperate and comply or be forced out of business.

During the mid-1960s and early 1970s, several big-brother—little-brother arrangements were developed by private, strong institutions with weaker institutions. They demonstrated that this kind of cooperative arrangement could work if the stronger institution shared in the revenue gained.

Dealing with Indirect Costs

In practically every instance, assisting agencies, as they are often called, have hidden costs that must be met either by the institution or from the overhead of grants. The federal government in recent years has been deeply concerned about hidden costs, and as a result many federal agencies are changing their regulations to authorize all direct costs but excluding indirect costs. The small, usually independent institutions raise the greatest objection to the exclusion of indirect costs because they sometimes must then rely on fund raising and revenue derived from endowment to remain solvent. If, further, an institution must cut into its endowment, it is a foregone conclusion that, without a financial windfall, that institution is headed for disaster. Consequently, for the institution, there is nothing left to do but to share, to consort, to comply with the regulations of cooperative foundations and, most specifically, federal agencies.

In most instances, both the cooperative foundations and the federal agencies want to take credit for their monies being used to improve or to make a contribution to the academy. As a result, some institutions encounter what they might consider undue intervention on the part of an agency to carry out productivity studies and evaluation projects to determine whether funds have been wisely used. In most cases, it is less whether the funds have been wisely used than whether productive results are manifest at the institutional level; consequently, the ripple effect into the community of higher education.

For colleges and universities to remain viable and competitive, amid declining enrollments and escalating costs—for them to maintain even present levels of survival, they will, of necessity, comply with government regulations. Any other course will be conducive to "going out of business."

8. COOPERATION IN THE HUMAN DIMENSION—BLACKS ON WHITE CAMPUSES

The Journey Begun, The Journey Ahead

PORTER L. FORTUNE, JR.

WHEN STUDENTS AT THE UNIVERSITY OF MISSISSIPPI elected a white "Miss Ole Miss" and a black "Colonel Rebel," their choice provided a striking visual symbol of change in the demography of academia. The number of black students enrolled in institutions of higher learning has more than tripled in the past fifteen years, and half of these students are on predominantly white campuses—many of which were once all-white.

Our society has made tremendous progress in expanding educational opportunity for black students, but progress has presented new challenges. Merely adding blacks to the enrollment on our campuses is far less an achievement than that for which we should strive: enabling and encouraging blacks to enjoy fully the benefits of university life.

I was not chancellor at the University of Mississippi in 1962 when James Meredith became the first black to enroll in a "white" institution of higher learning in Mississippi. I cannot speak firsthand, as can many of our faculty and staff, of the uncertain and demanding position in which the University found itself, of explosive tensions throughout our state, or of the 30,000 soldiers encamped near the campus. Nevertheless, there has not been a day since I came to the University in 1968 that some aspect of my responsibilities has not been affected by those events.

The full effect that the turmoil of 1962 has had on the University of Mississippi is difficult to describe. Our campus was torn by riots that left two men dead. Valuable faculty members resigned. The University's hard-won academic reputation was diminished. But perhaps the most unfortunate long-term consequence of the 1962 Ole Miss integration crisis has been a suspicious attitude toward the University which has lingered in the minds of some minority students. Ole Miss has labored diligently to dispel this atmosphere of distrust, and although problems remain, we have made progress.

Blacks make up nearly 8 percent of the University's enrollment today, and admissions officers and others on our campus are working steadily to improve that level. Black graduates appear generally to be pleased with their experiences at the University. A few years ago the University began conducting public opinion studies involving high school students, junior college sophomores, parents of college-bound students, and alumni of three Mississippi universities. This research showed that alumni who are members of minority groups are among the University's strongest supporters. I hope this support from minority graduates is an indication that Ole Miss has made an honest and concerted effort to meet their needs.

Our endeavors to gain the trust of black students parallel in some ways measures employed to disarm the adversary relationship between students and administrators that existed on many campuses in the late 1960s. A primary goal has been to establish effective means of communication between black students and the administration so that potentially difficult issues can be resolved before they reach the stage of confrontation. On our campus, a committee of students and high-level administrators meets regularly to discover, explore, and seek to solve problems that confront minority students. Even if surface tensions of the 1960s have eased, some distrust remains. More than ever before, sensitiveness to the needs and frustrations of all students, and especially minorities, is essential. I am convinced that administrators at Ole Miss consciously make an effort to give prompt assistance to black students who come to them with problems.

While my administration has worked for full integration of our campus, we have also encouraged black students in their endeavors to establish organizations that seek to support their group identity, cultural heritage, and specific objectives.

The University's efforts have been directed not merely toward opening the avenues of opportunity to all students, but also toward helping eager students whose previous educational experiences may not have prepared them well for the intellectual rigors of university studies. State-assisted institutions have an obligation to these promising students whose development has been hampered by circumstance. Recognizing this responsibility, the governing board of Mississippi's public universities has provided that 5 percent of our freshman classes may come from the ranks of students who show aptitude but do not meet admissions requirements. These students, many of whom are members of minority groups, receive special counseling and tutorial assistance through our Learning Development Center. While the center does serve the black students who would not otherwise be prepared for university course work, it is far more than a so-called minority remedial program. In fact, a majority of those who take advantage of the center's programs are white students who work with and beside blacks in an environment that is helping to build special bridges of understanding and support.

Many other institutions have employed similar strategies. I mention these only because their success at Ole Miss stands in dramatic contrast to the problems that beset our campus in the early 1960s.

As barriers have fallen and institutions have worked to provide greater opportunities for black students, the racial composition of the nation's university population has come to reflect more closely the makeup of the population as a whole. The increase in the number of black students on American campuses has contributed significantly to higher education's expansion during the past fifteen years. The Southern Regional Education Board reported in 1979 that since 1966 the number of black students had increased 277 percent, while white enrollment had gone up only 51 percent.[1] Blacks, who constitute 11–12 percent of our population, made up about 10.7 percent of the national enrollment in colleges and universities in 1976.[2] More than half of the blacks attending colleges and universities are enrolled in predominantly white institutions.[3]

Needed: Blacks on Faculty and in Administration

These changes have been accompanied by the identification of new needs, problems, and opportunities. Black students and professors at Ole Miss justifiably complain that the University's faculty, like those of most other predominantly white institutions, includes too few blacks. A more fully integrated faculty reduces the sense of alienation felt by many black students on predominantly white campuses. When a university has an adequate number of black faculty members, black students identify more readily with the institution, and their self-concepts and attitudes toward the institution change. No longer are they attending a "white" school; they are part of a multiracial institution. Increasing the number of black faculty members also can have a positive effect on white students. Obviously, greater interracial contact and cooperation increase mutual respect.

More pragmatic reasons also argue for increasing the number of black faculty members. On predominantly white campuses, black professors

---

1. Lorenzo Middleton, "Enrollment of Blacks Doubled Since 1970," *Chronicle of Higher Education*, January 29, 1979, p. 1.
2. Diane Ravitch, "Education Still Matters," *Phi Delta Kappan*, November 1978, p. 162.
3. Charles H. Lyons, "Access of Minorities: Blacks in the United States," *International Encyclopedia of Higher Education*, ed. Asa S. Knowles (San Francisco: Jossey-Bass, 1977).

usually assume a greater responsibility for counseling black students, a time-consuming activity that often can be undertaken only at the expense of the research and teaching duties that lead to promotion and advancement.[4] For formal academic counseling as well as for casual advice, students tend to look to faculty members with whom they identify most readily. This tendency may be greater for black students at universities where they make up only a small part of the student population. Many black students facing academic difficulty or having problems adjusting to the pressures—some of them self-imposed, some imposed by our culture—of life on a predominantly white campus quite naturally would be reluctant to turn to white faculty members or counselors for assistance. The shortage of black professors to perform this vital task on some campuses may be one reason blacks despair short of graduation at many predominantly white institutions.

For many of the same reasons, universities should increase the number of black administrators in responsible positions. All too often, presidents and chancellors do not have adequate information about how decisions under consideration will affect black students. If universities are really to meet the needs of minority students, minority groups must be represented at every level of authority, especially the higher levels. I am not suggesting that black administrators be hired to represent a black constituency. Rather, blacks should be integrated into the existing administrative structure, thereby enriching the store of information and experience on which collegial decisions are based.

Internal Grievance Procedures

Disputes are likely to arise in any academic setting. Students disagree with professors' evaluations of their work, with the decisions of professional school admissions committees, or with acceptance of transfer credits. Black students, keenly aware of centuries of mistreatment by a predominantly white society, are understandably sensitive in such situations, often believing that the disagreements are caused by racial prejudice. As a result, many disputes that should be resolved on the campus are settled in the courtroom. Universities should make all efforts short of compromising institutional and academic integrity to avoid litigation.

Fair and legally sound internal procedures for settling these disputes are the most effective means through which an institution can prevent the bitterness and heightened sense of distrust that are often the longest-lasting

---

4. Cleveland Donald and Lucius Williams, interviews held at the University of Mississippi, August 13, 1979.

results of litigation. For these procedures to work, however, students must believe that they are fair. Courts have told universities that grievance procedures must be clearly defined; to that guideline I would add "and easily understood." A complicated appeals process outlined in legalistic terms is almost certain to convince already suspicious students that an internal hearing is merely a kangaroo court.

Support Programs for Black Students

The use of standardized tests in admissions practices and in competence certification has given rise to many legal challenges in recent years, especially from minority students who assert that the tests are culturally biased and work to limit the upward mobility of blacks into graduate programs and professional careers. While experts continuously reevaluate these tests to ensure against cultural bias, universities should also be judicious in their use. In professions requiring standardized tests for certification or licensure of graduates, universities can provide special assistance for students who have difficulty taking such tests. Reviews similar to those conducted by law schools for bar examinations or by accountancy departments for the CPA examination could assist many students, as could programs to help students score better on standardized tests of all types.

Predominantly white institutions have a further obligation to provide financial support to programs that meet specific needs of minority students. Presidents and chancellors may hope that a university's programs are worthwhile for all students, but they cannot overlook the fact that students from minority groups have special needs and interests which are not fulfilled by programs designed to serve the largest possible group of students. My institution has, for example, increased its emphasis on black studies at a time when support is being withdrawn from similar programs on some campuses. This action is based on the belief that ethnic studies—primarily black studies in our region—are important academic pursuits and contribute to interracial understanding. Increasing a university's financial support for programs from which blacks derive the greatest benefit shows black students that the institution is as much concerned about their needs as about the needs of the predominant group.

Efforts toward creating a thoroughly integrated campus environment in the South have been frustrated by both black and white students who represent a generation that is ill-prepared readily to accept this new environment. Although white students seem to have become more tolerant than they were fifteen or twenty years ago, many of them have difficulty in accepting and understanding the black separatist movement that has developed in recent years. Open communication is particularly critical in this context, and universities should encourage dialogue that fosters mutual understanding.

For many reasons, predominantly white institutions should intensify their efforts to serve black students. Chief among these, of course, is the moral responsibility of higher education. For too long, many academic institutions joined other segments of society in relegating blacks to secondary status. The academic world is moving toward rectification and must not be content to stop with the progress thus far made.

Even more serious for the future of higher education is evidence of mounting strain between blacks and whites on some of our campuses. Last summer, a front-page article in the *Chronicle of Higher Education* described what the writers viewed as "simmering discontent" on predominantly white campuses, an "uneasy undercurrent" of racial tension. Interviews at universities around the country revealed that intramural sports have developed into interracial competition on many campuses, that black students believe white teachers underrate their work, and that collegiate racial disharmony is becoming increasingly widespread. One black staff member on a West Coast campus told the reporters: "In the late '60s, people confronted each other; today, black students and white students are missing each other. It is not an honest relationship; people are afraid to reveal themselves on all sides."[5]

Economic difficulties being predicted for the next few years are not likely to improve this situation. As inflation continues to erode the buying power of a family's income, black students will find it increasingly difficult to attend predominantly white institutions, even though the levels of financial aid have been increased dramatically. This factor may well send more black students back to the traditionally less expensive predominantly black colleges, causing a decline in minority enrollment at traditionally white institutions while intensifying the sense of alienation felt by black students who remain at those institutions. Black students on our campuses are also likely to feel greater pressures to achieve academic and professional success.

A further complication is the uncertain employment outlook for some fields that have traditionally attracted large numbers of blacks. A decline in employment opportunities, which would accompany any significant

---

5. Lorenzo Middleton and William A. Siever, "The Uneasy Undercurrent," *Chronicle of Higher Education*, May 15, 1978, p. 1.

economic downturn, is likely to find black graduates facing increased competition in the job market and encountering greater resentment from white applicants. As a result of all these factors, black students may become more demanding as they respond to pressures brought on by a period of slower economic growth.[6]

As higher education moves into a period of increased financial constraint, administrators will be tempted to allocate more resources to highly productive areas at the expense of programs that serve the needs of small numbers of students. Although belt-tightening will be necessary on many campuses, I believe universities would be unwise to sacrifice or restrict severely worthwhile programs that appeal primarily to minority students. A certain way to alienate black students and convince them that an institution is concerned only with serving its majority constituency is to cut such programs in times of financial adversity.

In large part, predominantly white American universities are only now beginning to serve the needs of minority students. Many institutions, unlike the University of Mississippi, have enrolled black students for decades, but until recent years few of them made special efforts to recruit black students, encourage their academic success, and fulfill their special needs.

Some Guidelines

In seeking to promote an environment of racial understanding and in encouraging the participation of black students in all aspects of university life, many institutions are going far beyond the activities I have mentioned. Their actions are commendable. I believe that predominantly white institutions should set at least these minimum goals for improving service to black students:

- Increase the number of black faculty and staff members.
- Concentrate on the selection of black counselors.
- Place qualified blacks in responsible administrative positions and train interested black professors for administrative roles.
- Monitor vigilantly affirmative action compliance at every level.
- Assure black representation on policy-influencing bodies.
- Establish legally sound institutional mechanisms for settling grievances to avoid racial polarization ensuing from litigation.
- Guard against racial bias in the use of standardized tests.

6. Donald interview.

- Provide financial support for programs designed to meet specific needs of minority students.

All of these goals have not yet been accomplished at the University of Missisippi. For example, Ole Miss has encountered great difficulty in hiring top black faculty members, who are attracted to other regions by significantly higher salaries. We at Ole Miss—and all of us in higher education—must redouble our efforts to overcome these barriers to improved service for black students.

Last year I was pleased to be host to some of America's leading historians in a symposium on changes in race relations since the Supreme Court's 1954 school desegregation decision. The conference itself was a significant and historic occasion for our campus. The scholars generally agreed on this point: "While the outward signs of racism are dead, institutional racism still exists."[7]

Eliminating institutional racism on predominantly white campuses will by no means be easy to achieve. But if universities do not zealously work to that end, they will bear far greater burdens in the future. Much has been achieved; much remains to be done.

Black Students, White Campuses— Variables That Affect Performance

LE VESTER TUBBS

BLACKS IN THE UNITED STATES are confronted daily by the inevitable consequences of living in a society where less than one hundred fifteen years ago their ancestors were slaves; where it was a violation of strictly enforced law for any citizen to be caught teaching them how to read or write; where less than fifteen years ago they could not, in many parts of the country, attend the same schools or use the same public facilities as whites. Many of these conditions have changed, and, even though some of these changes may be more of style than substance, they must be appreciated. Illustrating the distance gained is the attitude of former Governor George Wallace who, on June 11, 1963, stood in a doorway of the University of Alabama attempting to bar entrance to two black students.

---

7. Michael V. Namorato, ed., *Have We Overcome? Race Relations Since Brown* (Jackson: University Press of Mississippi, 1979), p. xix.

In October 1979, he stated that anyone who advocates returning to segregation "needs their head examined."

Coping with all the problems of a history of enslavement is something that all blacks experience in one way or another. Coping with the historical denial of quality education, however, is a more acute problem with which black students who attend predominantly white institutions of higher education now must contend.

In *Black Enterprise*, Elias Blake, president of Clark College in Atlanta, was quoted,

> I don't think there is any real deep commitment to the education of blacks that extends to the trenches of predominantly white institutions. These institutions were set up to serve a certain purpose, and they were never set up to meet the needs of blacks.[1]

Despite rhetoric concerning the response of white colleges and universities to black students, little has been done since 1826 when Edward Jones and John Russman (the first blacks in this country to receive college degrees) graduated from Amherst and Bowdoin respectively.

Returns on the Investment

Success or failure in society can be judged only in relation to each person's educational goals and life career. A first harsh reality that black students have to factor into their success-failure equations is that their degrees will not afford them the same opportunities in real income as their white counterparts may expect. Contemplation of the earning capacity a university degree will afford them has always been a practical and frightening consideration for black students and their families; in the 1980s, this contemplation takes on added importance.

For instance, Department of Labor statistics show that black families are much less likely than white families to have sources of income other than earnings. Whereas in 1979 three-fifths (58 percent) of all white families had income from dividends, interest, and rent, only 16 percent of all black families have such income. While the median income of black families increased by 3.5 percent (from $9,242 to $9,563) between 1976 and 1977, the median income of white families increased more than twice as fast, by 7.7 percent (from $15,537 to $16,740). Thus, the ratio of black to white family income fell from 59 percent to 57 percent—the widest gap ever during the 1970s. In fact, the closest black family income has been to white

---

1. *Black Enterprise*, May 1979, p. 29.

income is 6.2 percent in 1975.[2] Needless to say, the combined effects of recession and spiraling inflation over the last decade have not helped the economic situation or station of blacks in American society.

If income and material trappings are ornaments of success in today's society, how can a black student judge whether he has succeeded or failed when, irrespective of class standing or educational achievement, he is unlikely to earn as much as his white counterpart? Given this situation, what are the needs of black students enrolled in predominantly white institutions? Are their needs significantly different from those of their white counterparts? My experience in higher education in both predominantly black and predominantly white institutions over the past fifteen years has taught me that the needs of students, both black and white, are not significantly different. Any noticeable difference lies in the scope or the approach of the means that the institution employs in seeking to resolve the needs which separate these two groups.

The overwhelming majority of black students entering higher education are in need of financial assistance. Although the Congress and President Carter deserve commendation for their efforts in raising the levels of the H.E.L.P Loan Program, lack of financial aid continues to be a major reason why black students drop out of college. In addition to financial need, other factors militate against the collegiate success of black students.

Prior to entering higher education, most blacks attend public schools and lack the requisite intensive preparation necessary for success in university work. Yet, many of our universities still fail to make the type of commitments to developmental programs necessary to address these skill problems. Without a firm university commitment to address the needs of the capable but unprepared student, we can expect black students to see only the inevitable results that their inadequate preparation will produce and the likelihood that they will join the ranks of their brothers and sisters who have fallen victim to the revolving door syndrome.

Astin suggests that black students in white colleges have attrition rates 50 percent higher than either whites in white colleges or blacks in black colleges.[3] Most recent data suggest that that figure now exceeds 60 percent.

How the Variables Affect the Educational Experience

Black students' survival on white campuses depends on a variety of variables. Two, however, seem to be of foremost importance. First, the

2. *The State of Black America 1979* (New York: National Urban League, 1979).
3. Alexander W. Astin, *Preventing Students from Dropping Out* (San Francisco: Jossey-Bass, 1975).

institutional environment: upon entering predominantly white institutions, black students often are confronted with a feeling of isolation and find themselves subjects of overt discrimination by white students and professors alike. Many programs designed in the 1960s to make these institutions appear to be more hospitable toward blacks have, in recent years, been reduced or discontinued. The support mechanisms—both black student–based and campus-based—that emerged to assure that these institutions would be responsive to the needs of blacks are now floundering. A recent study by Donna Edwards on black student organizations on white campuses pointed out that race is no longer a sufficiently strong factor to maintain a black student organization. She indicated that students must be united by a common organizational purpose rather than a common racial identity.[4]

For the black student, the black political atmosphere and the white educational setting in which the black student operates often produce two opposing ideals. On the one hand is the preservation of the status quo intrinsically linked with white culture and its rewards of money and position. On the other hand are the countervailing values of "blackness"—values which, although not precisely defined, call for black people across the board to unite. In this context, the black college student feels called upon to respond both as a "student" and black person; however, his very position as a student—which at one time would undoubtedly have given him credentials for leadership—may now form the basis for charges of having "sold out."

The second important variable is the quality of the *instructional program*. John Gardner, in several of his writings, has cautioned teachers to avoid arrangements that diminish the dignity of the less able, to preserve the principle of the multiple chances, and to recognize that there are many kinds and levels of excellence.[5] The institutional reward system for faculty members on most predominantly white campuses are not congruent with the areas of concern identified by Gardner. Most campuses reward faculty on the basis of the quality of their research, their scholarship, their involvement in community services, and only lastly do they consider the quality of their teaching.

As we in colleges and universities focus on the 1980s and as we become increasingly concerned about competition and quality in higher education,

---

4. "The Black Student: Unity of Purpose," *Black Enterprise*, September 1979.
5. See Willard Abraham, *A Time for Teaching* (New York: Harper & Row, 1964), pp. 276–77, 381, 408–9.

in my view we must reevaluate the nature and scope of both the teaching processes and the reward system for excellence in teaching. National test scores clearly indicate that all segments of our college population can benefit from an improved quality of instruction. However, quality instruction is not the only thing that black students need in the classroom. It has been noted many times that students tend to achieve at the level expected by their teachers. Studies support the charge that white faculty are biased against disadvantaged students. Gamson, Peterson, and Blackburn, at the University of Michigan, found that among white faculty there was a persuasive ambivalence about black students in their midst;[6] that is, they often did not see them or even know they were in the classroom. These and other overt and covert hostile and nonsupportive attitudes are conveyed to black students in various subtle and not so subtle ways. In other instances, black students find themselves being called on by white professors only when issues concerned with blacks are being discussed. Many black students report they often feel that they are providing a "social experience" to both the professor and their white student colleagues.

An effective teacher must develop within the classroom a psychologically supportive environment. He or she must be able to communicate effectively with people of other races, ethnic groups, and cultures, particularly with respect to the subject matter presented in the classroom. In addition, the teacher must be sensitive to the additional stress that the minority student faces on a predominantly white campus.

Two Big Adjustments

Several research reports indicate that black students are highly motivated when they matriculate in our colleges and universities. Our faculty members must be trained to recognize and build on this motivation. In addition to these two major variables—institutional environment and instructional programs—other variables affect the life of black students in predominantly white institutions. Mitchem suggests two factors with which the newly enrolled black students must cope: (1) *a resocialization process,* a process that must create a positive outlook and minimize the effects of certain previous experiences that compete against the academic process and the ideas of the university; and (2) *the induction process,* a process that intro-

---

6. Zelda Gamson, Miriam Peterson, and Robert Blackburn, "Colleges, Clients and Controversy: Black Students on White Campuses," p. 16 (Paper presented to the 1978 meeting of the Association for the Study of Higher Education, Chicago, March 1978).

duces the student to the demands of the university and supports him through the inevitable shock of class and cultural tension.[7]

The life of a black student in a predominantly white institution is rough—I can attest to that. The black student encounters not only the normal pressures of student life but also other pressures in dealing with the white institution as a whole. Then there are the awesome pressures of handling the often-conflicting pulls of black student groups and the student's home and campus communities.

Prior to 1960 relatively few black students attended white colleges and universities. Today, more than one million black students are enrolled in predominantly white institutions, and if national statistics are correct, we can expect that over the next ten years blacks will become at least an increased proportion of enrollments. Therefore, I believe it is very important for members of the academic community, especially faculty members, to understand the variables that affect the performance of minority students on predominantly white campuses. This student is subject not only to the usual stress of a college student but also to the additional stress of being a minority student. It is very important for members of the faculty to understand this situation and to be more than academicians but also to be teachers.

I do not suggest that we lower standards. However, we must work toward teaching the unprepared how to achieve our standards. We must not give financial aid to students because they are black; rather, every student we accept who needs and merits financial aid should receive such aid. We must not change our curriculum to suit every passing fad; rather we must be creative and innovative and adjust where adjustment is needed. We must look at, and understand the needs of, black students if our institutions are to play their role in building a better society.

Black Students on White Campuses During Retrenchment

CLARENCE G. WILLIAMS

WITH PREDOMINANTLY WHITE COLLEGES AND UNIVERSITIES facing inflation and other financial pressures, black students on white campuses have

7. Arnold L. Mitchem, "Directions for Equal Opportunity in Higher Education: Financial Aid and Supportive Services" (Paper presented at the George Washington University Institute for Educational Leadership, Educational Staff Seminar, June 1978).

become, for many educators, a secondary concern. Yet now and for the past ten years, equal opportunity for minorities has been a continuing problem or challenge facing white campuses. Progress has been made in increasing minority enrollment on white campuses,[1] and several studies on the problems of black students on white campuses include sound recommendations to college administrators and leaders.[2]

Currently, my work is at Massachusetts Institute of Technology, a highly selective, science and engineering-based university. What follows draws on contacts with administrators, faculty members, and students regarding this subject. Though my comments may apply to graduate students, the attention is directed primarily to black undergraduates because my experiences are widely associated with this sector. Clearly, Mexican Americans, Puerto Ricans, and American Indians have many (and often different) problems in higher education that must be addressed if all minorities are to participate fully in the job market of our society.

On white campuses, some key problems related to black students appear to remain unresolved. To help meet these challenges, the white academic community must take responsibility for designing and instituting means to overcome problems. From my experience, I can recommend several guidelines that black and white administrators should consider to improve the quality of life and of participation for black students in the 1980s.

Problems and Challenges

Black students on white campuses will continue to encounter insufficient financial aid, negative recruitment and admission policies, and institutional racism. However, several other matters are dominant challenges to be confronted on white campuses.

First, the attrition rate of black students remains higher than that of majority students. The National Center for Education Statistics reported in 1979 that black and Hispanic enrollments have increased. For example,

> black and Hispanic enrollment rates for the 18- to 34-year-old age group increased by 5 and 6 percent, respectively, between 1970 and 1977 while remaining fairly constant for whites. . . .
> In 1977, 84 percent of whites, 70 percent of blacks, and 56 percent of

---

1. National Center for Education Statistics, *The Condition of Education, 1979 Edition*, by Nancy B. Dearman and Valena White Plisko (Washington: Government Printing Office), p. 91.
2. William M. Boyd II, *Desegregating America's Colleges: A Nationwide Survey of Black Students, 1972–73* (New York: Praeger, 1974); Charles V. Willie and Arline Sakuma McCord, *Black Students at White Colleges* (New York: Praeger, 1972).

Hispanics in this age group had graduated from high school. This represents an increase of 4, 12, and 6 percent, respectively, over 1970 high school graduation rates.

If these trends continue, the representation of minority groups in institutions of higher education will soon approach their representation in the general population.[3]

On the other hand, data on degrees awarded to racial and ethnic groups for the 1975–76 academic year show that most minorities are not represented in proportion to their college-age population. Blacks are underrepresented at all degree levels. While representing 12.4 percent of the college-age population, they account only for 6.4 percent of the bachelor's degrees, 6.5 percent of the master's degrees, and 4.3 percent of the first-professional degrees.[4] Therefore, the future suggests that more black students will enter higher education, but enrollments will still be inadequate in (1) the proportion of black young adults who graduate after entering college, and (2) the character or substance of the bachelor's degree received by those blacks who graduate.

In my view, the high attrition rate for blacks does not reveal the serious dropout of black students from the mainstream fields or occupations of the future. For example, in academic year 1975–76, education was the single most popular field for black bachelor's degree recipients. In traditionally black institutions during that year, 31 percent of all degrees conferred were in education.[5] Hence, if the black student dropout rate is combined with their high disproportion in the education and social science fields, then black students on white campuses could be significantly underrepresented in an occupational world of tomorrow based on science, mathematics, and technology. Too much attention, it seems, is given to the number of black students entering higher education. What needs greater attention is that black students do not acquire degrees of significant appropriateness at the same rate or same time as their white counterparts. Further, too many black students who get degrees will be unprepared to participate in some fields that will be in the mainstream of our society's activities.

Second, black and white students to a large extent continue to segregate themselves along racial lines, perhaps because both groups have been comfortable with the arrangement. However, this grouping appears to

3. *The Condition of Education, 1979,* pp. 91–92.

4. U.S. Bureau of the Census, *The Social and Economic Status of the Black Population in the United States: Historical View, 1790–1978,* Current Population Reports, Special Studies Series P-23, no. 80 (Washington: Government Printing Office, 1978), p. 87.

5. *The Condition of Education, 1979,* p. 214.

have greater negative effects for black students in the academic learning process. But white students too are cheated of acquiring reference points, tools, and experiences that will help them address and resolve future issues centered on race. First of all, many white campuses lack a critical mass (8–10 percent) both of diverse black students and of a representative professional group of black faculty members and administrators. Without such numbers, black students tend to withdraw to themselves. It is believed that all students can accept diversity among people when enough contacts under favorable conditions are made integral to campus life. We know, for example, that unless increased contact occurs among various groups under relatively favorable conditions, negative results are more likely than positive results.[6] Administrators on white campuses must become aware that unhealthy separation often is present within the student body despite an outward appearance of normalcy.

As for residential life, most black students appear to have black roommates and often live on residence hall floors with mostly or all blacks.[7] Willie and Levy found that the majority of black students on white campuses live in self-enforced segregation. Yet residential life should help keep communications open between black and white students and between black students and key college officials. If fruitful opportunities for dialogue (through residential or social experiences) between black and white students on white campuses are limited, hostility and lack of sensitivity will slowly but surely surface. As a consequence, the negative attitudes formed on campus will be transferred eventually to the future leadership of our society.

Third, academic and social advising continue to be less than satisfactory to enhance the survival rate and occupational outlook of black students. Three serious questions deserve consideration by academic communities. First, to what extent does the faculty's ability to generate academic achievement affect the academic advising of black students? Second, to what extent does academic advising affect retention within preferred major fields of students? Third, to what extent does academic advising affect the distribution of degrees awarded to black students?

The answers are obvious and of utmost concern since black students, it appears, are not fully benefiting from proper advisement. White faculty members in academic departments, particularly where black students

---

6. Mary S. Merritt, William E. Sedlock, and Glenwood Brook, Jr., "Quality of Interracial Interaction Among University Students," *Integrated Education*, May/June 1977, pp. 37–38.

7. Charles V. Willie and John D. Levy, "Black Is Lonely," *Psychology Today*, March 1972, pp. 50–52, 76–80.

historically have not enrolled in any sizable number, too often feel that the quality of the department declines with an increase in black students.[8] For example, Mingle's study found that white faculty intentionally communicated less with black students than with white students. In addition, he reveals, "When faculty believe that black students should meet the same 'standards' as whites, this tends to be translated into an unwillingness to alter traditional teaching styles or support institutional changes."[9] The shortcomings in academic counseling and teaching of black students thus are strongly associated with faculty attitudes and behavior at white institutions. The quality of academic advising in particular programs or majors within an institution is extremely important to black students, since a college degree alone (of virtually any kind) no longer guarantees employment opportunity and economic mobility. Morris, in his recent book, succinctly identifies the problem:

> Blacks more than whites in college tend to concentrate in a few undergraduate majors, particularly the humanities and education. This maldistribution not only predates the development of affirmative action but shows every sign of persisting. Moreover, the imbalance toward education and humanities, and away from science and technology, is aggravated in graduate schools. Unlike the distribution of blacks among institutions, however, the uneven distribution among programs has a fairly clear connection with economic mobility, and therefore a clear relationship with unequal education and economic opportunity.[10]

Although specialization decisions of black students do not prohibit other career choices, their choices often limit their future options. Thus, in academic advising, attention to the distribution of black students across major fields demands urgent consideration.

Maldistribution of black students across major fields on the undergraduate level means that the degrees awarded to them are distributed in the same biased and limited manner. That about one-fourth of all baccalaureate degrees granted to blacks in 1976 were in education points up the serious deficiencies in academic advising of black students on white campuses.[11]

Responsibilities of the White Academic Community

The principal responsibility facing the white academic community is to design and implement programs, changes, and innovations that enhance

8. James R. Mingle, "Faculty and Departmental Response to Increased Black Student Enrollment," *Journal of Higher Education*, May/June 1978, pp. 214–15.

9. Ibid., p. 213.

10. Lorenzo Morris, *Elusive Equality: The Status of Black Americans in Higher Education* (Washington: Howard University Press, 1979), p. 135.

11. Ibid., p. 176.

an environment in which academic, social, and personal achievement can be attained by black students. The responsibility resides with this community because it controls key components of university life—academic instruction, academic standards, and promotion of nonacademic programs. If black students are to have a fair chance at competing successfully, a few minimal essentials must be implemented by the white academic community.

First, clear, articulate policies must be developed and instituted regarding the presence of black students. To be effective, policies from the top administration should go further than simply equal treatment; they should include as well an affirmative action component.

Second, the academic administration is responsible for developing beyond the departmental level an active program to appoint competent black professionals as positive black role models (for both black and white students) *in decision-making, managerial positions* (vice presidents, heads of departments, etc.). Several appointments of this high calibre are essential in all institutions of higher learning, and such positions should not be confined to black or minority affairs. Because this issue is central, it needs elaboration. Today, most black administrators on white campuses are staff officers rather than line officers. In essence, blacks usually are staff members who have responsibility, but little power or authority in the formal administrative structure commensurate with their responsibility. It is critically important now to move from mere black presence (staff jobs that often are black-related) to full participation in decision making (line positions). Positive or negative relationships among black and white students are often based on whether they see and interact with an integrated administration.

Third, the white academicians hold responsibility to develop an effective, ongoing program that supports the recruitment and retention of black faculty. Cooperation among the black and white academic communities, particularly black faculty members, is essential in developing an effective program. A closely related program on the undergraduate level should be developed, where applicable, to identify and assist black students to pursue advanced degrees. Universities in particular should bear in mind that if the availability of blacks increases, the proportion of blacks to be employed on the faculties of higher education will increase.

Fourth, any institution that is seriously committed to affirmative action must establish an effective black undergraduate recruitment and retention program. One point about recruitment should be stressed here: The selection of black students to enroll in any institution should be based solely on the institutional academic resources in relation to a reasonable expectation about the student's ability to succeed. At M.I.T. we believe that an institutional commitment to the retention of minority undergraduate students must be expressed in very specific terms:

> [There are] six elements of our academic programs which bear on retention of minority students and which must be considered in appraising and building institutional commitment: (1) adequacy of financial aid, (2) effectiveness of advising, (3) program flexibility (ex. completing degree programs in five years as opposed to four), (4) efforts to ease the transition to university life (ex. prefreshmen summer program), (5) effectiveness and availability of academic support, and (6) willingness to recognize and sort out errors in judgment (in terms of admitting black students).[12]

To deal effectively with these six elements, an institution must be willing to give the financial support to operate such a program. Programs designed to increase the number of black bachelor's degrees require the expenditure of extra resources. Included in an effective program must be a sound evaluation process. For example, each institution should be concerned with the problems of retention within the major fields preferred by black students, as well as the distribution of degrees awarded to black students. Only ongoing evaluation can give proper answers and solutions.

A Few Closing Guidelines

- Educational enlightenment for all students is enhanced by having blacks represented in all phases of college life. Representation on the faculty, in the administration, and at all levels is a key sign that a successful affirmative program is at work.
- Programs designed to bring white faculty members in contact with black professionals who have status equal to or higher than their own will be necessary to change their negative attitudes toward teaching and academic advising of black students. The white majority in academic administration, with help from black colleagues, is responsible for seeking out positive mechanisms for their racial contacts and their discussions about the welfare of black students before serious problems surface. Lacking black-white, high-status professional contact in white academia, the two communities cannot engage in serious dialogue about black students, problems, and little change in attitudes of either can be expected.

12. Paul E. Gray, "An Institutional Commitment to the Retention of Minority Engineering Students," Proceedings of the Workshop on Retention of Minority Undergraduate Students in Engineering, Massachusetts Institute of Technology, 1977.

- Similarly, academic leaders must create mechanisms that encourage contact between black and white students. A positive environment for contact probably exists when white and black students interact in activities carrying more weight than the goals of either group.
- Essential to the growth and development of black students is participation by black role models in university decision making at all levels, particularly in the academic departments. Where the faculty includes blacks, black students are more likely to enroll and feel part of the academic community.
- Programs on white campuses where competent black faculty members and administrators have controlled the direction of academic, social, and personal services for black students have been a success and, in my view, still remain the most promising model for the next decade.
- Most institutions since 1968 have produced a sizable group of black alumni who can contribute insight into the problems of black students. This cadre of young professionals can be reached to only a limited extent through traditional alumni affairs methods. Communication with them may best be supplemented by (1) placing a black professional, preferably an alumnus, on the campus alumni office staff; (2) designing conferences for black alumni; and (3) developing other activities (such as telephone surveys) to solicit the opinion of black alumni on current campus issues.

Responsibility for academic and social growth of black students on a white campus must be shared by white and black professionals, and the effort put into the endeavor should produce success equal to that achieved by majority students. University leaders (presidents, deans, vice presidents, etc.) are responsible for ensuring that the educational needs of black students are met and that the necessary resources are available to foster an academic environment that is sensitive to communication between black and white people on campus. These elements are requisite to deal with the problems faced by black students before a crisis arises.

Black Students, White Campuses—
Student Perceptions and Institutional Response

EILEEN M. EGAN, S.C.N.

THOUGH TO DO SO IS TO DEPART from the scholarly tradition of impersonality in writing of concerns in higher education, I have decided to describe two personal experiences that have influenced my professional life with regard to black students on a predominantly white campus.

Two Personal Experiences of a Decade Ago

The first is the story of a young black woman who, accompanied by her mother and seven-year-old brother, came to seek admission to the college where I was external affairs vice president. It was a Saturday morning; most of the offices were empty; I was catching up with paper overload when the little family group knocked at my door. The young woman's name was Cathy; her little brother was George; I soon learned, from a devoted mother, that Cathy's father was a house-bound invalid. There was little that I could do except to visit a while, provide an application form, and recommend a return visit when the admissions office would be open.

I became somewhat personally interested in the applicant because of that chance visit. Sometime later in the semester, I inquired of the admissions officer about Cathy's application. It had arrived, I was told, but the test scores left something to be desired, and the admissions committee was reluctant to admit her. I indicated that I had visited with the family and that if family moral support might be expected to contribute anything to a student's success, this young woman would surely succeed. The admissions officer agreed to report my perception. Whether that report made the difference or not, I don't know, but the young woman was accepted with a recommendation for a lighter credit hour load during the initial year.

Shortly thereafter, I assumed new responsibility with the college as its president. Cathy's progress was unknown to me. I did, however, meet her occasionally because her work-study assignment was near my office. She seemed happy and contented. I would not be telling this story at all had tragedy not taken Cathy's life in a car accident on a rain-slick road on the day of her last final examination about a week before graduation. That tragedy brought the college community together in a way that was both unique and salutary. I learned that Cathy had become an *A* student during her last two years at the college,[1] that her student teaching practicum experience had been rated as extraordinary, and that the students and the staff considered her to be unusually gifted, both academically and personally.

The story has a touching sideline. Little George was so heartbroken at Cathy's death that, in an effort to distract him from his grief, his parents transferred him to a new school. By coincidence, the teacher who received him there was named Cathy. She had been a classmate of his sister at college, was able to share his grief, and thus help him to handle it. Just two

---

1. Rodney J. Reed, "Increasing the Opportunities for Black Students in Higher Education," *Journal of Negro Education*, Spring 1978, pp. 143–50, notes a similar incident.

weeks ago, I met Cathy's mother and little George in a local store. Little George is now well over six feet tall, is himself a college freshman, and still talks admiringly about his big sister, Cathy.

I cite this story as an example of the need to look beyond test scores in instances where they are considered as normative for admissions, of the need to understand the degree of the student's motivation, of the support of the family, and of any other predictors of success that may influence the admission process. When the student is a minority student applying to a predominantly white college, there is a distinct possibility that cultural difference may result in cultural bias, certainly not through intent, but by lack of intervention to understand the difference.

The second experience which I, as a white administrator, would like to share also occurred about ten years ago. As vice president for external affairs, it was my responsibility to represent the college at various community events. In the course of that activity, I met the principal of a then all-black junior high school who was a most sensitive and humane educator. At his invitation, I attended a holiday program at his school. It wasn't until I was seated in the auditorium where the students and some invited guests had gathered that I suddenly realized that I was one of only two white persons in the entire gathering of more than a thousand—a completely new experience to me. To be sure I had often been the lone woman, but I had never before been clearly a minority in a large majority of others. In that experience, I was the same, each other person was the same, but the sheer realization of imbalance made a lasting impression which the male-female imbalance had never effected. I was able later to share my reaction to the experience with my friend, the principal. He simply smiled knowingly and nodded his head wisely.

Shortly after I assumed the presidential role and directly as a result of that experience, I invited the black students on campus to meet with me. I told them I was there to listen to their perceptions, to their reactions, to their joys and discomforts as minority students on a predominantly white campus. For over two hours, I listened. From that session came the resolve to do two things: (1) to provide experiences for the white students on the campus which would sensitize them to the experience of being a cultural minority, and (2) to provide a broader base of dialogue and role modeling for the black students than had been available to them.

The resident community began a series of weekly dialogues at which the white students, at their own request, listened to their black colleagues. They were told what it was like to be a member of a cultural minority, how one missed one's music, one's cultural foods, and someone readily at hand to confide in. That series was followed by a second series, in which black community leaders were asked to participate in order to be both role models and exemplars for the black students present. The dialogues continued. Both groups responded favorably. More important, the black leadership in the student body emerged as articulate, competent, caring persons.

These events had their beginnings almost a decade ago. They took place at a college where there had long been a stated concern for the elimination of racism, at a college where the first black graduates received their diplomas in the very early fifties, before *Brown* v. *Board of Education*. Those graduates came to the church-related campus because it offered a program not available in the local municipal black college, which subsequently closed. Their presence on the campus was responsible for the demolition of color barriers in the city. At the time of commencement, the black and white community of students stood solidly together, despite opposition of the city fathers and merchants, insisting that they were one senior class and that all of their classmates or none would participate in the rental of facilities and the photographing of graduates. When a local photographer reported to the dean that the students were a problem in this regard, the dean responded, "It is you who have the problem."

Today's Experience

But each generation of college students is born and bred in a four-year cycle. The administrative lessons of a decade ago need to be kept currently applicable to each generation of students. Peterson and his colleagues report that the number of blacks on white campuses increased from less than 1 percent in 1940 to more than 7 percent in 1975.[2] That percentage has continued to increase. The little research available seems to indicate that there is no significant difference in quality graduate work between the black student who has attended a black campus and the black student who has attended a predominantly white campus. One study which compared 350 black American graduate students who entered master's or doctoral degree programs at the University of Illinois at Urbana-Champaign between January 1968 and February 1973 concluded that the two groups tended to perform equally well in graduate school, that there was not a significant difference in their graduate grade-point standing, and no significant dif-

2. Marvin W. Peterson et al., *Black Students on White Campuses: The Impacts of Increased Black Enrollments* (Ann Arbor: University of Michigan, 1978), p. 27.

ference was shown between the groups in the number receiving the master's degree and in doctoral-level retention.[3]

What is equally, if not fundamentally more, important but harder to get at is the degree to which those black students who have come to the white collegiate institution have grown and developed as persons as a result of that experience. If Reed is accurate in his assessment that "Perhaps the most pressing problem Black students face at large institutions of Higher Education is alienation,"[4] it behooves all of us at large and small institutions alike to attempt to improve the situation.

Why Choose This College?

In an effort to understand the perceptions of students at one institution and to compare and contrast their reactions with national reactions of black students, I circulated an open-ended instrument among the black students on the campus. To minimize any potential apprehension on the part of the respondents, the survey was hand-delivered by a small cadre of their number who agreed to help with the project. No attempt was made to obtain a statistically significant sample or, indeed, to obtain a 100 percent response. The aim was to provide a mechanism for tuning in to the feelings of those students who would respond.

The first question put to the students was, "Why did you choose this college?" The answers were in almost total agreement that the basis for the choice was either (1) a reputation for academic quality, expressed in those words, or the college's offering of a desired program, or (2) a reputation for the success of graduates of specified programs.

That very quality which the respondents indicated they sought became for some of them a problem to be surmounted, they noted. One student, who was interviewed at some length after returning the questionnaire, indicated that the quality of the program and the standards of achievement in its pursuit became a source of intimidation and of fear. The reaction was even more complex. The student feared that, having worked hard to achieve the standards and having done so, the other students might think that success was due to preferential, racially based treatment. The complexity of that double bind leaves such a student no out, no release from its noose. This student was unique in the complexity of the response; others simply

---

3. E. F. Anderson and F. A. Hrabowski, "Graduate School Successes of Black Students from White Colleges and Black Colleges," *Journal of Higher Education*, May–June, 1977, pp. 294–303.

4. Reed, "Increasing the Opportunities for Black Students," p. 145.

cited a quality program as both a sought-for goal and a critical challenge to be met.

What Pluses and Minuses at This College?

The second question of the survey asked the black students on this particular campus the following question: "What makes you, as a black student, comfortable on this campus?" One student answered "Nothing." The dominant response to this question, however, was that the individual was comfortable simply as a student—not as a black student. That thrust was typified by such remarks as, "I'm treated as a person"; "the student receives personal attention." A small number of students said that their choice and their degree of comfort related to the fact that they were older students for whom the atmosphere of the smaller collegiate campus was more comfortable than that of the larger university. A less frequent response was that the "Black students stick together on matters of concern." That the students spoke about the bonding of minority students confirmed the need for a critical mass on the campus, which has been noted by Willie and Sakuma.[5] Overall, the majority of responses from black students who spoke of their positive experiences seemed to place little emphasis on blackness. The general responses confirmed the findings of Boyd that black students do not espouse a separatist philosophy and that they generally do not want race to be the determining characteristic of either their friendships or academic activities.[6]

The question about being at ease on campus would be meaningless without a companion question which this survey asked: "What, if anything, makes you as a black student uncomfortable on this campus?" Again one student (a different respondent from the one above) answered, "Nothing," amplifying the response with the line, "I don't feel left out in any way." A variety of other responses included the following areas of student discomfort: lack of specifically black activities; small number of black educators; tension between loyalty to black friends and increased companionship with new white friends; signs of prejudice. These very areas were almost identical with those cited by Peterson and colleagues in their in-depth study of black students on ten white campuses.[7]

---

5. Charles V. Willie and Arline Sakuma, *Black Students at White Colleges* (New York: Praeger, 1972).
6. William M. Boyd, *Desegregating America's Colleges: A Nationwide Survey of Black Students, 1972-73* (New York: Praeger, 1974).
7. Peterson, *Black Students on White Campuses*, p. 39.

There was one amplification which the student felt strongly enough about to describe in an interview. On one occasion the student disagreed with a faculty member's procedure and expressed the disagreement, as the student described it, "strongly." The faculty member, in a conversation with the student after class, suggested that the student make an endeavor to surmount harbored feelings of hostility. This remark, the student resented as a behavioral stereotyping on the part of the faculty member, which the student judged would not have been made to a white student under similar circumstances. The student did not accept the stereotyping and explained to the faculty member that it was not a question of hostility but, instead, honest disagreement with the professor's manner of procedure. The student, in fact, was not at all hostile in the general sense of acting out of a repressed anger but was overtly angry over a specific incident. As the student described the situation for my benefit, I could not but agree that the student had a good grasp of the personal feelings involved and that the student's ability to describe the situation in an objective manner gave credibility to the perceptions that were present on both sides.

General Institutional Response

The two personal experiences discussed earlier related to minority experience as perceived by a majority administrator. What does the story of Cathy say to majority administrators? I believe it says that we can be key factors in helping black students succeed. Most of the smaller white campuses do not have open admissions; many of them have standards of admissibility to college. I suggest that the only standard allowable should be stated in the form of a question, Can we help this student to succeed? I believe that, in cases where preparation is inadequate and we know that ahead of time, we can provide support services before entrance to college and during the collegiate years. We can work to develop a supportive environment. We can encourage faculty development so that the black student will not experience the stereotyping and the cultural bias that may be present in an overt, albeit unconscious, way.

I believe that each of us who is a white educator working with black students should seek out the experience of being a minority within a black majority on at least one occasion. The experience is a conditioning of our behavior that will hardly occur unless we design its occurrence.

And I believe that the president should take the time to meet specifically with minority students to listen to their experiences, to evaluate the environment in which those experiences occur. And, finally, I believe in the president's responsibility to outweigh by presidential concern whatever alienation a century of history and present minority-hood may have produced in the black students who come to white campuses, for whatever reasons, in their search for the American dream.

American Council on Education

The American Council on Education, founded in 1918 and composed of institutions of higher education and national and regional education associations, is the nation's major nongovernmental coordinating body for postsecondary education. Through voluntary and cooperative action, the Council provides comprehensive leadership for improving educational standards, policies, procedures, and services.

LUCY
AND HER MANIFEST DESTINY

ILLUSTRATED BY DOROTHY KERNS

WRITTEN BY MARY FITZGERALD

Copyright © 2013 by Mary Fitzgerald

All rights reserved. No part of this book may be reproduced or transmitted in any form or by any means, electronic or mechanical, including photocopying, recording, or by any information storage and retrieval system, without permission in writing from the copyright owner.

ISBN: Softcover   978-0-9817811-1-2
Library of Congress Control Number: 2013910676

To order additional copies of this book, contact Mary Fitzgerald. School groups will receive a discount for orders of five or more books.

marytwickenham@yahoo.com

39499 N. Twickenham Rd.
Mitchell, Oregon 97750

Printed and bound in the United States of America by
Maverick Publications • Bend, Oregon

DEDICATION

To my dear friend, Sue Horton. I greatly admire the integrity and perseverance you showed while enduring hardships. Like Lucy, you would have made an intrepid pioneer!

CONTENTS

Introduction vii

Chapter 1 - Secrets Under the Attic 1
Chapter 2 - Letting the Cat Out of the Bag 13
Chapter 3 - Discarding Treasures 33
Chapter 4 - Across the Prairie 46
Chapter 5 - Lining Out the Adults 62
Chapter 6 - Trail Talk and Buffalo Chips 74
Chapter 7 - How Much Father, Father? 89
Chapter 8 - Dust and Distance 101
Chapter 9 - Bloody Beasties and Broken Dreams 119
Chapter 10 - Pain and Loss 130
Chapter 11 - Death on the Trail 143
Chapter 12 - Are We There Yet? 160
Chapter 13 - Drunks, Bloodsuckers, and Vermin 172
Chapter 14 - Death of a Loyal Friend 190
Chapter 15 - The God is Angry 205

Afterword 218
Acknowledgments 220
Bibliography 221

INTRODUCTION

In 1843, three Applegate brothers – Charles, Lindsay, and Jesse – joined the first major wagon train to leave Missouri for the Oregon territory. The journey, made with their families and with all their worldly possessions, was one filled with hope, hardships and heartache.

The oldest of the Applegate brothers' children, Lucy, was thirteen years old when she began the journey towards her manifest destiny. This book is the story of the trip as she may have experienced it.

My step-grandmother, Harriet Applegate Beckley Keyes, was the granddaughter of Charles and Melinda Applegate. Lucy's journey westward has been a fascination to me since I listened to Harriet's stories of her family when I was just about the age Lucy was when she traveled the Oregon Trail.

The people and the places contained in this book are real. The incidents, based on journal entries made by those traveling with the Applegates and on historical accounts, are told with the intent to entertain and to give the reader a sense of the hardships faced by Lucy and her family.

~ *Chapter 1* ~

SECRETS UNDER THE ATTIC

    She didn't like it, this being treated like a little child. Not when the adults in the kitchen below were discussing what just might possibly affect her whole life. Must be something very important and serious, Lucy was sure, or she wouldn't have been sent to bed early so she couldn't hear the adults talking.

    "Whatever they're mumblin' 'bout, must be 'bout us," Lucy muttered in her sister Ellen's ear. "An', here we are, put inta bed like little children." She straightened her body and, using a foot to give herself a slight push, impatiently turned over in bed. She jerked a tangled braid from under her shoulder and wiggled her length back into the depression in the feather mattress, pulling the patchwork quilt snugly around her body.

    She was jam-packed into one of the two narrow beds crammed into one half of the small attic in her family's home. She had been joined in her bed by three other wriggling girls trying to settle into the goose-down-filled mattress for the night, each one squirming to make a little nest. The second, smaller bed, held three younger girls.

    On the other side of the quilt hung to divide the dim room between the girls and the boys, she could hear her two brothers and six cousins. They were attempting to be quiet as they, too, worked to find comfortable sleeping positions in two beds, but Lucy could hear their turning bodies and, occasionally, a loud whisper.

"It's just not fair," she hissed, and her sister lying beside Lucy jerked her head away at the unexpected sudden burst of warm air in her ear and the tiny flecks of spittle hitting her cheek.

"I cook an' clean an' wash clothes an' change baby John's dirty rags all day an' then I get sent ta bed with…" and she paused for effect. Then, she hissed disdainfully: *"The children!"* She picked angrily at a dried scab on her chin, digging it off and flicking the offending skin into the dimness of the room. She gingerly felt the soreness on her chin and noticed a dampness that could only be seeping blood. Licking her finger, she used it to wipe away the liquid.

Lucy held her finger tightly against the sore left by the freshly picked scab in an effort to stop the slow oozing of the unseen blood, and her eyes strained as she squinted in the dim light of the attic. Through her narrowed eyes she could pick out the strings of dried apple rings and the shriveled green beans hanging from the rafters of the low ceiling.

Mother called the dried beans "leather britches," but Lucy and her sisters called them "tough sticks." Even after the dried vegetable was soaked for several hours before it was cooked and served with a meal, the beans were still tough and chewy. There was never a thought of not taking and eating the beans; children never questioned that they would take a serving of everything that was on the table and eat it without complaining. The girls swallowed the tough beans practically whole so they could get that unpleasant part of the meal over with and enjoy the remainder of the food on their plates.

Sometimes Lucy could hear better by focusing on something she could see, and she desperately wanted to hear whatever was being discussed by the men below. She squinted in the dimness of the room and concentrated on the leather britches hanging overhead. In the darkness of the attic, the shriveled beans looked especially unappetizing.

Lucy didn't consider herself an eavesdropper; she was just listening at a distance for the information that should be shared with her.

After all, she was twelve years old, almost an adult, and it was time her parents stopped treating her like a child.

She drew in a deep breath and smelled the dustiness of the room that was in need of a good sweeping and a scrubbing with her mother's lye soap. Lucy wiggled her nose and swiped a hand across her face and blew at the dust motes she could see in the dim light. The area definitely needed to have remnants of winter smoke and dust stirred around and tossed outside.

Overriding the other odors in the room was the unpleasant smell of seven young bodies with the lingering hint of sweat created by rambunctious frolicking in the hay mow that day. Added to the body stench was the stink that clung to an unwashed bare foot that had accidently squished into a fresh cow splat that had been hidden under loose hay in the barn.

"I s'pose *someone* stepped in a cow-pie again," Lucy hissed into the dimness of the room, holding her nose while looking in the general direction of a little sister. As she had finished milking, Lucy had seen Irene hastily wipe a large glob of manure from her foot with a handful of straw that had hidden the fresh pile deposited by the cow. Despite her efforts, the odor was still rank.

"When're you gonna learn ta wipe that stuff from in between your toes?" Lucy snapped. The only answer was a loud sigh in the small room.

She could detect, in addition to the odor of manure, the acrid smell created when some of the younger girls cuddled into the attic beds had made last-minute dashes to the outdoor privy a few seconds too late. It may be another few weeks or even a month before their mothers would allow the girls to wade in the shallow water of the river and splash off the daily accumulation of dirt.

In the meantime, the children carried their day-dirt with all of its odors into the night. Their baths, at the most only once every other week, were hurried affairs taken in the cool kitchen with a minimum of lukewarm water in the bottom of the small tub; often large portions of their bodies were only given a lick and a promise.

Furthermore, Lucy remembered, the children took their baths in order from the youngest to the oldest. The first and the littlest of the bathers would stick a foot into the water to test the temperature. Then, finding it to their liking, they would lower their little bare bodies into the tub. After sitting in the warm water for a few seconds, a smile of relief would shine on their face as a cloud of yellow water surrounded their bodies. Being the oldest child was definitely a disadvantage in more ways than one.

In addition to the dried cow manure and the unwashed bodies, Lucy could smell the unpleasant dirty-laundry odor coming from the pegs on the wall where the girls' soiled dresses hung, waiting to be donned in the morning for yet another day of wear. Lucy figured the ever-day dresses would almost stand by themselves before wash day would be declared. Her Sunday dress, worn only for church, was seldom washed.

"One more day," Mother or Lucy's aunts would say, but the next day would bring company to cook for or perhaps the weather would be too cold to stand in the yard over the wash kettle stirring the clothes with a large wooden paddle until they were clean. One more day would lead to one more excuse and the laundry might get done or it might not. Usually not. Not until the warmer days of spring.

Surely Angel Gabriel wouldn't allow heaven's angels to wear soiled, smelly dresses and trousers, the oldest Applegate child supposed, grinning wryly in the semi-darkness of the attic. Lucy figured that when she got to heaven she certainly would be able to bathe more often than once or twice a month, even in winter, and she'd have clean clothes to wear every day of the week.

She worked a finger around and around the thin brown strands of her braid, letting the fine locks slide smoothly in her loose hold. In the muted dimness Ellen could see her older sister working her hair with the motion that meant she was provoked. The nine-year-old had long since learned that when Lucy was doing the "hair thing," little sisters were wise to keep quiet.

"The grownups are plannin' somethin'," Lucy whispered in Ellen's ear. "I just know they are. An', I think we're gonna be part of it. It's not fair for them ta not share with me. I'm supposed ta act like an adult an' they're treatin' me like a *child!*"

The unknown secret being discussed below the attic in muted voices had been causing a growing enthusiasm between her father and his two brothers whenever they had met the past month or so. It was clear the excitement wasn't shared by her mother and her aunts.

In her mind's eye, Lucy could see all three of the women in their dark linsey-woolsey dresses with their prim white collars. They would be sitting with their chair backs against the wall and their eyes turned downward, quietly listening to the men's discussions. Their hands would be busy darning socks or mending trousers or dresses. As they worked, their heads would be canted to one side in order to hear their husbands' voices better.

Mother's sister, Aunt Betsy, was married to Uncle Lindsay, though Lucy didn't think the sisters looked much alike, other than they both had brown hair. Mother's face was thinner, her body a little heavier than Aunt Betsy's. And Aunt Cynthia...well, Aunt Cynthia looked like Aunt Cynthia. Seemed as if her mouth turned down at the corners constantly, making her look sad, and her body indicated that she had more of an appetite than the two sisters.

Lucy had observed that, when they were in a group, the men talked and the women listened. Always. The oldest Applegate girl wished Mother would say something. Or Aunt Cynthia. Or, Aunt Betsy. But, they never did; they just sat quietly and listened to the men talking with voices just low enough that Lucy couldn't understand them. The women were always knitting and mending, knitting and mending, and more often than not, during the daylight hours of the day, the children were sent out to the barn to play.

"An' I'm considered a child until Mother needs me ta help," Lucy thought silently to herself, patting her quilt rapidly, rhythmically, with her hand, exasperated at not being a part of the adults' secret. She sneezed at the cloud of dust she had stirred up from the dirty quilt and she slowed her patting.

Lucy didn't need to see him to picture her father's fleshy but stern face with his heavy black eyebrows above piercingly dark eyes. His mouth would be set in his usual no-nonsense manner as he listened to his younger brothers and he would be frequently raising his mug of what he called "bark juice," wiping a large hand across his mouth as he set his cup back down on the table with a soft thump.

The eavesdropping young girl could picture Uncle Jesse, the baby of the three brothers sitting at the table, listening intently from his place on the bench, serious as always. His head would be tipped downward as he cautiously contemplated what he was hearing, his chin jutting out, long nose drooping down to meet a large lower lip, the back of his head outsized and rounded.

"I don't 'spose anyone could call him a pretty man," Lucy thought wryly, and in the darkness she tried to imitate his looks, pushing her chin out and her nose down with her fingers. She instantly felt a pang of guilt for making fun of her uncle, remembering his kind nature, and she removed her fingers from her face.

"Looks aren't everythin'," she reminded herself. ""Purty is as purty does," Mother always says."

Uncle Jesse was more of a thinker than a looker. After thinking a few minutes about what he'd heard, he would lift his eyes and offer his carefully thought out words to his older brothers.

And Uncle Lindsay, with his straight mouth and his dark eyes deeply set under the bushy black eyebrows echoing the color of his thick hair, would burst into an animated dialogue and have his say when he was ready.

The kitchen would have plenty of heavy smoke from the brothers' pipes circling above their heads as they sat visiting. The upwardly drifting smoke mingled with the attic smells, and Lucy sniffed in irritation at the unpleasant combination.

Uncle Lisbon, the oldest of the four Applegate brothers, was absent, as usual. For the past few years Lucy had heard snippets of conversations from the three men seated around the table below, something about the Confederacy and slavery and Uncle Lisbon. She figured that her oldest uncle had different views on human bondage than his brothers, but she wasn't much interested in finding out more about that piddling stuff.

Lucy's biggest concern about her Uncle Lisbon was that she didn't get to visit with the fourth set of cousins. Lucy supposed her girl cousins would like to wade in the creek or play in the pile of grass stored in the hay mow in the barn just as much as she did, and the boy cousins would welcome a chance to outshoot Lish with their slingshots. It seemed silly that Uncle Lisbon's family didn't get together with the rest of them.

"You still awake?" Lucy whispered softly into her younger sister Ellen's warm ear, not ten inches from her own, and she moved her head even closer, gently blowing away the wheat-colored strands of her sister's fine hair that tickled her nose. She tugged to keep the quilt tucked tightly under her back, keeping the coldness of the room from her body.

"Shhh! Don't let Father hear you," was the soft answer from the ten-year-old. "An', quit blowin' on my face." Lucy felt a small puff of air on her own face as Ellen exhaled loudly in her direction, her breath bringing with it the unpleasant odor of teeth long overdue for a good scrubbing.

"Me, too," Susan murmured, her answer coming faintly from the far side of the bed. "I'm awake, an' I can't hear."

"An' me three," chimed in cousin Roselle, giggling softly from her place between Ellen and Susan.

"Can you hear what they're sayin'?" asked Susan quietly, wiggling her body enough that Lucy could hear her turning on the mattress. "I can't hear much a'tall."

"We're not s'posed ta hear," sputtered Ellen, a stray drop of her saliva landing on Lucy's cheek. "It's grown-up talk. Father an' the uncles are just makin' chin music."

"What's chin music?" The unexpected voice of her four-year-old cousin Theresa Rose in her ear jerked Lucy away from Ellen and she rolled her body over to face the little intruder.

"Cousin, I can't sleep," the tiny girl whined.

"Chin music's just talk. Go on back ta bed," Lucy whispered. She pushed her cover aside and rose to lead the little girl back to her place in the doubled beds where Lucy's younger sisters, Irene and Mary, cuddled together. She tucked the quilt under Theresa Rose and reached over to make sure it was tucked under Mary on the far side as well. She felt a soft lump under the cover and pulled out what she knew was the child's doll.

"Here's your baby," she told her cousin, handing her the rag toy. "Does everyone else have their baby?" and soft whispers reassured her they did. "They're tired. Be quiet so they can go to sleep," she advised the youngsters.

Lucy leaned over the cuddling girls, smelling the foulness of their unbrushed teeth and their night breath as she patted the three sets of warm cheeks lined up on the goose-down-filled pillow.

"Sleep tight an' we'll go feed the kittens their milk in the mornin'," she promised with a whisper. "But, you have ta close your eyes an' not make a squeak!" As she worked her way to her side of the bed, Lucy reached up and took her own rag doll, Sadie, from the shelf where she had placed her several months before.

"Won't hurt to cuddle her one last time," she thought defensively. This trying to be a grown-up was not always as much fun as she'd like.

Snuggling Sadie to her chest, Lucy grinned in the darkness when she heard the expected three sets of muted squeaks coming from the tightly bunched little bodies. The following trio of giggles gradually lessened, then ceased as the three younger girls drifted off to sleep.

"Won't hurt to cuddle her one last time."

"We'd better get ta sleep," Susan murmured drowsily. "We're apt ta get our necks wrung if Father hears us," and she was rewarded with giggles from the three other girls in her bed who could hear the softly spoken words. The thought of Charles hanging onto their heads and swinging their bodies in circles in the air until their heads popped off, much like chickens about to be plucked, was somehow gruesomely funny to the cousins.

"Shortess..." floated up to the bed in the attic. "...free for the takin'..." "...heathens..." "...oxen..." "...buffler..." The adults' voices occasionally drifted to the straining ears above, the isolated words and phrases like so many feathers floating in the darkness and making just about as much sense as goose down.

One by one, six of the eavesdroppers cuddled into their beds on the girls' side of the hanging quilt under the rafters drifted off to sleep. Lucy alone stayed awake. She strained to hear the voices from below and her mind latched onto an occasional word as it drifted upwards to the sleeping space.

She wondered if the boys jam-packed into the beds on the other side of the quilt that separated their sleeping space from the girls could hear any better. In the morning, she'd ask her brothers James and Lisbon and her cousins, Edward, Warren and Lish, if they'd heard any more than she had. Lish was two years younger than Lucy, but he seemed to hear better, and what he heard was easier for him to understand since he spent most of his waking hours with his father and he heard a lot of man-talk.

Just barely ten years old, his oldest son already did at least "half a man's work," Lindsay kidded. Lish helped his father with repairs and could cobble together almost anything made with wood, including mending a broken wagon wheel or overhauling a pulley.

Bright beyond his years, his studies came easily for him, and Lish finished his lessons quickly and always wanted to know more. He asked his parents questions unceasingly until one or the other would look him in the eye and declare, "Elisha, that's enough questions for today."

Lucy could tell from the glances shared between his parents that they were proud of their oldest child and she had the feeling that Lish knew that, too. He was wise enough to know, too, when he'd best keep quiet for a while.

Being the oldest of the Applegate cousins, Lucy felt stuck between being one of the children and being one of the adults. Her parents expected her to do the work of a woman which meant caring for the children during their waking hours and beyond and caring for the house and caring for the garden and caring for the milk cow morning and night.

"An' carin' an' carin'," she thought defiantly as she lay in her bed crammed against a little sister, longing to be part of the conversation below. "An' sometimes I just don't care." She grasped Sadie tightly against her chest.

Lucy found that growing up wasn't all it was cracked up to be. There was an invisible division between being a child and being an adult, and she'd be glad when she could prove to her parents that she was a mature human being and should be treated as such. Meanwhile, she guessed she'd have to be content with being either a child or a grownup depending on what her parents needed her to be.

Her ears strained to make out the words of her father and uncles below. Her sleepy mind wandered, set to roaming by those occasional phrases she could hear clearly. "…plenty a' milk an' eggs…" Lucy's thoughts drifted to reminding her little sisters to feed the chickens and pen them at night and to gather the eggs while she was occupied with milking Sukey.

She could almost feel the warmth of the milk cow's flank as she leaned her head against Sukey's side, her fingers wrapped around the large rubbery teats. Squeezing and pulling, squeezing and pulling, watching the thick streams of milk zip-zip into the pail until frothy foam formed on top. Her fingers squeezed a fold of the quilt covering the narrow crowded bed, and her hand unconsciously mimicked her thoughts as she kneaded the quilt.

She grinned in the darkened room, thinking of how she always squirted a few streams at the barn cats that showed up at milking time. The purring animals were amazingly clever at catching the warm milk in their mouths.

Occasionally, five-year-old Lisbon would appear at her side, squat down, and open his mouth, and Lucy would oblige him by squirting a stream or two into his opened mouth. The first burst of milk often splattered on the pint-sized man's face but Lucy's fingers would quickly adjust the stream until the warm liquid found its mark. With her little brother and the cats satisfied and wandering off, cleaning their faces before seeking other diversions, Lucy would be left alone to finish the milking.

Thinking of cats, she wondered when someone would let the cat out of the bag. She'd learned that adults could keep secrets locked up only so long. Then, just like children, they let the cat out of the bag and that was the end of the secret, which was often disappointingly uninteresting, anyway. She was sensing, however, that this big secret, whatever it was, might just be an enormous one.

"An' I'm supposed ta do Mother's work an' now I'm sent ta bed with the children?" Lucy complained silently to herself one last time, and she rolled onto her right side carefully so she wouldn't disturb the sleeping girls. Perhaps she could hear better out of her left ear. The men's voices were getting a bit louder, she thought, no doubt in part due to the increasing frequency of empty mugs being thumped on the table top and the cork being pulled out of Father's jug of blackberry wine with a loud "pop."

The talk became more animated, more rapid, until the words ran together in an incomprehensible buzz lost among the drifting smoke and the dried apples and the leather britches hanging above her bed, and Lucy slept.

~ *Chapter 2* ~

LETTING THE CAT OUT OF THE BAG

"Cousins! Cousins! Cousins by the dozens!" shrieked Ellen. Her sunbonnet tumbled off her wheat-colored hair and flapped against her back as she ran down the dusty road towards the two flatbed wagons, both half-obscured by the dust rising from the dry road bed. Though it wasn't quite summer, the heat was already building up for the day, promising an uncomfortably hot afternoon.

Her enthusiastic waves were returned by five vigorously waving hands in Uncle Lindsay's wagon and by an equal number in Uncle Jesse's, which was following closely behind. Rufus ran ahead of Ellen and her siblings, his cheerful barking joining that of the half dozen mongrels approaching. The noisy dogs added to the din of the dozen children calling out to each other, making for a boisterous, dusty reunion late on a warm morning in mid-May.

"Mother an' the aunts must be havin' a contest ta see who c'n have the biggest litter," eleven-year-old Roselle laughed to her cousin Ellen when she joined Lucy and Susan. She pointed at her mother and her two aunts, each of them holding a small bundled infant in their arms.

The four young girls stood watching cousins step from the wagons into the dust in front of Charles Applegate's two-story cabin.

Assorted sizes of bodies scattered from the wagons and the girls counted nineteen cousins in all, if the babies were to be included, and Lucy supposed they were.

"Mother has five an' Aunt Betsy has six an' Aunt Melinda has eight. Aunt Melinda's the winner! She's got the biggest litter!" Roselle declared, carefully brushing road dust off her long skirt. The girls burst into a fit of giggles.

"Litters, litters! Want ta see the new kittens?" An excited Mary reached for Theresa Rose's small hand and the entire group of girls turned as one, their backs to the adults gathered around the wagons. Though they'd never admit it, even to each other, each Applegate daughter was hoping to be overlooked long enough to escape the watchful eyes of her mother. If they didn't get inside the barn and out of view, they knew that they would be asked for help in preparing food for the two dozen hungry folks that would soon crowd into Melinda's kitchen for dinner.

"Let's hoof it," Lucy encouraged her younger sisters and cousins, her hand firmly planted on Roselle's back as she pushed her down the sandy path leading to the barn and, hopefully, moving out of her mother's sight. The girls gathered their long skirts in one hand, holding them up so they could move faster. Lucy urgently pressed her stumbling cousin past the corner post of the fence surrounding the young green vegetables growing in long rows.

"I declare! A June bug could scoot down the path faster'n you do!" she chided Roselle. "Scoot, Cousin, scoot!" and she kept her hand solidly on the back of the awkward girl, guiding her resolutely down the path.

Lucy hurried her younger cousin past the hollyhocks lining the path leading from the log cabin to the barn. Their bare feet thudded softly as they kicked up spurts of dust in the track leading to the cowshed, the sun warm upon their backs, the smell of water plants growing on the banks of the Osage River drifting along the path.

"Daughter!" Melinda's sharp voice rang out over the noise of the escaping Applegate cousins, and Lucy had no doubt which daughter that might be. She'd been caught again. "I need your help in the kitchen. Susan, you an' Ellen watch the children an' look for some more eggs."

Sighing, Lucy stopped her hasty retreat and looked begrudgingly at the backs of the younger girls hurrying happily down the path in front of her. Their giggles let her know they were well aware they were going to escape being cooped up in the house preparing food.

"Pooh!" Lucy muttered softly at the retreating backs. "I hope y'all stub your dirty little toes!"

Shrugging inwardly at the inevitability of helping her mother, she sighed as she raised her eyebrows and wrinkled her nose. Then, fixing a smile on her face, she started to turn to join the women standing near her mother's treasured rose bushes. She was almost knocked to the ground when a little body charging full-speed down the path to the barn ran full tilt into her.

"Watch where you're goin'!" Lucy barked, and caught her balance before she fell. Looking down at the small culprit, she saw her cousin Jesse, thick fluid oozing out of his ruined eye, the yellowish liquid mixed with road dust running down his face. She reached out and put a restraining hand gently on his shoulder.

"Just a minute, Cousin." She spoke gently to the seven-year-old as she grabbed his suspenders to hold him still. Lifting the hem of her apron, she carefully wiped the sticky fluid from the damaged eye and from his face. No matter how many times Aunt Betsy told him to be careful, he always smeared the seepage over his cheek when he clumsily used his shirt sleeve in an attempt to clean the discharge.

Jesse's eye had been ruined accidently with scissors years before and it seemed that no amount of salve or herbal teas or eye washes would heal the wound. The eye appeared to have a life of its own and, though she had grown used to it, Lucy still grimaced inwardly when she wiped little Jesse's face. All three Applegate families showed a soft spot for the lad, though he steadfastly refused to be coddled and demanded equal treatment.

"Go on, now," Lucy urged, and gave her pint-sized cousin a quick pat on his back before he bolted away to follow the other children to the barn.

"Bad eye or not, that little man is full a' dash-fire," Uncle Lindsay said proudly of his son. The family agreed that, despite his handicap, the youngster was full of vigor and manliness usually not shown by one so young.

"You need ta get the noodles made," Melinda instructed Lucy when she entered the kitchen. "But, first, the baby needs attention." Lucy knew what that attention would be. She could smell the strong odor of the soiled baby before she reached her parents' bed where her little brother John lay wrapped tightly in his small quilt.

She breathed shallowly while she unwound the blanket from the baby and removed his filthy diaper. Wiping the reddened skin as spotless as she could with a piece of muslin, she put a clean cloth on the child and then rewrapped him into his cocoon and placed him in his small corral of goose-down pillows that were arranged to prevent him from rolling off the bed.

Holding her breath, she carried the soiled rag at arm's length out the kitchen door and to the usual spot a short distance from the beaten path where the "attention" was taken care of. Stooping, she picked up a stick, scraped the solid stinking waste from the bit of cloth, and flipped it onto the ground. Then she draped the still soiled and wet diaper across a rose bush, careful to hook the fabric onto a few thorns. The stained material would remain airing out on the thorny bush until late in the day when Lucy did the last of her chores. She made a wry face as she thought of using the rinse water left from the supper dishes to wash the dirty diapers used during the day.

"An' just how many babies do you think I'm gonna have?" she asked the rose bush before she turned towards the house. "Just how many dirty diapers do you think I want ta change an' wash every day? Not a one, thank you very much!"

Inside the kitchen, Lucy lifted the top off the large cast-iron pot set on the back of the stove and sniffed the stewing hens that had been simmering all morning. Yesterday she had been assigned the task of catching three hens that weren't laying and then chopping off their heads and butchering them. The remains of those old gals were now tumbling slowly in the boiling broth. The meat falling off their bones showed it was time for Lucy to make noodles to add to the pot.

She opened the firebox and fed a few small chunks of wood into the opening, stirring the red-hot coals around to make the flames burn hotter.

"Are those bloody biddies just about ready ta eat?" asked Lisbon, hurrying into the kitchen with his cousin Jesse tagging close behind. The boys sniffed the air hungrily and flapped their hands at the flies that filled the kitchen and were buzzing around their heads. Lisbon rubbed his stomach in anticipation of Lucy's chicken noodles and dumplings.

"You shoulda seen them old gals when Lucy chopped their heads off yesterday!" Lisbon explained to Jesse. "Their bodies flopped around the choppin' block an' they did the dead chicken dance an' blood was a spurtin' outa their gory little necks." The storyteller mimicked the decapitated chickens' reflexes, his arms becoming flapping wings as he danced erratically around the kitchen, his tongue lying to one side of his opened mouth.

"Lucy held 'em by the feet an' dipped 'em into a big pot a' boilin' water an' made their feathers let go." He pinched his nose and made an unpleasant face. "You shoulda smelt the stink a' them ole wet feathers. Peeee-yew!"

Lucy had begun the unpleasant task of plucking the foul-smelling feathers from the hens while Lisbon, Susan, and Ellen stood nearby to help. As she threw the feathers into a pile beside the chopping block, the younger children would sort them, stuffing the smaller, softer feathers for pillows and mattresses into a cloth bag.

Lisbon had held up a severed head, working the beak as he gave his imitation of the dead chicken's voice: "And just why'd ja cut off my head, Miss Lucy dear? I gave you a egg for your breakfast ever day." Lucy giggled softly, remembering.

"An' what happened ta the old hen's head?" she prompted. She had snatched the head from her little brother's hand, she explained to Jesse, and had thrust it down the back of his shirt, laughing at his contortions as he shrieked and worked to get the clammy, bloody head out of his shirt.

Lisbon grinned sheepishly and nodded his head, remembering well what had happened to the chicken's head. He turned to proudly show Jesse the blood stain the hen's head had left on the back of his white shirt.

"At least you quit tormentin' me," she reminded him, grinning. "For a little while, anyway." She flipped a dish towel at the half dozen flies crawling over the table.

When the naked bodies of the chickens were free from their plumage, she had cut the carcasses open and, her nose wrinkled in disgust, she had removed the warm and moist innards, pulling out the edible organs and setting them aside.

"The gizzard for Father," she had explained to the children as she worked and sorted the pieces. "The heart for Mother an' the liver for James." She had thrown the remainder of the innards to the ground.

"An' the guts for Rufus an' the cats!" Her next job had been hacking the rubbery bodies into pieces of meat to be cooked.

"An' now, it's noodle time," she announced to the two young men watching. "Wanta help?" Lisbon nodded his head and grinned widely. He wiped an arm across his nose, and then pushed up his shirt sleeves. Jesse watched his cousin and then cleaned his nose with a finger, wiped his hand over his seeping eye, and rubbed his hand a few times on his trousers before shoving up his sleeves.

Lucy placed six eggs on the table. "You can each crack one inta the bowl," she directed. "Try not ta get any shells in there." Each boy thudded his egg against the table's edge and dropped the contents of the cracked egg, as well as several chips of the shell, into the bowl.

"Fish out the shells, you little ninnies," Lucy chided. As the boys reached into the bowl with their dirty fingers, she realized she'd forgotten to have them wash their hands first.

"Oh, well," she thought to herself. "The yellow yolk will hide the dirt an' it an' won't hurt the taste any."

"An' now, for each egg you put in the bowl, you have ta put an eggshell worth a' water in." The trio dipped into the pail of water Lucy placed on the table, dumping and counting as they worked.

Under Lucy's supervision, the boys reached hands they'd wiped on the legs of their trousers into the barrel of flour and dumped hands full into the egg and water mix. Stirring in enough flour to make stiff, slightly yellow dough, Lucy brushed breakfast crumbs off the table top and onto the floor. Then she scattered a cup of flour on the surface and dumped the large lump of noodle dough from the bowl and onto the spread flour.

As she was kneading the mound of dough, working in more flour, Lisbon handed her an almost perfectly rounded piece of wood about three inches in diameter and a foot long.

"You've watched me make noodles before, haven't cha, Little Man?" Lucy grinned at her little brother, and he nodded in agreement.

"An' next you roll it out," he explained to Jesse. "An' roll it an' roll it." His hand darted out and he took a little pinch of dough. Grinning, Lucy threatened him with the rolling pin and then she continued rolling until the grain of the wood was visible through the thin dough that spread over the table top.

Both boys, using the table knife Father had sharpened on his grinding wheel, took turns helping Lucy cut the dough into thin strips. Then, they hung the floury ribbons of dough to dry on long, reedy branches laid between two chairs. While the pasta dried, the young cooks brushed the flour from the table back into the barrel.

"Just why ja make the noodles an' dry 'em out an' then boil 'em until they're wet again?" Jesse asked.

"That's just the way it's done, Daughter," was the reply Melinda had given Lucy when she had asked the same question. It seemed to

Lucy that was Melinda's usual answer to most of the questions she asked her.

"That's just the way it's done, Daughter," Lucy had repeated sarcastically to herself, rolling her eyes after she had turned her back to her mother.

"That's just the way it's done," she explained to her helpers with a knowing grin, and she began to mix the dough for the dumplings. The boys looked at each other and shrugged as they waved away the circling flies. As long as the end result was noodles, they didn't suppose it made much difference why they were made the way they were.

"Cup a' flour'll make 'nough dumplin's for four people. Little spoon full plus a skosh of saleratus, half a little spoon a' salt, an' a dab of lard for each cup a' flour. Stir that up good until you can't see the lard an' then add enough milk ta make a stiff dough." She mixed the dumplings quickly as she talked.

"First, we have ta put the noodles in the pot. Help me drop 'em in, but be careful an' don't splatter the boilin' juice on your hands," Lucy directed the boys.

"But, Sissy, there's fly poop all over the noodles," complained Lisbon. Lucy looked; her little brother was right. She took a jar of ground pepper from the shelf near the cook stove, opened it, and dropped a pinch of the spice into the boiling chicken.

"Boiled fly specks!" she announced with a grin. "Stir it up an' you'll never know the difference!" Grinning, her helpers carefully dropped most of Lucy's noodles into the pot. A few fell onto the floor, however, and the young men quickly picked them up, wiped the strips on their trouser legs, popped the raw noodles into their mouths, and chewed happily.

"Mighty good fly poop!" Jesse grinned, his open mouth displaying a wet mass of dough, and Lisbon nodded in agreement.

"Dumplin' time," announced Lucy. "Drop a little spoonful a' the dough on top a' the chicken an' noodles, put the top on the pot, an' cook it 'til it's done. That's all there is ta it!"

Letting the Cat Out of the Bag

When the three brothers and their families accepted Father's invitation to "Put your nose in the manger," twenty-five people crowded around the table and perched on benches and chairs against the walls of the small kitchen. Lucy felt a surge of pride as she saw the simple yet ample meal sitting there, knowing she had contributed the large pot of chicken dumplings and noodles to the meal.

"An' we helped, didn't we, Jesse?" declared Lisbon, nodding his head proudly when Charles declared the chicken noodles and dumplings smelled powerfully good. "An' there was bunches a' flies an'..." Lucy reached over, grabbed his shoulder, and frowned at him as she shook her head slightly. Her little brother ducked his head, grinning.

"It's our secret, huh, Sissy?" he whispered. Lucy nodded her head, a grin on her face.

Wheat had dropped to fifteen cents a bushel, corn prices were so low Father grumbled about not being able to give it away, and sow-belly prices were dismal. With farming being so difficult and not at all lucrative, the men joked that one positive outcome was they may as well eat what they produced as the crops would bring in very little money at the market. Meals in the Applegate households were always substantial.

Towards the end of the spring of '42, family visits became more frequent, often lasting late into the night, the talk becoming more fervent and louder as the night wore on, and Lucy and her sisters and cousins no longer had to strain to hear the adults. The "winter secret" was no longer much of a secret and was discussed loudly and clearly and often. The Applegate men were talking of "perhaps" moving to the Oregon country.

"Perhaps, my foot!" Lucy told Roselle. "There's no "perhaps" about it," and she grinned at her younger cousin. "The adults have already made up their minds. They're just pretendin' to be thinkin' carefully about it. It's plain ta see they're all but packed up an' ready to move out. You just wait an' see. Father'll let the cat outta the bag soon 'nuff. He'll let us know their big secret, all right 'nuff."

"But, Cousin!" protested Roselle primly. "Father says "perhaps" an' we should wait for the adults ta tell us. We shouldn't try ta guess what adults are gonna do."

"Pooh! I don't give a fig 'bout "perhaps." I know better," was Lucy reply. "They're just makin' chin music, is all." She flipped her braids over her shoulders with a toss of her head. "Just chin music."

Unlike the late spring months when the listening children had only caught an occasional word drifting upwards to their space in the attic, they now had to bury their heads under quilts and pillows to buffer the men's voices that reminded Lucy of a gaggle of geese on the Platte River. Each man had something to contribute and each one had his say regardless of who might be talking at the time. Even Uncle Jesse grew animated and occasionally interjected his views.

"Seems like they forgot what they always tell us children, ta not interrupt." Lucy grinned as she whispered to Ellen.

"Do as I say, not as I do," her younger sister reminded her, and the girls burst into giggles at the phrase they'd heard countless times from adults. It seemed to Lucy that her sisters and her girl cousins didn't need much of an excuse to explode into a giggling fit.

"All this gigglin' makes my tummy smile," she whispered to Ellen, prolonging the fit of laughter.

"My tummy's downright amused," Ellen giggled, and Lucy's unexpected snort of mirth set the girls into a fit of merriment.

Talk around the table after the children had been fed and shooed outside or sent to bed was mostly about the poor conditions of the farmer in Missouri and what could be done about it. There were many slave owners moving into Missouri and farming had changed. The Applegate family, other than Uncle Lisbon, would have nothing to do with slavery, so their lives were necessarily harder than many of their neighbors, their expenses higher, and their profits lower.

"I'd not depend on another man's misery ta line my pockets," Father told Uncle Jesse. "Slavery would make a pretty bitter profit, the way I see it. That institution is the work a' Old Scratch, an' I won't have anythin' ta do with it."

Though the children weren't allowed to hear all the talk, the three brothers assembled in Melinda's kitchen often mumbled about their oldest brother Lisbon and his sympathies. Lucy sometimes felt a surge of compassion for the uncle who was absent and couldn't defend his position on slavery. She didn't feel her uncle could be influenced by Old Scratch; the devil would have a tough time of it if he tried to influence her Uncle Lisbon.

The children listened silently as they learned that the depression of the '30s had hit not only the Applegates but also their neighbors hard.

"'37 was the worst year, for sure," Uncle Lindsay informed his brothers. "But, there's no easy way to overcome our debts, despite the fact that life has been tolerable for us."

The three brothers talked eagerly about the reports from the Oregon country; it was said the grass grew as high as a horse's belly, the land was so fertile a man just had to drop a seed and it would grow, and the expansive land was offered free for the taking. Surely a move to the new territory to the west would be a boon to the three families.

"Well, then, just move!" Lucy thought impatiently, listening to the men's conversations. "Quit pretendin' the move is still "perhaps" an' just say we are goin'." Why the adults had to talk and talk when they'd already made up their minds to move was more than she could comprehend. She might be considered a child by the adults, but she knew they had made their decision already.

Lucy could sense excitement growing inside her twelve-year-old body; she was ready for an adventure and for a change from her daily chores. When she shared the feeling with her mother, Melinda frowned.

"We may not be makin' a whole lotta money," Mother snapped, "but we've got plenty ta eat an' clothes ta wear an' we can get by. We're doin' just a little better than last year. I don't want ta leave my family; I don't think Mother an' Father would make the move. An' my baby an' my roses," and Mother looked sadly around her. "This is my home."

Melinda sighed in resignation; both she and Lucy knew that, regardless of how the women felt, the men would be the ones to make the decision. Seeing her mother's sadness at leaving her home, Lucy knew she'd be wise not to discuss the matter any further with her.

Lucy asked Uncle Jesse to tell her of meeting and sharing stories with Baptiste Charbonneau, the son of Sacagawea, though she'd heard the story several times. The Shoshone Indian woman who had been a guide to the western coast of the United States almost forty years ago intrigued the young girl.

As Uncle Jesse shared his story, Lucy heard again how Sacagawea, who was only seventeen years old at the time, had traveled with the Lewis and Clark expedition in '04 to the Oregon country known as the Louisiana Purchase. She heard how Charbonneau had been born while his mother had guided the explorers westward, and Lucy was impressed at the strength of such a young woman. A trip to nearby Elm Grove was often a day-long undertaking for her family; she couldn't imagine a trip of an additional fifty miles, let alone a journey of more than a thousand or more.

"An', with a baby," Lucy remarked to Roselle. "With messy mossy diapers!" The girls had heard Aunt Cynthia say that the Indian mothers used moss for baby rags.

"Pretty scratchy, if you ask me," Roselle said, and she wiggled her bottom. "Can't even imagine that!" and the girls giggled.

"But," Lucy told her cousin. "What a wonderful adventure the trip ta the Oregon country would be. We would be able ta get away from the endless chores that fill every wakin' minute a' ever blessed day. I might not be as old as Sacagawea had been, not for 'bout five more years, but I'm strong an' I could do my share a' work on the trail." The listening girls nodded their heads in agreement, every one of them ready to start on the trail to Oregon.

"Yeh, 'n the ornery cuss likes ta parley as if he walked every mile a' the way himself," chuckled Uncle Lindsay, speaking of Charbonneau. "He's not a bit short a' good opinions a' hisself an' he does tend ta draw the long bow. But, exaggerated stories or not, he's been there."

Though the route that Meriwether Lewis and William Clark had taken was slightly different than the one proposed for the Oregon Trail, the dynamics of any emigrant's trip would be much the same. The Applegate men had listened as Charbonneau, always glad to be the center of attention, explained in helpful and perhaps a bit embellished detail the maps Lewis and Clark had brought back with them.

Lucy heard of Chimney and Independence Rocks. The Rocky Mountains. Forts Bridger and Hall and Boise. The Columbia River. Burnt River. The names all ran together, the landmarks something the men discussed and she didn't suppose she would ever see.

The children listening to their fathers discuss the move to the Oregon territory were to find that Charbonneau was not the only adventurer willing to share information of westward explorations. A fellow called Shortess soon became a household name. His booklet was thought by many to be the ultimate guide for emigrants to the Oregon territory, and the Applegates joined the hundreds of men who studied the contents faithfully. It seemed to Lucy that Father and his brothers could quote the information in Shortess's guide almost word for word.

Lucy noticed how Father and her uncles avoided looking at the women while they were discussing the distances and the hardships of the trail the explorers had blazed. She knew the men had already made the decision to travel that trail; she was impatient with their pretending they hadn't yet made up their minds.

Since that exploration led by Lewis and Clark, the young United States had suffered growing pains and the Applegate children learned some of their country's history during the family gatherings.

"I'm not sure why the folks have ta talk 'bout all this stuff," Ellen grumbled to Lucy. "S'not important t'us, I don't s'pose, and it's borin', borin', borin'!"

"They're settin' the stage for us, you ninny," Lucy whispered impatiently. "We'll understand soon 'nuff why we're goin' an' why it's a good move for us." She shrugged her shoulders in resignation as if to let her younger sister know the topics being discussed by the Applegate adults were for the more mature among the audience.

From Lucy's attitude, Ellen could tell she felt her younger sister was obviously not mature enough to appreciate the information. Ellen wrinkled her nose up at Lucy and turned away, fidgeting on the hard bench, her back resting against the cabin wall as the adults continued their talking.

Listening to the Applegate men was actually interesting, Lucy felt, and she knew she was learning about her country's history. The War of 1812; the building of the Erie Canal in '25; the making of a new union with the help of such strong-minded leaders as Andrew Jackson and Davy Crockett; the building of railroads to accommodate the movement of people and freight; Eli Whitney's cotton gin helping to establish ways of mass production; the settling of Texas; fur traders heading to the northwestern United States; the Trail of Tears when 15,000 Cherokee Indians from Georgia were moved in '38 to Oklahoma and a quarter of them died on the way.

"4,000 people," thought Lucy, doing the figures in her head. She looked at Susan and mouthed, "4,000 Indians." Ellen gave her a questioning look, so Lucy spoke softly in the crowded room.

"That's 'bout 4,000 people that died," she explained from her place on the bench crowded with cousins and shoved against the wall.

The girls thought of nearby Elm Grove and of all the people they knew and they whispered in their corner and counted on their fingers and decided among themselves that they might know a hundred people - maybe. A thousand people? Four thousand people? The number was impossible to think of, and the girls shrugged their shoulders and returned to their listening. To them, the stories they heard were as unreal as they were entertaining.

The older Applegate brothers were master story-tellers and they wove their personal and political views into their tales of a young country. The youngsters listening had begun to grasp the feeling of belonging to something bigger than the family assembled around the table after the dinner plates had been cleared. The adults were calling it a part of the United States' Manifest Destiny, a term the children were hearing but didn't understand.

Susan elbowed her older sister and mouthed the words, "You ask." Lucy squiggled nervously; children were to listen, not speak, and she didn't want to be banned from the room where the adults were so eagerly engaged in their planning. There was too much to hear. Ellen nudged her again and Lucy's own curiosity replaced her fear of Father.

"What does it mean?" she asked boldly during a lull in the conversation. "What's a "manifest destiny"?" Father raised his eyebrows as his eyes penetrated the dim corner of the kitchen, seeking his daughter from among the children sitting on the benches. Lucy could see him glance at Uncle Jesse and give him a quick wink, as if to say, "I'd better explain. Perhaps the women would like ta know, too."

"It's a pop'lar feelin' adults have; well, the Democrat-Republicans, anyway, that the United States is destined ta expand across the continent. "Manifest" means the idea is apparent, an' "destiny" means that it can't be stopped." Charles ran his eyes over the row of children and the women as if his penetrating eyes could implant in them the desire to join into the popular movement. Lucy mouthed her thanks and gave her father a smile when he looked her way. Then she ducked her head; she didn't want to seem to be sassy because she had spoken out when the adults were visiting.

"Folks who take part in the movement will be helpin' ta make history," Uncle Jesse commented. "The children will have stories ta tell their children an' grandchildren, for sure." He looked at the young Applegates sitting on benches lining the wall. "Who knows?

Perhaps someday, somewhere, someone will be writin' 'bout one a' you little hobbledehoys!"

Lucy scowled at James from her place on the girls' bench, thinking Uncle Jesse was talking directly to the boys.

"Always the boys," she thought. "Always the boys an' I don't s'pose we girls are important? I can't see Lish nor James nor any of the others changin' dirty baby rags an' makin' chicken dumplin's."

She wrinkled her nose at cousin Roselle and leaned over to whisper quietly. "An' the women do the hard work an' the men get the glory, I s'pose." Her cousin merely grinned at the sarcastic remark.

"Just because the government doesn't own the land in the Oregon country won't deter the courageous souls who chose ta leave their homes here ta colonize the lands west of the Rockies," Father commented rather pompously, scratching his thick thatch of dark hair. Lucy thought it sounded as if he were quoting from some pamphlet or other.

The Applegate brothers sat up a bit straighter at the table, puffing out their chests as if to assert their manliness. Lucy smiled from her seat on the bench in the corner where she sat with Susan and Roselle. There was no doubt among the girls just who Father and her uncles felt those courageous souls might be.

"If the soil in the new territory proves ta be as good as 'tis said ta be, our families can hope ta make our fortunes from the rich earth," Uncle Lindsay offered. "We know there's no assurance that the government will protect or help us in any way; that fact has been clear for some time now."

"There's strength in numbers," Father reminded his brother, "an' our family has always stuck together. An', we'll have some mighty good neighbors along with us ta help cover our backs, too."

The listening cousins heard how the movement was a private experiment and the emigration of '43 would be due largely to the efforts of Peter H. Burnett. His wife was in delicate health and he had even more delicate financial woes.

Letting the Cat Out of the Bag

"He's poor," Lucy explained "financial woes" in a whisper to Ellen who was sitting next to her with upturned eyes fastened questioningly on her older and wiser sister.

The move to the Oregon country would be an attempt to turn Burnett's fortunes around and start a new life. Burnett had made a concentrated and forceful campaign to encourage others to join his wagon train, and he was both surprised and pleased with the enthusiasm of the folks who stopped to parley with him, he told the Applegates.

The brothers had traveled to listen to Burnett speak and had lingered long after the dialogue was over. The Applegate men discussed emigration with the orator from every point of view they could think of, knowing the entire time they had already made the decision to emigrate. The effort to get enough people to begin the journey didn't take long, and Burnett planned to arrive at the rendezvous point on May 17, 1843. The Applegate families would be with him, Father told Mother, finally letting the cat out of the bag.

Lucy saw a look of bitter resignation pass over Mother's face and her shoulders droop as Father told her of his decision. Melinda was giving up the tiny sliver of hope she had kept that the family would remain in Missouri.

"I've known all along that your father had planned ta uproot an' move our family, no matter what my feelin's are on the matter," she commented bitterly to Lucy, both resentment and resignation showing plainly on her face.

Lucy heard of the decision without surprise. May 17, she thought. Ten days after she turned thirteen. She'd be a woman then; well, *almost* a woman, anyway. She had seen the Oak Grove girl who had married when she was still a twelve-year-old and had given birth to a child when she was hardly a thirteen-year-old. "Dirty baby rags an' pluckin' chickens!" Lucy wrinkled her nose. She was having enough of that without the bother of a husband, thank you very much.

On the other hand, there were some pretty handsome lads in Oak Grove that she'd been observing for quite some time. Leonard White

Lucy and Her Manifest Destiny

"*Charles helped his brothers build the covered wagons.*"

Letting the Cat Out of the Bag

had a huge smile and he flashed it often in Lucy's direction. Too, Robert Arthur wasn't bad to look at and he seemed to make a point of dashing past the Applegate girls on his bay horse whenever the occasion arose.

"A trip ta Oregon with those two might just be a great adventure," Lucy confided to Ellen with a grin. "An' who knows how many more fellas there'll be. Prob'ly dozens."

But, Lucy decided, it would be soon enough to think of husbands later, after the trip was completed. That is, if she decided she had any need for a husband. After all, husbands meant babies, and she'd had enough dirty diapers. She'd let the other young ladies worry about the boys for now; she'd worry about that problem later. First, the Applegate family had to get to Oregon and Lucy had to do her part.

Thinking of the adventure ahead, Lucy was thrilled. No more hoeing beans and pulling weeds. No more sweeping the kitchen floor or using a huge laundry paddle to stir dirty dresses in the washing pot filled with boiling water. The littlest of the children in the family could ride with Mother and their big sister wouldn't have to be responsible for them. For three glorious months, she would be part of a group of young people strolling beside covered farm wagons.

Perhaps Robert Arthur would pick a bouquet of fragrant prairie flowers and bring it to her. She and her sisters and cousins could wade in the ever-present streams the wagon train would follow. Lucy fantasized about meeting some Indian youngsters on the plains and striking up lasting friendships. There would be succulent berries growing abundantly beside the trail to Oregon and maybe Leonard White would catch fresh fish for her evening meals. Lish would probably shoot one of the huge buffalo that Lucy had heard would be grazing along the way, and there would be plenty to eat.

"I'll be thirteen years old when we leave home," Lucy mused. "An' when we get ta Oregon, I'll be thirteen an' a half. Somewhere along the Oregon Trail, I'll change from being a girl an' I'll become a woman. Somehow. I know it's part of my very own manifest destiny."

As she drifted off to sleep in the following months while the Applegate families prepared for their emigration, Lucy accepted the family's move westward as her personal goal, and her support for the migration grew. "Manifest Destiny," she murmured quietly and often, a smile on her face as she cuddled more deeply into the feather mattress, and the phrase became her personal mantra. "Manifest Destiny."

The unknown beckoned, filling her young mind with dreams of adventure on the lush grass-covered plains and over the beautiful mountains between Missouri and the Pacific Ocean. Had the young woman been able to foretell the harsh realities of the trail to Oregon, she may have embraced more of Melinda's skepticism and felt less of Charles's enthusiasm.

~ *Chapter 3* ~

DISCARDING TREASURES

Excitement about the coming emigration grew faster than the pile of coins in Father's cedar box under her parents' bed. Mother had gone to the garden to pick yet another pan of peas for Lucy to shell, and now would be a good time to check on the amount of money saved for the move from the family farm. Snooping into Father's treasure box wouldn't be wrong, she reasoned. The contents would affect her as well as the rest of the family, and the fact that she was prying where she shouldn't be seemed to be irrelevant.

Lucy pulled out the wooden box and hurriedly moved the coins into piles as she counted quietly, keeping an ear open for Melinda's heavy step on the kitchen porch. If she were found near the bed, she could tell Mother she was tending to baby John who was sleeping there; being caught with the "valuables box" open in front of her would be impossible to explain.

Lucy had not felt Father's strap yet, but she'd heard James's howls when he'd gotten the belt. Even worse than the pain of the belt would be the look of disappointment she knew she'd see on Father's face when he discovered she'd invaded his private space.

"Well, the money belongs ta all of us," she muttered to herself, justifying her snooping. "$135.67." Lucy frowned and counted the money a second time with the same results.

"Not enough ta even cross the Platte," she thought, and hurriedly scattered the coins in the bottom of the box, hoping they looked the way she had found them, and then hastily shoved the box under the bed.

"Plenty a' folks as poor as Job's turkey won't be able ta make the trip," Uncle Jesse had explained one night. "It's estimated the trip will take from about $500.00 to $1000.00 per family for outfittin'. With our big families, we'd better plan on saving up $1000.00 each, if'n we can."

To get enough money for the move, each brother would have to sell his holdings along with everything that the family couldn't take with them. The Applegate men had found there was no shortage of buyers for their land and equipment; the biggest problem was trying to get a reasonable price in a market glutted by the large number of people preparing to sell their holdings before moving to the Oregon country.

"Sellin's low; buyin's high," Uncle Jesse complained, and his brothers nodded their heads in agreement. They could get some of the cost of their emigration in cash but might have to rely on credit; perhaps Lisbon would act as banker for them, since he was staying behind, Father said.

"Poor Uncle Lisbon," Lucy thought. "He's always gettin' left out."

Lucy read the list of necessities the brothers had compiled and wrinkled her forehead in worry at the enormity of the task ahead for her family. Father had better get a whopping big price for the farm, or they wouldn't get very far from home. He had high expectations for what he thought they could buy; he seemed to think everything was necessary.

Covered wagon -- $70 (Maybe 2 wagons? Hold about 1600 - 1800 pounds each.)

Farm wagon -- $25 - 30

Cover for farm wagon: wagon bows, hickory: $3. Cloth: up to $1 yd. Make our own covered wagon? Good as buying.

Discarding Treasures

Ox -- $30 - $35 per head
Riding horse -- $75 or less
Pack horse -- $25
Cattle -- $8 - $20 per head
Milk cow -- $70 - $75
Tent -- $5 - $15
Nails -- $.07 pound
Rifle -- $15
Powder and shot -- $5
Shotgun or musket -- $10
Single-shot pistol -- $5
Hunting knife -- $1
Rec. for each adult -- 150 lbs. flour; 20 lbs. corn meal; 40 lbs. sugar; 10 lbs. coffee; 15 lbs. dried fruit; 5 lbs. salt; 1/2 lb saleratus (baking soda and baking powder mix); 2 lbs. tea; 5 lbs. rice; 15 lbs. beans)
Flour -- $.02 lb.
Corn meal -- $.05 lb.
Sugar -- $.04 lb.
Coffee -- $.10 lb.
Tea -- $.60 lb.
Salt -- $.06 lb.
Saleratus -- $.12 lb.
Rice -- $.05 lb.
Use our own beans and dried fruit. Enough?
Remember: coffee mill; coffee pot; fry pan; kettle; butcher knife; bread pan; tin table settings; candles; big wash tub; buckets; ax; shovel; hoe; hand tools; ropes. Keg of Mother's pickles!

Lucy saw the new owner of her family's farm ride into the yard one day and hand a small tote to Father. He pulled an envelope out of his vest and gave that to Father, too. When she next sneaked a peek into Father's box, her eyes widened at the amount of money she saw.

She thought Father had said he could only get a fraction of what the farm was worth; how could that be, given the large pile of money?

On top of the coins, there was a letter from the bank in town giving Charles the credit he needed to purchase livestock, equipment, and supplies for the trip west. Lucy couldn't read the signature scrawled at the bottom of the letter, which made the autograph look impressive and official for sure.

Lucy hurriedly read the letter, keeping an ear cocked towards the kitchen door, and then she closed the box and pushed it back under the bed with mixed feelings. She was swept up in the excitement of a new start in the Oregon country, but she desperately didn't want to leave her home and her friends.

At any rate, Lucy decided, there was no need to count the money any more. She had no say in whether or not she left her Missouri home, anyway, so she may as well forget about the money; Father would take care of that as he always did.

"Best start lookin' for a few cattle ta buy," Father advised. "Can pay for 'em when we get all the money for our land an' such. Applegate credit has always been good. Might have ta go a ways ta find enough animals. Other folks're lookin' for cattle, too." The next day he and his brothers left the corral early, riding on their favorite saddle horses, their older sons following on lesser mounts. Rufus bounced happily along with his people, overjoyed at having other dogs to romp with during the day.

Lish, the oldest at ten years old, was followed by the three cousins who were two years younger: his brother Warren, Lucy's brother, James, and cousin Roselle's brother, Edward. The "Eights," Lucy called them, as they rode off, and the name stuck. A year later, the family would be calling them the "Nines." The daily excursions to locate cattle for the emigration formed an even tighter bond among the cousins and they stuck together like a knot of the cockleburs that Lucy seemed to collect in the hem of her dress each time that she walked along the river bank.

Discarding Treasures

"*Surely Father wouldn't mind if she carried her treasures to Oregon.*"

The Applegate men's return each night was announced by Rufus's loud barking and the unhappy lowing objections of the cattle plodding wearily down the road. The makeshift cattle crew drove the complaining animals to a nearby field where they would be held until they were moved to neighboring grazing areas, awaiting their westward trek.

The boys, energized at the end of a long day by the appearance of their family who had been waiting at home, wore self-satisfied grins on their dust-covered, freckled faces. They showed off by loudly whooping and thumping their bare heels against the sweaty sides of their tired horses.

"We can break Babe an' use him in a team," Father told Lucy with a quick grin. "He's not too spoiled for that, I don't reckon."

The young ox befriended by the children after his mother died giving him birth had been given the name of Babe. The tag seemed to fit the wobbly little calf when they discovered him shortly after his birth. It had been Lucy's job to give some of the milk from her milk pail to the young calf each morning and night, and before long the orphaned animal had grown to a hefty size. He not only grew too big for his small pen in the barn but he also outgrew his name.

The young steer had bonded with Rufus, and at an early age the two animals were following the children while they were playing. Only when Babe decided to follow them inside the house did Melinda insist on his being penned up with the milk cow in her pasture near the barn.

After a day of gathering cattle and penning them, Charles would spend time training Babe to wear a yoke and to pull a light wagon around the barnyard. Lucy's father was sure the young ox would be a good addition to the two teams of oxen that would be needed for the trip, and the children were delighted they could take their pet along with them on their great adventure.

The best part of each day for the children started after supper was eaten and Father pushed his ladder-back chair away from the table, signaling the end of the meal. Lucy knew Mother would allow her to join the group for a time before she would be asked to help with the "women's work," as she called it.

Before Charles could stand fully erect, his seven oldest children would explode from their places at the family table and race outside. Father would spend the remaining daylight hours repairing the farm equipment he planned to take along to use on his new land. As he worked, his offspring would be put to work, proudly fetching parts and pieces for him to use.

Along with his never ending repair work, Charles helped his brothers build the covered wagons to haul the families and their belongings. Using well-seasoned hardwood, the three Applegate brothers built the big wooden boxes that would be the basis for the wagons.

"That looks like it's 'bout the size of Mother an' Father's bed," Ellen told Lucy, her eyes showing her surprise at the smallness of the wagon box. Each bed was about ten feet long, four feet wide, and two feet deep. Arched frames would be built on top and those would be covered with canvas.

Blacksmiths and wheel-makers were hired to build the moving parts for the wagons; part of the money from the sale of their farm lined these craftsmen's pockets when they left the Applegate farm. Lucy, standing near the new wagon, wondered how the family belongings could possibly fit into the little space provided for their possessions.

"Now, that's a fizzin' good wagon, if I ever saw one," Father said in satisfaction when he declared it was ready for the trip. He lifted the broad-brimmed hat he always wore when working and ran his fingers through his thick thatch of black hair.

"It might be first rate, all right," Mother said, shaking her head dejectedly, "but, Charles, it's so small!" She reached up to smooth her hair back and tucked the loose ends behind her ears and under the bun formed at the nape of her neck.

Lying head to toe, Lucy and Susan could touch both the front and the back of the wooden box on wheels; stretched out crosswise, they each had to bend their legs at the knees to fit their young bodies flat on the floor. Little two-year old cousin William had found he could peer over the top of the box of the wagon without standing on his tiptoes. When the canvas cover had been made, Uncle Jesse had to stoop to walk down the middle of the wagon without hitting his head on the wagon bows.

Father made wooden boxes to hold the family's possessions. When finished, they were pretty much all the same height, Lucy noticed. When she asked Charles why, he told her it was so a bed could be made on top of the boxes if need be.

"Father thinks a' everything," Susan commented, twirling a braid around and around her fingers. "When we get tired, we can crawl inta the wagon 'n take a rest."

"Has Father taken leave a' his senses? How does he think that small wagon can haul all our possessions to the new Oregon territory?" Lucy wondered aloud to Susan and Ellen. The two girls shrugged; such matters were of no importance to them. They were more interested in the thrill of the upcoming adventure.

Father had always seemed to handle the worrying for the family, though it seemed the constant look of anxiety on his face deepened as he prepared for the journey. Despite his fretfulness, there was no doubt in his children's minds that Charles was capable of solving any problems that might come up.

Mother and Lucy sewed pockets on the inside of the canvas top of the wagon, making the inside of the arched cover look like a well-patched tent. The pockets would hold items the family would use daily: tableware, ammunition, hairbrushes, muslin strips for bandages, salve for both humans and animals, and other necessities. Before attaching the pockets, the stiff water-proofed canvas must be punched with an awl so a needle could be forced through the hard fabric and the waxed thread pulled tightly.

Each pouch represented hours of work, and every time she sewed, her needle-pricked fingers left stains of blood on the tough material. After Lucy had stuck her fingers and bled at least a gallon of blood, she figured, beeswax was rubbed across each row of stitches on both sides of the canvas with the hope that rain wouldn't find a route through the cover and onto the goods packed inside. Lucy hated the job, and she scowled constantly as she worked.

Melinda stood looking at her belongs, a frown on her face. She had to make the hard choice of which family treasures to discard and leave behind in Missouri. The task seemed impossible. The belongings they took would have to fit into the wooden boxes that would line both sides of the wagon's box while leaving a small space down the middle for a walkway.

Mother wrapped a piece of flour sack around Grandmother's white china pickle dish with a pink rose pattern intertwined around the middle. She tucked it into the bottom of a flour barrel and then covered it with a few inches of flour. Next, she carefully placed a small teapot matching the dish into the barrel. Half a dozen more of the most precious of her dishes were carefully wrapped and cautiously tucked into the sugar and cornmeal barrels.

"We need a touch a' home where we're goin'," she explained to Lucy. "Wherever I can use Grandmother's dishes will be home. An', you can't learn ta be a lady if you have ta eat off a tin plate an' drink outta a tin cup."

"An' since when did china make a lady?" Lucy asked rebelliously in her mind, but she knew enough to keep her thoughts to herself. She flounced the skirt of her dress and did a mock curtsy and her mother frowned at her.

Her sorting and packing done for the day, Mother would leave the house and go up the worn path leading to the grave of the infant who had died the year before. She would remain there for a few minutes, looking at the little earth bath Charles had dug for the baby. Melinda had made the daily walk for a year, but she still returned to her kitchen wiping her reddened eyes with the hem of her apron.

Lucy didn't reckon Mother would ever really get over the loss of the child; none of her other eight offspring could replace the baby sleeping on the hillside overlooking the family farm. And now, the family would be leaving the little mite behind.

Lucy felt tightness in her throat and her eyes stung as she watched Melinda add flour and water to the sourdough mix that she would use for the next day's breakfast biscuits. The young girl knew her own sorrow at leaving her childhood home behind could hardly begin to compare to the grief of her mother.

Lucy's sadness lasted as long as it took her to turn around in the kitchen and spy the calendar standing on a shelf. Somewhere, just beyond eyesight, was May, 1843. A magical month. A magical year.

Lucy sorted through her bedroom for something special to take with her on the journey. Father had said each child could take only two small items because the entire family of ten would be traveling in a space with a base not much bigger than Mother and Father's bed. Lucy gently picked up Sadie, remembering that Mother had made the doll for her when she was only three.

The toy had been a constant companion for several years and her yarn hair had been thinned from being braided too many times. Sadie's round face was stained with dirt and grime acquired from a little girl's mothering. Sighing, Lucy straightened her doll's faded blue and white calico dress and arranged it over the thin rag legs before she placed Sadie on the hickory shelf in the bedroom, leaving her favorite toy for the next occupant of the house.

As an afterthought, she slowly changed the calendar next to Sadie to read "1843. May. Monday 19." Surveying her insignificant pile of belongings, Lucy chose a small hand mirror, a brush and comb set, and a string of blue beads. She rationalized that she could wear the beads so they wouldn't count as one of the two items she was allowed. She flipped her long brown hair behind her shoulders and surveyed her belongings.

She'd have to take the little cherry-wood trinket box Uncle Mac McClellan had carved for her. She couldn't leave that behind; his feelings might be hurt. Uncle Lindsay's family had "adopted" Uncle Mac when he'd shown up on their door step years before, asking for work.

He'd be seventy when the wagon train left home and headed for the Oregon country. Uncle Mac had been like a grandfather to all the Applegate children, acting as toy-maker and medicine man to the family. Cousin Alex had been named after Uncle Mac, cementing the bond that had grown between the Applegate families and Alexander McClellan.

Lucy rubbed her trinket box gently, thinking of Uncle Mac's greatcoat that reached mid-calf to his boot tops. It seemed to have endless inside pockets, and each of those pockets contained "nothing but useful magic." The old man's face, lined and darkened from years spent in the sun, brightened with a wide, contagious smile as he'd opened his coat to display the countless pockets inside. There were several little bags of medicines with which to treat any kind of illness or injury.

"Unca Mac! Unca Mac!" the littlest of the Applegate children would cry when they saw their adopted uncle coming. If they were lucky, Uncle Mac would pull out a small bag of peppermint candies to share. He carried small toys just often enough the youngsters gathered around him when he appeared, each sure that they would be the lucky recipient of the latest toy. No one had been able to figure out how he could remember whose turn it was for a new trinket but no one was favored over the other; the children were sure to keep track.

"A body'd think Unca Mac'd favor little Alexander McClellan," Lucy mused, looking at a small heart the old man had carved for her. She wiped a rivulet of sweat from her forehead. "But even if Uncle Jesse named little Alex after him, Unca Mac doesn't play favorites." She fingered the polished heart hung on a thin leather thong and then tied it around her neck.

As she looked at the slight pile of discarded belongings lying on her bed, Lucy resolved she would sew a pocket on the inside of her skirt to hold a few of her prized possessions. She couldn't leave behind everything. Not the rounded brown agate she had found in the creek that she called her good luck rock. Not the small needle case Mother had embroidered with blue flowers. Not the too-small peach-pit ring James had carved for her and she had never been able to wear.

Lucy picked up a muslin ball she had put aside into the pile of discarded items. She carefully unwound the strips of cloth decorated with a crudely stitched pattern of flowers.

"Poor Mother!" she thought. "Another one a those "lady like" things she wanted me ta learn." Lucy instinctively stuck a finger in her mouth as if to suck off a small droplet of blood as she remembered the many times she had poked her fingertips while struggling to learn to embroider.

"It'll make a fine trim for a dress bodice when you're done," Mother had promised. "Or, an apron."

As Lucy looked at the crudely done needlework, she grinned and added the wound muslin ball to the pile of treasures she would take with her.

"No one'll ever notice the poor job of embroidery on a gallopin' filly," she told herself. "It'll add a titch of color to somethin' someday."

Surely Father wouldn't mind if she carried her treasures to Oregon; they wouldn't take any room in the wagon, that way. And, it wasn't being dishonest. Not really. Lucy went to Mother's muslin bag of scraps and searched for the makings of a pocket – a large pocket – and began her project.

"Here's the medicine box," Mother told Lucy. "We'll have ta put it somewhere under something heavy so the little ones can't get inta it. If they drink some a' the laudanum, it could kill them."

"Why'd you take poison?" Lucy wondered aloud, wrinkling her nose at the thought.

"It's made outta opium, a strong drug," Mother explained. "It's good for really bad pain, but we'll have ta be careful ta measure out the right dose. The same for a lotta the medicine. Don't you ever give any ta your brothers or sisters. Ever." Mother paused for emphasis as her eyes seemed to bore into her oldest daughter's very soul, and Lucy squirmed as she lowered her eyes. "Usin' the medicine is somethin' ta be done only by Father an' me. We'll keep the box locked an' Father will have the key."

Lucy read the recommended list of medicines Mother had received from a doctor friend. She cringed when she read the word "purge." She knew what that meant: many trips to the outhouse. She didn't suppose there would be many of those on the trail. The best she could hope for, probably, were many bushy shrubs.

> Laudanum - (tincture of opium) Take 4 Ounces. Put 25 drops in water. Good for severe pain. Too much can kill a person.
> Calomel - Take ½ drachm or about ½ teaspoon. Use to purge the body.
> Castor oil - 1½ tablespoons. Use to purge.
> Turpentine - Use for linament on your family or the animals. Good for cuts on horses legs or sores rubbed on the oxen.
> Quinine - Use for malaria.
> Hartshorn - For snakesbites.
> Citric acid - For scurvey.
> Garlic - For tight chests and infections in the mouth.
> Pot marigold - For infections. Make a very strong tea, mix with lard.
> Peppermint - For upset stomachs. Make tea.
> Honey - Use for colds, mix with whiskey. Put on cuts, cover with bandage.
> Epsom salts - Dose, heaping tablespoonful in a cup. For purging or reducing inflammation. (Soak in very hot water.)
> Opium and whiskey - Very important. For many complaints. Dulls pains.

Lucy figured Mother could handle the medicine box for the family. She knew that Father, on the other hand, would dig into the medicine box and self-administer the whiskey "for many complaints." It seemed to Lucy that the box contained a disproportionate amount of whiskey.

~ *Chapter 4* ~

ACROSS THE PRAIRIE

"We're off ta a fizzin' good start, by cracky!" chortled James as he and his siblings skipped alongside Charles's wagon. Melinda perched beside Billy Doak on the hard, unyielding wooden seat. Her body wobbled back and forth on the narrow board as the wagon's wheels bounced on the uneven prairie sod, and her bonnet kept time to the jerking of her seat.

Irene clutched Lucy's hand. The little girl was sticking to her side like a cocklebur to a woolen stocking.

"Wherever I am, my little sister seems ta be right beside me," Lucy grumbled to herself. "I'm hopin' she'll get tired a' that 'fore long. Pretty hard ta impress a fella with a little girl stuck ta my side."

There had always been a strong neediness in the younger girl that had deepened Lucy's protective feeling towards Irene, and now she helped guide the four-year-old along beside the wagon. Though she grumbled about the responsibility, Lucy had to admit to herself that she would feel a bit incomplete without her little sister by her side.

Lucy ran her hands down the embroidered strips of muslin she had tucked into the front of her dress sash, run over her shoulders, and then tucked into the back. This was a special day, and the needlework added a festive touch to her dress. At the noon stop, Lucy knew, she

"This was a special day, and the needlework added
a festive touch to her dress."

would remove the muslin strips, wind them into a rag ball, and put it into her "secret" inside pocket in her skirt.

On May 22, the first day on the trail, the emigrants had set out with many of the women and children riding beside the drivers of the wagons on uncomfortably hard front seats, the wagons bouncing along slowly on the uneven prairie soil. For several hours, the travelers were focused on getting their teams lined out and into the column of wagons, keeping their place without running into the wagon ahead or lagging behind and slowing down the one following.

Not long after the beginning of the day's journey, the independent minded drivers in various wagons urged their teams away from the wagon they were following, moving to one side or the other, seeking a smoother route among the clumps of prairie grass. After a few miles, the jagged column was moving in some semblance of order and, as the thrill of the ride paled, many of the women and children jumped to the ground to join those walking. They could easily keep up with the lumbering, creaking wagons.

"Looks like everythin's hunkey-dorey," laughed James, flipping his dark brown hair off his face with a toss of his head and resettling his rounded hat back on top of his head. He stood watching the wagon train become as orderly as it probably ever would be, weaving around wild rose and western snowberry bushes.

"An' we young'uns are beginnin' our walk ta Oregon, one step at a time!" He left Mother, sunbonnet brim flopping erratically above her shaded face, clutching the edge of the board seat on which she was balanced beside Billy Doak.

Lucy could hear a loose wooden bucket banging against the side of the wagon bed; she'd have to secure it when the family stopped for noon meal.

"Unless Billy Doak takes care a' it," she thought. "Probably won't happen; he's been hired ta drive the wagon. James an' Lisbon will be busy twisterin' their cousins, so that leaves me ta take care a' the blasted thing!"

Baby John was being jostled from side to side in his small wooden box, and above the clattering wagon Lucy could hear unhappy squalls issuing forth from his confining container; he was not a happy emigrant.

The wagon hadn't gone far when Mother loosened her grip on her seat, reached around, and lifted the baby from his bone-jarring bed. Once he was out of the unsteady cradle and settled on a warm, familiar lap that cushioned the jolting, John gurgled happily and waved his pudgy arms excitedly. Lucy grinned at the youngest Applegate child enthusiastically kicking his legs beneath his long dress; he was on his way to his own manifest destiny.

James hurried to join Warren and Edward. The three cousins looked almost like triplets with identical dark hair framing their faces and their three sets of dark eyes twinkling with mischief. They all dressed alike; all wore the same style of rounded-top hat with wide brims, muslin shirts with five buttons at the neckline, and brown britches tucked into the tops of their shoes. The cousins walked alongside the wagons for a time and then ventured away from the slow moving column and began to explore the countryside.

"Stay close enough ta hear me call you," Mother reminded James, and he grinned and waved at her and was soon out of earshot along with his two cousins.

Lucy motioned to her three oldest sisters, grabbed Irene's hand in hers, and hurried ahead to join her cousins Roselle and Theresa Rose. They were walking beside Aunt Betsy who was gripping the edge of her perch on the high wagon seat and not looking as if she were enjoyed her ride at all. The strings on her bonnet had come untied, allowing her cap to slip to one side and Lucy smiled to herself at her aunt's lop-sided look.

"I'll give Mother an' the aunts one more day an' then they'll join us in our walkin'," Lucy remarked to the girls and the cousins all laughed and nodded their heads in agreement. She noticed later in the afternoon that it hadn't taken a day for the women to abandon their uncomfortable jolting places on the wagon seats.

"I think comfortable bottoms are more important than comfortable feet," she grinned to her cousin Roselle.

"Well, I'm thinkin' that some a' us have two pairs of shoes, so if'n one wears out, there's a spare," reminded Roselle.

"Well, we only have one pair each," Lucy told her, referring to her own family. "But, Father's got lots a' patchin' leather, too," Lucy added. "So. Looks like walk, walk, walk!" The travelers did just that.

The weather was clear and the road as good as possible, and the first day's journey to the Oregon country was a delightful beginning for the young emigrants cavorting across the prairie. Lucy and her cousins picked bouquets of coneflowers and sunflowers and, when their hands became too full, they discarded the most wilted of the flowers and picked more. She showed Irene and Mary how to pick apart the tiny prairie clover blossoms and suck the sweetness from the individual flowers. Irene soon tired of separating the petals and began munching on the entire blossom.

"Ya look like old Sukey!" Lucy teased her little sister, and was rewarded by Irene sticking her tongue out at her.

From a vantage point on the top of a small sandy knoll, the girls marveled at the sight of the white-sheeted wagons pulled by teams from their fathers' herds. The sight of so many wagons, so much livestock, and the hundreds of people all moving in a westward direction filled them with awe.

"Let's count the wagons," suggested Ellen, and for a time the girls stood tapping their fingers in the air as they pointed at each of the wagons moving slowly in a dusty and jagged line below their vantage point. Their voices grew louder and louder in an attempt to keep track of their count and to cover the conflicting numbers spoken by their sisters and cousins. The counting soon turned into giggles and the Applegate girls discarded their task and resumed their walk, avoiding the clumps of needle-and-thread grass that stuck to the hems of their dresses.

"Anyways, there are 'bout a hunnerd wagons. Father said," reminded Lucy, pushing her fly-away hair behind her ears and jerking on her bonnet strings. "An' 'bout seven or eight hunnerd people." She fanned her warm face with her apron.

"Or maybe a thousand!" contradicted Rosalie, grinning at her cousin. She lifted the skirts of her green calico dress and twirled in a circle.

"Or maybe a whole lot!" chimed in Irene with all the wisdom of a four-year-old, and the youngsters joined hands and skipped happily on the prairie, full of joy and excitement about their new adventure. Their long skirts swirled in the soft breezes blowing gently from the east and the warm softness of the prairie sod felt comfortable under their bare feet. The girls had all discarded their shoes shortly after the day's trip had started, tying them to their dress sashes, and keeping them ready for wearing through rocky stretches.

"Our manifest destiny is off ta a beautiful start," Lucy told the younger girls. "It's goin' ta be a grand journey. A seventeen-hundred-mile journey. Maybe two thousand miles. Father says."

She looked at her cousins and sisters, noting that all their faces had already reddened from the warm spring sun. "An', we'd better keep our sunbonnets on. Everyone's face looks like a little tomato and you know what that means. We're gonna start hurtin' 'fore long." She moved her hand across her neck, wiping away the drops of sweat that had formed.

The girls all reached guiltily for the sunbonnets hanging by their ties down their backs and settled the hats on top of their heads. Lucy supposed that would last ten minutes, at least, and she grinned and shrugged her shoulders. Sunburn was nothing that a little bit of lard spread on their faces wouldn't cure, she supposed.

With all the innocence of youth, the youngsters gamboled through the first days of their travel, exploring and wondering at each new flower, each new shiny pebble, and each new vista spied over the top of the next rise. While the adults in the emigrants' wagon train had a more practical view of the hardships ahead, none of the pioneers were prepared for the adversities and the sorrows they would soon begin to experience.

Snuggled under her nine-patch quilt with twelve-year-old Susan, eleven-year-old Ellen, seven-year-old Mary, and four-year-old Irene, Lucy tried to lull herself to sleep by counting the stars twinkling brightly in the night sky she could see through the open tent door. While the prairie sod in her family's tent provided a mattress for her young body, it wasn't as soft as the feather bed left behind. Lucy fitfully tossed and turned, looking for a comfortable spot for her tired young back.

She listened to the last discordant strains of a not-too-distant fiddle fade into the night and thought she recognized "Oh, Susannah!" though it was played in a way she'd never heard before.

"The poor fellow is playin' the tune the cow died a', for sure." Lucy thought. No matter how poorly played, the music seemed somehow strangely comforting, and it soon became a reliable part of the routine of night camp.

At a nearby campfire a man guffawed loudly and was hushed by a scolding wife. A dog barked and was joined by several more before the pack quieted, and the animals reminded Lucy of poor Rufus, left behind. An occasional oxen lowed and Lucy could hear a lone horse stomping his feet. As she listened to the camp sounds, man and beast alike slowly quieted, then drifted off to sleep.

Lucy's mind wandered back to the past few days on the trail and to the past several months of preparing for the trip to Oregon. She thought of Robert Arthur, full of dash-fire, racing past her on his bay horse and of Leonard White's never-ending broad smile. As she wriggled under her warm quilt, she wondered where her place was in all this nonsense. She supposed she'd find out soon enough, and she felt the excitement of the unknown deep inside her young body as she drifted off to sleep.

The emigrants met the first obstacle on their journey when they came to the Kansas River on May 24. It was on the banks of that waterway, too high to be fordable, that Lucy and her sisters saw their first "wild natives."

The youngsters were fascinated with the strangers though, from a distance, the young men didn't look that much different from the emigrants, the girls thought. They didn't wear war bonnets nor did they carry bow and arrows or spears; rather, they wore what appeared to be cast-off clothing that looked much like that the men in the wagon train wore. Disappointingly, instead of war-paint, their sun-weathered faces were covered with broad smiles of welcome.

"So much for all the stories we've heard 'bout the heathen natives," James groused, picking absent-mindedly at skin peeling from his sunburned face. The children watched as Father and his friends enlisted the help of the friendly Flathead Indians. The natives seemed to be eager to help the wagon train to cross the river.

Because of the number of wagons to be ferried across the river, the emigrants knew they would be at the crossing for a few days, and the women and children took advantage of the pause in their trek to Oregon.

"We'll get some clothes washed," Mother planned as she reached her arms behind her back to untie the sash of her stained apron. "And it'll be a good time ta do some bakin'. And vistin'." She was speaking to Lucy, who planned to avoid the family's campsite and Mother's chores as much as she could.

Lucy looked around for her younger sisters, hoping they would share the tasks. Susan and Ellen had already slipped away from the family wagon, as Lucy had noticed they seemed to do when there was work to be done.

"For sure," she thought, "Irene and Mary will cause more work than they will do." She felt she should be proud that Mother and Father depended on her to help with the younger children, but she'd rather be playing with her sisters and cousins. She shrugged her shoulders and sighed.

Lucy nodded her head at Mother and made a big show of taking the milk bucket from where it set just inside the wagon's entrance.

"I'll get Sukey milked," she volunteered, though she knew she was expected to do the milking. She lifted the pail slightly in Mother's direction, hoping the smile on her face as she hurried to do her chores would keep Mother from asking her for any more help just yet.

As soon as she had milked Sukey, Lucy took the pail of fresh milk to the wagon, careful to keep the canvas cover between herself and Mother so she wouldn't be seen, and then she hurried off to join her cousins. Lucy didn't feel too guilty; after all, Mother could find her if she really needed her.

Standing near the morning campfire while nursing baby John, Melinda moved so the shade from her bonnet's wide brim would shelter her child's face. She watched Lucy sneak quietly away from the wagon, and she grinned, knowing full well what her oldest child was up to.

"Best let the youngster enjoy a little fun time with her cousins while she can," Melinda thought. "There'll be all too few precious minutes later on for her ta be a child." She blew a loose strand of hair from her face and wiped her forehead. The warm morning was shaping up to be a hot day and she would enjoy the slight shade offered by the willows.

"You young'uns stay back, now. You hear?" Charles ordered the group of children crowding close to the natives.

Though he took the lead in pressing as closely as he could to the foremost Flathead warrior, James was poised to turn and dash away if he saw any indication the young brave might somehow mysteriously find a tomahawk and attack him.

"I ain't 'fraid a' them fellas," James muttered to his cousin Edward. "Ain't 'fraid a bit," he repeated, though he stood poised for flight. His brothers and cousins had his back, he thought, but a fellow just had to be ready. Lucy noticed with a slight grin that Warren and Edward clung to James so tightly they appeared to be part of his shadow.

"Brave souls, I declare," she thought to herself as she observed the Nines, though she'd have to admit she was more than a bit nervous herself.

It was obvious to Charles that the bunch of young Applegates would cause great damage to each other in their haste to get away if any of the Flatheads so much as scowled at them. Grinning, Charles lifted his hat, ran his fingers through his thatch of dark hair before settling his hat on his head once again and returning to his work.

The young'uns stood the required distance from the men, watching interestedly as two canoes made of black walnut were lashed together to form a platform that would ferry each wagon, one at a time, to the western shore.

From her viewpoint on the river bank, well away from the waterway, Lucy plucked a willow leaf from a slender branch and absently nibbled on the sprig as she watched James Nesmith and several of the other young men swim beside the canoes, helping to keep them on the right course.

Cousin Lish, his hat wedged tightly onto his head, slipped into the flowing water and swam beside the men. Lucy knew her cousin had often sneaked away from home and secretly swam in the Osage River; his mother would have skinned him alive if she had known of his furtive escapades. For some unknown reason, Aunt Betsy was dreadfully afraid of the river.

"I swear ta my time. If'n Lish doesn't quit grinnin', he's goin' ta swallow half the Kansas!" Susan exclaimed as she stood watching her cousin's obvious joy at being in the river. She had joined Lucy on the muddy bank and started to chew on her own sprig of willow but she spit it out quickly when the full bitterness of the leaf filled her mouth.

As the girls watched from the eastern bank of the river, they saw Alexander Zachary take his turn and cautiously move his wagon onto the tipsy boards perched on the two canoes. His wife, a look of terror on her face, and ten wriggling and exuberant Zachary children were crammed together tightly in the small wagon. The young'uns reminded Lucy of a basket of fishing worms.

"I hope they make it ta the other side 'thout crawlin' out inta the river." Lucy laughed nervously and Susan joined in.

Lish paddled lazily some ten feet away from the down-river side of the slow-moving makeshift ferry bobbing steadily across the current, and Mr. Nesmith swam abreast of the large raft on the opposite side.

Lucy's attention was caught by the flash of a red-wing blackbird darting past, and her eyes followed its path to the safety of willows lining the bank of the river. The musty odor of the wet bank thick with grasses contrasted with the freshness of the breeze blowing from the prairie. The young woman allowed her eyes to wander over the scattered wagons waiting their turn at the crossing and knew that somewhere in the group were the Applegate families.

An alarmed shout from Susan caused Lucy to spin around. The canoes had neared the western bank of the waterway and a collective gasp went up from the crowd as they saw the raft carrying the Zachary family slowly begin to sink in a current flowing rapidly near the bank. The wagon with its cargo of emigrants and all their provisions was soon immersed in the river.

Lucy felt her stomach churn and she sensed she was about to witness a drowning. She held her breath as one member of the family, then another, surfaced and was helped to the shore by Nesmith and the young Flathead men who plunged into the water to help in the rescue. Lucy panicked. Where was Lish? Had he drowned?

Then she spied a little boy clinging tightly to an ox yoke, floating downriver in the fast water. She watched in horror as his light raft swirled in the current, moving faster and faster. The tiny man wasn't making a sound and Lucy stood helplessly, clutching her hands tightly, sure that he would be swept away, never to be seen again. Suddenly, some of the Flathead youths began to run down the bank and got ahead of the accidental sailor, plunged into the water, and pulled him to shore.

Lucy finally located Lish on the far bank and she saw him looking at her and slowly shake his head. Though she couldn't see clearly, she knew he was mouthing the words, "Don't tell Mother." Lucy nodded. No need to worry Aunt Betsy needlessly. She clutched Susan's shoulder, putting a finger to her lips and shaking her head at the younger girl, asking her silently for her muteness, and was rewarded with a few nods.

All at once she realized how close they had been to witnessing the death of the small Zachary boy, and she sank onto the muddy ground rutted by the many wagon wheels driving onto the ferry, her legs suddenly and unexpectedly too weak to hold her upright. Her eyes unaccountably filled with tears and she wiped them away with the hem of her long apron. She blew her nose loudly on the fabric, adding mucus heavy with trail dust to the tear-dampened skirt.

"Are you all right, Sissy?" queried Susan. Her little sister hesitatingly patted Lucy on her shoulder.

"I'm fine," retorted Lucy, pulling back from the comforting hand. "I just got somethin' in my eyes. Must be a piece a' sand or somethin'," and she wiped her hands quickly across her cheeks, forcing a wan smile onto her face.

"'N I got some blasted sand burrs in my skirt. Need ta pick 'em out," and she bent to her task, tugging the stickery seeds from her dress, waiting for the tears in her eyes to subside. She rose to her feet.

"We'd better go see if'n Mother needs our help," and the girls moved away from the bank of the Kansas River, Lucy clinging tightly to her younger sister's hand as they made their way through the massed wagons waiting their turn at crossing.

Father finished his nights rounds early that night and, before he sat by the family's fire for a last cup of coffee, he rummaged through a trunk and pulled out the family Bible. Joining his family, he sat down, leafed through the book, and then made a selection.

"The book a' Joshua talks 'bout crossin' the River Jordan," he began. "Not sure exactly where I read somethin' 'bout the Lord helpin' folks cross the river, but He for sure helped us today. Need ta remember that. I'll just read a few verses here."

As she listened to Father's reading, Lucy felt Mary cuddle up to her on one side, Susan and Ellen on the other, and she nestled Irene on her lap. Mother sat nursing baby John and an impatient James and Lisbon squirmed as they sat on the ground by the campfire. The thought crossed her mind that, as important as the words she heard were, it was also important to just be close to the warmth of the fire and surrounded by her family.

As Lucy bounced Irene on her lap, she pretended to listen to Charles's deep voice droning on and on. What she was really concentrating on, however, was the music she heard from several wagons away. She wished she were dancing to the tune of the fiddle instead of sitting on the hard ground, listening to her father's uninspiring voice.

The near disaster of the Kansas River crossing flowed from the children's minds almost as fast as the running waters of the river. The morning after the Zachary family had nearly met with disaster Lucy finished milking, hurriedly deposited the milk in the family wagon, and started to sneak off to join her cousins for a morning of exploring the countryside. Father had said it might take four more days to get everyone across the river, and Lucy planned to spend as much of that time with her cousins as she could.

"Daughter!" Lucy heard Melinda's sharp voice. "I need help with the washing. When that's done, you'll be free ta go."

"Help, indeed," Lucy thought. "You mean you want me ta do the laundry for you. And just where did little Miss Ellen and Miss Susan run off to?" With a big frown on her face, she took a bundle of dirty clothing from her mother and stomped off to the river. She found a shallow place where the water ran rather swiftly over rounded river rock. The smooth stones would make a good wedge for the washboard used to scrub the clothing, Lucy decided.

Wading several steps into the river, she bent to her task, grabbing a shirt that belonged to one of the boys from the pile of dirty clothing.

Across the Prairie

She wetted it in the cool water and then rubbed a large bar of lye soap over the garment. Scrubbing the fabric against the corrugated tin on the washboard was the part that Lucy hated. She had to scrub the fabric against the ridged tin until the shirt was clean and her knuckles were red and sore.

Satisfied that the piece of clothing was clean – well, clean enough anyway -- she rinsed it and waded to the shore. She placed her wet bundle on a small patch of grass where the clothing would accumulate until she was finished rubbing her knuckles raw.

"And I don't 'spose I'll get any sympathy for that," she muttered to herself, looking at her reddened hands. When all of the clothing was washed, she would hang it on the branches of the shrubs lining the river.

"'Least the hangin' won't cause any blisters," Lucy groused to herself.

She reached for the next piece to wash and saw that it was one of the two pairs of pantaloons she had brought with her. Looking around to make sure one of the boys wasn't nearby to see her underwear, she quickly dunked the undergarment in the water, soaped it, and started scrubbed away.

Hearing footsteps, Lucy, startled, looked up to see Robert Arthur approaching.

"Where in thunder did he come from?" she wondered and looked desperately around for a place to hide her pantaloons. There was nothing but the pile of laundry and that was just far enough away that she couldn't reach it without Robert seeing the unmentionable she was holding. She quickly wadded the pantaloons in a ball and, keeping her eyes on the approaching young man, she stuck her underwear under her foot, holding it under the running water and out of sight.

"Nice day," Robert declared with a smile, and he stood on the river bank looking down at Lucy. He began talking without pause about the weather and the cows and the Zachary family and the nice day and… Lucy soon tired of listening. She nodded, smiled, and fretted.

Lucy and Her Manifest Destiny

"When all of the clothing was washed, she would hang it on the branches of the shrubs lining the river."

Lucy could feel the lump under her foot that she knew were her pantaloons, and she hoped they wouldn't come loose. She had no idea what she'd do if Robert saw her underwear. She'd probably just simply die of mortification, and her face turned red at the thought.

"Well, 'bye. Good talkin' ta ya." Robert mumbled his farewell to Lucy and left her standing in the river clinging to her washboard. When the young man was out of sight, she reached down to retrieve her pantaloons. They were gone. Gone down the swiftly running Kansas while Robert rambled away and she had apparently been standing on a river rock.

"They're probably twenty miles downriver by now, way the water's a goin'," Lucy thought. "And I'll just have ta wear my one pair of pantaloons all the way ta the end a' the journey." She sighed in resignation. "I s'pose they'll be good an' ripe by then."

~ *Chapter 5* ~

LINING OUT THE ADULTS

"Hurry! Hurry! Hurry!" Lucy scolded Irene. "They're going ta vote and I want ta see!" She kept a firm grasp on her sister's tiny hand, dragging the little four-year-old behind her. The scuffed toes of the tiny girl's buttoned boots bounced on the uneven ground as she tried to regain her footing. Her tiny face, shaded by her sunbonnet but reddened already by the sun and wind, had acquired a darker hue in her effort to keep up with her big sister.

"Breaked de arm, Sissy!" she complained in her high-pitched whine. "Breaked de arm!"

"Oh, honestly!" Lucy groused and she scooped up her pint-sized sister and tossed her up in her arms. She clutched the light body tightly to her chest and hurried up a slight grass-covered rise for a better look at the excitement below.

Panting from her run up to her vantage point with the weight of Irene in her arms, Lucy stood still for a time to regain her breath. Warm spring breezes played with her long, fine brown hair hanging below her bonnet, and as she set her little sister on the ground, she finger-combed the tickling strands of her tresses and tucked them behind her ears.

Lucy inhaled the fresh grass fragrance mixed with the occasional odor of the large herd of cattle milling around not far from the group of immigrants. Father was there somewhere, she thought, keeping an eye on his "investments," as he called the herd of cows belonging to the Applegate brothers.

"Sukey is there somewhere in the herd," Lucy told Irene. "Help me find her." She and her little sister looked for the milk cow's light brown body among the red-brown of the beef animals. Then she remembered Father had tied Sukey to the back of their wagon so she'd be ready to travel. She didn't tell Irene that; looking for the milk cow among the herd would give the little pest something to do.

And Babe, the poor boy. He was missing out on the fun of being with his friends and stood near the wagon, ready to be hitched with his three team mates. She hoped the pets were as excited about the coming trip as she was, but she somehow doubted they were. Nonetheless, Lucy felt a certain comfort that her two of her three favorite farm animals would accompany her on her trek with her family. She already deeply missed Rufus.

Despite the children's pleas, Charles's face had darkened and his eyebrows knitted together in anger as he adamantly roared that the family didn't need a dog to cause trouble with the livestock. The children had all known the subject was closed and was not to be mentioned again. When Father said something, he meant it. End of conversation.

It didn't seem fair to the youngsters that they hadn't been able to bring their Rufus when there were dogs constantly running around the wagon train, barking and causing havoc with the cows. Lucy sighed; Father knew best, she supposed, but she couldn't help thinking he was being a bit mean making the decision he had about leaving Rufus behind.

Strewn about on the seemingly endless Kansas prairie below her were what looked like far more than the thousand people Uncle Jesse had said were part of the 1843 wagon train to Oregon. The emigrants in their assorted collection of 110 or so mostly white-topped wagons gathered on the early-spring green prairie were an impressive sight. The people seemed to be somewhat oriented towards a dozen or so men barely separated from the large assembly of the Oregon Emigrating Company, as they called themselves.

Before they had left Independence, Missouri, on May 22, under the guidance of their leader, John Gantt, Lucy had heard Father and her uncles talking about the group meeting to decide on a set of "traveling" rules. Gantt would be a good leader, Father and his brothers agreed. He'd be aided by a council of men who would help lead the group and enforce and mediate any disagreements of the rules. These officers were to be elected now that they had reached the Kansas River, which was less than a week's travel from their starting place.

Gantt had been a captain in the U.S. Army, Uncle Lindsay had explained, and he had made his living in the fur trade. He'd been willing to guide the wagons to Ft. Hall in Idaho for $1.00 per person. The captain seemed like a capable sort, Lucy had thought as she watched him ride past on his long-legged bay.

Lucy admired the way Gantt sat tall in his saddle, his back ramrod straight, with a posture reminiscent of the commanding officer he'd been in the Army. She was sure the families were right in placing their fate in his hands as far as the wagon train's route went. There would be nine men elected to help him keep the emigrants in check in their daily dealings with each other.

"That will be no easy task," Uncle Lindsay had remarked ruefully, and his brothers had nodded in agreement.

"There're more'n a handful a' hugger-muggers hangin' 'round, that's for sure," Uncle Jesse complained. "I hate ta have the underhanded, sneakin' fellows along, but they'll come in handy when there's work ta be done."

"If'n they were children an' disagreed, Father's hand would put them in their places in a minute," Lucy mused in disgust. "And just why does it take nine men ta settle an argument among adults when Father can handle problems by himself? You'd think their brains would be bigger than children's and they could figure out their problems on their own. I guess their brains are just too little for their bodies."

Lucy was to find it would be the personal interactions between the strong-minded travelers that would cause more disasters, more hardships, and more grief than any other preconceived notions of problems for the emigrants.

The emigrants had crossed the Kansas River on June 1, and the crowd was abuzz with excitement, eager to learn who would lead the group for the remainder of the roughly 1,700-mile journey. Several names had been heard around the campfires at night, but Lucy didn't recognize many of them; they weren't fathers of her friends, so she'd had no occasion to meet them and she wasn't particularly interested. Father and her uncles would care for the Applegate families and that took care of her worries about that.

Lucy could hear names called out by men in the crowd below her vantage point, and she watched the nominees step out some distance from the expectant mass of humanity. She put Irene on the ground and clutched her tiny hand firmly in her own, not wanting her little charge to run away to join the group of emigrants below. A slight breeze was fluttering the long skirt of the blue calico dress she wore for this important occasion, and Lucy smoothed it against her willowy frame, straining to hear while scanning the crowd for the sight of any young man that might catch her eye.

She watched as the named candidates self-consciously separated from the main group; those in favor of that nominee formed a line behind him. Ultimately, the candidates with the longest lines would be the winners of the prairie election and would assume the positions of leaders of the Oregon Emigrating Company. Lucy's smile widened as the lines formed on the grassy carpet and Irene jumped up and down enthusiastically, a big grin on her face as she watched the excitement growing below.

Cousin Roselle joined the two girls on the knoll, carrying her two-year-old brother, William Henry Harrison.

"Such a long name for such a little man," Lucy laughed at her cousin as Roselle said his name and ordered him to stay put when she placed him next to Irene. The girls laughed together, watching the crowd below while keeping a firm grasp on the hands of their younger siblings.

As the four Applegate youngsters observed the gathering of emigrants, the leaders of the lines began to walk across the prairie, stringing out to allow for a better comparison of the length of the ranks. They moved slowly at first as their lines grew in length, then faster and faster until they were running slowly, the people following them keeping pace and laughing as they ran.

Lucy held Irene's hand tightly and laughingly ran with her cousins, moving to be parallel to the long lines of voters. They passed Dr. Marcus Whitman, who, with his wife, Narcissa, had established a mission in the Walla Walla Valley near the end of the Oregon Trail.

"Hi, Docta!" shouted Irene as she ran past, waving at the minister who would be helping to make the emigrants' journey a little more comfortable with both his medical knowledge and his pioneering information. Dr. Whitman waved back, a brief smile on his lined face, but he didn't join in the merriment.

"Was Dr. Whitman too serious?" wondered Lucy as she flashed a smile in his direction and continued to tug her little sister parallel to the lines of emigrants. She'd overheard Father and Uncle Jesse chuckling one night, when she was supposedly asleep in her attic bed.

Her ears had perked up when she heard that Henry Spaulding had proposed to Narcissa. The lady had refused and Spaulding had instead married a neighbor lady, Eliza. Later, Dr. Whitman had married Narcissa. The two couples became close friends and not long afterwards, in 1836, the Whitmans and the Spauldings had traveled together to set up the mission in Walla Walla.

"Kinda tight quarters for a slighted love," Father's voice from below the attic had carried a hint of laughter.

"Just a bit a' gossip." Mother's sharp voice had caused Lucy to wonder what the problem was. She had failed to understand what difference it made, anyway. She just felt comforted to know that Dr. Whitman would be on the wagon train to help the travelers. She only wished he would relax for a few minutes and join in the fun the group of pioneers was having.

Lucy threw her head back and laughed loudly at the sight of her Aunt Cynthia hiking up the billowing skirt that seemed large enough for a small tent. She was exposing her sausage-like legs crammed into high-topped shoes as she plodded along as fast as she could beside the mass of merrymakers, a large smile on her face. Everyone was caught up in the excitement, and Lucy knew they were forgetting the talk of what could lie ahead of them in the next four months. The crowd seemed lost in a few minutes of insanity before reality set in.

"We're votin', Irene! We're votin'!" Lucy laughed as she ran across the prairie, moving around larger clumps of grass and jumping over shorter ones, her full skirt held up with her free hand. Ellen and Susan had joined the girls and ran with her. Mary and Theresa Rose ran up to join the group of giggling girls.

"We boatin'! We boatin'!" Irene agreed, the laughter in her thin little voice reflecting the girls' merriment.

After the lines of voters regained their election-day decorum, the girls listened from their place on the edge of the crowd and heard that Peter Burnett had become captain of the wagon train. James Nesmith was elected orderly sergeant. Who either man was, the girls had no idea; apparently the majority of the wagon train members felt they would be good leaders.

As for Lucy, she knew she'd better find her family's wagon and quick; Mother would be expecting her to help with the children while she got the wagon ready. Leonard White materialized out of the throng of folks hurrying to ready their wagons, his usual wide smile lighting his face.

"Great deal a' excitement ain't there?" he asked, nodding his head towards the crowd.

Lucy and Her Manifest Destiny

"She was exposing her sausage-like legs crammed into high-topped shoes…"

"Purty excitin'," Lucy replied, twisting her body slightly to swish her long skirt. Somewhere behind her she could hear Ellen and Susan snickering, and Lucy's face reddened. She was glad she'd donned her good calico for this important day, and she flipped her head back, tossing her tresses gently in the spring breeze blowing the scent of young grasses across the prairie. Who cared what her little sisters thought?

"I gotta get back ta Mother," Lucy explained to the young man with a smile, edging away towards the general direction of the Applegate wagons. She reached out to her littler sisters and Mary and Irene each grabbed a hand.

"See ya 'round," Leonard said, smiling broadly, and, tipping his hat with an awkward movement of his hand, the sixteen-year-old disappeared into the crowd.

"I hope so," Lucy thought to herself with a beam, thinking the journey to the Oregon country was definitely looking better every day. Then, half dragging the shorter legged Irene and Mary by their hands and with her following of tittering sisters and cousins following closely behind, she hurried to find her family's wagon.

"You certainly took your time getting' back ta help me," Melinda Applegate scolded her daughter as Lucy neared her family's large canvas-covered wagon. "John needs dry clothin' before Father gets here. Make sure the others are all here an' stay by the wagon so we'll be ready ta go. I need ta get the rest a' those things picked up an' packed away," and she gestured towards an assortment of belongings strewn about near the wagon. "Get the children collected up."

Her mother gathered up the skirt of her long brown linsey-woolsey dress as she carefully climbed the sturdy ladder-like steps into the wagon. Lucy began rounding up her siblings. Susan and Ellen stood near the remains of the dead campfire, each poking in the ashes with a long stick and flipping chunks of charred wood at each other.

"Stop acting so childish!" Lucy scolded her younger sisters. "Honestly, you need ta grow up!"

James and Lisbon hurried to Lucy when she called them over from Uncle Lindsay's wagon. The boys were still full of excitement after running across the prairie with the crowd of immigrants, and they threw fake punches at each other. As they dodged and feinted in mock battle, Lisbon let his guard down and James made a quick grab for the back of his younger brother's hand. Grabbing a small pinch of skin, he twisted suddenly.

"Ouch! You twistered me, you big bully!" Lisbon screeched, looking at the reddened blister-like welt on the back of his hand.

"Get over it!" James admonished his little brother as he sneaked a look into the family's wagon to see if his mother would come charging out to settle the dispute.

Melinda stuck her head out of the rear opening of the wagon and scowled at the boys. "Seems you have some energy ta spend," she informed them. "James, pack those things on the ground over here so I can stow them away. Lisbon, you scatter the campfire around an' make sure there are no live coals left. Then both a' you boys fetch a pail a' water ta carry along with us so we'll have some at our first stop."

Melinda's head disappeared into the wagon and then reappeared a few seconds later. "And, no more twisterin'!" she ordered her sons, and then ducked under the canvas cover to complete her packing.

"That'll last 'til she's outta sight," Lucy thought, and was proven right. Before the boys began to do the chores they'd been assigned, James stole a quick glance at the wagon opening and then sneaked a hand over to Lisbon and left another twister on the back of his little brother's hand. The younger boy jerked his hand back quickly, but kept any burst of pain to himself; he apparently thought he already had enough chores.

"Boys!" Lucy sniffed and turned to her task of gathering her siblings for Mother. She took Irene by a hand and pulled the tot's other hand away from her nose where she had been industriously working her index finger. With tightly bundled baby John rolling from side to side on the quilt spread on the grass, Lucy had her three brothers and four sisters all collected.

"Eight little Applegates, all ready an' accounted for, Mother," she informed Melinda.

"An', being the oldest child, an' a girl at that, I'll be expected ta be the keeper a' the little brood that will always need ta be fed or ta have a smelly an' wet diaper changed," she thought. "Mother'll have her arms full a' baby John ever blasted wakin' minute a' the day."

"I s'pose I'll have ta try ta keep them outta the fire an' outta the creeks an' outta trouble. An' away from those strange Indians I've heard stories 'bout." She scowled at the six children fidgeting under her scrutiny. "In other words," she told herself, "I'll have ta help Mother keep the children from unintentionally destroying themselves through their own carelessness." She sighed.

"And don't you ever, ever, *never* get inta Father's medicine chest," Lucy ordered the assembled children, accentuating each word with a shake of her finger. James stuck his tongue out at his bossy older sister and Lisbon, watching his big brother, did the same. Lucy sighed. She knew that she was for sure not leaving all of her responsibilities behind at the family's two-story log cabin.

"I may as well be the maid," Lucy thought. She often wondered if her parents had planned for their first child to be a girl just so Melinda would have help with the ensuing brood of children, which Lucy was sure had been acquired to help her parents on their farm.

"Hello, Lord," she imagined Charles had prayed. "I want my first child ta be a girl so we'll have a caretaker for the rest a' the children. Then, I want a few more girls ta help her an' Mother, an' then I want a whole passel a' boys ta help me. Thank you an' good night." Usually, what Father wanted, Father got. There was no doubt in Lucy's mind the Lord would see things Charles's way.

Now, it seemed, there might be yet another baby on the way. Mother hadn't talked about it yet, but before they had left home Lucy had noticed her hurrying out the back door of their home, rushing to reach the side of the space cleared away from their home before she bent over, retching. Often during the day, Lucy could see Mother loosening the top button of her dress, pulling at the fabric, swallowing over and over as if to keep her nausea at bay.

"Looks like a baby ta me," the young girl thought, but she'd not yet heard her parents discussing a new addition to the family. "Father probly doesn't know yet, but he'll know soon 'nuff. I s'pose he'll want 'nother boy ta help him on the farm when we get ta Oregon. He'll prob'ly get a son, for sure, if that's what he wants."

It was beyond her to understand why Mother would want to put up with one more mouth to feed, more diapers to wash each day, one more cranky baby to cut teeth and keep the family awake at night with fretful cries.

"I s'pose that's where I come in," she sighed in resignation.

Lucy unwrapped the baby, replaced his wet rag, and then straightened John's long dress and placed him on his back in the little quilt-lined hickory-wood box. She loved her little brothers and sisters, she supposed, but they seemed like such nuisances much of the time. Lucy frowned. She didn't see why she'd want to get married and repeat her mother's life, sacrificing her own freedom to focus only on caring for a demanding husband and a challenging brood of little diaper-wetters and nose-pickers.

Lucy could see Mother quietly looking at her offspring gathered near the wagon, her eyes falling on each child as she accounted for everybody before the day's travel began. The youngsters could scatter until the nooning, they were told, but then they would need to hurry back for a second inventory, then again when the family stopped for the night. In between counts, they could explore and cavort at will with their cousins, but they were warned to not stray far from the wagons.

"Stay close enough ta hear me callin' you," Mother directed. After the first day, Lucy supposed Melinda would have to have a mighty loud voice if the children were to hear her calling them.

"You boys check with Father before you go galavantin' off. He might need some help."

"Yes, Mother," James agreed, nodding. Lucy knew full well he and Lisbon would hurry to join their cousins and put Father out of their minds as soon as they left their wagon.

After the initial trial of lining out the wagons and getting everyone heading in roughly the right direction, Lucy found she was enjoying her new-found freedom. Carrying baby John or towing Irene along didn't seem an imposition as long as she could be with her cousins and little sisters, keeping an eye out for the young men. There seemed to be no shortage of those; they dashed past on their horses quite often or they walked past on unknown errands, and Lucy had a smile ready for them all.

"It would be hard ta pick who is the most handsome," she laughed to her cousin Roselle. The eleven-year-old agreed with a nod of her head and a shrug of her shoulders.

"Boys are always sneakin' extra pieces of bread an' butter or pullin' my braids," she complained to Lucy. "I don't see how good looks can improve them any."

"Children!" Lucy huffed, and she turned away.

~ *Chapter 6* ~

TRAIL TALK AND BUFFALO CHIPS

A group of riders was approaching the emigrants, and the drivers of the wagons pulled up their teams and sat quietly, awaiting the arrival of the unfamiliar horsemen. Robert Arthur sat astride his bay horse, his mount's eyes fastened on the approaching group of brown and white pinto horses carrying natives on their backs.

"Looks like some of those Indians we keep hearin' 'bout," Ellen whispered nervously to Lucy. The girls huddled together near the Applegate wagon, brushing hair away from their eyes. The strong breeze brought the smell of sage warmed by the early afternoon sun, and Lucy supposed she would forever remember the fragrance of the shrub when she saw a native.

Captain Gantt rode out to meet the warriors, estimated by the men observing from the wagon train to be about ninety strong. His followers watching from a distance were apprehensive as he slowly but steadily approached the unfamiliar people.

"By cracky, looks like one or two hunnerd of 'em!" exclaimed James excitedly. "We'd better watch out for 'em. Get ready for a fizzin' good fight. It's goin' ta be a bad one." He and his cousins huddled together, peering out from behind Lindsay's wagon.

Lisbon brandished the pocketknife he held in his hand. "Just let 'em try anythin'," he declared. "We're ready for 'em, ain't we Sissy?" He looked at his big sister for approval, ready to defend her at any cost, and the excited young lad wiped a stream of mucous from under his nose and onto his trousers.

"I think it's gonna be fine," Lucy reassured him, a hand on his shoulder. "You'd better put that thing away 'fore you cut yourself or one a' us." She smiled nervously at the six-year-old's ferociousness towards the unknown strangers parlaying with Captain Gantt. Truthfully, she was also feeling more than a little apprehensive. She didn't think anyone knew what to expect; she knew without a doubt that these were the murderous heathens they'd heard about.

Tension built among those watching the captain and the group of strangers as the Indians gestured. Their horses stood shifting from one foot to the other, bruising the grass with the weight of their bodies and causing a grassy smell mixed with sage to drift towards the watching emigrants. One of the horses snorted and tossed his head; at the sound, James jumped behind Lucy and gripped her shoulders tightly, peering around her to watch the group of men.

"Get ready, Sissy," he whispered nervously near her ear. "Get ready for a humdinger of a fight."

While watching Captain Gantt talking with the natives, Lucy mentally tried to prepare a course of action should the Indians attack. The only place to go would be inside the family's wagon, and that would be precious little protection. It would be more like corralling the children so they'd be easier for the Indians to round up and carry away to spend the rest of their lives being slaves. Lucy's eyes darted around the campground, but found she couldn't come up with any other plan for shelter. With luck, she may not need to do anything.

The fellow who seemed to be doing most of the talking gestured towards the waiting Applegate family, and Lucy drew in a sharp breath and held it. She'd heard stories of scalping and she stood there trembling, waiting for the inevitable attack.

Then, Captain Gantt reined his horse around and, his body as parade-ground perfect as always, rode towards the waiting wagons. The group of natives remained where they were, watching the horseman ride toward his people, and Lucy imagined they were impressed with the captain's air of authority.

The captain would later relate the gist of his conversation with the warriors. They were a party of Kansas and Osage Indians and carried with them a Pawnee scalp, which was complete with ears decorated with beads. The Nines would all later make claims that they had seen the scalp, which had been divided into several pieces, but Lucy pooh-poohed them.

"The war party was too far from the wagons for you little hobbledehoys ta see any such a thing," she scoffed.

"Did too!" scowled James, thrusting his chin forward.

"Did not!" Lucy smiled. "How could you see it if you were hidin' behind me?" Wrinkling her nose dismissively at his claim to fame, she ended the conversation by turning to join her sisters.

"Did too!" her younger brother indignantly insisted to her back, and Lucy merely shook her head with exaggerated movements, rolling her eyes and relishing the opportunity to taunt James.

Regardless of the mutilated scalp, Captain Gantt agreed to give the Indians some food. He explained to Charles that one of the Indians who spoke English well claimed the party had not eaten for three days.

"Better ta give 'em the provisions instead a havin' 'em steal some cattle later on," the captain explained, and the men in the party of emigrants quickly agreed.

"Better 'n gettin' attacked, for sure. Best part ways with the natives soon's we can," Charles allowed.

The meeting up with the war party carrying the grotesque Pawnee scalp would be the only sign of a warring people the emigrants would encounter on their trip. Daily, however, someone would mention the shriveled ears, the withered cheek and the straggly scalp Captain Gantt had seen. The awareness of such a gruesome sight would reinforce the need for the wagon train to proceed with caution through the natives' land.

"And I did too see the scalp with the ear," James would remind Lucy each time he heard mention of the hungry group of natives. "Just 'cause you couldn't see it, doesn't mean I couldn't see it." Lucy would silently move her lips in exaggerated mockery of her little brother's indignant words and then turn away with a smile, feeling she would always be the winner in that contest.

The emigrants were kept in extremely loosely organized columns that gathered together when they halted for the day. Each night the wagons were driven into a circle that had previously been measured and marked out by a pilot, each driver stopping so that there was but a wagon length separating them. Men used the oxen's yokes and chains to connect to the wagon in front, making a corral for the animals. That the circle was formed by the wagons in such a short time, sometimes as little as fifteen minutes after the lead wagon had halted at the spot designated by the pilot, always amazed those watching.

As Billy Doak unhooked Babe and the other three oxen from their wagon, Lucy would grab her milk bucket and hurry to catch Sukey and tie her to the family wagon before she could wander off to join the other cattle. Bent over her milk bucket, Lucy would keep a wary eye out for the oxen teams as they were unyoked and let loose to graze on the blue-stem grass, silky prairie clover, and scrubby brush.

The animals that looked so huge lumbering across the prairie were even more intimidating up close. Their large bodies, covered with trail dust and bits of the wild roses and western snowberry shrubs they'd rubbed against, were streaked with foul-smelling sweat by the end of the day. Lucy milked quickly so she could get some distance between herself and the large smelly beasts.

Sukey was giving less milk than she had at home in Missouri, and Lucy could finish her milking much faster than she had before the trip began.

"At least there's still plenty for us," she told Mother. "An', the cream is still good an' thick. I'll put it in the churn an' we'll probably have butter by tomorrow night." Melinda nodded absently, glad for Lucy to take over the problem of making butter.

The slightly yellow cream would rise overnight to the top of the milk pail that Lucy had set aside after the evening milking. Each morning, she would skim the heavy cream from the milk and put it in the churn hanging from a peg driven into the side of the wagon. The milk was hung next to the daily pot of beans that would soak all day and would be cooked and ready to eat within an hour after the wagon stopped for supper.

The churn was a wooden bucket fitted with a tight top with a hole in the center that Father had drilled. To finish making the churn, Father had stuck a dowel he had carved from a maple limb through the hole and to this he had attached a wooden paddle.

It would take three days, sometimes, to get enough cream to make about a pound of butter, but the results were worth the wait. Lucy had to finish the chore of churning the cream by working the paddle up and down until globules of butter formed. The jolting wagon, however, had done much of the work for her, and she found making butter much easier on the trail than at home.

As Lucy, Susan, Ellen, and Mary towed Irene away from the family tent and towards a small thicket of rose and snowberry bushes so the girls could relieve themselves one last time before crawling between their quilts, they could hear the nearby thuds and grunts of a fisticuff. The emigrants had been told, among other rules of behavior, there was to be "no physical resolutions of differences," and though the sounds of the fight could be heard clearly, no words were being spoken in the cloudy night.

"Some folks seem ta be hard of hearin'," Lucy whispered to her little sisters. "Wonder who it is an' what they're fightin' 'bout?" She peered into the darkness that hid the grunting men.

"We'll just look for blinkers in the mornin', Sissy," replied Susan. "Those black eyes really show up, don't they? I need ta go now," and she moved towards the group of bushes.

"Just try not ta tee-tee on your dress again," Lucy begged Irene. "I don't wanta crawl inta bed with your wet dress on my leg."

"But it's so hard ta not have a seat," whined Irene.

"Get used ta it," Lucy advised. "It's not the worst thing that'll happen ta us 'fore we're done travelin'," and she bundled her skirt in her arms as she raised it and squatted. She teetered on the uneven prairie sod, looking at the night sky bright with stars, hoping no stranger would pass nearby in the night. This embarrassing position was definitely not one she'd ever considered as she'd sat on a solid oak seat in the family's backyard privy in Missouri.

"I never thought I'd ever tee-tee ta the tune of a fiddle," she giggled to Ellen, listening to the strains of the instrument somewhere in the ring of wagons. The girls broke into giggles, then laughter as they struggled to keep their balance.

"Girls! Control yourself!" Mother ordered them, and the hilarity turned to suppressed snorts as the girls tried to obey.

The sisters were to notice fewer fights as the trip wore on, and then the fracases seemed to stop – or, at least the girls heard no more sounds of fist fights during the night and they saw only an occasional blinker or split lip. They did continue to hear, though, for the duration of the trip, words of abuse tossed back and forth between the emigrants.

"Looks like the young men finally realized they can't drive a team if both a' their eyes are swollen shut," Father remarked to Mother after supper one night.

"No matter if they are in full-mournin' or half-mournin'," Mother commented. "Both eyes black or one eye black." She made a wry face. "They all act like a bunch a' hard-cases without the sense of a goose. They need ta quit actin' like hobbledehoys an' grow up. Maybe some folks need more work ta do durin' the day so they won't be so full a' Old Scratch when night comes."

Lucy and Her Manifest Destiny

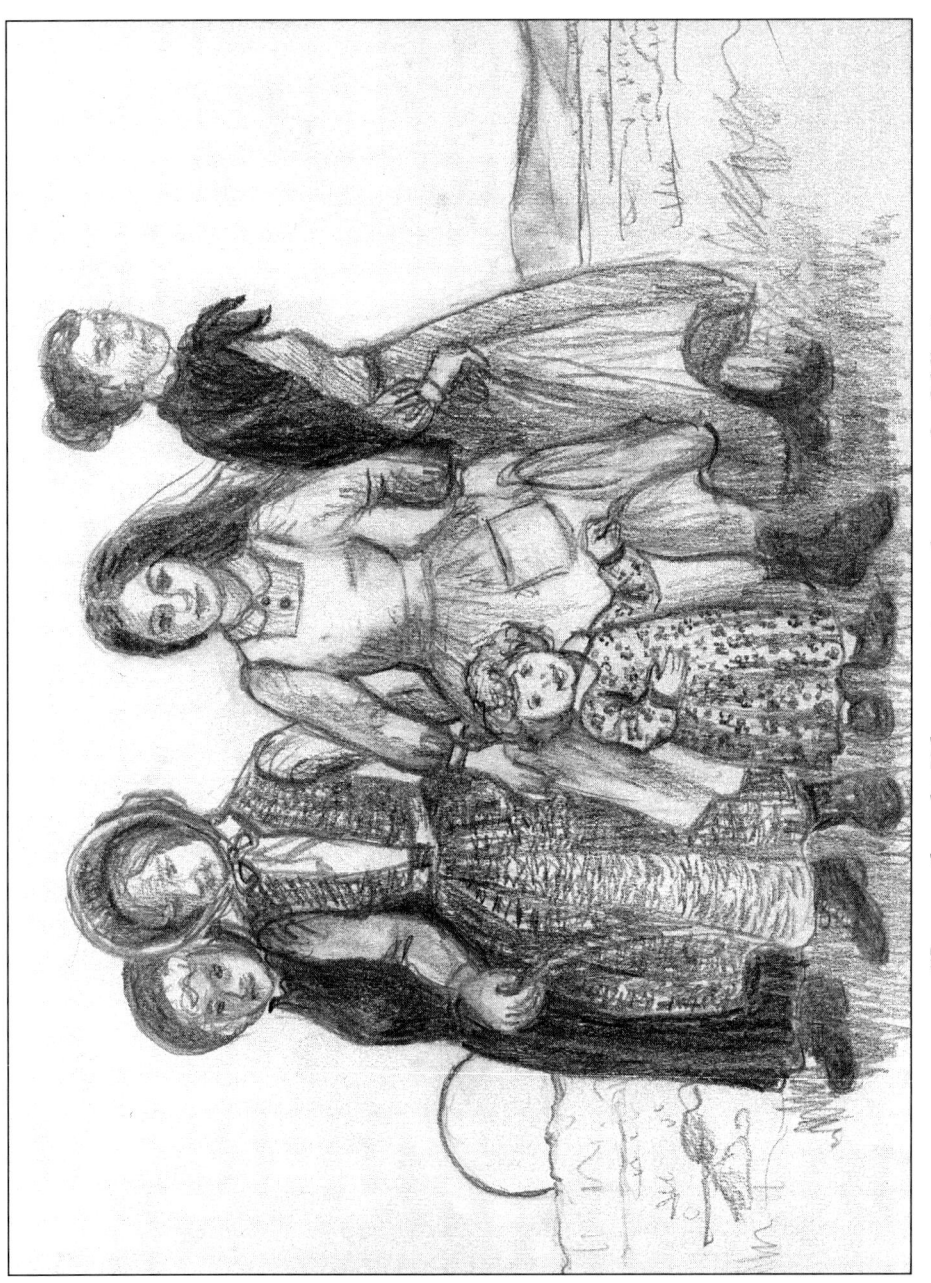

"*I never thought I'd ever tee-tee to the tune of a fiddle.*"

Trail Talk and Buffalo Chips

She had her own young men to worry about. Each night she rubbed salve on new cuts and scratches and dug slivers out of bare feet and splinter-festered fingers. Though the children's faces were turning darker each day and they sunburned less, they still asked for a dab of salve or lard each night to rub on their faces and chapped hands.

Clothing seemed to develop new holes each day and, for the first few weeks of the journey, Melinda automatically dragged out her mending kit each night after the evening meal. Soon, however, her increasing exhaustion and the sheer number of little rips and tears in everyone's garments overwhelmed her and she cast aside any attempts to mend. She reasoned that the Applegate's clothing was no worse than that of the other folks they were traveling with.

The young men weren't the only emigrants who couldn't work together without disagreeing. Lucy and her sisters and cousins heard disputes daily as they walked past the lumbering wagons or listened at a distance to the men guiding the teams of oxen. Certainly, her younger brothers weren't immune to fighting among themselves.

"Shut your bone box!" James yelled at Lisbon one day when his little brother provoked him for some slight unknown to Lucy.

"James!" admonished Melinda. "Wherever did you hear that? You're not ta use such language," and she grabbed her son's shoulder and shook him.

"The fellas all say it," James muttered, looking down and scuffing the toe of his shoe in the dirt.

"I don't want any son a' mine soundin' like a little saucebox," Mother warned. "Now hoof it on out ta Father and take him a drink of water." She dabbed at her face with her apron, wiping it free of sweat and pushing back the damp strands of hair that clung to her forehead under the brim of her sunbonnet.

Lucy watched James and his cousins fill pails of water half full and begin their trek out to the cow column. Father had said the cows were almost two miles from the family wagon, and Lucy supposed that by the time the Nines got there, they would have practiced every naughty word they could think of.

On June 8, after several heated discussions between those who had cattle and those who didn't, Peter Burnett resigned as captain. Lucy overheard Father explaining to Mother that Burnett had found that while their leader, John Gantt, had made several trips across the plains with small groups of disciplined men, trying to ride herd on a large group of independent-thinking emigrants who were unused to following orders was a different journey.

William Martin, who had been elected to replace Burnett, had little experience with managing a wagon train let alone a group of almost a thousand strong-minded individuals. There was just too big of a gathering of "gentlemen of four outs" – without wit, without manners, without money, and without credit – for Martin to expect harmony. He was to be reminded daily of the depth of the determination of the men in the wagon train. There would be much conflict among this group of strong minds before a truce of sorts was reached.

As Lucy and her family hiked across the prairie, they found they had best keep eyes peeled for piles of fresh oxen or horse dung. A misstep often resulted in the unpleasant chore of wiping the soft manure off bare feet with a handful of grass. Scrub as she might, the acrid odor of fresh manure would follow her until she could wash in the water of a creek or of a river.

She was glad to hear that the men had finally come to their senses when they decided the need for grazing for the animals necessitated the livestock be moved a great distance from the main caravan of wagons. Charles explained the large group of animals might travel as much as five miles away from the wagons some days.

The Nines looked at each other in dismay when they heard Uncle Jesse would move the cows even further from the route the wagon train was taking. That meant they would have to lug drinking water for the men even further.

"Best we can hope for, I guess, is that the men drive those cows close to water ever step a' the way," James muttered dejectedly to Warren and Edward.

"We won't have so many stinkin' piles ta step in," Lucy remarked to Roselle. "An' the Nines'll be too tired from luggin' water ta the men ta give us Old Scratch when they come back. Makes ya almost feel sorry for them." She grinned at her cousin. "Almost," she added.

Her cousin nodded. "A girl doesn't have ta be the oldest cousin ta figure that out." She wrinkled her sunburned nose and gave Lucy a teasing grin.

Father explained that the large company which had left Elm Grove was unmanageable, in part because of the need for grass for the animals and in part because of the group's aversion to all discipline.

"Too many hugger-muggers," Father told Mother. "Too many young'uns full a' Old Scratch. If they weren't so rambunctious, always ready ta fight, our lives would be a lot easier." He shook his head ruefully, hoping the decision to split up the emigrants would help prevent some of the fights that had been occurring. The wagon train was divided into four divisions and a captain and an orderly sergeant were elected for each.

As the Applegate brothers had a large herd of their own, Uncle Jesse was elected to be in charge of the cow column. He quickly learned that cows, no matter how skittish, were much easier to contain than the independent-thinking men who formed the wagon train. He would have about sixty wagons and a couple thousand head of cattle to be responsible for on the way to Oregon. Listening to Martin rambling on and on about problems he was having with the men under his leadership, Jesse appreciated his four-legged charges even more.

Robert Arthur, astride his bay horse, galloped up to Lucy. The warm summer breeze caused his long blonde hair to flop despite the tattered hat he had crammed onto his head. He pulled the animal that was covered with splotches of sweaty foam to an abrupt stop a short distance from Lucy. Sitting astride his mount, he looked down from his lofty perch and grinned mischievously when she hurriedly stepped back.

Uncomfortable with being so close to the unpleasant smelling large animal, Lucy tried to hide her uneasiness as she fished around in her mind for something to talk about.

"I'm Uncle Jesse Applegate's niece," she explained to Robert Arthur, wanting to share the important news of her uncle's assignment. "Or did you already know that?" She bunched part of her skirt up to hide a large stain left by a spilled plate of beans.

From the way the young horseman grinned down at her, Lucy realized he had known and she also sensed that he wasn't as impressed with her uncle as she was. She wiggled her bare feet in the grass, trying to cover what she knew were dirty toes, and she was at a loss for a topic of conversation.

"Uh..." she began, and then stopped. "Uh, what?" she asked herself. She rubbed some sweat from her neck and pushed a few damp strands of hair from her face. "What is there ta talk about?" She searched her mind for something intelligent to say, her face taking on a rosy glow.

"Mmm...," Robert contributed, and then fell silent. He pulled the reins of his horse to the left, then to the right, making the horse throw his head and pull at the bit impatiently.

Apparently Robert had no idea of what to say, either. He merely grinned again and nodded his head before reining his horse away from Lucy. A large glob of sweaty foam slipped from his mount's side and towards Lucy as he dug his heels into the bay's sides and thundered off across the prairie.

"Sissy's got a beau!" teased Mary.

"Sissy's got a beau!" chimed in Irene and the two barefooted girls laughed as they sped away repeating the chant.

"Honestly. They are such babies," Lucy remarked to Susan and Ellen, trying to keep a grin from forming on her face as she tucked her fly-away brown hair behind either ear.

Trail Talk and Buffalo Chips

"Hmmmm," was the only comment Susan made as she raised her eyebrows. Ellen wisely kept silent, though she grinned widely.

Lucy sniffed and turned from her sisters. "Funny," she thought, "how they are nowhere to be seen when there are chores to be done. But just let Robert or Leonard ride up and – surprise! There they are!"

"I think my hands will always smell like buffalo chips," Lucy said disgustedly to her little sisters, wrinkling her nose at the unpleasant odor of the fresher of the huge animals' dung. The heat of the merciless sun beating down seemed to intensify the unpleasant stink.

The three girls were scrambling through the cropped grass, avoiding the newest of the buffalo manure and stooping to pick up the flattened rounds of dried dung and tossing them into the large tin bucket Lucy was lugging. Until they had crossed the wide prairie and the home of the buffalo, gathering buffalo chips would be a daily chore, both Mother and Father had assured them. There just wasn't any wood available for the campfires.

Thwap! "Have a chip!" Susan chortled.

A lightly tossed tan-colored chip about ten inches in diameter hit Ellen in the back as she bent over a pile of the prairie fuel. She grabbed two dried chips of her own and threw them, one after the other, towards Susan. The little sister dodged them with a big grin on her sunburned face, and then she stooped to replenish her ammunition.

Lucy accidentally got in the line of fire and the handful of dried dung intended for Ellen showered Lucy instead. Some of the tiny particles clung to her sweating face and neck.

"Girls! Stop that!" Lucy ordered in her sternest older-sister voice. She brushed a dusting of the dried chips off her cheek and her dress bodice. "Honestly, you two are actin' like such babies!" The "babies" each responded with well-aimed rounds of buffalo dung missiles, hitting their nagging bucket carrier with a fresh barrage.

"You asked for it!" Lucy shrieked, and reached into the bucketful of campfire fuel. As the chips were thrown back and forth, they

Lucy and Her Manifest Destiny

"That's for skippin' out on helpin' with supper," Lucy shouted.

broke up into smaller and even smaller pieces and Lucy joined her younger sisters with giggles and well-aimed dung.

"That's for skippin' out on helpin' with supper," Lucy shouted and pelted Susan's back with a large disc of buffalo dung.

"That's for not helping Mother take care a' baby John!" she laughed at Ellen, and she covered her younger sister's hair with a well-aimed handful of small dried chips.

Fortunately, the excrement was aged and dried and surprisingly odor-free, not fresh and soft and foul. The fracas ended with the three sisters sitting in the middle of the battle scene, laughing and brushing the ammo from their clothing. Lucy wiped the sleeve of her dress across her face, cleaning the remaining manure dust from her mouth, though she knew there would be a dusting of the chips in her hair until she could brush it out.

"Back ta work, you two scoundrels!" she ordered as seriously as she could, trying to keep from smiling. The three girls began their gathering again, rested by their short break from work. They began picking up chips in earnest, knowing they needed to take a full bucket to their mother before the wagon stopped for the night and she would begin cooking supper. Lucy looked furtively around, hoping there were no young men who had witnessed her little burst of childishness.

"Honestly," Lucy thought as she followed the younger girls in their zigzag pursuit of the dried rounds. "Those two could exasperate Old Scratch." But, the diversion had been harmless and there was still plenty of time for them to dump their first bucket of chips and return for more. Later wagon trains would have to wander further and further from the trail to gather chips, Lucy supposed, and she was grateful for the abundance of the dried buffalo dung close to their route.

Lucy wiped a trail of sweat from her face as she watched her brother James and the other two of the Nines, Warren and Edward, gathering fuel some distance from the three sisters. The cousins could be really mischievous, but they were naughty with smiles on their faces, Lucy supposed.

She thought of how in Missouri the boys had been practically glued together. Nowadays, on the trail, the only time they were forced to be separated was when they had to report to their respective family so their parents would know where they were. The young men were often heard discussing their plans to share a farm when they got to Oregon and were old enough.

For now, however, the trio of cousins seemed to be content to hunt buffalo chips together and they laughed and made a game out of what seemed to Lucy to be an unpleasant chore. Lucy knew that at least once during their foray for fuel, a fresh pile of manure would be flung at a cousin, causing a short free-for-all with soft buffalo droppings. The boys usually ended their day with new waste stains on clothing that could never be washed clean.

"Edward, James, an' Warren, the chip boys!" Lucy dubbed them.

"Oh, buffalo chips!" James grinned, and then he silently formed the phrase with his lips.

"Don't you dare slip and say that "s" word," Lucy warned her brother and cousins. "You'll get the soap, for sure." She had seen James have his mouth washed out with soap when he had slipped in one of Sukey's offerings and had uttered the forbidden word.

"It's the same stuff, you ninny!" James reminded her. "Both are dirty words!" and he crumbled a large buffalo chip in his hands and sifted it into the breeze, grinning in delight when Lucy backed away from him to avoid getting the dried dung dust on her skirt.

"Buffalo chips" was the closest to prohibited words Lucy heard The Nines utter, and for reasons unknown to Lucy, no one ever corrected them. Lucy supposed there were more serious problems than three little sauceboxes for the parents to contend with. As long as the boys continued to lug their fair share of buffalo chips into camp, the families could pocket any of their naughty little sayings.

~ *Chapter 7* ~

How Much Father, Father?

By mid-June, with new leaders and new divisions, the emigrant train had settled into what would be as much of a daily routine as possible. No matter where Lucy would look on the trail ahead or to the side or to the back, there were canvas-covered wagons bouncing over the uneven ground. Lurching from side to side over irregular ground, stirring up clouds of dust and with the earthy fragrance of the grasses and shrubs crushed under heavy hooves and heavier wagons, the emigrants' progress was easy to see and smell.

Gone was the original mental picture of the newly outfitted wagons on the first few days of the journey, all lined out in organized columns, all traveling in orderly lines. The most that could be said about the group was that they were all traveling in a westwardly direction.

An unrelenting sun beat down on the travelers and added to their misery. Despite their mother's admonitions to keep their sunbonnets on, the girls more often than not pushed them off their heads and let them hang down their backs, enjoying the coolness of their sweat-dampened scalps drying in the breeze.

Lisbon began to ask daily, "How much father, Father? Are we there yet?" His parents soon grew tired of answering him and ignored him. Lucy followed their lead; the little man presently dropped his questioning and plodded alongside the family wagon, one determined step at a time. Lucy could understand Lisbon's questioning. After all, she couldn't picture how far a hundred miles were, let alone a thousand; how could a little boy of six be expected to understand?

Often when the sun beat down during the heat of the day, the younger children tried to stay in the shade of the wagon, making their pathway veer first one way, then the other. By late afternoon, their clothing was damp with sweat, their reddened faces reflecting the misery of their exhausted bodies. Had they known the daytime temperatures sometimes reached a hundred degrees, they would have been even more miserable.

The feeling of excitement and adventure was weaker than it had been the first week of travel and the feeling of the glorious adventure dimmed. Lucy could feel a growing current of unrest constantly flowing along with the emigrants, and she was no exception.

The scenery began to look the same every day. Rolling prairie covered with clumps of sand blue-stem or needle-and-thread grasses, accentuated with wild rose and western snowberry shrubs. Lucy tired of gathering the wild asters and silky prairie clover for bouquets, only to discard them within a few minutes.

Far to the south, she could occasionally see the peaks of an unknown mountain range breaking the monotony of the distant horizon. The landscape seemed as tedious as her days had become.

She knew that she was considered one of the children until the time came for a dirty diaper to be changed or a young child to be watched. Or, Sukey to be milked. Or, butter to be churned. She was left out of conversations between the adults, just as she had been before leaving Missouri.

Watching Mother and her aunts plodding alongside the wagons, Lucy saw they always had a baby in their arms, the child often nursing as their mothers walked. John was about a year old, as were Aunt Betsy's Lucien and Aunt Cynthia's Gertrude. Each of the women was carrying around twenty pounds, she supposed, and it had to be exhausting to pack that much weight.

"Mother an' the aunts have the hardest time a' this journey," she decided, speaking to Susan and Ellen. "How'd ja like ta pack twenty pounds for two thousand miles?"

"Father says only 'bout seventeen hunnerd," reminded Susan.

"Whatever," Lucy retorted, scowling and flipping her hair off her sweaty face.

With Lucy's encouragement, her sisters gathered large bunches of prairie coneflowers and sunflowers and presented them to Mother and the two aunts. The women wearily smiled their thanks and clung to the bouquets of fast-wilting wildflowers, along with their babies, until the girls had wandered off. One by one, the women let their wildflowers fall to the ground where they lay until they were tromped underfoot by a following team of plodding oxen.

Awakened at 4:00 in the dawn of June 18 by the night sentinels' discharged rifles, the sleepy travelers dragged their weary bodies from their beds to prepare for the day. Men and the older boys hurried to points beyond the perimeter of the encircled wagons to relieve themselves before moving to the area where the livestock had been held.

The herd of a few thousand oxen, horses, and cows had been night-pastured on the nearest grass, almost half a mile from the circled wagon train. The families had pulled close together the night before, following the established custom of chaining the tongue of one wagon to the rear of the next. The result was a strong barrier encircling a corral about 100 yards wide.

Now, in the early morning light, the livestock was moved towards the encampment, and team oxen and saddle horses were driven inside the circled wagons to begin preparing them for the days' travel. The men knew that they must be ready to go when the signal was given at 7:00. Those who weren't prepared would have to fall in at the dusty rear of the train for the day. No allowance was made for laggards.

"We'll get the yoke for you, Father," James volunteered unnecessarily. He knew Charles expected him and Lisbon to drag the heavy yoke beam and the two bows, as well as the harness leather, into position for their father and Billy Doak to place on the oxen.

"That maple yoke weighs 'bout sixty ta seventy pounds," Father had remarked, so I don't 'spect you'll be able ta lift it onta the oxen's necks for a few years. Ya need a few more 'taters 'n gravy under your belt." It took both boys tugging on the heavy piece of hardwood to ready it for placing on the team.

Charles lifted the yoke beam with its two arches carved out to accommodate the oxen's necks, and he balanced it on the two animals standing side by side. He then reached out his hand for the U-shaped bows, one for each yoke mate. Those he quickly placed curved side down around the team's necks, forcing the ends upwards through two holes in the yoke beam to hold them in place.

"Poor Babe. That hard wood is makin' his neck an' shoulders sore. He's a puller, though. I knew he would be," James said proudly as he gently ran a hand over the hide on Babe's shoulders where the bow had worn the hair away.

Charles stooped to pick up the leather lines and swore as he saw a piece of leather nearly worn through. He looked around to determine how soon the wagons would be moving. He reached into his pocket for his knife, quickly cut the broken part of the leather strap away, and reached for his belt.

"I don't plan ta eat dust all day," he explained to James and Lisbon, eyes widened as they backed away from their father and his belt.

"This'll do 'til I can mend it proper," and he replaced the missing part of the leather line by drilling holes with his knife tip and lacing the belt into place with parts of both of his leather shoestrings.

There were sixty wagons in Charles and Melinda's group, divided into fifteen platoons of four wagons each. Each platoon took turns in the lead and Lucy knew that while their wagon was second in line today, tomorrow it would be in the lead, which was the desirable position. However, the following day they would be relegated to the rear of the column and would have to eat dust all day.

"An' breathe dust, an' blow dust an' snot all day long," she thought wryly, looking at her soiled apron. She looked forward to the next wash day, which would be Lord only knew when. Handkerchiefs weren't an option, she'd learned the first few days of the journey; they were just one more thing to keep track of and the aprons could be washed anyway, Melinda had told her daughters when they complained.

"'Juh see that soldier over there?" James would ask, pointing to the left with a finger resting under his nose. "The one with a stripe on his pants?" and he would wipe the mucous on the side of his trousers and give Lucy a mischievous grin. His older sister would turn away, exasperated, despairing of ever teaching her brother to be a little gentleman.

Early in the morning, a few days after Father had mended Babe's leather lines, women and the older girls left the ring of wagons. Each one grabbed a handful of grass as they walked, and formed their own circle within a small grove of two-foot-high rose and snowberry shrubs.

Lucy remembered she had noticed the day before that her younger sisters had discarded their bloomers; they were in the way, they declared. "'Sides, nobody sees my bottom," Irene had explained wisely. Lucy continued to contend with the one undergarment she had left. She was determined she would be a lady, regardless of where she was.

In the dim light of the beginning day, the women held their full skirts outward to the side to form a privacy screen while each took her turn squatting in the center for her morning toilet. They broke out of their ring and hurried to their campfires to prepare a hasty breakfast and to ready their wagons and their broods for the day's travel.

She grabbed the family's milk bucket and rushed to find Sukey. She milked quickly, missing Lisbon who was still sleeping. Though the cow was giving less milk, Lucy would still give her little brother half a dozen squirts each morning if he showed up. He would gulp the warm milk, his mouth kept open for the next burst. Finished, he would wipe his mouth with the palm of a grubby hand and clean it on his pants. Then, grinning his thanks, he would scoot off towards the family wagon.

"So this is our grand trip ta Oregon," Mother grumbled as she tucked the cast-iron pot into the flames of the cooking fire Father had hastily built before he hurried off just at false dawn to get the oxen ready for the day's journey. They hoped to make fifteen miles that day and breakfast had to be eaten and the wagon train ready to move out shortly after the sun had begun to shine its early morning light on the prairie grasses.

Mother measured oatmeal into the simmering water, a small handful of the dried and milled oats for each member of the family, and stirred the contents of the pot with her long-handled wooden spoon. Suddenly, she clamped a hand over her mouth, handed the spoon to Lucy and hurried away from the morning fire. She could be heard retching violently just beyond the circled wagons.

"Oh, Lord! I'm not ready for this," she muttered to Lucy as she returned, wiping her face with her apron and making her way back to the cook fire. Lucy sighed, tucked her hair behind her ears, and kept stirring the pot of oatmeal. The hunch she'd had before the family left their Missouri home had been true. There'd be another little baby before Christmas for Mother and Lucy to take care of.

"Actually, for me ta take care of," Lucy thought ruefully. "Mother will have her long period a' recovery from the baby being born, an' then she'll start another baby an' the chores will begin all over again."

Mother had cooked a substantial supper the previous night, making sure to bake enough sourdough biscuits for breakfast and for dinner at the noon stop. She had learned that there wasn't always enough time for baking in the morning before beginning the trek for the day. Already, the emigrants had found that occasionally there would be no time for breakfast.

The noon break would sometimes be short and hurried, if they were lucky enough to be able to stop at all. At other times, the wagon train might spend several hours nooning so that the women could

How Much Father, Father?

"She grabbed the family's milk bucket and rushed to milk Sukey."

bake and do laundry and the men could mend harness or make other necessary repairs to equipment. Lucy couldn't figure out the schedule. The men didn't seem to know a day ahead of time just what the next day of travel would involve and the women had to be prepared for whatever situation might arise.

Whatever surprises the changing schedule brought, Lucy knew her part was rushing her little sisters through their morning jaunt to the tee-tee circle or to a convenient shelter of brush, rushing to milk Sukey, rushing to help with breakfast.

"An' rushin' an' rushin' an' rushin'," she thought to herself. "But, at least the rest a' the day I get ta be with the cousins." She thought a few seconds and then amended her thoughts. "Well, a lotta the day, anyway."

"Cut an' butter these an' give 'em ta the children when they come out," Mother ordered, and she wiped a loose strand of hair from her face and tucked it behind her ear. "And, it's time ta wake 'em up." She handed a pan of cold biscuits to Lucy, who was standing next to the early-morning fire, her eyes still heavy with sleep. Her hair was uncombed and her muslin dress wrinkled from having been slept in the night before.

"An' the night before. An' the night before that," Lucy thought unhappily, half-heartedly trying to smooth away the night-wrinkles in her soiled apron and skirt. For the first week of the trip, Mother had insisted that ladies wore nightdresses to bed and her daughters were going to be ladies. Then, practicality had set in.

With the neighbors sleeping only fifteen or twenty feet away and night trips to the nearest bushes often being a necessity, ladies had to put a proper wrapper over their nightdresses before making the trip to relieve themselves. That took time. Too, when the alarm was sounded each morning, the camp had to wake up and eat breakfast and be ready for the day's journey, often within an hour. Changing from night clothing to day clothing just wasn't practical.

"Change the baby while I pack," Mother directed Lucy as she finished dishing up the cooked oats and wiped the last of it from the

How Much Father, Father?

pot and flipped it onto the ground. "An' make sure the children all have lard on their faces. That might help with some of the soreness an' the peeling. If Uncle Mac stops by, you might ask him for some more salve, if he has any. We're out." Melinda wiped her glistening face with her apron; the day was already shaping up to be a hot one.

Lucy's face was dreadfully sore from sunburn, even as it slowly turned into a deep tan. Each day the soreness seemed to get worse, despite her trying to keep her bonnet on and her face coated with a layer of lard. The other children were the same; the boys seemed to take great delight in peeling the dead skin from their faces, wadding it in little balls, and throwing the soft missiles at any child within hitting distance.

As the children's faces burned and cracked and peeled and sometimes bled, Uncle Mac tried to rub his own special salve on each face, assuring the youngsters they'd soon adjust to the sun and would look just like little Indians. The old man's calloused fingers rubbing his magical salve on her face did make Lucy feel better, and it wasn't just her face that benefited from Uncle Mac's care.

His ministrations were the only time she was given some attention solely meant for her; at all other times, she was lumped together with her siblings. As long as she could remember, she had been responsible for her younger sisters and brothers, and there never seemed to be time for anyone to focus on only Lucy. She felt warmth from more than Uncle Mac's fingers and she always reveled in his gentle touch on her face, regardless of how sore it was.

Still not fully awake, Lucy stumbled towards the small family tent in the half-light of the dawning day to carry out her mother's orders. Lifting the flap, stained from countless dirty hands opening the closure, the odor of the baby's dirty diaper and the smells of the family crowded into a small space for the night filled Lucy's nostrils.

"Pheww!" she muttered. "An' I suppose Mother will feed us beans for supper again tonight." She grimaced at the thought; Father insisted the family sleep together in the small enclosure for safety.

Lucy and Her Manifest Destiny

Surely, Father would change his mind after tonight and allow Lucy and her sisters to sleep outside the tent.

"It's not fair that Father an' Mother sleep outside the tent," Lucy thought. They spread their bedroll near the entrance to the shelter and would roll under the wagon for protection from rain if need be, but they escaped the family tent at any rate. Lucy supposed the nights Mother joined the children in the tent were not her favorite.

As if to accentuate her thoughts, she heard a loud burst of explosive gas from the boys' side of the tent as Lisbon rolled over under his quilt and relieved his bloated stomach for the first time that day. James giggled and then loudly contributed to the rank odor.

"That's rude!" Lucy admonished the boys and covered her nose and mouth with her hand, a scowl on her face. The boys were neither quiet nor ashamed at the relief they began to give their stomachs by expelling sharp bursts of foul gas. One of her sisters joined in, then another and another, and there was a short, but enthusiastic concert as her siblings giggled and vented their night vapors.

"Children!" Lucy ordered sharply. "Stop that or I'll tell Father!" As she turned towards the door of the tent, the movement caused her to lose control, and she joined in the explosive chorus with such a resounding and unexpected noise that she startled herself.

"Children!" Father's voice boomed from near the entrance of the tent and he lifted the stained flap to determine the cause of the commotion and then quickly dropped it and backed away. The tent had grown instantly and deathly silent at Charles's appearance. Lucy stood at the door, humiliated. She'd been caught acting like a child.

She turned her head towards her siblings, grimacing and looking each one in the eye, shaking her head slowly as she did so. No one made a move.

"We have ta go out," she finally whispered in resignation to the silent children. Her shoulders slumped. Father would never forgive her. She was supposed to be an adult, and here she was, acting like a child.

The children each crawled out from under their night covers and slowly dragged towards the tent door and joined a waiting Lucy. Squaring her shoulders and taking a deep, if silent breath, through a mouth covered with her hand, she opened the canvas flap and stepped out to face the music.

Charles stood there in silence, a stern look on his face as he watched each of his disgraced children stumble out the door. There was no shoving as they huddled there in a tight group, ready for whatever punishment their father might mete out.

Lucy feared he would give the boys the belt, and she'd seen the welts the leather strap could leave on her brothers' legs. What fate awaited her and her sisters, she couldn't fathom. Being stared at by the nearby emigrants was humiliating; she knew she'd be asked later what the cause was for the early-morning discipline. How could she truthfully explain without revealing how crude she'd been? How unladylike? She hung her head in shame. She wouldn't be able to lie.

Her head turned downwards, Lucy sneaked a look at Charles and saw his hand reach towards his belt. It wasn't there. She remembered just about as soon as her father apparently did that he'd had to use it to mend Babe's harness. He had no belt; instead, he'd strung a leather thong between two loops in his pants, snugging the looseness of his waistband together and tying the thin piece of rawhide into a tight bow.

Lucy thought of Father whipping the boys with that limp piece of cured cowhide and she felt a burst of laughter building inside her. She hastened to cover her mouth and faked a cough. Peering at Charles from under her eyebrows, she thought she could see a quick look of amusement flick across his face; apparently he was having the same thought about the floppy piece of rawhide.

Father stood looking at his children in silence for several moments, watching their unease, knowing they were fearful of the punishment they knew they deserved for such poor manners.

"You young'uns need ta get ready for the trail," he finally said. "Grab a biscuit an' some oatmeal an' get your mornin' chores done."

He began to turn away and then stopped, and his massive head swiveled towards the children. "Tonight, you boys spread your bed outside the tent. You girls can leave the flap open so they can move inside if it gets too cold." His face showed no emotion, but Lucy could see his eyes dancing as he turned away from his brood.

~ *Chapter 8* ~

DUST AND DISTANCE

There was last minute frenzy as the wagons prepared to leave camp. This was the part of the day Lucy felt the greatest excitement, knowing how many tasks were required of everyone for the wagon train to spring from a dead sleep to travel mode in such a short time.

Standing near the family's tent, waiting for Father and Billy Doak to take it down and pack it on the wagon, Lucy breathed deeply. The prairie air was clear and fresh, free from dust for a few hours and, also, free from the loud disputes she heard too often during the days.

In the early mornings there was no time for argument between fractious men in the wagon train; for a few hours everyone seemed too focused on preparing for the day to spend time in disagreement. Lucy knew she was not the only one who hated the constant dissension among the travelers and she knew, too, the morning respite from the constant bickering was welcomed by everyone.

At exactly 7:00 each morning, the clear notes of a trumpet sounded over the prairie. The ringing sound always sent a tingle of excitement down Lucy's spine and she found herself looking forward to the melodious announcement that it was time for the pioneers to begin their trek for the day. The last note hadn't faded away before the wagon drivers cracked their whips over the oxen teams and they moved forward, the oxen occasionally bellowing in protest at the weight they were pulling. It wasn't long before the protesting animals quieted down and settled into the drudgery of the day.

Harness leather creaking, wagon wheels squeaking, a loose bucket thumping loudly against a solid board, the emigrants began to roll forward. The lead wagon was followed by the rest, though the drivers didn't keep in a straight line. What one driver found to be the best route might look too rocky to the next man, and the wagons each sashayed slowly on their chosen route, their canvas covers bouncing across the prairie, all rolling toward their evening resting place.

One of the wagons needed to make a last-minute repair and Lucy saw that it had been left behind to catch up as best it could. For the rest of the day, the poor souls making the repair would be reduced to traveling in the dust of the preceding train. The captains of the wagons made an attempt to rotate the wagons so each emigrant could take a turn being in the lead. Unfortunately, break-downs didn't figure into the lineup; the damaged wagon would take its place at the end of the line and would have to work its way up to the front.

Lucy and her little band of sisters and cousins strode as far to one side of their family wagon as Mother would allow them to. That was the only way to avoid the main cloud of choking powder. On this day, the dust-eaters would travel from twenty-five to thirty miles, the greatest distance they had traveled in a single day. Father had said they were about 270 miles from the rendezvous point in Missouri, and they were now on the great Platte River.

Susan tripped in a rut on the grassy prairies, and Lucy reached out a hand to steady her. "Where'd those ruts come from?" the irritated girl asked, steadying her feet and rearranging her long skirt.

"Father said the buffalo travel ta water every day. They travel in single file an' head straight ta the river. They have made the trip over an' over again, using the same route, an' these ruts are the result a' those heavy fellows playin' "follow the leader." Lucy grinned. "Father said that's what happened ta the wagon that didn't start with us; it broke an axle in a rut last night."

"An' I s'pose our wagons are gonna leave big ruts, too," groused Ellen. "They're far heavier 'n a big buffler."

"Prob'ly," Lucy agreed. "But I s'pose the rain'll wash 'em all away 'for long." She studied the pathway trampled into the soil by the buffalo. "Or not. Might be here a while, all right."

The girls squatted down near the path traveled by the buffalo and put their hands to the bottom of the rut, measuring the depth. Their fingers touched the bottom and their elbows were only slightly above the level of the sides of the buffalo path. Then, putting their arms sidewise in the furrow, they found they could comfortably touch their fingertips and their elbows on either side of the groove.

"Is that why Father has an axle tied onta the side a' our wagon?" Susan asked as she scratched first one itchy arm pit, then the other. "I thought he was bein' silly, but I guess not." Her dress was soaked through with sweat, as were those of her sisters.

"Father knows what he's doin'," Lucy assured her little sister. "Always." Then, silently, she told herself, "I think." She absently fanned her flushed face with her apron, relishing the bit of a breeze it created.

By noon the wagon train had covered an estimated twelve miles, the cloud of dust growing in size as it floated further and further back, increasing in size and density with the passage of each wagon. A heavy haze covered the last of the emigrants in the slowly advancing column.

An order from the captain was passed to the drivers of the wagons: stop briefly to grab a cold biscuit or some dried fruit for lunch and to give the oxen water and a rest, and then be ready to roll again when the signal was given. Today was a good one for covering miles and the emigrants would travel until there was only time enough to prepare for the night before darkness settled in.

Lucy and her four sisters made their usual tee-tee circle, their wide gathered calico skirts fluttering in the prairie breeze. Each girl clutched a handful of the softest grass they'd been able to find.

"Where's an elm when you need it?" Susan joked as she heisted her long skirt and gathered it in her arms before squatting down in the center of the makeshift circle. Her sisters joined her in laughter.

The girls remembered that the first day of their journey they had been eager to arrive at Elm Grove. Each of them had pictured a large stand of huge trees gathered together to provide a haven of shade for the wagon train. When they had reached the first stop after their rendezvous point, they had found one elm stump, one old tree, and one small sapling. Lucy and her sisters had been highly amused at the unsuitable name for their first encampment.

"Oh! A bee!" squealed Ellen from her place on the circle and she dropped her skirt and began swatting at the offensive insect.

"Grab your skirt, you little ninny!" ordered Susan sharply, unable to get to her feet quickly from her squatting position. Her face reddened at the thought of exposing her bare bottom to the wagon train.

Lucy giggled, and then Ellen, grabbing her skirt again, joined in. Little Mary jumped from one foot to the other in mirth, flipping her skirt up into the air. Susan finally gained her feet and reluctantly but helplessly joined her sisters in laughing at the incident.

"Boys are so lucky," she complained, and her sisters nodded their heads in agreement.

"In more ways 'n one," Ellen commented. "My bottom's sore from wipin' it with grass." Her comment brought knowing laughter from her sisters.

"Use your skirt, you ninny," advised Susan. "It'll dry." Ellen wrinkled her nose in disgust, but Lucy noticed her little sister seldom snatched a handful of grass after that.

"To be truthful," Lucy thought silently a few days later, though she'd not admit to Susan that she'd been right, "a skirt *is* much softer than grass."

James might have argued with his sisters about the luck in being a boy, had he heard them. Father had given him and Lisbon the nooning chore of pushing a small bit of grease around the hub of each wheel, using a stick they had found on the ground as a tool. Each day as the wagon train ground to a slow halt in the middle of the day, the boys would dash to the family wagon.

The young men would snatch a cold biscuit from Mother, take a bite, and place it on the top of the high, dusty wagon wheel to keep it away from the ever-present mongrel dogs sniffling past, searching for a drop of food. The boys would dig out a glob of lubricant from the grease bucket and dab a dollop of the heavy oil onto the wheel's axle. They always managed to get a smudge of grease on their fingers, which they transferred to their biscuit when they grabbed it to take a bite. The boys almost never had a noon biscuit without the taste of axle grease on it.

While the boys greased and the girls tee-teed, Father watered the oxen from a large bucket and checked their yokes and harnesses. The oxen's necks were showing the results of the rubbing of the heavy yokes, but it couldn't be helped. They'd get tougher as the trip wore on, he supposed. Meanwhile, he'd best keep a bit of salve on Babe's neck.

As Mother nursed baby John, she stroked dust from his cheek and Lucy could see her sigh. Lucy knew she was remembering the poor little mite left behind in Missouri. Leaving the unnamed baby in the small grave was, for Mother, one of the hardest things she'd had to do in her thirty-year lifetime.

Lucy knew all too well that Mother would never return to place flowers on her eighth child's tiny grave. She saw Melinda's lips moving and knew that she was praying silently and fervently for the safe birth of the tenth child she was carrying. Lucy supposed that Father felt mighty bad about the baby left behind, too, though she had never heard him say a thing.

"Men seem ta keep their feelin's bottled up inside more'n women," the young girl concluded, speaking softly to Susan. Her younger sister, also watching Mother, looked at her and nodded silently in agreement. Both girls sat quietly, wiping their faces with apron skirts they had dampened with water, enjoying the cooling effect of the water evaporating from their warm skin.

"C'n you imagine?" Lucy muttered to Susan. "Ten children before Mother turns thirty? 'Most one a year? Not for me, thank you very much." She daubed her damp apron on her neck, wiping away small traces of sweat.

No matter where she looked, Lucy could see women and children resting in the shade of their wagons. She watched them slumped wearily in the shade of the wagons, wiping their faces and sharing drinks of water from tin dippers. She supposed everyone was just as tired as she was.

Father walked up to Mother to get a handful of biscuits for his noon meal and it seemed to Lucy his feet were dragging in the dust, scuffing up tiny clouds of dust. He remarked that they'd made almost ten miles so far that day, and he seemed mighty proud of the distance they'd covered.

"No wonder I'm a mite tired," Lucy told Susan. "An' just think how tired Mother an' the aunts must be, packin' all that weight." The break was over too soon. When the lead wagon began to move forward slowly, the women and children got to their feet slowly and began their afternoon trek, one weary step after the other.

Lucy noticed the children didn't tend to stray so far from the slowly moving wagon in the afternoon as they had in the morning.

"Wish we all had horses to ride, like Father an' a lotta the men do," Ellen complained, and Lucy nodded her head in agreement.

"It'd be a long run for him ta get ta the herd, though," she said. "He needs his horse." She grinned mischievously. "An' the Nines need ta walk ta lug that pail a' water out ta 'em. Uses up some a' their orneriness!"

"Pick up wood as we go along an' put it in the wagon for our campfire tonight," Father had directed the children just before they had left camp that morning. His voice had seemed to take on an added gruffness since they had begun trekking westward, and his brows seemed constantly knitted together in worry.

This morning Charles had pulled back on his horse's reins, halting the animal for a few seconds before dashing off for the day. He had looked down at the youngsters scattered around his wagon, lifted his hat, and resettled it on his head. Lucy thought he looked as if he had suddenly realized the eight children belonged to him.

"No wood, no cobbler!" Charles had threatened in an unusually deep voice, his eyebrows pulled together in a mock ferocious scowl. Then he had grinned slightly at his own teasing before he reined his horse away from the children, his grin the first sign of joshing Lucy had seen from him since leaving Missouri. She supposed there was a lot for him to be worrying about, all right, but the slight show of humor from her father brightened her day.

Throughout the day, the children picked up an occasional piece of driftwood or a dried willow branch from the ground to toss up into the rear opening of their family's wagon. By the time the wagon train would make the evening stop, they knew the accumulation would amount to very little, but each stick would help.

The day was warm, the drive monotonous, and under the summer sun Father, who had tied his horse behind the wagon to drive the oxen for a spell and to give Billy Doak a break, nodded sleepily. He drove for a time and each time his head drooped down towards his chest, he jerked upright, forcing himself to stay awake. When Father's uncustomary rest was over, he gave the lines to Mother, who took her turn guiding the wagon across the prairie. Father untied his saddle horse from the rear of the wagon, heisted himself into the saddle, and rode off to the cattle herd.

Once, Mother's head bobbed sleepily down on her chest, her bonnet shading her face from the bright sun, and her eyes closed. Her oxen team ambled up behind the wagon she was following, which had been slowing, then had stopped, and she could feel her own team hesitate, waiting for guidance. Tugging on the leather straps to direct her team around the wagon in front, Mother noticed the driver of the team with his head on his chest, fast asleep, his oxen also dozing in their traces.

She knew exactly how weary the driver must have felt as he had slid into an afternoon nap. She'd let someone else wake him, and she looked at Lucy and her little group of followers and put her finger to her lips, gesturing to the sleeping driver. The children cooperated with glee, greatly exaggerating quiet footsteps as they tiptoed past the stilled wagon wheels.

"Let's pick some flowers," Susan suggested, and the five Applegate sisters, accompanied by Lisbon, veered away from their family wagon, telling Mother they'd be back soon. Spring rains had given the prairie vegetation most of the rainfall it would get until fall and the sunflowers and gaillardia were blooming in clumps of yellow and orange. There was an occasional blue flax blossom to break off from a long, fibrous stem and add to the bouquet of gaillardia. The children stooped to pick the flowers and tucked a blossom into each sister's hair.

A prairie chicken exploded from its hiding place near a clump of grass, startling Irene, who squealed and dropped her handful of flowers. Her sisters whooped in laughter at the sight of their frightened sister, each glad it hadn't been her who had been only a yard from the frightened bird.

"There goes our prairie chicken an' dumplin's, flyin' away!" Susan laughed.

Over the creak of the wagon wheels and the pop of an occasional whip, there could be heard the shouts of the cattle drivers herding the reluctant bawling cows and oxen that were stubbornly resisting the day's march. The horses and mules had seemed to accept their westward trek soon after the journey began, but not so the oxen and cows, who appeared to object every step of the way. It seemed to Lucy that they were always hungry or thirsty or tired, and she felt sorry for the young men who had to push them across the prairie each day. It was no wonder their tempers grew shorter as the days grew longer.

Dust and Distance

"...the oxen and cows appeared to object every step of the way."

The girls watched as Father rode towards the cow column led by Uncle Jesse. He reined his horse to the top of a low ridge where he could escape the dust for a few minutes and as he sat watching the herd below, he lifted his hat to wipe sweat from his brow. Lucy could see him absently-mindedly scratch an irritated armpit, and she imagined he'd welcome a bath. The advance scout had reported there would be an abundance of water for the night camp near the river, and the emigrants looked forward to a good washing.

From Charles's elevated position above the noise and the dust, the scene of the prairie below covered with an abundance of spring grasses was spectacular. Rose shrubs and snowberry bushes added color, and Charles could see patches of silky prairie clover on the rolling terrain. He thought of the men and women who were the backbone of the mass of wagons and livestock moving over the landscape. The whole panorama was comprised of individuals who independently had their own agenda for the move to the Oregon country.

There were the Applegate families who had left behind a failing economy and farming business and were looking forward to a more profitable venture in the west. There was the Burnett family, hoping to gain enough success to pay off debts in Missouri. There was the Ford family, as well as a majority of the others, looking forward to obtaining some of the land that was supposedly free for the taking. Too, there were those named and unnamed individuals who had departed eastern lands a few steps ahead of the law, hoping to leave their pasts behind.

Musing, Charles watched the wagons driven by the individuals responsible for the forward movement of the emigrant train meandering westward. He knew they were undertaking a journey that only the strong could complete.

The success of the settlers would depend on their determination and their creativity in meeting each obstacle that arose on the trek of almost two thousand miles over prairies and mountains, through thick forests and over treacherous rivers, up and down steep hills that even

Dust and Distance

horses would hesitate to attempt, and through lands dominated by what were perceived to be hostile Indians. The emigrants had to be a special breed of people to even begin the journey of unknowns. They had to have gut-deep pioneering souls and the determination to succeed; they were a special breed; they were men and women of destiny.

"This is the stuff we read 'bout in history books," he mused, "though I doubt anyone will give us much thought. Hunnerd years from now, all anyone'll remember is that we reached Oregon country an' began building it up." He sat quietly for a few more minutes, watching the moving wagon train and the stock below.

"Pretty lofty thoughts," Charles snorted, bringing himself back to the reality of the journey, and he tugged at his horse's reins to begin the descent down the sloping rise towards his brother Jesse. The grandiose picture from up on the ridge soon gave way to the actuality of the dusty grind of the daily movement across the rutted prairie. Realism took over as cows balked and bellowed, wagons risked breaking axles in the deep ruts, and disputes broke out between the emigrants over real and imagined slights.

Although he couldn't hear the words, Charles could tell from the angry gestures made towards each other by two young men mounted on prancing horses outside the moving column of wagons that the council would have a hearing after supper that night to settle a dispute.

"'Druther deal with obnoxious, balkin' oxen than with rambunctious young men," Charles thought as he pulled up beside Jesse.

"What's wrong with 'em?" he asked his brother, pointing to a wagon that had pulled off to one side of the route, the owner having pitched a tent and built a fire. This had necessitated the cows be driven around it; one more irritation for the day.

"Woman's violently ill," Jesse replied shortly, indicating the matter was not to be discussed. "Old sawbones Whitman is takin' care a' her." Dr. Whitman had proved to be a valuable addition to the wagon train and the brothers left the woman's fate, whoever she may be and whatever the problem, in the good doctor's hands. As for the

Applegate brothers, for now they had bawling cattle and squabbling young men to worry about.

An advance scout had marked a grassy stretch of prairie near the Platte as the place for the night camp. The lead wagon reached that point as the evening light was fading and the protective night circle was made. The creaking wagons slowing to a stop, the dust settling as the oxen were unyoked and driven to their night feeding ground with the horses and the cow column.

Evening shadows were long, the campfires burning low, and the children were taking one last trip for their evening toilet while the ladies made their final tee-tee circles of the day. Hearing the clattering sound of a wagon approaching, Lucy looked up and saw Dr. Whitman entering the camp. He was followed closely by the missing wagon that had irritated Father when he found it stopped in the middle of the cow column's path.

"All's well," the doctor smiled at Lucy's parents. "Mother and child are fine."

"Easy for you ta say," Lucy thought with irritation, thinking of the delivery of Sukey's last calf not more than a few months before the family had tied her behind the wagon to begin the journey to Oregon. The process of the birthing had held a fascinated Lucy spellbound and she had longed to rush to the moaning milk cow and offer her comfort but Father had forbidden her to enter the barn during the birth.

Crouched quietly in the early evening shadow outside the barn, she had watched the birth from her hiding place as she leaned against the still-warm wood of the building. She had clasped a hand over her mouth to prevent any sound from escaping. If Sukey's struggles and moans were an indication of birthing, Lucy figured she didn't need to have anything to do with the whole process, thank you very much.

Watching Dr. Whitman tiredly walk his horse towards his waiting wife, Lucy felt a slight twinge of doubt of the overall honesty of the good doctor. "All's well," she mumbled softly, thinking of the pain she had witnessed her favorite milk cow endure. "All's well, indeed."

Dust and Distance

The council of men handled the disputes of the day and Lucy could hear a violin playing "Oh, Susannah!" while young men and women danced on the uneven prairie grass. Mother had given Lucy a resounding "No!" when she'd asked to join the young folks in the dance. Lucy, tired from her day's trek, really didn't mind much; her request had merely been made from habit and she hugged John close, gently rocking him to sleep, and she felt a weariness creep over her tired body.

In the distance the melancholy voice of a flute could be heard as groups around campfires paused in their last conversations of the day. It had been a good day, with only one broken axle, a new emigrant had been added to the wagon train, and the council had just three disputes to settle that night.

"We need ta appreciate days like this," Father told his family, yawning and stretching as he prepared to leave the campfire for his bed. "There'll be some pretty tough days ahead. Now, off ta bed with you young'uns." Lucy and her four sisters crawled under their large quilt and the little ones were asleep before Lucy could admonish them to hold still.

The boys, their bed outside the tent now, wriggled only a short time before they were silent. The twenty-five miles plus that day had been an exhausting walk for young folks and Susan's gentle snoring and a little snort from Mary were the last sounds Lucy heard before she joined her little sisters in slumber.

Within ten minutes after the lead wagon stopped the next day, James had unloaded the day's accumulation of wood from the wagon and started Mother's cook fire. Finished with that chore, he removed his hat and beat it against his leg several times to rid it of dust. Settling his hat back onto his head, James grinned at the young men who were sauntering towards the family wagon.

"Here come your beaus!" teased Ellen, grinning at Lucy. She was rewarded for the comment with an elbow jabbed sharply in her side.

The girls had noticed soon after the trip began that there were several young men, unmarried as far as they knew, who happened to stroll by just before supper. Robert Arthur and Leonard White seemed to stop by almost every night.

The fellows would join Father as he sat near the campfire waiting for Mother to finish cooking the meal. While visiting, the boys would sneak flirtatious looks at the Applegate sisters and longing looks at the large cast iron pot of food nestled in the heat of the cook fire.

"I wonder what the fellows find more interestin', us girls or the food?" Lucy commented wryly to her mother. She was more than sure that any affection they may have was just cupboard love, the men pretending to love the cooks so they could have some of their food. Melinda looked at her daughter and reminded her that the way to a man's heart is through his stomach.

"Fiddlesticks! Cupboard love has no place in my heart," Lucy retorted.

When supper was ready, the children were called to the family's cook fire and Mother asked Lucy to ladle portions of the meat and vegetables onto their little tin plates and hand them a buttered sourdough biscuit.

"I declare, my arms are going ta fall off, luggin' baby John all day. He's a heavy, wigglin' little bundle an' I'm purely wore out, Daughter. I need you ta do the rest a' the supper chores for me." She sank to the ground, clearly tired from the day of carrying her youngest child.

As Lucy cared for the younger children, she was aware of the young men continuing to sit by the campfire. When Father offered them a plate, they eagerly accepted. Lucy gave them the same portion she had given the children, no more and no less.

"I'm needin' ta eat, too," she thought defensively. "Looks like Mother fixed just enough for us an' didn't add an extra tater ta the pot for comp'ny."

The nightly routine of the young men stopping by just at meal time continued for several weeks until Mother noticed their supplies were dwindling much faster than she had planned for. After she talked this over with Father, the young men were politely but firmly told the family had to ration their food if it were to last the trip.

At first, it had seemed unfriendly to Lucy for Father to tell the young visitors the family didn't have extra food to share. After all, she had seen the boxes in the wagon bed crammed with food when Father had loaded them in Missouri. On top of that, she liked having the young men around the family campfire.

She hadn't yet decided which one was the cutest, but it was amusing to listen to them compete against each other for her attention. Leonard more often than not just sat with the group, a big smile on his face. Robert seemed to never sit still, fidgeting on his rock seat as he tried to appear enthralled with Charles's stories, though Lucy noticed him sneaking glances at her from the corner of his eye. Surely there was enough food to share.

Deciding to check out her parents' honesty about the food supply, she inspected the food boxes. Taking inventory, Lucy could see how fast the contents of the food boxes and crocks were disappearing. She sneaked a few slices of dried apples and hurriedly stuffed them into her mouth and chewed slowly. She noticed a small number of little white worms wriggling among the leathery fruit and she carefully picked them out and discarded them.

Lucy had to admit to herself that, once again, her parents had known what they were talking about when they had decided to quit sharing their food so freely. She knew she would miss the young men around the campfire, but she was consoled by the fact that they had so far always managed to find her during the day.

"Mother, may I use the last a' the dried apples ta make an apple pandowdy for Ivan's third birthday?" Lucy asked Melinda. "It's June 24 an' his birthday will be tomorrow. I'm sure Aunt Betsy would be glad ta have me make it for her. 'Sides, I noticed there are a few worms in the apples an' we better use 'em up." Melinda agreed; she was glad to let Lucy take over any of the cooking she wanted to.

The first thing Lucy did the next morning was to put the last of the family's dried apples into a cast iron pot, cover the fruit with water, put the lid on the top, and hang it on a peg driven into the wagon box. By the time the wagon train stopped for the day, the apples would be soft enough to make into a pandowdy.

"That's the last apples for a few years," Mother reminded Lucy. "It'll take a while for any apple trees we plant ta produce fruit."

"Don't s'pose the Indians'll have any apple trees planted, do ya?" Lucy teased Melinda, and was rewarded with a frown of disapproval. Then, more seriously, Lucy promised, "I'll make the best apple pandowdy you've ever tasted. Somethin' ta remember 'til we get more apples ta cook."

When the wagon stopped that night, Lucy carefully skimmed off a few dead and bloated worms that were floating on the top of the apple water and tossed them away.

"Whatcha doin', Sissy?" asked Irene who was, as usual, underfoot as Lucy worked. Ellen and Susan always seemed to have something to do, far away from the work, Lucy thought, but she could always count on Irene being nearby and in the way. Mary seemed to always tag along with Ellen and Susan and that was just fine with Lucy; one little nuisance was all she needed to contend with.

"Chunkin' debris," Lucy answered with a mischievous smile at Irene. She drained some of the water from the swollen apples and nestled the covered iron pot into the bed of glowing red embers of the fire.

While the apples were cooking, Lucy mixed her standard dumpling dough in a large bowl, adding half a cup of sugar to the batter and another half a cup of the sweetener to the apples. She smelled the cooking fruit and then sniffed again. The apples seemed to smell rather bland, she thought.

"Does this smell right ta you?" she asked Irene. Her little sister sniffed and then wrinkled her nose.

"They ain't good smellin'," she ventured. "They need more smell."

"Spicy, you mean," Lucy told her. "They don't smell spicy an' good. Hmmm." She looked for Mother so she could ask her for advice, but Melinda was nowhere around the family wagon. Shrugging, Lucy decided to be self-sufficient.

Looking in Mother's cooking supply box, she saw nothing but salt and pepper. No cinnamon. No nutmeg. She sprinkled a few pinches of salt over the apples and stirred that into the dessert, but the salt did nothing to improve the fragrance of the boiling fruit.

"Hmmm. 'Spose pepper'll help any?" she asked Irene, and the little girl merely shrugged as she stood twisting a lock of hair around her finger.

"It's awful good in chicken dumplin's." Irene remembered, nodding her head.

Lucy sifted a few pinches of the spice on top of the apples, stirred it in, and sniffed.

"I think it needs more," she told Irene. "'S not smellin' spicy 'nuff." She added a few more pinches of pepper for good measure, smelled the boiling apples, and sneezed. "I'm sure that's a good plenty," she said nervously, and then dropped the sweetened dough on top of the boiling apples and covered the pot.

After the dumplings had cooked for ten minutes or so, she removed the top, smelled the dessert, and frowned.

"Still not smellin' spicy," she sighed. "But, it is what it is."

The younger children finished their dessert quickly and then licked their plates clean. Lucy hesitantly took a bite of the apple pandowdy. The dumpling topping was good and sweet, but the apples… well, the apples certainly were spicy, and not in a good way.

Lucy chewed her pandowdy slowly, her eyes misting as she looked downward, and a deep feeling of shame overcame her. She'd used the last apples the family would have for the next two or three years or more, and she had totally ruined them. She'd definitely kept her promise to Mother to make an apple pandowdy she'd remember.

She sneaked a look at the adults sitting around the fire sharing Ivan's birthday treat. They were exchanging amused looks with each other and she knew they were sharing her thought that pepper had not been a good spice to use in apple pandowdy.

"Fly specks, Sissy," Lisbon whispered to Lucy, a wicked grin on his face as he held up his spoon with a few specks of pepper clinging to it. He was rewarded with a frown from his sister.

"Mighty sweet dumplin's, Lucy," Father commented, and her uncles grinned and nodded in agreement.

"Thanks," Lucy mumbled, keeping her head towards the ground. "What else have they been untruthful about?" she wondered. Then, thinking the comment through, she decided the adults *were* being truthful. The dumplings *were* good; the apples, however, were terrible and the adults were being kind enough to not comment on them.

"Mighty good dumplin's," Uncle Mac agreed, nodding his grizzled head. "Sweet."

~ *Chapter 9* ~

BLOODY BEASTIES AND BROKEN DREAMS

"Buffler! Big herd a' 'em!" shouted an excited scout as he dashed towards the moving wagon train, his saddle horse dripping with sweat.

A group of a dozen or so excited young men hastily mounted their horses and angled off from the path of the wagon train, galloping in a northwesterly direction towards the buffalo. As they dashed across the prairie, one of the riders touched a hand briefly to his dilapidated slouch-hat and grinned at Lucy. She smiled back and gave him a quick wave, though she was not sure who he was.

She noticed the men leaving the wagon trail were heavily armed; there was constant worry about the Sioux Indians who had driven the buffalo away from the trail traveled by the emigrants. The risk of the hunt would be worth it, though, as there was always a need for meat for the travelers. The Applegates were not the only family whose food boxes were dwindling.

It was June 30, Ellen informed Lucy that afternoon, as the men returned to report they had shot some of the adult buffalo that had been located near the Platte River. They intended to skin them and use their shaggy brown hides to make boats for fording the river. Lucy knew without being told that every scrap of meat would be used to feed the hungry travelers.

Lucy and Her Manifest Destiny

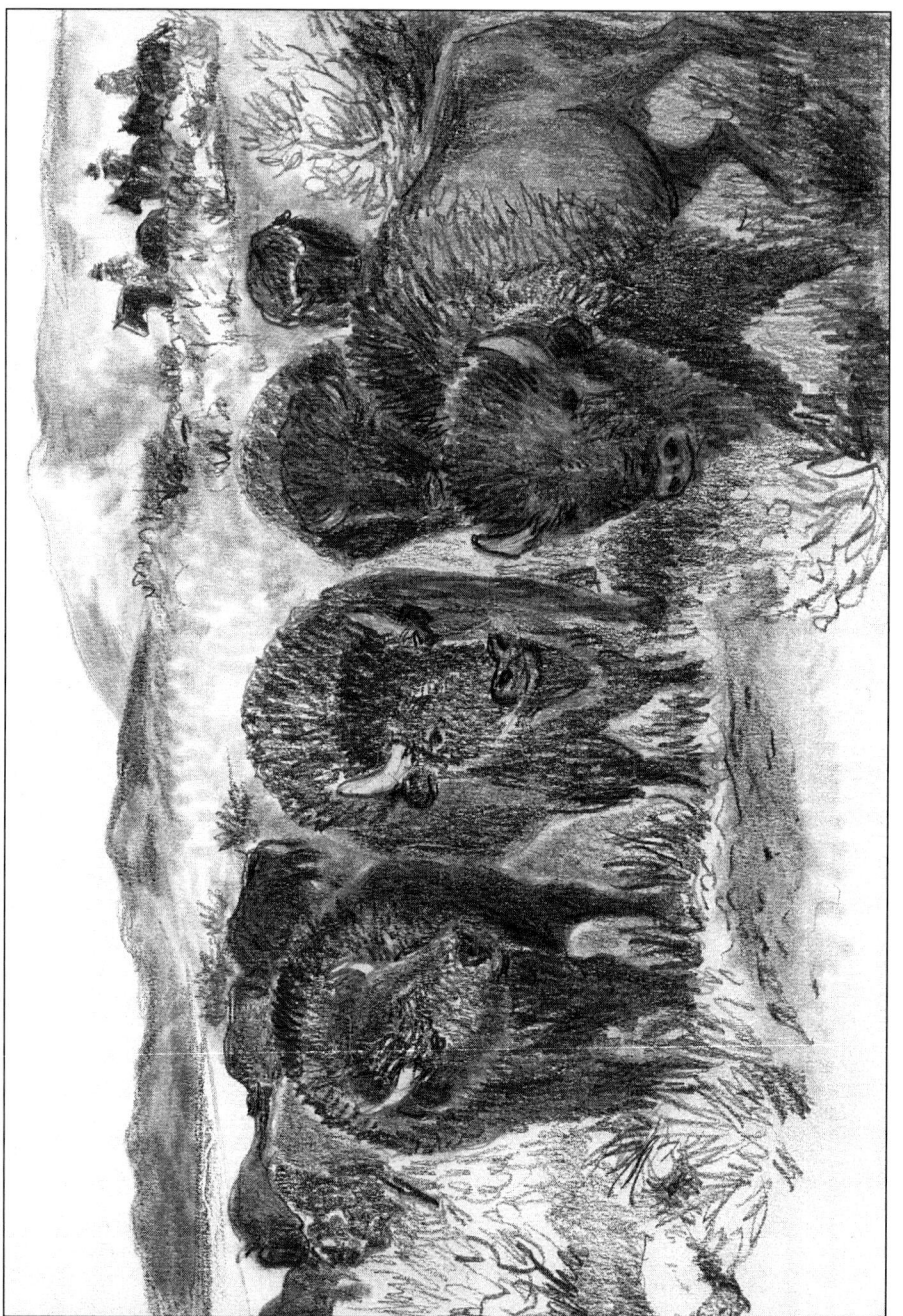

"*Buffler! Big herd a' 'em.*"

Bloody Beasties and Broken Dreams

When the stampeding herd of buffalo had put some distance between themselves and their fallen companions, the children hurried to join the hunters gathered around the huge bodies lying near a cluster of snowberry bushes in the bottom of a small gully. The wagons left their intended path for the day and trailed slowly to the carcasses.

Lisbon rushed towards the downed buffalo and skidded to a stop just short of the first huge animal lying in a heap.

"By cracky! They're big bloody beasties, hain't they, Sissy?" he shrilled in amazement as he marveled at the size of the creatures. "They're big bloody beasties, by cracky!" When he stood next to one of the dead animals, he could barely peer over the carcass at Lucy and his eyes widened in surprise.

Lucy and the girls kept their distance from the bloodied bodies, their noses wrinkling in disgust.

"Eeeee-yew! Those beasts stink!" Ellen declared, and the girls all daintily pinched their noses. "An', they are huge!"

"They're a tad bigger'n our old stewin' hens, all right," Lucy declared, and the girls tittered. They'd not been allowed to attend the butchering of large animals back home in Missouri, as that was not considered ladylike, Mother said. These animals were definitely much larger than an old stewing hen.

"I get the wishbone!" Irene declared, sending the assembled group of children into hoots of laughter.

The Nines gathered near the skinning crew surrounding the dead animals and each boy was fingering a pocketknife in the pocket of his trousers. Lish was allowed to pull back on the large hind leg of a huge shaggy carcass bloodied from several gunshot wounds. He leaned backwards and pulled fruitlessly with all his might, his feet slipping time and again on the slick grass. He was grunting with his efforts until Uncle Lindsay took pity on him and, grinning at his son's efforts, helped Lish pull back on the leg.

The men worked to slit the soft belly skin open and spread the cavity wide to expose the still warm intestines. An unpleasant odor rushed from a gut that was inadvertently gouged with a sharp skinning knife, and the digested grass spewed over the opened cavity.

A big glob of blood splattered on Warren's face, and, grinning, he swiped at it with his forefinger and wiped some on James's and Edward's foreheads, giving the Applegate cousins identical streaks of red. The three lads began to shuffle in a circle, tapping their hands over their mouths as they chanted nonsense words, acting out their version of the Indian dance they'd heard the men discuss. Father stopped them with a frown; the men had serious work to do and the young folks needed to quit their nonsense and give the butchers room.

After the adults had removed the thick hides, they were dragged away from the bloody carcasses. A second group began preparing the skins, scraping the larger bits of flesh and fat from near the edges of the still warm pelts in order to make the job of punching holes for leather laces easier. That job would come later in the day, after the daily routine maintenance had been done on wagons and harnesses.

A half dozen bloodied young men butchered the dead animals, cutting up the meat and dividing it among a long stream of waiting children. The youngsters took on an air of importance as they lugged pots full of the still warm flesh to the women waiting in camp.

When all the usable parts of the animals had been tended to and the men had left for other jobs that needed to be done, the Nines, with expectant grins on their faces, kneeled by the piles of glistening intestines. They began sawing on the refuse, tossing pieces to the dogs gathered around the carcasses.

"Let's make a ball!" suggested James, the ringleader of the Nines, "just like Father did when we butchered our pigs last fall." He reached for a bladder half-full of urine and then held on to the slippery orb while his cousin Warren sawed across the tough tube connecting it to the carcass.

"Phew! Stinko!" Edward wrinkled his nose as he squeezed the remaining urine onto the grass, splattering his cousins' pant legs and shoes with the pale yellow liquid. The three young men set the bladder aside and began probing a second pile of intestines, then a third, looking for more bladders. Their pocketknives got a workout as they scraped bits of flesh and fat from the tough outer membrane of the bladders until they were satisfied with the results.

The Nines had drawn an appreciative audience of younger boys and were rewarded with comments of disgust and admiration. Finally tiring of the cleaning of the buffalo bladder he was working on, Edward glanced at James, then at Warren to see if they were ready to blow into their bladders to make a ball. Each of the three hesitated to put the cold, gristly, wet mass to their mouth, each waiting for the others to make the first attempt.

"Dare ya!" James said, knowing that Warren wouldn't pass up a dare. The crowd of admiring boys watched as Warren put the small opening of the bladder to his mouth. He blew. And blew. And blew. His cheeks puffed out until they hurt, his face turned red, his eyes watered, and an enormous snort of air and mucus escaped through his nose as his body shook from his efforts.

"Here! Let a man help you!" scoffed Edward, and he put Warren's clammy limp bladder to his lips. Blow as he might, however, the sagging bag continued to flop down. James took a turn, as did another young man, then another, but to no avail.

"Not as easy to blow up as a pig bladder," Edward said in disgust. "Who needs a ball anyway?" and he tossed the flaccid organ onto the pile of entrails where a camp dog sniffed it, then hoisted a leg to mark the reject as his own. The gathered boys giggled and turned from the piles of offal to find other means of amusement.

Lucy and her female entourage had been keeping well away from the butchering, not wanting to get involved with all the blood and guts and hides. After the boys were out of sight somewhere in the willows lining the riverbank, Lucy looked at Susan and Rosella questioningly. Not a word was spoken, but each of the girls gathered up her long skirt and slowly approached the large piles of discarded innards, carefully avoiding the patches of blood scattered around in the grass.

Susan wrinkled up her nose but took a step closer; Ellen followed and Lucy was right beside her. Mary and Theresa Rose bravely

Lucy and Her Manifest Destiny

pushed past the older girls and, bending over, reached out to touch a long green intestine glistening in the afternoon sunshine.

"Oooh! It's slimy!" Mary squealed. Jumping back from the offending object, she slipped in a pooled spot of gore and sat with a thump on the blood-spattered grass. Lucy jerked her to her feet, but not before the skirt of her little sister's dress had acquired a large blood stain.

"For a seven-year-old, you sure are a ninny!" admonished Lucy. "Off to the river with you," and she grasped Mary's hand firmly in her own, leading her to the Platte to wash her skirt. The other girls followed into the shallow water near the bank and soon they were all washing their skirts and splashing the water on themselves and at each other.

Their shrieks of laughter brought Mother and Aunt Betsy to the river and Lucy spied the women with a guilty start.

"Sounds like you're havin' fun, Daughter," Melinda said, a fleeting smile flickering across her face. She nodded her head in approval and jiggled baby John as she talked. "Best enjoy yourself while you can."

Irene ran up to her mother, her skirt gathered up in one hand and a river mussel in the other. The large smile on her face showed her delight in finding the freshwater shellfish, and Melinda reached out to take it.

"Best put it back in the river," she advised her little daughter. "It would miss its mother if you take it away from its home."

Lucy saw a look of sadness flit across Mother's face and she knew Melinda was thinking of her own mother whom she would never again see. A pang of sympathy filled Lucy.

She felt a twinge of guilt as she thought of the fun she was having. Perhaps Mother would begin enjoying the adventure soon, she hoped. She'd attempt to help her as much as she could and try to make the trip easier for her and for the unborn child she was carrying. This afternoon, however, she planned to just be one of the young'uns and enjoy the break from traveling.

The sun had moved low in the western sky the day of the buffalo hunt. Half a dozen men worked on the freshly skinned hides, using awls to punch holes in the tough pelts and sometimes in their own fingers, resulting in a few explosive curses. Warren grinned at James, and Lucy knew that the Nines would be adding a few new words to their trail vocabulary.

"Why is it that the naughty words seem ta have a catchy ring ta 'em?" she thought wryly, as she found herself repeating some of the words in her mind, though she had no idea exactly what they meant. She supposed she might just save a few of them in the back of her mind to pull out and use when the right occasion arose.

After a sufficient number of holes had been punched in the buffalo hides, the men laced the pelts together with thin strips of cowhide. Other men worked at making boats by covering wagon beds with the pelts, flesh side out. A few cow skins taken from animals that had died on the trail were added to the boat-making effort.

"There's old Sam," James said, pointing to one of the cow hides. "I'd know his brindled hide anywhere."

"Least, he can do a little more good," Edward nodded wisely. "Those streaks a' black in his gray hair give the boat a bit of class."

The Nines discussed for a few minutes the fact that nothing on the trail was wasted, though a great deal had been discarded. "Guess we're learnin' what's necessary an' what's not," James pointed out. "I'd better hoof it ta camp when Father calls. I'd hate ta have him decide I'm not useful an' leave me beside the trail!" The cousins guffawed loudly at James's wit and Warren punched his cousin's arm lightly before resuming his observation of the men.

Watching her brothers and cousins, Lucy perceived that their trousers and shirts were decidedly the worse for wear, the trials of the trail obvious. Rips and tears in their garments had not been mended and trousers were being washed only when the boys swam or played in the river water. A grin flitted across Lucy's face.

"That is, unless the boys decide to go skinny-dipping an' leave their dirty britches on the bank."

No one had taken the time or energy to cut hair and the boys' heads were all topped with unruly shocks of blond, brown or black. Faces were tanned and many had lighter patches where sunburn scabs had been picked and torn off.

"It's a sorry looking bunch," she told Ellen, nodding her head towards the group of boys. "Their sit-upons have a lot a' flags a' distress pokin' out, don't they? She pointed to the shirt-tail sticking through a hole in Warren's trousers.

"It'll get worse, I'm thinkin'," remarked Susan. "It'll get worse," and she scuffed a dirty bare foot on the ground, rubbing away some flakes of loose skin from her heel. "'Sides, have you looked in a mirror lately?" she asked her older sister. Lucy frowned. She hadn't, nor did she want to.

For some of the boats, a willow frame was used for the rims and the ribs, and fresh hides were stretched over these. Left in the sun for the hides to dry and shrink, the relatively waterproof conveyances became known as buffalo boats. Some of the canoe-like boats were lashed together to make a raft. Once loaded with the emigrants' wagons, the rafts would be attached to long ropes and towed across the river by horses and young men.

The weather was pleasant and while the men were occupied with the making of the buffalo boats and the crossing of the South Platte, the women made use of the lay-over to do laundry, mending, baking, drying of some of the buffalo meat, and visiting.

The children played in the only grove of trees they had found on the banks of the Platte River. The cottonwoods and willows provided firewood for the camp and stick horses for the youngsters to ride while galloping madly through the camp among the cook fires. Sometimes their flexible steeds knocked about pots and pans and caused havoc around the campfires. However, the weather was pleasant and mothers were getting sufficient rest so the rambunctious youngsters were merely shooed away with admonitions to keep their horses under better control.

As Charles poked the last of the evening firewood towards the center of the dwindling flames, Lucy overheard Mr. Nesmith proudly tell him that Mr. Stewart had been presented with a daughter, though he made no mention of the mother.

"Seems men take the credit for everythin'; surely, Mrs. Stewart had a major role in the episode, hadn't she?" Lucy thought wryly, watching the two men visit. Father's face had seemed to merely darken during the journey while Mr. Nesmith's had taken on a ruddy color interrupted by patches of peeling skin. Regardless of the changes in their appearances, it was apparent to Lucy there had been no changes in what was expected of their wives.

Mr. Nesmith grew serious, shaking his head from side to side as he shared the news that a rifle had accidentally gone off when a careless sentinel had mishandled it, and the shot had broken a mule's neck. This was the most serious accident that had occurred so far on the trip from the reckless use of firearms, he declared.

"Judging from the way a lot a' folks handle their rifles, more accidents had not occurred because a' great good luck, not by precaution," Mr. Nesmith observed.

"You've got a point there," Father agreed. "Sometimes I think we're our own worst enemy, though I think we best keep an eye out for the Indians. They aren't slackers, for sure. They work hard 'nough ta make a livin', all right." He thought quietly for a minute and then grinned. "Even if it's a livin' from us," he added.

The sentinels had been keeping their eyes peeled for the natives and though the wagon train had not been attacked, as had been feared would happen, several cows and horses had been driven off by the natives and then had been returned for a payment.

"They're pretty good businessmen, aren't they?" Uncle Lindsey groused, though he had no choice but to pay the ransom for his livestock.

Lucy wondered, as she saw Father gather some coins from his hoard in the wagon to give to the Indians, just how much money there was left in the box. Surely, there would be plenty to finish their journey to the western part of the Oregon territory. But, then again, maybe not. Who knew what unknown expenses would come up? She certainly had no idea. She knew Father had a pretty good handle on everything so far, but it seemed there were many little surprises on the trail that were causing the lines on Father's face to deepen.

"Or, maybe it's just the dust is gettin' ground deeper an' deeper inta his face," Lucy concluded, "an' that's makin' the wrinkles stand out more." She rubbed at her own face and was rewarded with small snakes of dust rolling into her hand. Disgusted, she wiped the dirt onto her skirt.

"I don't suppose I'll ever really, really be clean again," she complained to Ellen. Her younger sister replied by rubbing her hands across her own face and presenting Lucy with a dozen dirt-snakes, smiling drolly as she did so.

The few Indians the emigrants encountered appeared to be somewhat shy, though friendly. This train was the first that had crossed the plains, with the exception of eleven wagons the year before, and the natives and the emigrants shared a natural curiosity.

The Nines were itching to get closer to the strangers, hoping to inspect their clothing which looked disappointingly like rejects from the white men. Too, they were curious about how the native children's lives differed from their own, but their parents ordered them to stay well away from the unfamiliar people. Mother and Father warned the children to not wander far from the encampment for fear the Indians may be interested in hauling off little light-haired children.

"Somewhere in a teepee on the prairie an Indian mother is prob'ly tellin' her children ta stay away from the people in the wagon train 'cause they might kidnap little dark-haired children an' haul them away in the strange boxes on wheels," Lucy joked.

Melinda frowned as she smoothed her hair back into the ever-present bun at the nape of her neck, settled her bonnet more firmly on her head, and gave Lucy a stern look that put an end to the teasing.

The Fourth of July was celebrated with the emigrants swimming and fording the Platte, moving their wagons and stock across the river which flowed in a fairly straight west-east direction. The men found that the buffalo boats proved to be adequate for ferrying the emigrants across the waterway.

"Old Sam is helpin' us one last time," Lucy remarked to Ellen, pointing out a hide on the buffalo boat being loaded with a wagon. "His brindled hide adds a bit a' color ta the brown boats, doesn't it?" With the vision of the little Zachary boy still vividly in her mind, Lucy breathed easier when the last wagon had made the crossing with no mishaps.

"Thanks, Sam," she thought.

~ *Chapter 10* ~

PAIN AND LOSS

"We're 'bout 400 miles from Independence," Charles told Melinda as he sat eating supper. He wiped the last of the bean juice from his plate with a crust of bread and settled back for a rare visit with his family before he began his nightly after-supper rounds. To Lucy, his voice seemed filled with a hint of self-importance at being part of the first major effort to travel to the Oregon country.

Mother sat quietly, as usual, nursing the fretting baby John and making no comment. She occasionally rotated a shoulder, trying to ease some of the soreness caused by lugging the heavy child all day.

"Even baby John is gettin' tired a' this manifest destiny," Lucy thought silently, watching the fretting child. "An' I don't s'pose he cares 'bout being written down in the history books, for sure."

James, sitting on the far side of the fire, suddenly began pulling himself backwards with his hands as he dug his heels into the ground and pushed. Lucy giggled. Her younger brother looked like an inverted spider, and she knew that was what he must have seen. James didn't fear much, but for some reason the tiny creatures scared him nearly half to death and could always make him run a Missouri mile without stopping. Lisbon stomped on the tiny offender and grinned

Pain and Loss

at James, who gave him silent thanks. A sheepish look covered his face, and Lucy grinned.

"James's fear of spiders might just come in handy someday," she thought to herself.

Lucy's attention went from her brothers and back to her father. Listening from her seat on the ground, she felt a great pride in him as she watched his face lighted by the flickering orange flames of the family campfire, but she felt that his appearance wasn't as impressive as his actions.

The coat Father wore day and night was showing the effects of the journey; dust and dirt coated the shoulders and the back, those places where Charles's hands couldn't handily reach as he swatted at himself to remove the dust each night. She noticed a few three-cornered tears in the front of his coat. A larger one on an elbow seemed to strain downward to meet the garment's worn cuff, and Lucy knew there was a long slash on the back of Father's coat that exposed the wool lining.

"There's more'n a fair amount of hugger-muggers in our group," Charles remarked ruefully. "An', there are those that are as poor as Job's turkey always trying ta cabbage onto somethin' that isn't theirs."

Father shifted his weight to rest more comfortably on the flat rock he was perched upon. Lucy wondered if the grimace that passed quickly over his face was from his sit-upons grinding into the hard rock or from remembering some of the rambunctious fellows and their antics.

"Maybe a tad bit a' both," she thought.

"We've been on the trail long enough that folks oughta be lined out an' things oughta go smooth," Father continued. "Other than the constantly laggin' herd a' cows slowin' us down an' the few river crossin's which took time, we've been movin' pretty steadily westward." Mother, as usual, had no comment, and Father rose to make his nightly rounds before climbing into his bedroll.

"Remember what Dr. Whitman advised us ta do," Charles reminded as he left the family's night fire. "Travel, travel, travel." The good doctor had assured them they wouldn't reach Oregon unless they traveled, and travel they would.

James grabbed the large skillet from where Mother had set it near the campfire and, using his opened pocketknife, scraped off a few scraps of meat sticking to the pan and popped them in his mouth, chewing with relish.

"I want some scabs, too," insisted Lisbon, reaching out a hand for a scrap of meat. "I stomped the spider for ya. 'Member?" His older brother frowned at the reminder of his backing away from the tiny creature for which he had developed an unreasonable phobia.

James removed a small piece of burnt meat from the pan and stuck the reward in the shape of a tiny morsel resting on the tip of his knife into his little brother's mouth. After sharing a few more hurried scrapings of the skillet, James closed his knife, stuck it into his pocket, and hurried to join Father.

Watching her father leave, the glow of the campfire fading on his face as he moved away, Lucy wished silently that Mother would do her part by at least verbally supporting Father. She didn't openly oppose Charles but she didn't offer any encouragement, either. She looked after the family's basic needs, but she seemed to be barely involved in the move westward. She and the aunts just kept plodding steadily along, exhausted from lugging fidgety babies all day. Mother just…well, she just *was*.

The wagon train reached Chimney Rock on July 10 and they camped near the landmark in a space where there was plenty of clump grass, prairie clover, water, and buffalo chips for their night camp. Lucy was impressed with the column of clay and sandstone that rose about 150 feet above a 200-foot mound on the prairie. The sandy rise to the chimney was covered with a sparse collection of clump grass and cactus scattered among fallen sandstone rocks of varying size.

The Nines had been voicing their impatience in reaching the goal that had been taunting them for two days. They were among the first of the children to scratch their names in the light brown sandstone

Pain and Loss

base of the chimney, and Lucy and her sisters scraped their names into the soft sandy rock soon afterwards.

"Wonder how long our names will last?" Ellen asked.

"'Til the wind wears it off, Silly!" Susan teased, and Ellen stuck her tongue out quickly, her back turned towards Lucy so her big sister wouldn't reprimand her.

Seeing the look on Susan's tanned face, Lucy had a good idea what had taken place, but she merely grinned and began to lead the way back to the wagon train. "Children!" she thought, slipping slightly in the surrounding base of soft soil leading down from the butte.

Her body gained momentum as she slid and slipped down the sandy slope, and her feet began to trip her up. She saw she was headed towards a large patch of cactus and she turned her body sharply, losing her balance and sitting with a resounding thump squarely on top of a mound of the spiny plants.

Instantly, sharp points of pain shot through her buttocks and she opened her mouth to scream but no sound came out. The burning sensation was beyond words, and she sat where she had fallen for half a minute, afraid the agony would increase if she moved.

"Are you okay, Sissy? Are you okay?" asked a concerned Lisbon, reaching out a hand to pat her on the shoulder. Ellen and Susan reached Lucy a step or two behind Lisbon, and soon half a dozen curious children surrounded Lucy.

She sat on her cactus throne, her rump afire with embedded spines, glaring at the ring of youngsters, the pain in her backside making her want to hurl insults at them. Lucy dug deeply into her mind, searching for just the right invective. Somehow, it seemed to Lucy that using some of the trail vocabulary she'd learned would lessen the sting, but she couldn't for the life of her pull up one single word that seemed appropriate.

"I'm fine," she scowled, gritting her teeth. "I'm just fine. Now get on back ta camp. Mother's callin' you." The spectators stood for a short time and then wandered towards the waiting wagons. If Lucy wasn't crying, there was no entertainment to be had there at the foot of Chimney Rock.

"Wait a minute, Ellen," the impaled girl called, and her younger sister turned back, a questioning look on her tanned face. "Help me up," Lucy directed and held up a hand. She grimaced as Ellen helped her to her feet and the cactus spines seemed to dig even more deeply into her rump. Twisting her head around, Lucy could see several thorny cactus pads attached to her skirt.

"Pull 'em off, you ninny!" Lucy ordered. Each time Ellen tugged at a flat oval pad, her older sister uttered a sharp "Ouch!"

"You left some there," Lucy complained, rubbing her rump through her skirt. The fiery sensation was still strong enough to bring tears to her eyes each time she moved.

"I got 'em all," retorted Ellen, crossing her arms defiantly and scowling. "And, you're the ninny. Who'd sit on a cactus?"

"I didn't sit on a cactus. I fell on it," Lucy snapped. "There's a big difference, you simpleton!" She took a step forward and felt several shooting pains in her backend. Pulling the back of her skirt away from her body, she scowled at Ellen.

"You left some spines in my bottom," she accused her sister. "Pull 'em out!"

"Pull up your skirt," directed Ellen. "I can't get the stickers out if I can't see 'em."

"No! Someone'll see my pantaloons," Lucy retorted, tugging her skirt downward defiantly.

"No, they won't," Ellen assured her confidently. "They'll see your bottom 'cause you'll have ta pull your pantaloons down so I can see the stickers." Lucy glared at her younger sister and the two girls stood glowering at each other for a time, unsure what to do. Looking around, Lucy could see no one behind her on the rock; everyone seemed to have headed back to the wagons that were beginning to move away from the landmark.

"Fine, then. I'll just squat down an' you can get 'em out," Lucy barked. She pulled her skirt up and her pantaloons down, careful to

Pain and Loss

shield her backside from anyone but Ellen. There was a short but painful session at the base of the landmark as Ellen pulled and Lucy yelped and the cactus spines were removed, one at a time.

"Don't you dare tell anyone I had cactus stickers in my bottom," Lucy scowled at Ellen. She reached out quickly and, grabbing the loose skin on the back of her younger sister's hand, she twisted, hard. Ellen gave out a sharp yell of pain.

"There's more where that came from," Lucy threatened. "If you dare tell one single soul you took stickers outta my bottom, I'll twister you every day a' the week. Do you understand?"

Ellen nodded her head and rubbed the back of her twistered hand. "I understand," she muttered angrily. "But, you didn't have ta twister me. I was just tryin' ta help."

"I'm sorry," Lucy relented. "Thanks. But, don't you dare tell a single soul. Promise?" She held out a hand with crooked fingers poised for twistering, and Ellen nodded.

The sisters hurried to catch up with the departing wagon train. As soon as they reached the family wagon, Mother began to fuss at Lucy because she'd been lagging behind when she needed help with the baby; his bottom was getting mighty sore from not getting his wet diaper changed often enough and Melinda was hoping Lucy could be a bit more responsible.

"Sore bottoms are just no fun," James grinned at Lucy, and rubbed his backside. Lucy sighed. She supposed she'd never hear the end of the cactus episode. Honestly, James was such a baby. Shielding her face from Mother, Lucy stuck her tongue out at her younger brother.

Nearing the Black Hills on July 14, Uncle Lindsay's wagon, jolted apart by the ever-increasingly rocky road, broke down. The Applegate men surveyed the broken, patched, and re-patched wood on the wagon. Charles looked disheartened at the contorted trunks of the mountain mahogany growing along the rock-strewn route the wagons were taking.

Lucy and Her Manifest Destiny

"Uncle Lindsay's wagon, jolted apart by the ever-increasingly rocky road, broke down."

Pain and Loss

"The Indians supposedly use the wood for their war clubs and tools," he told his brothers, "but it's too small and crooked to be of any use for patchin'."

Uncle Jesse, mounted on his saddle horse, was taller than the shrubs nearby. He reined his horse around and rode off over the rolling hillside, searching for any piece of wood among the sage and mahogany bushes that could be used. He returned in half an hour, shaking his head.

"No sense wastin' time tryin' ta repair it," Uncle Jesse told his brothers. "It wouldn't work. We'll just hafta change it inta a cart." He gathered the necessary tools from his own wagon, and the three Applegate brothers began working on the necessary overhaul.

While the brothers were occupied with remodeling the wagon, Uncle Mac peeled some of the bark from a gnarled mahogany bush. He cut the bark into small pieces and stuffed them into a small, soft leather sack. Pulling the drawstrings tight, he stowed his bag in one of the many inside pockets of his greatcoat.

"Good for coughs," he explained. "Make a tea. Might come in handy later on." He winked at Lucy and turned to help the men with their wagon remodeling.

Aunt Betsy turned from the broken wagon clutching baby Lucien tightly in her arms, and Lucy could see the tears welling in her eyes. There was no doubt the few dishes her aunt had tucked into the trunk of her family's clothing would have to be left behind. Lucy knew that when her aunt had begun packing their belongings for the move, Uncle Lindsay had ordered her to not include them in the wagon.

"I informed him there was no way I'd leave every single thing behind," Aunt Betsy had told Mother. Uncharacteristically, she had stood firmly against her husband's wishes. It was going to be a long trip to Oregon, Lindsay knew, so he had wisely, if not reluctantly, agreed Betsy could take her family's china with them. Now, it seemed, her single small victory would be taken away from her.

"We can put some a' mother's dishes in our flour barrel," Melinda offered quietly to her downhearted sister. "It's gettin' lower by the day, an' there's room." Aunt Cynthia, too, volunteered some room in her wagon, and Aunt Betsy selected a precious few possessions to stow in the women's wagons.

Melinda glanced furtively at Charles, working alongside his brothers, and her eyes fixed on Betsy in an unspoken agreement that the men didn't need to know everything that went on. She kicked defiantly at a prairie coneflower nearby, dislodging the plant that dared to be in her way.

"God wouldn't a' given women brains if He didn't intend for us ta use them once in a while," she whispered to Betsy in passing, and her sister nodded her head firmly in agreement. She pulled her hand from a fold in her skirt and gave Melinda the small glass dish she had concealed there.

Lucy surveyed the makeshift cart standing on the sandy, rock strewn slope covered with the scrubby looking mahogany bushes and sparse grass. The new contrivance was only half a wagon long, which meant that it was now about four feet long and still just four feet wide. When Aunt Betsy's family arrived at their destination, all they possessed would be on that small cart. Even with the boxes piled high in the bed and tied on securely with ropes, there was a large mound of belongings that would have to be left behind.

Each person in the family was allowed one change of clothing, and all but a few essential cooking utensils were left with the hope that someone coming along later would be able to use them.

"We can cook an' eat together," Melinda offered, and Lucy smiled to herself. Aunt Betsy could be Mother's helper now, and Lucy would have more time to spend with cousins. Perhaps a little bit of good was coming out of the mishap, though the sorrow on Aunt Betsy's face made Lucy feel more than a little guilty for welcoming a new assistant cook for Mother.

As the shortened wagon began to move away from the mound of Lindsay and Elizabeth's belongings, little three-year old Ivan rushed from his mother's side and threw himself on the ground, and his arms encircled a large cast-iron pot.

Pain and Loss

"Chit-un dump'uns!" he screeched, tears flowing over his cheeks. "Chit-un dump'uns!"

Lucy gazed at the tiny man hugging the discarded container, his tear-filled eyes fixed on her as he shrieked over and over: "Chuzin Wucy! Chit-un dump'uns! Chit-un dump'uns!"

"Quiet'n that young'un, 'Lizbeth!" ordered Uncle Lindsay and, clenching his jaw, he turned away, leaving the screeching boy in his mother's care. Lindsay took his place beside the team of oxen and, cracking a whip to get the animals started, he rejoined the procession of emigrants, the two wheels of the cart bouncing along behind the oxen in front.

Lucy hurried to her cousin's side and dropped down onto the ground beside him. She smoothed his hair away from his face and wiped at the tears flowing over his wind and sun-roughened cheeks.

"It's fine," Lucy crooned, reaching an arm around the frail little body, drawing him close to her. Ivan nestled against her, his sobs shaking his body. "It's gonna be fine, little man," his cousin murmured. "Cousin Lucy can make chicken dumplin's in Aunt Melinda's pot. When we get ta Oregon, I'll make you a big, big pot full a' chicken dumplin's an' you can eat all you want."

"Oh, Chuzin Wucy!" Ivan moaned. "Oh, Chuzin Wucy!" and he squeezed her tightly, hiccupping. "I'se hungry for chit-un dump'uns."

"Let's get Lish an' James and Edward ta kill us a prairie chicken for chicken dumplin's," Lucy offered. "Maybe we'll see some today. Maybe tomorrow. How's that sound? Maybe I can make you some prairie chicken an' dumplin's. How'd that be?"

Ivan nodded and his sobs dwindled, and then stopped, and Lucy wiped his face again with an apron soiled from trail dirt and tears and mucous.

Lucy nodded to Aunt Betsy that she had the situation under control. Her aunt, eyes brimming with tears and arms full of a fussing one-year old Lucien, nodded her thanks and stumbled away. With several backwards glances, she joined the group walking away from the belongings and the memories she'd been forced to leave beside the trail.

Lucy tried to console Ivan. "It's hard, little one. It's hard, I know. We all have to make sacrifices on our way to Oregon. But, once we get there, it'll be worth everythin'. You'll see. An' Cousin Lucy'll make you all the chicken dumplin's you can eat. Promise. Pinky promise." She held her hand out to Ivan, and he managed a shaky grin as he extended his hand and linked a very dirty little finger with his cousin's.

"Pinky promise," he echoed.

"The poor little man just can't understand all this," Lucy thought. She realized her little cousin was crying for more than a cast-iron pot left beside the trail.

He was only three years old and he'd been uprooted from his home and was expected to walk close to two thousand miles – well, maybe only seventeen hunnerd. The trail was rough going for the adults, let alone for a child with ill-fitting shoes that were badly worn.

Ivan had suffered from sunburn and wind burn and bug bites and twisters. His mother was forced to give him a little less food each day in an effort to stretch the family's dwindling supply. He had been too hot under a relentless summer sun and too cold in a wet bedroll. The poor little mite was just plain old bone tired.

"An' now he has ta leave his chit-un dump'un pot behind," Lucy thought, "an' walk pert near two thousand miles? He's only three years old. Even I can't understand all this. Father an' the uncles tell us this is best for all of us, but sometimes I wonder. This manifest destiny is dreadfully hard. I just hope that it's worth it in the end."

Lucy struggled to her feet, reaching down to help her little cousin to his, and, clutching hands tightly, the two children resumed their trek. Every fifty feet or so, Ivan looked back over his shoulder towards his family's pile of belongings beside the dusty trail.

Pinky promise," Lucy reminded him each time.

Pain and Loss

"Pinky promise," Ivan would repeat, his thin voice quivering, and he stumbled alongside his cousin, his blistered feet tripping occasionally on the rocky path they were following.

"Let's look for lizards," Lucy encouraged Ivan and Irene. "Betcha I can find more'n you can." The younger children eagerly took up the challenge, and soon Ivan appeared to be somewhat distracted from the loss of his chit-un dump'un pot.

Ellen and Susan, walking side by side as usual, stumbled on a snake curled up beside a sage brush and their startled and shrill screams stopped the group of children in their tracks. The two girls were screeching, the other children jumping up and down with mirth, and Uncle Mac came running to see what was causing the commotion. By the time their savior arrived, the frightened reptile was nowhere to be seen.

"Was it a rattler?" the old man asked. "Did it have rattles on the end a' his tail?" No one could answer. The snake had been long gone by the time the youngsters had reached the terrified girls.

"Walk wide 'round those fellas," Uncle Mac advised. "One bite an' you're a goner, fer sure. Keep your eyes on the ground when you're walking. I knew a fella onct, lasted five minutes after he was bit. Bad pison," The old man started to leave the group of frightened children, then turned to give a last word of caution.

"An' watch out fer scorpions. Those little fellas 'bout this long," and he held his thumb and index finger about two inches apart. "Their little tails are curled up like this over their backs." He demonstrated with a curved finger. "Their pison's 'most as bad as a rattler's." Uncle Mac left the group of sobered children to continue their walk.

Leading the cluster of nervous children through patches of sage brush and clump grass, Lucy saw Ivan occasionally pause in his search for the elusive lizards and cast a lingering look backwards on the trail. A gopher scurried across their path and once a sage hen exploded nearby, causing a chorus of shrieks from the youngsters.

Susan found a burrowing owl who sat wisely surveying the exploring children. Watching the inquisitive bird rotate his head as he surveyed first one child, then another, the children were soon laughing and limping along the trail, feet sore, legs tired, and sweat rolling down their bodies.

As she walked along with the younger children, Lucy looked back from time to time at Aunt Betsy's belongings. The pile appeared to grow smaller and smaller as her steps took her further and further away from the possessions being covered by a fine coat of dust from passing wagons. She had no inkling that the sadness she felt for Aunt Betsy and her family would be overshadowed soon by another, much deeper sorrow.

~ Chapter 11 ~

DEATH ON THE TRAIL

"Next stop, Ft. Laramie," Charles reminded his family after the evening circle had been formed, cook fires built, and supper finished. He sat near the campfire, his patched shoes reaching towards the warmth of the flames as the cooling breezes of the evening began to blow the blaze first one way, then another. Lucy thought that his body slumped a little more than usual and that Father looked tired. Very tired. The stains and little rips in his shirt and trousers only added to his look of weariness.

"We're 'bout a third a' the way there. We've come 'bout 600 miles so far in just 'bout two months." The pride of the completion of the trip to this point was heard in his satisfied, though tired sounding, voice.

Lucy gave her father a puzzled look. An unspoken question formed in her mind as she did some figuring. If the wagon train had only come about 600 miles in about 60 days, that meant an average of about ten miles a day. At that rate, the almost 2,000 mile journey would take about 200 days. No matter how poorly she was at doing arithmetic in her head, she didn't suppose that meant the trip was going to take the four months or so they'd hoped for. More like six months, the way she figured it.

Lucy and Her Manifest Destiny

James sat contentedly scraping the skillet and then sharing the meat scraps with his younger siblings. Lucy noticed her parents didn't bother to caution him about sticking his sharp knife blade into their mouths. She wished James would offer her a piece, but she supposed he thought she could get her own scabs; the small crusty pieces of the fried meat that had been left in the pan were her favorite treat.

"Least, with all a' us scrapin' an' cleanin' the pans an' plates after meals, I don't have ta work very hard at washin' the dishes," she thought. She knew that as she tidied up the supper dishes she'd wipe the cooled pan with her finger and lick it clean, relishing the lingering flavor of the meat fried in bacon grease.

She studied her brother carefully; he'd recently begun to twister the younger children more and more. It seemed to Lucy that he was taking his frustrations of the journey out on the little folks, and she didn't like it. She tried to talk with him about his meanness.

"So, tattle on me," James taunted her. "Don't ferget, Father whups the tattletale first afore he whups the fella doin' somethin' wrong," and, sticking his tongue out at her, he turned and walked away.

Charles usually excused himself soon after he'd wiped his supper plate clean with the last bite of his biscuit, and then hurried out to check on his herd of cows, making sure they were settled in. Tonight, however, Father commanded the children to remain seated around the family's fire after finishing their meal. The youngsters stole questioning glances at each other, wondering what was so important that Father didn't rush away from the family to tend to his chores.

"I want you children ta stay away from George Beale," Father ordered his children in a voice intended for their ears only. The random flashing of the flickering flames highlighted one part of Father's face, then another. The wavering light gave him an eerie look and added to the mystery of the sudden lecture.

"Why?" Lucy wondered, puzzled at the command, and she lifted a fold of her dress and carefully picked out some sand burs the long skirt had collected that day. She looked at her siblings gathered beside Father and could see the confused look on their faces. They all

Death on the Trail

knew that Mr. Beale had taught school in Missouri for a while and had hit Cousin Jesse with a switch, an event the young man boasted about when he was out of hearing distance of his parents.

"Gettin' switched by the school master is a badge of honor for the boys," Lucy whispered to Ellen, "an' surely doesn't make Beale a bad man." Also, the Applegate brothers had hired the dark-skinned, black-eyed nineteen-year-old Beale to drive a wagon, loaded mostly with bacon and flour, for them. Why would Father and his brothers hire someone they didn't trust?

"Just stay away," Father said sternly, looking each of his children in the eye until they turned away. Charles rose to his feet, giving one last intensely dark look at each of his offspring in turn, and then turned to do his night chores. As usual, James and Lisbon tagged along with him, thereby escaping having to help Mother prepare the younger children for bed.

"Whatever is the matter with Father?" Lucy asked her mother when Charles was out of sight in the darkening night. "He's acting strange. I thought we were s'posed ta be kind ta ever'one."

"Just do what he says, Daughter," Melinda urged. "Sometimes we don't have to know why. Father knows what's best," and she sighed, pushing a fly-away strand of hair behind her ear.

"Just 'nuther grownup secret," Lucy thought. "An' I don't s'pose I'll ever know what's wrong with George Beale. Must be one a' those fellas Father says left Missouri a step ahead a' the law."

"Let's get ready for bed while the men are gone." She led the girls into the night for their last toilet break of the day and found a small stand of mahogany bush to aid in forming a circle. Somewhere in the darkness a coyote howled.

"I wish he'd shut up!" complained Susan. "I don't like his moanin'. He oughta try ta change places with us for a day."

"He's not complainin'," Lucy assured her. "He's laughin' at your bare bottom!" and the girls forming the tee-tee circle tittered. Lucy knew that in the center of the circle the darkness hid an indignant Susan sticking out her tongue as she squatted in the grass.

Several days later, six-year-old Lisbon grew tired of dragging along behind the wagons. He looked at the upward slope, the way forward strewn with rocks of various sizes and scrubby brush. The weary lad decided to disregard Father's orders and sneak into Beale's wagon to hitch a ride.

"My legs are just so tired," he complained to Mary. "My ankles keep twistin' and my shoes have holes in the bottom and I can feel ever rock I step on. Don't you dare tattle on me or you'll get twistered good."

His sister, stumbling slowly along behind Beale's wagon and absently chewing the end of a braid of her hair, made no comment. Lisbon crawled onto the slow moving wagon and worked his way forward among the large wooden barrels of flour. He found a big copper box placed behind the driver's seat and quietly crawled in. He let the lid down so softly that Beale had no idea he'd picked up a hitchhiker.

Melinda was concentrating on her footing as she cradled John in her arms and picked her way among the rocks. She failed to see her young son crawl onto the wagon and hide in the box. She thought he was walking with his Aunt Cynthia and his cousin Alex as he often did.

"How far is it ta Oregon?" Ellen asked Mother. They'd come about 600 miles, Father had said, but he'd forgotten to say how much further they had to go. "I'm gettin' purty tired a' all the dirt an' grime an' this supposedly glorious trail," she grumbled.

"It's a ways further," Melinda comforted her daughter, wiping a tiny rivulet of sweat from Ellen's scowling face with the hem of her apron. "Still a long ways," and she watched Beale's wagon begin to move up the rock-strewn hill in front of them.

"Hard ta believe I've packed little John 600 miles. He must weigh twenty pounds, at least. No wonder my arms an' my shoulders an' my back are tired, even if I'm gettin' used ta it." She worked her way around rocks of differing sizes, stumbled over a few small, loose pebbles, and caught her balance.

"Guess it's no wonder my soul's kinda gettin' tired, too," she mumbled in words barely audible to Ellen and Lucy. She stooped to pick a sand burr off the hem of her long dress. "An' I'm getting' tired a' these blasted burrs, too."

Mother hoped to sleep under a roof at Ft. Laramie, if the family could find a place in the barracks, and Lucy shared with her that a real bath in a real tub would truly be welcomed.

"For all a' us," her oldest daughter muttered wryly, looking at their tattered and stained dresses, the grunge around their fingernails, and the filth ground into their chapped hands.

Heaven only knew how long it'd been since she'd given her long, dull hair the recommended one hundred strokes at night. Seems there was no need for braids any more. They just came undone and were a bother to plait, anyway. She scratched her scalp absent mindedly and, seeing that her fingernails had removed trail dirt from her head, she itched and scratched until her scalp was sore.

The heavy Applegate supply wagon driven by Beale began inching slowly up one of the few steep hills the emigrants had encountered on their journey. It began to move forward more slowly and then even slower. Beale cursed and cracked his whip over the oxen's back, again and again, but the animals couldn't maintain their pull against the heavy weight. The wagon stopped and then began to roll backwards, gradually picking up speed.

Lucy could see Babe and his team mate straining against the pull of the wagon, their muscles tightening, their backs bent as they leaned forward. Lucy leaned her body forward as if that motion would help the animals pulling the wagon. Babe's hooves began to slide on the rocky incline as he and his teammate were pulled backwards by the heaviness of the load. Beale turned the air blue with a string of cuss words and jumped from the wagon and left it and his unknown passenger to their fate.

Lucy felt a grip of fear deep in her stomach as she watched the out-of-control wagon rush in reverse down the hill, gathering speed and heading on a collision course with a following wagon. Holding

Lucy and Her Manifest Destiny

her breath and clenching her fists in terror, she saw a rear wheel hit a small boulder on the rocky hillside, causing the runaway wagon to bounce to one side, just missing a collision with the wagon behind it.

The heavy freight wagon clattered backwards down the stony incline, dragging the struggling oxen with it. A rear wheel hit a large rock with a resounding crack and a barrel of flour was catapulted onto the rocky hillside and shattered when it landed, the flour dusting the nearby shrubs and grasses. The wheels sent rocks and dust flying until the runaway wagon ground to a stop, miraculously still upright.

A flour-covered Lisbon, tears streaking down his face, emerged from the mess. No one realized just how badly hurt the little man was; they thought the tears were mostly from being scared and knowing Father would be disappointed at his disobedience.

Lisbon sat near the still wagon, tears flowing down his face as he sobbed quietly. He received little attention, other than from a stray dog that gently nudged the boy with his nose and licked the tears and flour from his face.

"I want Rufus. I want Rufus," Lisbon sobbed quietly, putting his arms around the mongrel's neck and laying his face against the matted fur, but no one was listening to him. They were more concerned about the loss of the precious flour that had to last the family until their journey's end.

Mother and Lucy and Susan carefully scooped up what they could of the flour scattered on the grass and put it into any container they could find. Lucy shook a flour-covered sunflower over a barrel, adding a few spoonsful of flour to the container. Mother sighed in relief when she saw her prized dishes were whole and she carefully tucked them into an unbroken flour barrel.

Father let Lisbon know that he was terribly disappointed his son had disobeyed his orders. Lucy listened to Father's tongue-lashing and felt it was worse than any punishment he could've given with a belt. She knew he was disappointed that his son had disobeyed him, but she knew, too, that her little six-year-old brother was weary from his long days of walking mile after mile. Father should take that into

Death on the Trail

account, she figured, and not be so hard on him. She scowled darkly at his turned back.

No one knew just how scared Lucy had been as she had watched the runaway wagon drag the protesting, bawling oxen backwards down the hill. After supper she headed towards a thicket of bushes. In the darkness of the night, she carefully removed her soiled pantaloons and buried them, unwashed, under a large moss-covered rock.

"An' that's my last pair," she thought. "So much for bein' a lady." She flounced the skirt of her dress a few times, actually enjoying the lack of a restrictive undergarment pulling at her legs.

"Good-bye, pantaloons!" she whispered into the stillness of the night. "Good-bye, Lady Lucy!"

After the initial shock of the accident and the relief the family felt at Lisbon surviving, they largely ignored him. Lisbon, though badly injured internally, knew better than to complain about his pain. Knowing he'd defied his parents, the youngster moaned quietly to himself, apparently feeling he was being justly punished.

Shortly after the accident, Lisbon began having seizures and they soon became a daily occurrence. Before long he was confined to the jolting, uncomfortable wagon, the ride jarring his injured body unmercifully. The Applegate family had no way of knowing that later he would be restricted to a wheelchair and, eventually, he would become totally bed ridden.

When Lisbon's pain became unbearable, Father would mix a few drops of laudanum into water and let him sip the liquid slowly. When his son's head nodded and Charles knew he'd soon sleep, he would recap the bottle of the laudanum and water mix and tuck it back into the medicine chest where it would be locked up until it was needed again. Lifting the six-year old carefully, Charles would lay him on the makeshift bed on top of the boxes in the wagon. Everyone seemed to be relieved on those days Lisbon was able to join the children in their westward walk.

"Yiddo yady Yucy, sittin' on a cactus," chanted Irene. "How many stickers? Well, just ask us!" Lucy frowned down at her little sister and opened her mouth to ask her where she had heard that rhyme when Ivan chimed in.

"Widdo wady Wucy! Her's sittin' on a chacus," smiled the little man, bouncing along in time to the words. The hot afternoon sun beating down on his upturned face caused small rivulets of sweat to run down Ivan's face.

"Little lady Lucy, sittin' on a cactus. How many stickers? Well, just ask us!" James's beaming face left no doubt in Lucy's mind that he'd been the author of the offensive poem.

Scowling, Lucy dropped Irene's hand and stomped away from her young tormentors. Her anger delighted the children and Lucy was to hear the chant frequently the rest of that and following days.

""Revenge is mine," saith the Lord," remembered Lucy. "Or somethin' like that. Well, I'll just have ta help Him out a bit," and she stomped alongside the family wagon, a frown covering her face, plotting her revenge. The heat of the day did nothing to lessen her fury and, as she wiped sweat from her face time after time and pulled at the dress sticking to her body, her anger grew.

From the sounds of Father's enthusiasm about reaching Ft. Laramie, Lucy had imagined it would be a large settlement and she looked forward to seeing the encampment. This would be the first community the wagon train had come to since leaving Missouri. Mother hoped to replenish her supplies there and Father wanted to lay over a few days to repair wagons.

As the Applegate wagons bounced and creaked their way slowly up to the military establishment, Charles commented that he found the size of the fort to be smaller than he had anticipated. Lucy heard many folks expressing similar surprise and disappointment. The log stockade itself was about 150-feet long on each of the four sides. The walls were bordered on the outside by small cabins, their roofs ending about three feet from the fort's barricade.

Lucy surveyed the surrounding countryside. A small group of teepees stood nearby, and to the south of the fort far away across the prairie she could see some mountains. Closer, to the west, was a tall mountain top standing above those nearby. Father identified it from his map as being Laramie Peak.

There were a few scraggly white firs not too far from the fort, and some green alder bushes grew along the North Platte River. Uncle Mac said some of the trees were Rocky Mountain maple and box elder, but Lucy thought they were mighty puny compared to the trees near her old home in Missouri. The fort was just as unimpressive to the children as were the trees.

"Surely this is just a small part a' the town," she told Susan. The girls looked at the small stockade with its cluster of cabins in disappointment. Even with the few worn looking Indian teepees nearby, there wasn't much to look at.

"I don't think much a' this Ft. Laramie," Susan commented wryly, wrinkling her nose at the small settlement. "An' those teepees look like they've seen better days. Pretty scroungy lookin' leather coverin', if you ask me."

Mother and the girls walked past the Indian encampment as the family made their way towards the fort. They watched a few Indian women stirring a pot of food tucked into their campfire. Observing strands of unwashed hair blowing around their darkened faces and seeing their soiled garments, Melinda wrinkled her nose in disgust.

"Seems they don't much care 'bout their appearance," she sniffed. "Seems they'd have 'nuff water ta wash up a little." She walked a bit further before adding another comment. "Least they could do is comb their hair a little." Mother walked a short distance before adding, "And I s'pose my dream of a bath was just that – a useless dream."

Lucy couldn't help but think that Melinda's hair seemed just as dirty as that of the stooped old squaw bending over a smoking campfire, shoving firewood into the flames much as Mother did each morning and night. The only difference in the dirt their clothing showed was that Mother's dirt was ground into linsey-woolsey while the old Indian woman's dirt was ground into buckskin.

"I'd hate ta tell you this, Mother," Lucy thought, "but you two women are more alike 'n you imagine."

After a quick survey of the meager supplies offered for sale in the small and dim provision room, Melinda complained to Charles that goods in the small fort carried big prices. Coffee and brown sugar was each $1.50 a pint and the poor-quality calico was $1.00 a yard. She knew she could do without the fabric to make dresses for her girls.

"No need ta dip inta the cash box for that cheap calico," she told him. "There's plenty a' scraps and thread in the rag bag ta see us through 'til we can find some decent fabric. There'll be other rips 'n holes 'fore the journey's end." Secretly, Melinda had no intention of doing any mending; the effort would be a futile attempt that would be undone as soon as she'd knotted the last thread, she knew.

"Powder's $1.50 a pound," Charles told her, "but I need ta replace what I used on the buffalo hunt." He counted the money carefully out of his wooden box and then retraced his steps to the fort where he bought what he needed.

"The fellow didn't even hesitate when he told me how much the gunpowder was," he complained to Melinda, hefting the small bag he had purchased.

While Mother sat near the family wagon cuddling John and visiting with the women, the older children tried to appear nonchalant as they strolled, again and again, past the Cheyenne chief and some of the Indians who were lolling near him beside the fort wall.

The natives were as disappointing to the children as the fort was to the adults. Only a few of the Indians were dressed in the leather garments the children had heard they wore; most seemed to be clothed in castaways from the white men who either lived at or had passed by the fort.

The Indians seemed to be friendly enough, though most of their language was unfamiliar to the young emigrants, which made the natives all the more fascinating. The strange language mixed with just a few words of barely understandable English made up in part for their disappointment at the clothing the strangers wore. For days afterwards, the younger of the children would explode into gibberish, uttering nonsensical words, declaring emphatically that they were "talkin' Injun."

The road that had done so much damage to Uncle Jesse's wagon became rockier and the traveling became rougher after they left the fort.

Clumps of grass became more abundant and there was more of the pesky sage and mahogany brush to wind through. Wagons bounced over an increasing number of rocks, the jolting exhausting the drivers as bodies were jerked first one way, then another.

Irene fretted incessantly about her feet hurting until her sister picked her up and packed her for a while. "Good thing she's so tiny," Lucy thought. "Not much heavier'n baby John, 'n Mother has to lug him around all day." She looked around and could see several youngsters riding in their family wagons, choosing uncomfortable bottoms over even more sore feet.

Thinking to give his tender feet a rest from walking on rocks, six-year-old Joel Hembree had decided to ride on the family wagon. He explained to his father his ankles hurt from twisting when he stepped on loose rocks and his knees hurt from the falls he'd taken. He hung onto the edge of the wagon seat, proud to ride next to his father regardless of the punishment he was receiving from the jerking of the wagon. He grinned down at his mother walking beside the wagon, the erratic bouncing of his perch popping his mouth open and shut.

The son was named Joel Jasper, the father Joel Jordan, and sometimes Lucy was confused when folks talked about Joel Hembree.

Lucy and Her Manifest Destiny

"Irene fretted incessantly about her feet hurting until her sister picked her up and packed her for a while."

"And we can't even call 'em by their initials," she commented to Ellen as the sisters watched the Hembree wagon bounce along the route. "J. J. for both a' 'em! Who'd do that ta a child?"

"J. J.," laughed Ellen. "J. J. an' Sarah."

It was July 18 and the child Sarah Hembree was carrying would be born in a week or so. Lucy could see her giving her enlarged stomach as much support as she could. As she walked, she kept a hand nestled under the large bulge.

Lucy figured each step on the rocky road would jiggle that poor unborn child all over the place. Sarah's feet, already swollen when the day's journey had begun, must be throbbing incessantly; Lucy's were, and she wasn't packing any additional weight. Poor Sarah must be packing twenty or thirty extra pounds, Lucy guessed.

She noticed Sarah watching her son riding in the family wagon, bravely hanging onto the seat, Lucy supposed Sarah was wondering if the child she carried would be a little sister or a little brother for Joel. A little girl would be nice this time, Lucy thought. She could see Sarah give Joel a weak grin and then focus her attention on the uneven path she was following.

The incident happened without warning. Lucy was concentrating on the next likely place to put her foot when she heard the loud creaking of a wagon wheel jolting over a rock, then an anguished shout from the older Joel Hembree.

Young Joel had been thrown from his perch by the last bounce of the wagon over the large stone, and his father had been unable to grab him as he tumbled off his seat. Before his father could stop the forward motion of the oxen, two wheels of the heavily loaded wagon had run over the slight body.

Whipping her head around, Lucy saw her young friend's body on the ground just behind the rear wheels of the wagon, his arms and feet flailing feebly in the dirt, his head moving slightly from side to side. A rivulet of blood ran out of the little boy's mouth and pooled on the ground under his sunburned cheek. Joel's parents reached the barely moving body at the same time, and Sarah, kneeling down beside her son, began to shriek inconsolably.

Charles stopped his team a short distance behind the Hembree family and hurried forward. He stood there a minute and then turned away and stepped into his wagon, unlocked his medicine chest, and took out the bottle of laudanum mixed with water. He poured half a cup of the opiate mix and handed it to Joel's father. The worried parent lifted his son's head slightly, and the little boy screamed in pain at the movement.

His father poured a trickle of the drug-laced water into his mouth. Again and again the father administered the laudanum. Again and again the little boy shrieked. Finally, he quieted and ceased moving his arms and legs, though he still uttered an occasional moan.

Charles offered the father an enameled cup with a small ration of whiskey in it. Watching Joel swallow it down in one gulp, Lucy realized the liquor was, indeed, a much needed drug.

The broken body of the slight boy lingered through the long night. Lying in her bed, Lucy could hear Sarah crying and, occasionally, uttering a loud shriek that pierced the darkness. Each time the scream came, the children awoke and began crying and Lucy and Mother cuddled first one and then another child through the long night.

Little Joel's death was the first for the wagon train. It was a sobered group of emigrants that gathered for the funeral the morning after the accident. The crowd watched as Joel Hembree, tears flowing silently over his weather-beaten cheeks, carefully laid the small bundle that was his son into the elongated hole that had been dug near the trail.

"Sissy," whispered Irene while tugging on her sister's skirt and watching a sobbing Sarah kneeling beside the grave. "Where's Joel?"

"Shhhh. He's wrapped in the bundle," Lucy whispered back.

"Was he cold?"

"He was cold. Very cold," Lucy answered. "The blanket will keep him warm," she added softly. "Now, shush."

Lucy watched Mary and Irene chewing on the ends of their braids and Ellen and Susan standing with their arms around each other for comfort. The Nines stood with sobered looks on their faces, huddling together for the funeral services. All the children stood with tattered clothing and unwashed hair and faces, and Lucy could see the adults hadn't cleaned up any better than the youngsters.

Lucy thought of how much store had been set in getting tidied up for church or for a funeral in Missouri. As she stood looking at the rag-tag group assembled to pay their respects to the Hembree family, she understood that looks weren't the most important thing in the world.

"It could have been any of us, Lord," Lucy thought. "It could have been any one of us. Thank you for sparing my family."

"The Lord is my shepherd..." began Dr. McLaughlin, reading from his tattered Bible, and Lucy's mind tuned out immediately.

"And just where was that shepherd when His little lamb needed Him?" she thought defiantly, thinking of Joel lying on the ground, blood seeping out of his mouth, his arms and legs flailing weakly, his mother's screeching through the long night. She'd have to give some thought to that shepherd thing, for sure.

On the other hand, Lisbon stood nestled against her side while Irene and Mary each clutched one of her hands. Those little ones had been spared, and Lucy gave God a quick "Thank you, Lord" for that. The whole death and life thing was just a bit too hard for her to grasp, she supposed. She'd just have to let God take care of it.

As the group of emigrants mourned the loss of one of their children, Lucy tried to rationalize her feelings. She supposed she'd better sit down and do some reading in the Bible the first time she had some extra minutes.

Lucy imagined that each parent watching the Hembree family grieve was sharing the same thought: that could have been their child, lying there. A stone marker had been crudely engraved with Joel's name and a note tied on a stick gave the information that the six-year-old was the son of Joel J. Hembree, and that he had been killed by a wagon running over his body.

Reading the crudely lettered notice, Lucy thought it ironic that no mention was made of his mother; surely she was as much a parent as the father. There were some things the young girl just couldn't understand, and her throat tightened as she placed the polished rock, carried in her secret pocket since she'd begun her journey to the west, near the note-bearing stick.

"Leavin' some a' my belongin's beside the trail somehow doesn't seem important anymore," Aunt Betsy told Mother and Lucy. "I just don't see how I could ever get over leavin' a child behind on the trail."

Melinda nodded; the child she'd left in Missouri would at least have her family there to care for the grave. The Hembree family would have to rely on passers-by to honor their son. Standing near the fresh grave, the sisters reached for each other's hand and squeezed tightly for a time, each lost in her own thoughts, each wondering what the remainder of the trip had in store for her own family.

Helping her little sisters prepare for bed that night, Lucy looked into the clear sky bright with stars and wondered which one was little Joel's. Her little sister watched her with interest.

"Does God really have a star for ever'body that dies?" asked Irene, wondering if the story she'd been told was really true.

"Ever'body has their own star," Lucy assured her little sister. Tucking her under the quilt in the tent, Lucy bent over the young girl and gave her an uncustomary kiss on the cheek. "Now, sleep tight," she murmured, and Irene reached from under the covers to give Lucy a tight hug and then lay quietly for a few minutes.

"Sissy, will he be lonely?" Irene asked in a tiny voice.

"He'll have a lot a' angels with him," Lucy assured her little sister. "For each star in the sky, that's someone there ta take care a' Joel." Satisfied, Irene cuddled closely to Lucy and soon her sister could hear her soft snore.

Lucy lay sleepless, thinking of the events of the past few days. The breaking up of Aunt Betsy's wagon, Lisbon's injuries from the runaway, and the death of little Joel had shattered her belief once and for all that the trip on the trail was going to be one glorious day after another.

"Guess I have ta be more uv a help ta Mother an' Father," she thought. "They can't take care a' all the little ones. Not all at once." Lucy raised her head up and counted the lumps under the quilts that were her younger siblings.

"All the little Applegates accounted for, Lord," she thought. "Thank you." She rested her head on the quilt again. She realized all too well that the trip towards her manifest destiny was proving to be much harder than she had thought before leaving Missouri, and she wondered what disaster might strike next.

"Not *if* there'll be a disaster," she thought, "but what *kinda* disaster."

~ *Chapter 12* ~

ARE WE THERE YET?

"How much father, Father?" James sighed, scuffing his feet in the dust near his rock seat. "Are we almost there yet?" Traces of sweat had made light paths on his dirty face which was framed by his long, unkempt hair. With his tattered and grungy shirt and with his equally filthy and well-worn britches showing large holes in each knee, Lucy felt he was a most pathetic sight.

"It's a long ways, Son," was the answer, and Charles pushed the end of a half-burnt stick into the campfire. He watched James as his son absently picked at a large scab on his cheek. The large brown crusty spot was the result of the severe sunburn he had suffered the first week on the trail. Despite repeated scolding from both his parents and his older sisters, James wouldn't leave the scab alone. Charles supposed he would wear a scar from the sunburn for a long time.

"Independence Rock next. I've heard it's pretty impressive," Charles offered encouragingly. "We'll get there tomorrow." The children looked at their father, waiting for more information.

"Made a' granite. Purty hard stuff. You'll find it's considerable harder 'n Chimney Rock. Kinda hard ta write on, I've heard." His deeply set dark eyes reflected the flames from the campfire as he looked up at his children.

"Only 'bout a hunnerd 'n thirty feet high," Charles added, "but it's been easy ta see for a while, hasn't it? Ifn you wanta pace it off, you'll find it's 'bout a thousand an' nine hunnerd feet long an' 'bout eight hunnerd an' fifty feet wide." He grinned at James.

"Fact," Charles added, "some folks say it looks like a giant white whale a layin' there on the prairie."

"Humpff!" snorted James. "Never saw a whale."

"Why Independence Rock?" Lisbon asked. "Why's it called that?"

"It's sorta a' guide," his father answered. "If we wanta get ta our destination 'fore cold weather sets in, we need ta be at the rock by Independence Day. July 4."

"We're late, ain't we?" It wasn't a question but rather a statement from Susan, the child who kept track of the dates. "It's July 27 a'ready."

"We're doin' fine," Charles responded. "We're doin' fine." He prodded another stick into the dying fire. "We're doin' fine," he repeated and stared somberly at the flickering flames. "We'll make up the days. Just have to push a little harder, is all." He sat quietly for some time before rising tiredly to make his nightly rounds.

"Yiddo yady Yucy," chanted a voice softly from the children's bed, and the whispered chant was taken up by first one child, then another, until their collective voices became loud enough for Melinda to hush them. Lucy scowled in the darkness and she turned her body away from the younger girls sharing her bed on the hard prairie ground.

"Oh, how I miss my Sadie," she thought, and she pictured the doll as she had last seen her. She'd been sitting on the wall shelf where Lucy had left her, next to the calendar that read "1843. May. Monday 19." Lucy's arm curled to her chest as she remembered how her doll had felt.

"I guess I'm too old for toys," she supposed. "But, somehow, lugging baby John and Irene around just isn't the same as my little Sadie."

Independence Rock was a welcome diversion for the children, and as soon as their wagon had pulled into the evening circle made near the Sweetwater River, the youngsters hurried to the rock. Despite Father's warning that the rock would be hard to write on, each of the older children picked up a rock to use as a writing tool.

Lucy carried a small piece of granite in her apron pocket and, upon finding a spot where her feet could stand securely, she scratched her name: "Lucy Applegate. 1843." Her writing tool barely left a scratch, try as she might to make the marks deeper. Father had been right, as usual.

Then, with a grin on her face, she etched the initials "R. A." as far as she could reach to the right. Changing the rock to her left hand, she wrote an awkward looking "L. W." "No need ta play favorites," she thought, looking at the initials with satisfaction. As she descended the slight rise near the base of Independence Rock, she kept a wary eye out for clumps of cactus.

Making her way to her family's wagon, she felt the prick of a sand burr in her skirt. Leaning to pick up her skirt tail and remove the prickly seed, she spied a large patch of the offending plant. Lucy started smiling.

That night, before Melinda could ask her for help, Lucy grabbed the quilts to make the children's beds. As she flipped the last top quilt onto the bottom one, she turned to James, who was sitting nearby.

"Ja see that bunch a' enormous black spiders today?" she asked. "Next to that pile a' rocks we had to go 'round? *Big* guys, they were."

"Were'nt no spiders," James retorted, scowling at his sister.

"Was too. 'N I saw a bunch a' scorpions right by 'em. Little tails with their stingers all curled up," and she curved a finger to demonstrate. Out of the corner of her eye, she could see the flickering of the dim fire light reflecting off Susan and Ellen's faces as they sat looking at her, listening to the exchange with wide eyes.

"I s'pose the rattlesnake I saw a few feet away was after himself a good scorpion and spider dinner. Ya s'pose?" Lucy's eyes widened questioningly as she turned away from the children.

She began to skim cream from the top of the meager pail of milk and placed it in the churn. As she worked, she kept an eye on the children and grinned mischievously when Mother declared it was bedtime.

The children crawled between the quilts Lucy had spread for them. Immediately, they began shrieking hysterically and frantically crab-walking backwards out of the bed, throwing quilts in every direction.

"Scorpions!" screeched Susan, and she raced towards Lucy for protection.

"Rattlesnake!" screamed Ellen, dashing towards her older sister.

"Spiders!" howled James, throwing his quilt off and jumping from the bed, his eyes wide with fright as he looked in the dimness of the night for the one small creature that could put fear in his heart.

"Bug-us-es," shrieked Irene, and Lucy broke into loud laughter as Mother, eyes wide, hurried towards the children. She approached the bedding and cautiously lifted the top quilt to see what was causing the commotion. As she did so, she released the pungent odor of a quilt freshly wetted by some frightened child. Father, dashing up to his family in alarm, grabbed a half-burned stick of firewood, ready to kill whatever was threatening his children.

"Sand burrs!" Mother declared. "Nothin' but sand burrs and a wet quilt. You children get back ta bed." She turned to finish her night chores and Charles dropped his weapon.

"Yiddo, yiddo Applegates, sleepin' on sand burrs!" Lucy giggled as she chanted just loudly enough for the children to hear. She watched with satisfaction as the children attempted to clean the stickery seeds from their beds.

"You're not funny, Lucy. Not a bit funny," snipped Ellen, picking a knot of sand burrs from the quilt. "You didn't have ta be so mean just 'cuz of a little poem."

In the near-darkness, Lucy grinned widely, though she said nothing. She was almost certain that she would hear no more chants about "Yiddo yady Yucy."

On August 3, the emigrants came in sight of the impressive Rocky Mountains with their caps of everlasting snow. Lucy, concentrating on the glaring whiteness of the mountain tops, felt an involuntary shudder race through her body. The grasses seemed thinner, the shrubs clinging closer to the ground as if for protection from the cool winds blowing from the snow-covered highlands.

"I hope we can pocket the trip over those mountains," she remarked to Susan. "Looks mighty cold ta me." Although they were majestic in appearance, Lucy knew the snow meant cold, pure and simple.

"Father'll take care a' us," was the reply, though Lucy thought her little sister looked somewhat dubious.

The heat of the prairie gave way to slightly cooler temperatures as the emigrants approached the mountains. The path became rockier and the emigrants, as they plodded along, concentrated on the ground and tried to avoid stumbling on the stones. The younger children began to whine.

"I'se got busters an' boozes," complained Irene as she limped beside Lucy late one afternoon, clutching a wilted sunflower in her hand. "Me yeggs is tired."

"Just a few more steps an' then we'll rest a bit," Lucy encouraged her. "Count 'em with me. We'll take ninety-nine steps an' then stop ta rest while we count ta ninety-nine. Then, we'll take a hunnerd an' fifty more an' then rest while we count ta a hunnerd an' fifty." Her little sister looked at her dubiously.

"But, Sissy, I can't count ta a hunnerd. You know that!" She threw away her sunflower in exasperation.

"I'll do it for you. I'll say the number an' you repeat after me. Ready?" The two sisters picked their way along the trail, counting together. Occasionally they failed to see a rock and, stepping on it, turned their ankles and soon Irene tired of the game.

"I'se tired a'ready," she moaned to Lucy and the little sister sat on the ground, refusing to walk further despite Lucy's urging. "Me yankles hurt," Irene wailed. "Carry me, Sissy. Carry me," and she reached her arms up to her oldest sister.

Her older sister looked at the miserable girl huddled on the rocky patch of ground. Her own ankles and legs hurt and, furthermore, Lucy could feel blisters burning on both of her feet and one of her knees had a sharp ache from hitting a rock when she'd fallen. The thought of both little Joel Hembree who'd never be able to walk again and of her own personal misery overcame the patience she'd been exercising.

"You know what, little miss?" she snapped at her sister. "You know what? *My* yankles hurt an' *my* boozes hurt an' *my* busters are bleedin'." Lucy's voice rose. "An' you know what? *I've* still gotta keep walkin. Furthermore, *you've* gotta keep walkin', you spoiled little girl. We've got a long ways ta go an' whinin' won't help a bit. An' furthermore, if you'd rather, we can make you a dirt bath an' leave you beside the trail like we did little Joel. Howdja like that, little miss?" Lucy squatted beside her sister and began to scoop a depression in a patch of soft dirt near her little sister.

Irene jerked her head upright and her eyes widened at the unexpected outburst from her big sister. She sat quietly for a minute, her surprised eyes locked onto Lucy's. Then she held up a hand in resignation, a silent request to be helped up from the ground.

"Can ya help me count ta a hunnerd, Sissy?"

Lucy could tell that the more pleasant days, free from the heat of the prairie, were doing very little to alleviate some of the arguments the men seemed to be having. She wondered with an inward smile if they, too, had busters and boozes on their feet. The earlier enthusiasm felt at the beginning of the trail had been replaced by a general unrest among the adults. Lucy recognized that for everyone in the

Lucy and Her Manifest Destiny

wagon train, the thrill of the journey had worn just about as thin as her threadbare calico dress.

From inside the children's tent, Lucy listened to her parents visiting near the evening campfire and she strained to hear their words.

"One man wants ta go faster, the next one in line wants ta go slower," Charles was complaining to Melinda. "One wants ta cross the river here an' another wants ta cross there. One wants ta go this way an' one wants ta go that way, an' another wants ta go any direction but the right way." Lucy could hear her father poking a stick fiercely at the dying embers to emphasize his frustration. "I can see why Jesse chose the cow column over ridin' herd on the wagon train."

Each day seemed a repeat of the one preceding: one weary step after another. The oxen plodded tediously along, picking their way through rocks and around an occasional scrubby juniper or pine or shrub. Babe lost a shoe somewhere among a stretch of rock-strewn trail and the children looked long and hard for the precious piece of shaped flat iron, but had no luck finding it.

Their favorite ox was limping that night when Father returned from his day of riding with the cow column, a worried frown adding an extra crease to his tired face. When the wagons were circled, James helped Charles replace the lost shoe on Babe's hoof, noting it was the last one in their stock.

"We're all practically barefoot," Father said tersely, looking at his boots with the strips of rawhide wound around them. "Our shoes weren't made for walkin' this much."

"I think Sukie is tired, too," Lucy told Mother. "I think she's startin' ta wonder along with the rest a' us just how much father we have ta go. She's only givin' a few cups a' milk ever day." The milk cow's supply of milk was dwindling, despite the hands full of grass the children pulled as they walked along and tried to encourage the family pet to eat.

"We're all tired, Daughter," Melinda said quietly. "An', we'll be even more tired 'fore we get ta the trail's end." She pulled her wool shawl more tightly around herself and the fussing baby John and leaned her body towards the fire.

"You'll need ta start mixin' water in with the milk. Don't let the children see you or they'll complain. Mix it half an' half, 'bout. There's just not enough ta go 'round 'lessn you do."

"They won't like watered down milk," retorted Lucy, balking at her mother's suggestion. "Just wait an' see. They won't drink it."

"Just do what I say, Daughter," Melinda ordered sharply, and Lucy turned away in a huff. She would find out her mother knew best; not one of the little Applegates turned up a nose at the weak milk.

With reluctance, Lucy told Lisbon she could no longer give him squirts of Sukey's warm milk; there just wasn't enough to share. Her little brother merely shrugged; he was already being given smaller portions of food, so no more milk squirted fresh from Sukie was just the way it was going to be.

Lucy thought of her home in Missouri and she thought of Sadie, left behind on the shelf three months before. In her mind's eye, Lucy could picture the doll sitting beside the calendar with the date of May 19, 1843. She supposed it was a picture she would never forget; an image of an easier time and an easier life. Somehow, this reaching her manifest destiny was even harder than she had imagined it would be.

As the wagon train approached the Rocky Mountains, the air became cooler, the hills covered with more trees and smaller vegetation. The lush grasses provided abundant feed for the livestock and relief from wagon-produced dust. The path said to be the shortest one through the mountains was chosen by the scouts and seemed to be tolerable.

"Tolerable has taken on a whole new meanin'," Lucy thought, following her family wagon bouncing its way through a meandering pathway among rocks and shrubs. "I 'spose it's tolerable 'cause I didn't break a leg and just sprained my ankle." She limped along, tugging on Irene's hand and jerking it unnecessarily when her little sister stumbled. Off to one side Ellen and Susan stumbled through a

Lucy and Her Manifest Destiny

"Lucy could picture the doll sitting beside the calendar with the date of May 19, 1843."

rock-strewn pathway, working hard to avoid turning their ankles on the uneven trail.

Later, Lucy would hear some of the emigrants say the route was tolerable because there had been no deaths on the shortcut. It was tolerable because no broken wagon had to be converted to a cart. Tolerable because none of the travelers had been injured badly, nor were any killed. Tolerable because the wagon train was more than halfway to the journey's end and, Lucy supposed, once over the top of the Rockies, the path would be mostly downhill all the way. 'Least, that's how she envisioned it in her mind.

After the wagon train made an uneventful crossing of the summit of the Rockies on August 7, the only difference they would note for a while, Father said, would be that the water would now be flowing to the Pacific Ocean.

"An' what difference does it make which direction the water flows?" Lucy grumbled to Susan. "Water always flows downhill. If it starts flowin' uphill, that's when we oughta be concerned. Pacific? Humpff!"

The one blessing, Lucy supposed, was that there were evergreen trees and their fragrance was a welcomed change from that of the prairie sage brush. And, dead tree branches made a bigger firewood pile faster than sage branches.

"I s'pose that's two blessin's," the weary traveler admitted to herself.

Lucy's feet were sore from stumbling through the miles of the rocky route the wagons were taking and she had twisted her ankle on a loose rock, then fallen and skinned her elbow. Her mood matched the darkness of the rain clouds she could see building in the west, and as she watched them, she supposed the family would sleep in a leaking tent under wet quilts that night. Again.

Each day was a repeat of the one preceding: one tired step after another. Reaching a designated point somehow didn't seem like much of an accomplishment after almost three months on the trail and with hundreds of miles yet to go. Ft. Bridger was the next goal; Lucy wondered if the stockade would be as disappointing to the emigrants as Ft. Laramie had been. She didn't know how it could be.

The children were tired; most of them had walked the entire distance from Missouri. Their sunburns had finally healed, though many of the children bore scars where scabs had been picked off over and over. Their faces had tanned and their bodies were hardened from their daily exercise. Too, the children were beginning to noticeably lose weight. Most of the families were beginning to ration their food, portioning out the meals, and it seemed to Lucy that she was always hungry.

"Father says we've traveled more 'n a thousand miles," Lisbon bragged. "I bet I've walked 'bout two thousand miles so far, with all my explorin' an' gettin' firewood an' stuff. Think so, Sissy?" and the six-year-old looked to Lucy for affirmation. Lucy nodded her head in agreement; he was probably pretty close to right, she figured, and it wasn't worth arguing even if she disagreed.

"An' I bet James has twistered me ever mile a' the way, too." He held up an arm with fresh bruises.

"We'll get 'im," Lucy promised Lisbon. "We'll get 'im."

The air was becoming thinner, the breezes cooler, reminding the emigrants they had miles to go before winter set in. Just after daylight on August 12 when the last sound of the waking bugle had died away, Lucy opened the flap of the family's tent and found a heavy frost covering the camp. When she stooped to get a dipperful of water to dump into the oatmeal pot, she discovered that a layer of thin ice had formed in the water pail.

"Hurry, children," she directed her brothers and sisters. "It's time ta get up. Get some more clothes on. It's gonna be cold this morning. We have ta hurry ta the tee-tee circle 'fore it's time ta leave."

"I don't hafta go, Sissy," whined Irene. "I a'ready did. I wanta stay here where it's warm," and she tried to snuggled more deeply under the quilt. Lucy could smell the fusty ammonia smell of the wet bed and knew her little sister truly didn't need to join the other children.

"Maybe you don't need ta join us," Lucy admitted, "but you're gonna be mighty cold with that wet dress. Better get your dry one on."

"But, Sissy!" whined Irene. "I don't have 'nother dress. Just me Sunday dress."

"Put your Sunday dress on over the top, then," snapped Lucy. "You'll freeze if you don't get more clothes on. You'll dry out soon's the sun comes up, an' then you can take the good dress off."

As she hurried the younger children through their hasty breakfast, Lucy could feel a sense of urgency among the adults as they prepared to break camp. The call of the birds flying overhead seemed shrill in the thin air, the winds stiffer, and the cold more penetrating despite the extra layers of clothing the children had put on.

"An' it's off ta Bridger's fort," Lucy informed her little sisters. "S'pose it'll be more impressive 'n Ft. Laramie?" She was answered by silent shrugs and the children resumed their plodding towards their destination.

~ *Chapter 13* ~

DRUNKS, BLOODSUCKERS, AND VERMIN

On August 14 the Applegates reached Ft. Bridger, which was situated on Black's Fork of the Green River. To Lucy's amazement, the Green River was truly green. Lined with cottonwood trees, the river offered an abundance of fish to supplement the travelers' dwindling food supply.

Built on a large flat plain a seemingly long distance from tree clad mountains, the fort was not an especially impressive sight, Lucy didn't feel, but it was at least a sign of civilization.

A herd of twenty to thirty goats and a few sheep could be seen a short distance away, and Lucy supposed the cows they could see grazing in the lush meadow some distance away belonged to the fort. The gathering of Indians around the garrison added some interest to the small stockade which was surrounded in part by a picket fence.

"There's only 'bout four or five cabins," she told Susan, surprised there weren't more. "An' those are purty miserable lookin' log houses, but it looks like they're buildin' some more. The cabins look to be 'bout sixteen feet by sixteen feet – or less. Prob'bly less," Lucy figured aloud.

"How many Indian lodges are there?" The girls disagreed on the number, but they all counted twenty-five, more or less.

"I don't think much a' this Jim Bridger's fort," Ellen told Lucy, disappointment plainly written on her face. "I'd heard so much 'bout old Bridger being the "Daniel Boone a' the Rockies," an' the least he could do is have more supplies."

"He's got the usual," Mother reminded her. "Flour, lead, knives, hats, coffee, sugar, an' what-not. An', a' course, spirits an' Indian things. Considerin' they just started buildin' the fort a year ago, I s'pose it's not bad."

Lucy and her sisters each clutched a hand as they moved between the piles of deer, elk, and antelope skins in the dimly lit cabin serving as a store. The girls found a stack of deer-skin pants and another of moccasins, and they fingered the garments. Lucy boldly lifted the light tan leg of a pair of pants and rubbed the leather against her cheek, marveling at the softness.

"How'd ya like ta wear a pair a' those?" Ellen grinned. "Bet they'd be mighty comfy!" She wiggled her bottom.

"Ellen!" exclaimed Susan, her eyes widening. "That's awful! Ladies don't wear britches, you silly!"

"But I'd like ta try," Ellen responded wickedly. "How 'bout you, Lucy? S'pose they'd feel good?"

"We'll never know, I s'pose," Lucy grinned. "But it sounds like a mighty good idea ta me." She swished her worn skirt.

Perhaps, the children told each other as they left the fort behind the next morning, they would find more excitement at Fort Hall, some 150 miles distant. The image of the inconsequential settlement of Ft. Bridger faded almost before the dust from the emigrants' wagons had settled to the ground.

Lucy and the other children found Soda Springs to be a fascinating phenomenon when the family reached that point ten days after leaving Ft. Bridger. Lucy counted ten springs sparkling upwards among the lean grasses: six large ones and four smaller ones. The water bubbling up had the taste of soda without flavoring, and each child took a sip, making faces at the strange-tasting liquid. Nearby was a small hole from which gas escaped. Taking a dare from Lish, the Nines each took a whiff of the air which caused them to feel slightly nauseous and light-headed.

"We're drunk! We're drunk! We're drunk!" the Nines chanted, stumbling on small rocks and bumping into each other. Lucy and Ellen, watching, giggled at the boys' antics.

"Children! Shame!" Aunt Betsy scolded. "Get away from that sody water!" The cousins immediately sobered up, ducked their heads, and shuffled away from the springs. The girls waited quietly until the boys and Aunt Betsy, clutching a complaining Lucien in her arms, moved on. Curious, they approached the escaping gas and inhaled deeply. The vapor tickled Lucy's nose, making her sneeze, and her head feel light.

"I'm drunk," she whispered to Ellen with a wicked look on her face, pretending to stumble as she walked in circles. "I'm drunk!"

"Me, too! I'm drunk!" Ellen replied in a soft voice, joining her older sister in the game.

"So there!" Lucy whispered defiantly, her eyes following Aunt Betsy as she moved slowly down the trail, the brim of her sunbonnet bobbing in time to her heavy plodding steps. "It's okay ta have fun once in a while. So there!" and she took another deep whiff of the sulphurous gas, then gasped as the strong vapor permeated her head and caused her to feel slightly dizzy.

"So this is what it feels like ta drink bark juice," she told Ellen. "I don't think much a' it, myself."

"Me, either," agreed Ellen and hiccupped.

"I can see it! I can see it!" James shouted as he came running towards Lucy and her entourage of children the day of August 27. "It really shows up! Come see," and he turned to lead the youngsters to the top of a slight rise.

Off in the distance, they could see the palisade surrounding the garrison that was Ft. Hall. Tall light colored adobe walls formed the enclosure around several wooden cabins and store houses. From where Lucy stood, she could see two high guard towers jutting high above the fence.

"We're close ta a thousand 'n fifty miles from Missouri," Father said proudly as he rode up to where Mother trudged along with a fussing baby John. "We're more'n half way there, Melinda." Her response was a weak nod, and Charles, after sitting watching her quietly for a few seconds, reined his horse around and rode off towards the fort.

The emigrants found that Governor Grant, the commander of the fort, held fast to his belief that wagons could not be taken any further on the trail to western Oregon.

"'Snot been done," he declared to the men listening. "You prob'ly can't make the passage 'thout losin' a lotta wagons an' animals, an' it'd be mighty hard on the women an' children. By the time you spend half a day goin' that way, you'd think Old Scratch hisself had 'hold a' ya." He shook his head emphatically.

"Might be possible, but I just don't see how, lessn' ya switch ta pack trains," Governor Grant continued. The remainder of the way was tough and treacherous, he warned, and would be by far the most perilous part of their journey. He recommended the wagon train head to "Californy," a much safer route.

As the Applegate brothers listened to Grant, they thought of Lindsay's wagon. They feared the possibility of having to pack their provisions on their oxen's backs and walking the remainder of the journey if they continued on the planned route.

The brothers gathered around Charles's campfire and discussed the next leg of their journey. The trail so far, though there had been mishaps, had been fairly easy to travel.

"Though I 'spose "easy" has a diff'rent meanin' now 'n it did back home," Lindsay offered ruefully, sullenly poking a stick into the coals at the edge of the campfire. Lucy wondered what the men would do while they were sitting around the campfire if they didn't have sticks to stir things up with.

Lucy and Her Manifest Destiny

"We're more'n half way there, Melinda."

The brothers had many misgivings about the most arduous part of the trip to Oregon. After much discussion, however, the Applegates and their following were determined to try the route with the resources they had.

"Dr. Whitman insists we can make it, an' the good doctor hasn't given us any bad advice so far," Lindsay reminded his brothers, and they agreed. After waiting a few days for the stragglers in their train to gather at the adobe fort, they would resume their push towards the Oregon country.

Lucy, standing just out of sight of Father and the uncles, gripped cousin Roselle's hand tightly as the girls listened to the adults making their decision.

"Hope we don't have ta go through what poor Aunt Betsy did," Lucy whispered, and her cousin tightened her grip on her cousin's hand in silent agreement.

"I hate ta see Gantt take leave a' the wagon train." Father swirled the last of his cooled coffee in his tin cup as he visited with his brothers. "He's fulfilled his contract, though, an' he's done a mighty good job of it. He's been a good man, an' we'll miss him, for sure."

His brothers nodded in agreement, both Lindsay and Jesse poking at the campfire with long sticks, moving the burning branches further into the flames. Gantt was unfamiliar with the territory beyond Ft. Hall, and, his guiding over familiar territory done, he planned to join the emigrants heading south towards California.

Lucy hadn't been aware that John Gantt would be leaving the wagon train. She watched as he rode away from the wagons the next morning, stop at the top of a small rise, and turn in his saddle to give a final wave of goodbye to the emigrants watching from below.

Lucy waved back vigorously but knew that the wave of one small arm would not be seen by the guide looking down from his vantage point. As the guide turned in his saddle, lifted his reins, and rode out of sight over the ridge, Lucy felt uneasiness creep into her mind; could anyone else guide the emigrants as well?

Gantt was not the only man the emigrants would lose. Lucy's feeling of apprehension at Gantt leaving the emigrants increased when she heard that Doctor Whitman was also planning to leave the group soon. He would guide them as far as the Blue Mountains before going ahead to his mission in Walla Walla to prepare for their arrival. He assured the emigrants that he would send an Indian scout to the train to help pilot them through the Blues.

There had been no more buffalo chips for the campfires since the wagon train had left the Ft. Laramie country and the children had adjusted to new night chores. As the wagons crawled slowly westward, the group relied on sagebrush for cooking. Though it was plentiful, the three-foot-high shrub burned quickly and the children had to make numerous forays to gather enough fuel for preparing the evening meals.

"Be sure you look for ticks," Lish told the group of wood-gatherers. "They like ta hop onto your ankle, crawl up your leg, sink their little teeth into your hide, an' suck out your blood." He laughed as the girls lifted their skirts to inspect their legs.

"They do not!" Mary frowned. "You're just being a big bully!"

"Unca Mac says," reminded Lish. He'd been waiting for just this minute. "Looka here!" and he pulled up his shirt tail, exposing a blue ball the size of a marble, stuck to his belly. Dropping his shirt tail, he reached into his pocket.

"All you need's a good toad sticker," he explained as he opened the blade of his pocketknife. "Just stab the little beast!" and, lifting his shirt tail, he did so. The girls jumped back and shrieked with disgust as blood spurted out of the tick's bloated body.

Grinning in satisfaction, Lish slowly pulled off the shriveled tick and headed towards a pile of sagebrush branches beside the trail. The girls looked at each other, eyes wide. Well. If Unca Mac said, it must be true, and, furthermore, Lish had demonstrated that if Lish said, it must be true. They agreed to inspect each other at the end of their wood gathering.

The first half-dozen wagons to push through the heavy sagebrush found it to be troublesome, even though the shrub would snap and was soon ground into small pieces by the following wagons. Lead wagons had to change their teams often, as the animals quickly grew weary pushing through the sagebrush thickets.

Advance scouts on horseback attempted to find the easiest path through the shrubby obstacles, resulting in a zigzag course for the emigrants. Even with the altered route, however, the passage was rough on the stock and the way forward was slow.

By the end of each day struggling through the sagebrush, the emigrants were covered from head to toe with a layer of the flour-like powdery dust from the sage that had been ground into an ashy residue that floated in a heavy cloud over the wagon train.

"My nose is pert near plugged with dust," Susan whined.

"Well, clean it on your apron, you ninny," retorted Ellen.

"Children!" Lucy admonished her younger sisters. "Try ta be a bit more pleasant ta each other." She stumbled on a sage branch lying in the trail the girls were following.

"Oh, fiddle!" she groused as she rubbed a knee she had twisted. "Just clean your nose, you ninny!" she snapped loudly at Susan, and limped along in the sage-laden dust cloud with her sisters.

Lucy stumbled upon a miserable Lisbon huddled next to a broken sagebrush, his head resting in the crook of his elbow.

"What's wrong, Little Man?" she asked, kneeling beside him. Lisbon held up a hand and forearm for her inspection, displaying half a dozen twister bruises on the sage-scratched skin.

"James," he sobbed.

"Soon," Lucy vowed, hugging her little brother. "Soon. I think I have a plan. Promise." She had no plan, really, but she knew there'd be an opportunity soon. "I'm puttin' my mind ta comin' up with a real good plan real soon."

Babe had lost weight since the beginning of the trip, despite treats the children slipped to him when they could. Lucy and her siblings often walked as closely beside him as Billy Doak and Mother would allow, encouraging him to pull harder. When their team pulled aside to allow the following team to break through the heavy sage, the children smiled; poor Babe needed a rest. They patted his thick hide wet with sweat from his efforts, crooning softly to him as they fed him the small bunches of grass they had pulled.

"Babe was only this high when he was a baby," Lisbon said, and held a hand up to Babe's stomach. "An', now, he's a big boy." Lucy's six-year-old brother ran grimy hands through his wheat-colored hair, unintentionally wetting it with sweat from Babe's side and causing the thick mop to stand upright on the top of his head.

"I'm glad we gotta at least bring Babe with us," Mary sighed, and Lucy nodded. Looking at Susan and Ellen and Mary and Lisbon, she knew they were all thinking of Rufus and remembering that Father had demanded he be left behind, despite the children's pleas to bring him. Lucy supposed that a small part of her would never forgive Father for deserting Rufus.

Ellen exhaled slowly and leaned a cheek against Babe's thick side. "I love you, Babe," she said softly, patting the ox with a grubby hand. Her matted hair had escaped the braids Lucy had tried to plait without combing, her dress was tattered and soiled, and Lucy wondered if her little sister would ever be clean again.

Lucy thought Lisbon was an odd looking little lad with his unruly hair sticking straight up from his head, but, looking around at the others, she could see he looked no worse than the rest of the children. This morning there seemed to be no child without dirty and straggly hair, unclean faces covered with sunburn scars and scabs, scratched hands with broken and filthy fingernails, and tattered clothing.

After the day's struggle through the sagebrush, every child's face and the backs of their hands showed numerous new thin, bloody scratch lines from the shrub. Ellen's nose had started to bleed when a sage branch had snapped back, hitting her on the face, and she had smeared the blood over her cheek and upper lip before Lucy could pinch her sister's nose and stop the flow of blood.

"You're not a purty sight," she teased Ellen, wiping at the dried blood with her apron skirt.

"So," retorted Ellen. "An' you're not a purty sight, neither!" The sisters stood glaring at each other, each one knowing full well no one was a pretty sight just right then.

"An', don't you dare spit on that thing an' wipe my face with it," Ellen ordered, pointing at Lucy's apron skirt.

"Fine. Just stand there an' be ugly," Lucy spat out and turned away from her younger sister in disgust.

Lucy suddenly realized that the children's faces weren't quite as round and plump as they had been in Missouri. With their unwashed and unkempt hair framing dirty faces and their thin bodies covered with tattered and filthy garments, the youngsters seemed to have aged several years since beginning their trek westward.

Mother's meals weren't as bountiful as they had been at the first of the trip westward, despite not inviting anyone but family to share meals with them. While the children each were served their portion of the food, Lucy knew those portions were much smaller than they had been a month previously.

Furthermore, when each Applegate had received a fair share of the prepared food, there was nothing left in the pan for a second helping. James was always quick to grab the pan for scraping just as soon as it was set down. Lucy could see that her brothers' britches all seemed larger and that her sisters' dresses were looser than they had been.

"When did we get this way?" she thought, wondering at how such a deterioration of the children's appearances could happen so fast and yet so gradually that she had been unaware of it. She half-heartedly smoothed her apron and wiggled her legs; she found she was enjoying the freedom from her previously constricting pantaloons and grinned to herself at her wickedness in leaving her underwear under a rock.

Somehow, the thought of freedom from her previously restrictive undergarment gave her the boost of energy she needed to complete the push through the sage.

"I wonder how many other pantaloons have been left beside the trail? We're no different than anyone else on this journey," she thought in resignation. "No worse off and no better."

Off in the distance she could see a rider sitting on his horse, a rifle cradled in his arms as he rode beside the herd of cows limping slowly past.

"'N even the men an' the cows an' the horses are lookin' tired 'n sore," Lucy thought. "I don't have it so bad. Not really." She fastened her eyes on a shrub a few hundred feet ahead and, a step at a time, worked her way around rocks and towards her objective. That reached, she spied another shrub to use as a goal, and she plodded onward, Irene in tow, a following of youngsters trailing behind.

Lucy found it hard to imagine how Cousin Jesse's injured eye was feeling. Each time she saw him, his bad eye was oozing liquid, his tanned cheek covered with the dried matter mixed with trail grime, the shirt sleeve he used to wipe the injured eye equally filthy. She'd given up on her attempts to keep her young cousin's face clean, and apparently everyone else had, too. Damaged eye, encrusted face, soiled shirt and all, the little man still determinedly kept up with his family and cousins.

"I knew the trail would be long," was Melinda's only comment as she stooped over the campfire, feeding sticks into the flames flickering over the top of the fire trench. The emigrants had learned the fire burned more quickly and used less fuel if a small trench about two feet long, six inches wide, and ten inches deep was dug to build the fire in. Too, the wind wouldn't put out the flames, and the large iron pots could rest on the sides of the trench, making the cooking easier and faster.

Mother quickly used up the few armloads of branches that had been gathered and tossed into the wagon that day. The children were all relieved that there was plenty of firewood to gather. No one complained about the absence of buffalo chips.

"I don't see why Mother needs ta use so much firewood," complained James. "After all, we're the ones who have ta find it an' lug it ta the fire." Lucy scowled at him.

"Seems some folks like ta complain a lot," she snapped, "but they're always at the front a' the line for supper an' ready ta stick their nose in the manger." Her younger brother held a hand to his face to hide the tongue he stuck out at her, and then he turned and stamped away to find his two favorite cousins.

The wagon train bounced and wound its way westward towards the Snake River, then south along the river for some distance. Their progress could be marked by a thick cloud of disagreeable dust. The emigrants breathed in the heavy powder with every breath, coughing and spitting and drinking small sips of water to ease the dryness in their mouths.

The noon break was welcome, as the animals and emigrants alike could rest and enjoy drinking enough water to clear the dust from dry throats. The river was broad and fairly still, the water very clear, and the Nines immediately decided to take a quick dip in the river to wash off trail dirt.

Watching the trio of Applegates disappear into a willow thicket and soon afterwards appear in the slow-flowing water, Lucy was struck with an idea. It was time for James's payback.

"Revenge!" Lucy whispered to Lisbon with a huge smile on her face. "Hurry! Round up the girls for me. Wait for me ta tell you when ta start walkin' t'wards the river."

With a finger over her lips to caution her little brother to be quiet, she stealthily moved towards the thicket of willows. It didn't take long to find the boys' britches, and James's were easy to identify; they had several large blood stains from his helping to butcher the buffalo and one trouser knee sported a three-cornered tear.

"Havin' fun?" Lucy yelled to the Nines, and the three young men halted their splashing each other and looked in alarm towards the bank where a grinning Lucy stood waving James' britches.

"River's mighty clear, ain't it?" she teased, and the trio looked at the clear stream flowing slowly past. They immediately began to stir the mud with their feet, clouding the water.

"Put my britches down!" ordered James, a large scowl on his face. "Put 'em where you found 'em!"

"I think I hear Lisbon an' the girls comin'," she informed them, raising her voice to cue Lisbon it was time for him approach the river. She waved James's britches over her head. "I'm thinkin' they'll love seein' the clear river water!"

"Give 'em to me, Sissy," James ordered, moving slightly towards the bank, stirring the mud constantly, glancing downward to ensure the water was cloudy. "Give 'em! Please." He advanced another step, stopped and stirred the river bottom, then retreated a few steps as Lisbon appeared at the river's edge with his older sisters and a few cousins.

"What's it worth?" Lucy taunted. "Maybe no more twisterin' little folks? Huh?" and she grinned widely, whipping his trousers again.

"Lucy Applegate! You give me my britches!" James screamed. "I'll twister you every day of the week if I want to!" James stirred the mud, Lucy waved his trousers, and the watching crowd of children began to laugh loudly.

"James!" The children heard Charles's voice from the direction of the family wagon. "James! Time ta get goin'."

"Gimme my britches, Lucy Applegate! Gimme 'em right this instant!" James blustered.

"No more twisterin'?" Lucy prompted him.

"James! Hustle on now." Father's voice sounded mighty impatient as he roared his son's name. Lucy, Lisbon, and the children stood on the bank, wide grins growing even wider.

"I think I hear Father callin' ya, James," Lisbon chortled, cupping a hand to his ear as if to hear better. Irene giggled and Ellen snorted loudly.

James knew he was whipped, no matter what he did. Either whipped by giving into Lucy's demand or whipped by Father for not obeying. Father's whipping would hurt a whole lot more than Lucy's. He stirred the mud, a dark scowl on his face.

"Okay. No more twisterin'. Gimme 'em now," and he held out his hand.

"Pinky promise?" Lucy teased. "Pinky promise? No more twisterin' the rest a' our journey?"

"Pinky promise," James nodded grudgingly. He held up his hand, defeated, his little finger crooked. Lucy motioned Lisbon to enter the water, and, with a wide grin on his face, the younger brother waded towards the older, his finger extended.

"Pinky promise!" Lisbon declared triumphantly.

By nightfall when the wagons circled for the night, Lucy knew her face was streaked with dust mixed with tears from irritated eyes. She only had to look at any of the other emigrants to know they were mirroring her own face. She brushed the alkaline dust from her faded and worn calico dress in disgust.

Looking around for any signs of Robert Arthur or Leonard White, she was relieved when neither of the two young men was in sight; she'd hate for them to see her.

"Oh, how I wish I could be clean again an' my eyes an' nose free from this blasted never-ending filth," she complained to Susan and Ellen. Her two sisters merely nodded tiredly, not bothering to answer. They each had their own burden of dirt to bear; complaining had so far not prevented the buildup of grime. Ellen dug a finger into her nose and wiped it on her skirt, then lifted her apron to blow her nose.

There were plans to cross the Snake the next day, and Father talked about them as the three Applegate brothers and their families joined in a group around the campfire. Talk was that the crossing would be successful if the emigrants would follow Dr. Whitman's advice to fasten their teams together for support while crossing the river. The children listened to the adults discussing the crossing.

"What would we do if we fell out a' the wagon when it's goin' 'cross the river?" Ellen fretted, twisting the end of her long wheat-colored braid around and around a finger. Her dread of rivers equaled that of her mother's.

Lucy shrugged. "Hang on tight, you ninny," she advised her little sister.

"You could swim across," Lucy added softly to her cousin Lish, looking around to make sure there were no adults within hearing. "It won't be any worse than the Platte. All that sneakin' 'way from chores at home an' goin' swimmin' might come in handy." She grinned as she chided him; it seemed good to find something to joke about.

"Yeah, but I've gotta drive the wagon so Father can help with the stock," Lish answered. He squared his shoulders and dug in his nose with a grimy finger, removing a large glob of mucous and dust and wiped it on his already heavily soiled shirt. Lucy knew he'd rather be working with the cows, but she could see him puff out his chest as he thought of the importance of doing a man's work by driving the family safely across the fast-flowing Snake River. Lucy wrinkled her nose at her cousin's conceit.

The next day, most of the emigrants followed Dr. Whitman's advice on linking together their teams and their crossing was successful. One independent young man, thinking that with a strong carriage and a good team he could make the crossing on his own, ran into trouble when he reached deep water. Seeing his dilemma, someone helped him to safety by throwing out a rope to tie around his oxen's horns and guiding the carriage and the wiser young man safely to the far bank.

Another man, riding a mule, unfortunately left the shallow part of the river and rode into a deeper place, resulting in both the man and the mule being drowned. Few of the pioneers noticed him and his animal disappearing quietly, leaving no trace of their existence.

Drunks, Bloodsuckers, and Vermin

"That's why we have leaders," Father told Lucy as she watched a group of emigrants search for the man. "We'd best follow their orders." A sobered group of emigrants watching the event determined they would follow the route established by the leader when crossing the Snake a second time near Ft. Boise in a few days.

As they circled the wagons near Ft. Boise late in the afternoon of September 19, Lucy remarked to Mother that she found the stockade similar to Ft. Hall, though it was supposed to be about ten years older.

The adobe walls surrounding the fort's cabins and storage houses had been built in '34 by Dr. McLoughlin and the Hudson's Bay Company, Father had told her. It seemed the folks running it had more than enough time to lay in a good supply, but it didn't seem like much, a trail-weary Lucy grumbled.

"Small supply, high prices," she complained to Mother. The fort didn't look any more promising than the previous forts that had disappointed the emigrants with their meager but high-priced supplies.

"It's a goal, Daughter," Melinda replied. "It's a point to reach an' means we've come a certain distance on our trip. Then, before our dust settles on that fort, the men are talkin' 'bout reachin' the next point on the map. It's all part a' the trip," and she sighed as she turned away, signaling the end of the conversation. As an afterthought, she turned to face Lucy.

"At least it's not surrounded by that miserable sage," Mother added, a twisted grin on her face. "I've had quite enough a' that blasted stuff ta last me a lifetime, ticks, dust, an' all."

Lucy watched with curiosity as a group of Indians walked into their camp, carrying dried salmon to sell. The large carcasses were blackened and the odor of the drying fires lingered on the meat. The unfamiliar smell was not at all unpleasant, Lucy thought, as the Indians mingled with the emigrants. She watched the men slapping at their bodies occasionally and scratching various body parts vigorously.

"What's their problem?" Susan asked Lucy as her older sister pulled her away from the group of traders.

"Lice!" exclaimed Lucy, and the girls moved quickly away from the trading session. Before entering the tent that night, Melinda asked the children to check each other for the pesky little creatures. "I think I see one," Lucy told Susan, lightly tracing the tip of a finger across the back of Susan's neck, mimicking the feel of a louse on exposed skin.

"Get him!" exclaimed Susan, cringing and moving her neck closer to her big sister for some help.

"There he goes!" Lucy squealed, moving her finger once again across her sister's neck.

"Ouch!" He's bitin' me!" her little sister squealed.

"He's gettin' away. Hold still while I get him," the prankster ordered, and began to lightly slap her sister's shoulders. "There he is!" Slap! "There he goes!" Slap! "He's a fast little guy!" and, unable to contain herself any longer, Lucy broke into laughter.

"Oh! You're awful! Get away from me." An indignant Susan moved her shoulder away from Lucy's hand and stomped off to the far side of the campfire. Lucy and Ellen delighted in taunting their sister the remainder of the night, slapping their shoulders each time they noticed Susan watching them. The target of their amusement spent the remainder of the time scratching her body in various places, scowling at her sisters as she did so.

Crawling under their quilt that night and hearing Susan slap and scratch, however, Lucy and Ellen regretted their prank. They began to imagine the light tickling of lice on their bodies and they slapped and scratched themselves to sleep.

Despite being plagued with lice, the Indians provided the emigrants a welcome break in their monotonous diet. Smoked fish was a new experience for most of the group. The children, especially, ate until they quickly finished every last morsel of the salmon. They went to bed with full, if aching, stomachs.

The river near Ft. Boise looked ominous. A strong wind formed high swells on the surface, and the emigrants camped for the night, hoping for better conditions the next day. Before dark, some of the wagon beds were blocked up six inches to keep them from getting into the water.

"If we get into deep water, the beds'll float right off," Father grumbled with a look of worry on his dark face. Although they considered the alteration of their wagons a hazard, most of the emigrants took a gamble and raised their beds. Fortunately, all the wagons were taken across safely the next day and the contents remained dry.

"One more hazard reached an' mastered," Father said with satisfaction that night. "One step closer ta our destination," but his face still carried what seemed to be a perpetual worried look.

"An' just how many more hazards will we face?" Lucy thought. "How could they be as bad as Lisbon's wreck an' losing Joel?" She was to find out.

~ *Chapter 14* ~

DEATH OF A LOYAL FRIEND

A few days later, on September 23, the wagon train reached another river that presented an entirely different problem from any the wagon train had so far encountered. Lucy, surveying the waterway from a small knoll, thought that Burnt River was hardly deserving of the name river. It seemed scarcely the size of a large creek at this point.

She could see that the riverbed was bordered by steeply sloping hills lined with timber and brush. The passage would be through a narrow valley squeezed between two ranges of high mountains. The reason for the name Burnt River was obvious. Wild fires from the past had left behind charred remains of tall trees. The towering black sentinels stood high in stark contrast to the greenness of the valley floor.

"We don't have the time an' the manpower an' the tools ta clear the banks a' their brush," Charles groused. "We'll be forced ta drive through that rocky riverbed when thick growth on the bank blocks the way. It's gonna be a tooth-rattlin', wheel-breakin' ride." He looked worriedly towards his brother's wagon, cut in half.

"We'll just have ta move the wagons ta the banks when we can, gettin' short breaks from the bone-jarrin' ride over the rocks." He walked around his wagons, tying the loads more securely, hoping to protect them against the expected jolting.

Though the wagons inched forward slowly through the constricted route, the progress was almost unbearably noisy, penetrating Lucy's ears and seeming to throb in her body. Wagons bounced and clattered noisily from one rolling rock to another, and frequently a wheel would splinter, causing loud shouts of alarm and frustration.

Loose buckets and crates banged on the sides of wagon beds and animals bawled or whinnied as both cows and horses slipped on one treacherous rock after another and fell to the rocky riverbed. The trip up the river valley was a body-bruising, wagon-destroying passage, and the roughest part of the journey up to that point.

"More new words we dasn't use," James grinned wickedly at Lucy, who stood with her hands over both ears as a nearby teamster berated his yoke of oxen.

Small children screamed in pain as they stumbled on round stones that turned, causing them to fall head first and bruise their knees and jar their arms when they attempted to slow their fall. Lucy led her brood of children out of the riverbed and onto the bank, where they walked around the thick shrubs as much as they could. Too often the underbrush became impenetrable and the children had to drop back into the route the wagons were taking.

"I'm worried about Mother's china," Melinda complained, but she made no move to inspect it. Whatever happened would just have to happen; they had to move forward.

There was no room for a wagon to pull out of the way of the one following in the narrow riverbed. When a mishap occurred, the men behind would hurry to help with repairs so the delay would be as short as possible. Tempers became even shorter than the stops to mend damages, and Lucy and the children ducked their heads as the air seemed to turn blue with the men's shouted oaths of frustration.

Already weakened by the hardships of the trip to this point, the gaunt animals were having a tough time with the passage as the men walking beside them urged them on. Babe was stumbling through the rocky pathway, moaning softly as his tender feet grew even more sore with each step he took. James, stumbling along beside him on the gravelly passageway, murmured words of encouragement. More than once he had to jump clumsily to one side to avoid being hit by Babe as the large ox slipped on a rolling rock and his massive body lurched sideways.

Over and over the emigrants questioned the wisdom of Dr. Whitman who had contradicted Governor Grant, saying the passage was possible. Everyone knew, though, that there was no turning back at this point. One wagon overturned twice in one day but, being righted with the help of ropes secured to the frame and pulled by horses, the driver once again took his place in the line of wagons.

The three-day trip through the Burnt River valley made lasting impressions on all members of the wagon train. The men were impressed that they had overcome the sheer hardship of traveling the restrictive Burnt River route. The women were impressed with how well the flour had protected their dishes. The children were impressed with the new and colorful vocabulary they had learned from men struggling with animals and wagons through the unforgiving rocky passage.

From Burnt River, the group traveled to the Powder River for an overnight stay and then proceeded to the Grande Ronde.

"This has got ta be the most beautiful valley in the world," Lucy proclaimed, breathing in deeply the fragrances of the lush vegetation. The Blue Mountains surrounded the valley and rich green grass covered the fertile prairie that was encircled with tall timber. Running through the valley were several streams. Emigrants of all ages tugged off worn boots and tattered stockings and let the cooling waters soothe their trail-weary bruised, blistered, and swollen feet. The Nines joined friends as they improvised fishing poles and began to catch supper for their families.

The wagons had hardly finished making their night circle when a group of Indians approached the emigrants. Though they had determined through their previous meetings with them that the natives were harmless, the children nonetheless eyed them warily.

Susan immediately started scratching at herself when she spied the poorly dressed assemblage approach the wagons, and she kept her distance from them. Each brave carried small leather bags which they opened to display what Lucy thought looked like small dried onions.

"Dried camas," explained Uncle Mac. "They dry it on hot rocks." The roots proved to be quite good, and it was a welcomed addition to the dwindling supply of food. The next day, their adopted uncle showed his following of young folks the onion-like green leaves of the plants and the children delighted in digging in the soft dirt for the edible roots. The bulbous plants were plentiful, and many of the children overate, filling their shrunken stomachs for the first time in several weeks.

"My tummy's sore," Lisbon whined to Lucy after the youngsters had dug camas for several hours.

"How many camas did you eat?" his sister asked curiously.

"One," was the reply, and the little man looked at the ground and scuffed the worn toe of his shoe back and forth.

"How many?" Lucy asked again, raising her eyebrows.

"One."

"Be honest now. You know you dasn't lie," he was reminded by his oldest sister.

"One!" Lisbon declared vehemently. He stood silently a minute before giving in to Lucy's unrelenting stare. "One – at a time," and the matter was closed.

"This valley's got ta be 'bout a hundred miles around," estimated Uncle Jesse. "What a great location for raising cattle." Several of the emigrants had gathered to discuss the possibility of settling in the large valley.

"Looks like this could be the country we had hoped ta find in Oregon," Father exclaimed. "This is all a man could want. I doubt we will find anything better anywhere else. Too, it's the first of

October and winter will soon be upon us. We'd be wise ta settle here." However, when the Applegate families, along with others in the wagon train, took inventory of their supplies they found the lack of adequate provisions dictated they push on.

"Maybe we can come back later," Uncle Mac suggested. The brothers nodded slowly as they decided against giving up their goal of settling in the western part of the Oregon territory.

"If we were well supplied, we might well have settled here at the foot a' the Blue Mountains," Charles told Melinda.

"It is what it is," was her reply, and her shoulders drooped in resignation.

Lucy sighed as she heard the decision to push on. "I'd be content ta stay in this little spot a' paradise and never, ever travel another step," she told Roselle. The next day, the girls resumed their despondent plodding alongside the wagons and Lucy wished silently that she had Sadie to carry rather than Irene to tow along the trail.

Dr. Whitman left the emigrants and traveled ahead to his mission to prepare for the arrival of the wagon train. He wanted to stock his store so that much-needed supplies would be available for the travelers when they arrived. On top of that, he explained, there were two expectant women at his fort who were close to their time and he had promised to be there for their deliveries.

Lucy supposed he had to carry through with his plans to leave the wagon train at this point, but she didn't like it. She and her family stood silently, watching with regret as Whitman, his wife Narcissa, and the Spauldings rode away from the group.

The good doctor had promised to send an Indian guide to escort the wagon train. He also planned to leave notes on poles to direct the emigrants on their way, but that seemed like very little comfort. The warm feeling of security that washed over her each time she had seen Dr. Whitman was replaced with a feeling of trepidation as she watched him ride away.

Death of a Loyal Friend

"...Lucy wished silently that she had Sadie to carry rather than Irene to tow along the trail."

There was no road through the Blues. Again, Governor Grant's words rang in their heads as the men were forced to cut their way through fallen timber with axes dulled by overuse. There were no grindstones on which to sharpen the axes; the men had left the heavy grinders in Missouri. About forty men worked to hack a passage for the wagons, their hands becoming blistered, their backs sore, their arms numbed from constantly thudding their axes down upon the tough trees.

Lucy noticed that some of the men in the wagon train had sneaked furtive glances at the toiling wood cutters before they turned away and began to busy themselves with other tasks, real or imaginary. Those who were working to clear the passage grumbled but it looked as if they decided they could spend their energy more wisely if they concentrated on removing the timber from the proposed roadway.

"I'll remember those young nobs," Uncle Lindsay grumbled when he stopped to swipe the sweat off his forehead. He rested his dulled ax on the ground for a minute or two, flexing his shoulders for relief from the constant thudding of the tool against the downed trees.

"I won't forget their fimble-famble an' all the reasons they made up ta keep from helpin'. Those lame, prevaricatin' excuses they're making now that there's man's work ta be done won't help them any when we settle an' they come beggin' for help." He resumed chopping at the wooden barricade, his motions intensified by his anger.

Lucy wondered where Robert Arthur and Leonard White were; their help would certainly be welcomed.

"On second thought," she told herself, "maybe not." She picked at a festering scab on her chin and looked at her ragged and soiled dress and ran her hands over her dirty and unkempt hair. Lucy knew she looked every bit as shabby and disheveled as did her sisters.

"Those fellows had better just stick ta their cows. It's no wonder they prefer them ta me; I look like such a fright." She pushed her flyaway hair behind her ears. "'Sides, I have young'uns to care for. Don't have time fer boys."

Death of a Loyal Friend

The heavy fragrance of the pine and fir trees filled the air as the older children struggled alongside the men and women through the deep forest duff, helping to drag branches and other debris out of the way. Emaciated oxen, already trail weary, were hitched to the large trees to drag them aside and the wagons inched forward on the crude road.

Mother and Lucy and her sisters often caught their long skirts on snags and tore the bottom edges even more. Their hands and arms became scratched and cut from protruding branches. The littlest of the children whined, the older youngsters complained loudly, and Lucy wondered, as she toiled through the timber, just how wise Father had been to begin the trip from Missouri.

Before they could ford the Grand Ronde River flowing through the valley, men had to shovel a roadway down the bank of the river and up the other side for the wagons' passage. As the emigrants hacked and bounced and struggled through the Blue Mountain timber, following the path set by the Indian pilot Dr. Whitman had provided, they often camped in the tall timber within sight of the previous night's camp.

The days were getting shorter and cooler, but the work of clearing a passage kept the emigrants comfortable during the day. Lucy struggled from a deep sleep and peered through the tent flap to see a snowfall of about two inches.

"That's to be expected for the first a' October, I s'pose, but it's gonna do nothing but add ta our misery," she grumbled, and shook Ellen's shoulder to awaken her.

For a short time the younger children whooped in joy as they played together in the light snow, making packed ice balls to throw. Their hands soon became cold, though, and the snowball fights quickly lost their importance.

"Me hands are cold, Sissy," whined Mary, her fingers white with cold even as she rubbed them together firmly to warm them.

Lucy and Her Manifest Destiny

"Get some stockin's on 'em, you ninny," Lucy scolded. Climbing up the few steps leading into the wagon, she reached into the clothes box, scrambled the contents, and pulled out the first two small stockings she could find: one a dirty gray color and the second an even dirtier gray.

"Put these on," and she pushed the stockings on her seven-year-old sister's hands.

"I don't know why we left all our mittens behind. I s'pose 'cause it was May an' warm when we left," Lucy explained.

"Me, too. Me hands are cold," complained Irene, holding out sore, reddened hands to confirm her complaint, and Lucy again found stockings for a little sister and was rewarded with a quick hug around her legs.

"I'm cold, too," complained Lisbon, stomping his feet. Lucy could see a swollen bare toe, irritated by the snow, sticking out of a large hole in his boot.

"Where are your stockin's, Little Man?" she asked in disgust. "Ever' six-year-old should know they need ta wear stockin's."

"I couldn't find 'em. Not this mornin'. Not yesterday mornin', neither," Lisbon wailed, dancing up and down in place to warm his feet. "Not before, neither."

Sighing, Lucy climbed the steps to the wagon yet again, searched through the family's box of clothing for a third time, and found two stockings; mismatched, too large, holey toes and all, they were the best she could do.

"Sit down," she ordered Lisbon, and unlaced his boots. The stockings were too large, but that allowed her to turn the holes in the ends under her little brother's feet so that there was no bare skin showing under the large hole in the sole of his boot.

"That's the best I can do," Lucy sighed. "Anyone else not able ta dress themselves this morning ta keep the cold out?" she added sarcastically.

James sidled up to Lucy and looked around to see if there were an adult nearby. He turned his back to his older sister, pulled up his coat tail, wiggled his backside, and showed her the hole in his trousers that was large enough to allow his underwear to poke out.

"Sissy, me buttocks are cold!" he whined in mock anguish. "Me sit-upons have a hole in 'em!"

Lucy's looked at her brother's torn trousers with the flag of distress poking through the huge rip. She could hear Susan snickering, and Ellen snorted loudly.

"Your buttocks are gonna get whupped if you don't get them busy!" Lucy reminded her little brother. Turning, she winked at her sisters.

"Now, ta work, you lazy bones! No more fimble-famble. Lame excuses won't get us through this mess a' trees."

The youngsters began their chore of tugging tree limbs out of the trail marked the previous day, snow shaking off the branches as they were dragged to one side. Every so often, Lucy would hear a muffled, "Me buttocks are cold!" from one or the other of her sisters or brothers and there would be a burst of loud giggling from those close enough to hear the complaint.

As the children worked, their bodies warmed in the coldness of the day, both from the weak rays of sun that shone upon the clearing and from the little bit of merriment they were enjoying.

Father, pausing in his chopping of a large branch, looked at his brood of children questioningly, wondering at the source of their hilarity. Wisely, he decided the cause of their mirth was for them alone to share and, even more wisely, he didn't ask questions. Lowering his head, he resumed his hacking.

The cattle frequently wandered off, hiding in the lofty trees, and were a constant source of frustration as the men of Uncle Jesse's cow column struggled to keep an account of the animals. Lucy often heard men's tempers explode in violent outbursts. The constant shrill voices of irritated women and the constant bickering of children dampened her spirits even more.

She tried to keep her head down and focused on moving one more bit of underbrush and one more long branch at a time and her hands blistered and popped and bled. Her nose ran and she swiped at it half-heartedly, wiping her hand on her long coat, and she could see no one who wasn't doing the same.

"We've become quite a sight," she thought. "We've had ta pocket a whole lot we never had ta in Missouri, but I suppose we can put up with our misfortunes a little longer. I guess we'll put up with anything ta reach our manifest destiny," and she wrinkled up her nose in disgust. "Father says," she mumbled sourly. "Myself, I don't much care for this makin' history."

During the second day's struggle through the deep timber, Babe, straining to pull the wagon over heavy brush and past a downed log, lost his footing and Lucy heard a loud snap just before his huge body thudded to the ground. Father skirted trees and jumped over smaller vegetation as he ran to the collapsed ox in alarm. The children were only a few steps behind.

Babe, his massive body straining in the wagon's harness, moved his broad head slowly from side to side, making a depression in the soft forest duff. The children's pet ox lowed softly, brown eyes opened wide in pain. Lucy could see the jagged end of an ivory-colored leg bone protruding from brown hide and she noticed blood running slowly and steadily out of the open gash.

Father bowed his head and briefly covered his eyes with a roughened hand. Watching him, Lucy felt her eyes burn as she realized what had to be done. She had witnessed injured animals on the trail and knew there could only be one outcome. She bit her lip and clutched at a fold of her faded blue calico skirt, keeping her eyes focused on Babe's huge flailing head with his deep brown eyes wide in fear and pain.

"Let's go for a walk," Father said hoarsely. Lucy touched her fingers to her lips, kissed them, and blew the kiss to the steer that had been her pet since birth. Unshed tears filled her eyes as she clung to

Mary and Ellen's hands and stumbled through the heavy brush and away from Babe.

Gesturing to George Beale and Uncle Mac, Father picked up Irene and, with Mother carrying baby John, they led their brood away from the fallen ox. The family struggled around timber downed for the roadway and then pushed through the thick brush for a few hundred yards before stopping. Sinking onto the forest floor, Mother cradled baby John in her arms and the children huddled together and waited for the shot they knew would come.

When the loud crack of the rifle sounded, the children jumped and gasped. Lucy and Mother sat with arms supporting the youngest of the sobbing children. Lucy wished fleetingly that just once she could trade places with one of the little folks so that she, too, could be wrapped in warm arms and consoled.

She stole a glance at Melinda and saw her mother's eyes were tightly closed and tears were flowing slowly down her face. The lines on her mother's face seemed deeper, her dry and brittle hair more mussed than Lucy had ever seen. The corners of Melinda's mouth turned downward and her shoulders slumped forward as if the weight of caring for the children was too much for her.

Lucy gently brushed a loose strand of hair off her mother's face and tucked it behind her ear. She supposed that, in many ways, she had somehow taken over the role of being the caretaker of the children. She knew that she had to be strong. Mother needed her now more than ever.

Lucy tightened her grip on Mary and Susan's shoulders and pulled them even closer. Father stood quietly for a few brief minutes, at a loss for words. He watched his family grieving and then, without a word, he set Irene down on Lucy's lap and turned to help the men butcher Babe.

"I hate the Oregon Trail!" sobbed Mary, and Lucy and Melinda sat quietly with the group of mourning children.

Lucy and Her Manifest Destiny

After struggling through the timber, the emigrants found an Indian village and prepared to camp near the natives early the evening of October 6. Almost before their wagon had stopped, Susan began scratching her body until she noticed Lucy, a grin on her face, watching her. She stopped immediately and stuck her tongue out at her older sister, then turned away with a loud, "Humpff!!"

They found the Indians had an abundance of peas, corn, and potatoes to trade. As they had long since run out of vegetables, the famished members of the wagon train gladly traded the Indians articles of clothing for the fresh food. There seemed to be no objection to the worn garments the emigrants offered for the produce; anything presented was accepted in trade. The travelers feasted hungrily. By the end of their first meal of fresh vegetables in several months, the Applegate children's stomachs were so full they ached.

Finished with her meal, Lucy belched uncontrollably and loudly in a most unladylike way and, embarrassed, hurried to cover her mouth. A fleeting grin flew across Melinda's face when she saw it was Lucy who had made the rude noise but she made no comment.

James, sitting nearby, nodded and smiled his approval and whispered "Bully for you!" The Nines tried to imitate Lucy until Father ordered them to stop.

"Got one over on ya, didn't I?" Lucy muttered in James's ear, and he grinned and nodded in agreement.

On October 10, the wagon train camped about three miles from Dr. Whitman's mission, which consisted of one adobe building near the settlement of Walla Walla. The emigrants stayed at the camp site for four days, physically and mentally exhausted. They needed to rest and recuperate from their struggle through the timbers of the Blues and from the strain of the trip up to that point. Bodies were tired and sore, tempers were short, and there seemed to be no lack of petty and childish outbursts from the men. Dr. Whitman bore the brunt of much of the acrimony and Lucy listened to the exchanges with disgust.

She understood from listening to Father and her uncles that the missionary had laid in a supply of goods from which the travelers could replenish their supplies. He had himself paid a price twice what the emigrants would have paid at home in Missouri. Dr. Whitman added an amount to the goods to make a profit and the prices seemed exorbitant to the members of the wagon train who were almost all as short of money as they were of good nature.

The high cost of the purchases resulted in some of the emigrants refusing to pay what the doctor asked. Father told Lucy that this, in turn, would eventually lead to several families running out of necessities before the end of the trip and having to beg for some of the already scant provisions of their fellow travelers.

"Have they forgotten all that Dr. Whitman did for us?" she asked Charles and Melinda. "Has everyone forgotten how much we owe him? How many times his medicine helped us? How many times his wise advice got us through some tough situations? Without his help, we couldn't have made it this far. I just don't understand." Charles stamped away from his family, his face showing disgust at his fellow travelers.

Mother shrugged and made no comment. She had more immediate concerns; her family was worn and ragged from the trip, she was heavy with her unborn child, the remainder of the trip harbored unseen hazards, and she had to improvise the best she could to make the family's food last until they reached their destination. Worrying about the adults' temper tantrums wouldn't change her family's situation any.

Ft. Walla Walla wasn't even a day's ride from the Whitman Mission and was located on the river for which it was named. The terrain was totally opposite that through which the wagon train had just traveled. The soil around the area seemed sandy and barren and there were only a few cottonwood trees immediately on the streams. Other than that, there was not a tree in sight of the fort.

"So this is the great Oregon country?" Mother asked Father as they stood beside their wagon on October 16 when they stopped near Fort Walla Walla. Lucy watched her survey the barren land and the wide Columbia River with unease.

The emigrants had struggled 202 miles from Ft. Boise in the past twenty-four days, most of the travelers in the wagon train had literally walked their way from Missouri, and some had left members of their family in graves beside the Oregon Trail. Now Melinda appeared to doubt their efforts had been worth all their sacrifices if the scene stretched out in front of the family was what they had suffered such hardships for.

"It's not all like this," Father assured his family, though Lucy could sense that he had misgivings, also, as he looked at the surroundings. This was totally different than the paradise-like valley of Grande Ronde they had rejected as a potential home before they had begun their struggle through the forested Blue Mountains where they had lost their beloved Babe.

Lucy could see that Charles looked slightly stooped and she knew that the burden of keeping his family safe on their trip to Oregon had taken a toll. She had not really paid attention to Father, other than try to do as she was told to avoid his piercing dark eyes shooting a look of disapproval her way.

"Poor Father," she thought. "He's really had a hard time, I s'pose. I hadn't really thought a' that before. It's been a struggle for all of us."

She stood silently for a time with her parents, looking at the barren land. "The struggle that cost Babe his life," Lucy thought, and at the remembrance of the gentle ox, her eyes filled with tears and she turned from the ragged and weary group assembled on the banks of the Columbia.

~ Chapter 15 ~

THE GOD IS ANGRY

Some of the emigrants decided to drive their wagons to The Dalles and go from there on boats down the Columbia. They planned to remove the wheels from their wagons and put them on the rafts, using the canvas tops as shelters for the trip. Others in the wagon train, including the Applegate families, chose to leave their wagons and cattle at Walla Walla and float the river in boats. After they were settled at their destination, they would return to gather their belongings and their livestock.

The boats, about forty-five-feet long, five-feet wide, and three-feet deep, were made of the light but tough cottonwood trees found near Ft. Walla Walla. The lightness of the materials would make the vessels capable of being carried on the shoulders of forty or fifty Indians when they reached the falls near The Dalles. These porters were said to be able to carry the boats for perhaps three-fourths of a mile without setting them down. Once around the falls, the boats would be let back into the river by means of ropes.

"Who will milk Sukey?" Lucy worried aloud to Charles. "And are you sure Uncle Jesse will come back ta get her and the rest a' the cows?" She thought of Rufus left in Missouri and Babe left in the

Blues, and she swallowed a lump in her throat as she thought of the possibility of losing yet another pet.

"Dr. Whitman will make sure she's well taken care of," Father answered. "There's a whole passel a' young'uns that need the milk. And, you'll finally have a break. She'll join the herd a' Uncle Jesse's cows an' go the rest a' the way with them. You'll be milkin' again 'fore you know it."

The Applegate families purchased boats for their trip down the Columbia and stowed their necessary provisions into the vessels. Each time Lucy carried an armful of supplies to the boat the family would be traveling in, she wrinkled her nose at the new smell to add to those she had encountered on her journey.

She had gone from the fresh fragrance of the prairie grasses to the choking sagey scent of the dusty trail to the smell of the almost impenetrable forest. Now the unfamiliar damp odor of the flowing river seemed to assault her senses, almost as if to signal the presence of something sinister. She didn't like this new smell.

The night before the beginning of their watery journey, the three Applegate families sat around the evening campfire listening to Uncle Mac relate an Indian legend he had heard that day.

"Seems," he began, "that the People a' the Columbia used to have a hard time a' it, gettin' 'cross the river. They asked their Great Spirit, Manito, ta help them, an' he built a substantial stone bridge for the Injuns. The People were afraid it would wash away, so they gave it the name Bridge a' the Gods, hoping that would appease Manito.

"About that same time, he also sent his three sons ta earth. There was Multnomah, the mountain the locals call Mt. Rainier. A second son, Klickitat, or the totem-maker, is called Mt. Adams. The third son was Wyeast, the singer, and we know that as Mt. Hood."

Uncle Mac shifted on the large rock where he perched, enjoying being the center of attention, and he gave a knowing wink to Warren. The young man gave an awkward wink to the storyteller in return, screwing his face to one side as he did so.

The God is Angry

"Then, a beautiful woman came along and that is when the troubles started." Warren and his fellow Nines kept their focus on Uncle Mac and nodded their heads knowingly.

"Squaw Mt. was a beautiful young lady an' she moved between Klickitat an' Wyeast. The brothers grew jealous over the cute little mountain an' began ta fight. The earth trembled, ash covered the land, an' the mountains began ta throw rocks at each other."

Lucy looked at her cousin Roselle, wrinkled her nose, shook her head, and mouthed the words, "No way!" Uncle Mac, however, continued his story and everyone, including adults and children, listened closely.

"The brothers threw so many huge boulders at each other that the stone bridge broke in half an' fell inta the river. His sons an' their fightin' angered Manito so much that, in punishment for their behavior, he caused the huge rapids just below the bridge." The storyteller paused and grinned at the circle of trail-weary Applegates.

"You'll believe the story when you hear the sound a' the rapids tomorrow," he promised. "The God Manito is still angry at his sons, an' he's not quiet about it." The Nines grinned admiringly at Uncle Mac. "You'll see," the old man assured them, nodding his head. "You'll see. The god is still angry."

Lucy watched Mother set her jaw and clutch little John tightly as she stepped into the wobbling boat. She refused to allow James to ride with the other two Nines; she wanted to have him close to her on the ride down the river. Lucy saw Melinda caress her growing stomach as if to reassure the child she was carrying that all would be well on the river. Then Mother's eyes wandered to check her children, making sure they were all present and safely installed in the cottonwood boat.

At first, Lucy feared the feel of the craft. She had never traveled over water before. The unfamiliar movement of her seat from side to side, coupled with the unseen bottom of the river, which was who knew how far down, was unnerving, to say the least. With a

Lucy and Her Manifest Destiny

death-grip she clutched the side with one hand, her other arm wrapped tightly around Irene.

"I don't like boats. I don't like boats a little bit," Irene announced, her voice trembling. Her little sister was squeezed against Mary, sitting next to Ellen, who was clutching her side of the boat as tightly as her oldest sister.

The Indian guide stood in the front of the craft, a red bandanna tied around his head, directing the men who guided the boat. Eventually, the boat settled into the current of the Columbia. As the roll and pitch of the vessel lessened, so did the grips of the Applegate family, though no one let loose of their hold on the solid wooden sides of their transport.

"I hafta tee-tee," announced Irene loudly.

"Shhh! You'll have ta wait," Lucy whispered, her face reddening at the thought of her little sister talking of such a personal matter in front of strangers. "We'll stop after a while. Just wait."

"But I can't wait. I have ta stop now!" whined the four-year-old, squirming on the hard seat. Lucy put a finger to her lips, trying to quiet her sister. The progress down the river couldn't be stopped for such trivial matters, she didn't reckon.

"Squat down." Melinda's voice came quietly from behind the girls. "It can't be helped."

"But I can't!" contended Irene. "There's no room." She stuck out a chubby leg, touching the plank seat in front of her to demonstrate the lack of space.

"Then just wet your dress," Lucy muttered, scowling at her insistent little sister. A moment later, there was the warm scent of fresh urine and Irene's body relaxed in Lucy's grip.

"Problem solved," Lucy thought. "I'm sure there could be worse things happen."

As the boats approached the falls they had heard so much about, the rumble of the water grew almost unbearably loud. "The god Manito must surely be angry," Lucy declared, though she doubted anyone heard her. "Very angry, indeed."

The God is Angry

"I don't like boats. I don't like boats a little bit," Irene announced, her voice trembling.

Lucy and Her Manifest Destiny

The reverberation of the water rushing through the rapids boomed through Lucy's body and made conversation difficult, if not impossible. Indian guides stood at the front of the Applegate boats, steering the crafts through the rocks, dashing sprays of water hitting their bodies and trickling into the oversized canoes. Soon, Irene's indiscretion was covered with river water thick with foam.

The pioneers kept their death-grips on the sides of the boats and each other, white knuckled, their bodies tense. A feeling of doom permeated their bodies as the sound of the cascading river increased and they were pushed by the force of the water into a narrow trough, measuring less than sixty feet wide. Tall forbidding black rocks loomed threateningly on either side of the constricted channel.

The girls looked around to ensure the other boats were still with them; as long as the Applegate family was together, surely they would be safe.

"I'se scared, Sissy," Irene screamed into Lucy's ear. "I'm berry, berry scared!"

"Hush! So am I," Lucy shrieked back at her, her voice shaking. The children huddled in fright and when she turned towards Mother, she could see her mouthing the unheard words to hold on tightly.

"We'll be fine. We'll be fine. We'll be fine," Lucy chanted.

Without warning, the boat carrying Warren, Lish, Edward, and Uncle Mac flipped over in the turbulent water. Lucy watched in horror as her cousins and the old man were flung into the white water and disappeared from view.

"Don't look!" shrieked Melinda, and all the children swiveled their heads and looked. They focused their eyes on the boat that was being tossed and rolled in the foaming rapids. Suddenly, Lish's head popped up and he began swimming towards the bank of the river. His body was whipped back and forth in the frothy, swirling water until he was thrown with force upon the rocky shore.

When the family was able to pull their boats to the shore to aid Lish, they saw he had landed with such power that many bones in his body were broken. Though they knew his body was damaged badly, they were unaware that the smashed body would never heal properly and would cause him much discomfort in later years. His family huddled consolingly around him on the wet and rocky shore, thankful he was safely on land, not yet thinking of the damage done to his body.

The frantic Applegate family and their friends stumbled alongside the river, lurching among the rounded rocks, looking both upstream and down. Tears ran down the faces of Father and her uncles as they called in vain for Edward and Warren and Uncle Mac. Lucy could see their mouths moving but their voices couldn't be heard over the cascading water booming through the narrow chute of the Columbia.

She saw James, mouth trembling and eyes filling with tears, break away from the group of searchers and stumble to a willow thicket. She followed her little brother and found him huddled against a large boulder, shoulders heaving as he sobbed loudly. Sinking to the ground beside him, Lucy put an arm around James.

"It's okay, James," she said, patting his shoulder. "It's going to be okay. You're going to be okay." Her little brother shook his head and continued to weep inconsolably.

"Why, he's just a little boy," Lucy thought in amazement as she encircled his thin body with her protective arms and felt his small, bony shoulders. Cuddling her sobbing brother to her chest, she realized just how small he was. She wondered why she hadn't thought about that before. James had always been the little brother following along behind her to find ways to torment his older sister. He had seemed to have the mission of making her life miserable on the trail, and, actually, he was just a little boy.

"Just a little boy," she repeated to herself. "And, Father expected him to be a little man and help him ever step of the way. He got to be a little child sometimes, but mostly he had to be a man." She hugged him tightly as James leaned against her chest.

"Oh, Sissy," he sobbed. "I'm gonna miss my Nines. My own special Nines."

"I know," she crooned, trying to quiet him. She held him and rocked him back and forth on their seat of small rounded rocks. "I know." And she thought again that her brother was just a little boy and she cradled him and wiped his face with her soiled apron and let him cry.

Search though they might, the bodies of Edward and Warren and Uncle Mac were never found. It would do no good to blame the Indian pilot whose lack of skill was later said to be the cause of the accident, but there remained the fact that all the other boats had made the passage safely.

The miserable family huddled around a large campfire that night, gathered tightly together for comfort. Forever after, Lucy would associate the damp smell of river rocks nestled on a muddy river bank with doom.

"It's not fair," Mother's voice burst out, tears flowing freely over her lined face and down to her set jaw. She pulled her shawl tightly around her thin shoulders as she glared defiantly at Father. Melinda sat perched on a large rounded rock, rocking back and forth and holding baby John tightly to her breast with one hand, her other hand caressing her large stomach rounded with the unborn child.

"The boys walked almost ever blasted step a' the two thousand miles from Missouri an' here we are just a few days from our journey's end. Ta have it end like this is just not fair. An' poor Unca Mac. This gettin' ta Oregon just doesn't seem worth the price we had ta pay."

"Unca Mac did the best he could," Uncle Lindsay mumbled. "That heavy old coat a' his prob'ly pulled him down, an' his boots prob'ly filled with water purty fast. Didn't have a chance."

"He was a tryin', though. He was a tryin'." Lucy saw Uncle Jesse's eyes fill as he ducked his head. "He just couldn't reach the boys."

"He'd a' made it if he hadn't been a tryin' ta help the boys," Father added softly. "He'd a' made it."

Lucy could hear the defeat in her uncles' voices, the deep bitterness in her mother's, and she felt pity for Father. He had absolutely no control over the misfortunes the family had gone through. He and his brothers were trying to make life better for their families. Why couldn't Mother understand that?

Charles sat quietly for a few minutes. His eyes focused on the toes of his boots, patched crudely with scraps of cow hide and thin strips of deer skin. Slowly, he raised his massive head and looked soberly around the campfire at the circle of Applegates huddled on the bank of the foreboding Columbia.

Father took in each pair of haunted eyes set deeply in faces weathered from months in the sun, scars and scratches on many of them. Each Applegate seemed to be pleading silently for guidance. He looked at the raggedy and tattered clothing his extended family wore, their thin and stooped bodies, and he knew without doubt their souls were just as ragged and worn as what he saw.

"We'll find a safer route," Father promised the gathering. "Lindsay an' Jesse an' I. We'll just have ta go on an' finish our journey. Right now, we've the rest of the family ta take care of."

Before Father ducked his head again to focus on the ragged cow hide squares on his boots, Lucy saw tears begin to overflow his eyes. Lucy knew he wouldn't wipe away the signs of his sorrow; crying was for children and women. The silent emigrants sat lifeless for some time with even the children not moving. Then Charles struggled to his feet and left the glow of the evening fire, stumbling on water-rounded rocks, and he was followed closely by his two brothers.

The families did little talking that night. It seemed to Lucy that her sisters hugged her extra hard before they crawled into bed and even Mother gave her an unaccustomed squeeze as she passed John to her for a dry cloth. Crawling under the patched and dirty quilt that had covered the girls for the past five and a half months, Lucy didn't bother to squirm to find a more comfortable sleeping position; she knew she would sleep little that night.

Long into the night, Lucy thought of childhood treasures left in Missouri and of dusty miles and of sore feet and of sunburned faces.

"Oh, Sadie, Sadie. How I miss you," she whispered, and her arms unconsciously wrapped around a remembered little rag doll as she hugged herself.

She thought of Babe and of the Nines and of little Joel Hembree's small grave beside the trail. She mourned for the two cousins she had lost that day and of Uncle Mac. She thought of Mother's expanding stomach and of the unborn child who was no longer a secret. She thought of helping Father and Mother establish a home and a future for the new baby and for the younger children in this Oregon territory.

Finally, tiring of laying in the crowded tent and still being wide awake, she slowly wiggled out from under the quilt, careful not to wake her sisters as she left the shelter.

Lucy picked her way cautiously through the maze of smoothed rocks strewn about on the sand, past a few clumps of willow, and then chose a large boulder to sit against. Leaning back against the stone, her head tipped back, she gazed at the darkened sky with its sparkling jewels of stars.

"Which star is Edward's?" she wondered. "Which one is Warren's? And which ones are Unca Mac's an' Joel's?" She sensed rather than heard someone approach, and Father sat down near to her.

"Can't sleep?" he asked in a low voice. Lucy shook her head. Charles's presence felt warm and comforting in some way, though he sat a foot or so away. Looking up at her father, Lucy could see in the dim night light the thick dark mane of hair above his jutting brows and deeply set eyes, his large body trail-worn and muscular and large. His presence overshadowed her, making her feel small and yet somehow protected. She couldn't remember ever sitting this close to him before.

"Can't sleep?" she questioned him softly in return and could see him shake his head.

"It's been a long day," Charles said quietly and sat for a time without speaking. "A long trip." Father and daughter sat quietly on the banks of the Columbia, listening to the rolling waters, the cry of night birds, and the occasional plaintive call of a lone coyote somewhere in the darkness. The dank smell of the always damp sand was broken by an occasional whiff of the river willows brought by the cool breeze blowing softly up the river. Lucy pulled her shawl more tightly around her shoulders.

The two weary travelers sat quietly, each lost in private reveries, and suddenly Lucy realized her father had moved nearer to her and had a comforting arm around her shoulder and was pulling her close. She snuggled against him, absorbing his warmth through the tattered and stained coat he had worn each day since leaving Missouri. Leaning her head against his massive chest, she could smell the mingled trace of countless campfires and dust and cattle and tobacco, and somehow she felt reassured by the familiar scents.

"You've done a remarkable job on the trail, Lucy girl," Charles's quiet, deep voice broke the silence. "I couldn't a' made the trip 'thout you."

She tipped back her head and looked up at her father's face, surprised at the remark and unsure what he meant. Father seldom talked to her, other than a sentence or two, and she could never remember actually sitting down with him for a visit. There had always been children around, it seemed, and he was much too busy to chat with a little girl. Over thirteen years, and this first conversation was uncharted territory for her; she had no idea what to expect.

"Your mother's been sick the whole trip," he continued. "It was tough for her, an' the children woulda been miserable 'thout you. I wish you coulda had more time ta enjoy yourself, but you did what had ta be done." He shifted his weight and pushed his mane of dark hair back from his face with his free hand. "An', you did it well." Then, tenderly, his rough hand smoothed a fly-away strand of hair from his daughter's face.

"You left Missouri a girl an' somewhere along the trail, you left your childhood behind an' became a young woman. Your life will never be the same." He sighed. "An' sometimes that can be a good thing."

Charles squeezed Lucy's shoulder gently. "It'll take strong people ta succeed in this young state. You have what it takes. You'll be fine." Lucy could only nod in answer; she didn't know how to comment on the unexpected remarks.

Her father removed his arm from around her shoulder and opened his coat, reaching to an inside pocket. "I brought something for you," he said softly. "I wasn't sure when ta give it to you, but I figured you'd want something ta remind you a' home." Charles hesitated awkwardly and then continued.

"She's been at the bottom a' the medicine chest the whole trip and is probably a bit rumpled an' squashed, not ta mention she reeks ta high heavens a' the medicine from the broken bottles. But, here she is," and he reached out his massive hand that dwarfed the small rag doll he held.

"Sadie!" Lucy squealed, then clamped a hand over her mouth and reached for her treasured doll and hugged the ragged body close to her chest. "Oh, Sadie, Sadie, Sadie! Oh, Father, Father, Father. Oh!" and suddenly, for the first time since leaving Missouri, Lucy broke into sobs, collapsing against Charles's chest.

She wept uncontrollably for a long time and her father held her close, patting her back awkwardly, wiping her tears with a soiled coat sleeve as Lucy cried for all those losses she hadn't previously allowed herself to mourn.

Her tears were for her lost cousins and for Uncle Mac and for little Joel and for the other emigrants left beside the trail. She thought of Rufus waiting in vain in Missouri and of Babe who had given his heart and his soul and, finally, his life for the family as he toiled towards the new land.

As she clutched her childhood doll and leaned against her father's chest, Lucy sobbed quietly as she thought of the runaway wagon that had changed Lisbon's life forever and she thought of lousy Indians and the rocky Burnt River passage. Her thoughts drifted from buffalo boats to the large boats carrying her family to this camp on the Columbia. She shuddered when she pictured Lish's body, tossed about and broken but alive. Finally, her sobs subsided and she sat up, wiping her eyes on the skirt of her faded calico dress, then blowing her nose loudly on the tattered hem.

"It *has* been a long trip, hasn't it, Father?" she said in a trembling voice. She could feel as much as see him nod his head. "But, we're almost there. The trip is almost done." She sat quietly, her head bowed, thinking for a moment.

"I guess," and she paused, sitting upright and squaring her shoulders. "I guess we can say I've reached my manifest destiny," and she smiled weakly. Lucy could see Charles reach out his arms in the dim light and she nestled against him as he enveloped her in a tight hug.

"That you have, Lucy girl. That you have. You've surely reached your manifest destiny."

AFTERWORD

For Lucy and the other members of the Applegate families, the remainder of the trip down the Columbia River to Ft. Vancouver was made uneventfully, their minds numbed by the drowning of two of the Nines. The family had known before leaving Missouri that they would face hardships on the trail; despite that knowledge, the loss of the two young men who would never fulfill their dreams of sharing a farm in Oregon with their cousin James made reaching their final destination bittersweet.

After spending the winter of '43 at the abandoned Willamette Mission north of Salem, Lucy moved with her parents to Polk County where they settled on a donation land claim. Baby Albert, who was born in December of the year the Applegates reached Oregon, was joined later by Harriet, Thomas, Jane, Fanny, George "Buck", and Milton. Including the infant who had died in Missouri, Charles and Melinda had sixteen children.

In all, Jesse and Cynthia would have twelve children, as would Lindsay and Elizabeth. The Applegate families would figure largely in early Oregon history. Jesse and Lindsay were probably best known for joining thirteen other men in 1846 to find a southern route from the Whitman Mission to the Willamette Valley, their sons' deaths the impetus for their efforts. This southern route became known as the Applegate Trail.

In 1865, Lucy and her family were to receive news of George Beale. Beale had murdered a man for his money, was found guilty, and was hung in Salem. After the hanging, the Methodist establishment wouldn't permit him to be buried in the cemetery. A sympathetic farmer, who declared he didn't profess to being a good Christian like all the Methodists, allowed Beale to be buried on his farm.

While still a young woman, Lucy was injured and became blind in one eye. She would never marry, and spent all her adult life helping others. She was fondly referred to as "Aunt Lucy." Lucy died at the age of eighty in 1910.

ACKNOWLEDGEMENTS

Heartfelt thanks go to my friend Dorothy Kerns who graciously shared her artistic talent by creating the wonderful illustrations for our book.

A special thanks to Bobby Ferenstein for meticulously editing the first draft of <u>Lucy</u>. I am grateful to my husband, Tom, for editing the final copy for errors – twice! I'm indebted to Ali Osborn, a gal just about the age of Lucy, for giving me her point of view on the content.

Mary Fitzgerald
May 24, 2013

BIBLIOGRAPHY

Applegate, Shannon, "Skookum,"Corvallis, Oregon. Oregon State University Press. 1988.

Flora, Stephenie. "The Emigration to the Oregon Country in 1843." http://www.oregonpioneers.com/1843

Flora, Stephenie. "Emigrants to Oregon in 1843." http://www.oregonpioneers.com/1843

http://www.en.wikipedia.org//wiki/Fort_Boise

http://www.en.wikipedia.org//wiki/Fort_Hall

http://www.en.wikipedia.org//wiki/Fort_Bridger

http://www.en.wikipedia.org//wiki/Fort_Laramie_National_Historic_Site